WEAPONS OF CRITICISM

WEAPONS OF CRITICISM

Marxism in America and the Literary Tradition

Edited by Norman Rudich

Ramparts Press

Palo Alto, California 94303

809
R833 w

Library of Congress Cataloging in Publication Data

Main entry under title:

Weapons of criticism.

Includes index.
CONTENTS: Rudich, N. Presses.—Rudich, N. Introduction.—Criticism in history: Jameson, F. Criticism in history. Finkelstein, S. Beauty and truth. LeRoy, G. C. Literary study and political activism. Stratman, D. G. Culture and the task of criticism. Baxandall, L. Literature and ideology. Robinson, L. S. Criticism and self-criticism. San Juan, E., Jr. Art against imperialism for the national liberation struggle of Third World peoples.

[etc.]
1. Literature, Modern—History and criticism—Addresses, essays, lectures. 2. Criticism—United States—Addresses, essays, lectures. 3. Communism and literature—Addresses, essays, lectures. 1. Rudich, Norman.
PN701.W4   809'.04   74-9178

"Spirit of Nelson Guiding Leviathan" reproduced with the permission of the Tate Gallery, London.

Published by Ramparts Press, Palo Alto, California 94303

Library of Congress Catalog Card Number 74-9178
ISBN 0-87867-056-4 (cloth)
ISBN 0-87867-057-2 (paper)

Printed in the United States of America

The weapon of criticism obviously cannot replace the criticism of weapons. Material force must be overthrown by material force. But theory also becomes a material force once it has gripped the masses.
— Karl Marx, "Toward the Critique of Hegel's Philosophy of Law: Introduction"

To my parents, Joseph and Jeannette, with loving gratitude
for their devotion and self-sacrifice.

CONTENTS

PREFACE

The main inspiration for this collection of essays in Marxist literary criticism comes from two sources: a discussion group sponsored by the American Institute for Marxist Studies (AIMS), 1968-1970, and the forum on "Marxist Perspectives in Literary Scholarship and Teaching," sponsored by the Radical Caucus (RC) and held at the 1972 national convention of the Modern Language Association (MLA) in New York. That inspiration spread to individual contributors as the volume grew.

Our AIMS discussion group was aware of a developing change in the social and political atmosphere both at home and abroad. The political activism of the 60's made our deliberations something more than the morale-building exercise of a few isolated intellectuals on the Left. The movements for peace in Indochina, for civil rights, for women's rights, for social justice and democracy provided a context which enabled us to understand that we were a sign of the times.

We came together in New York once a month from various towns and cities of the Northeast in order to review the present state of Marxist literary scholarship and criticism, and for the purpose of contributing, theoretically and practically, to its further development. At each meeting a member of the group would read a paper of scholarly, critical, or theoretical interest covering a broad range of problems in the interpretation of past and present literature. We represented various backgrounds, professions, and interests, and the generations who are now between twenty-five and sixty years old. There were university professors of literature, an American historian, art and music historians, journalists, independent scholars and critics, and graduate students. Some are well-known on the Left for their many activities and publications, some less. The fidelity of the attendance was proof that all of us felt a need to test our ideas in discussion with friendly but intellectually demanding co-workers in the field of Marxism and literature. The years of cold war and reaction in the United States had kept most of us isolated in our research as well as in our political concerns, and our work had suffered as a consequence. Some were Marxists, some close to becoming Marxists, and others simply convinced that the Marxist method

The editor takes full responsibility for all the ideas and opinions expressed in this Preface.

9

in the analysis of cultural phenomena is important for anyone doing serious research today. Ideological diversity and political allegiance were no barrier to free and open debate. On the contrary, because this diversity reflects accurately the present state of leftist thinking in our country, it enabled us to locate the most pressing problems of Marxist literary theory which needed to be solved before we can move forward with renewed confidence. Seven of the present essays come directly out of the AIMS discussion group.

The Radical Caucus of the MLA has been active in the Northeast for a number of years. Although its orientation cannot be described as specifically Marxist, it has provided a point of convergence for a number of scholars and university teachers of literature representing a broad spectrum of political ideologies with at least this much agreement: that it is necessary to change the present policies and structures of American political and intellectual life if we are to avoid physical and moral decomposition. Some of the salient radical tendencies which find expression in the RC are Feminism, Bi-dialectalism, various nuances of New Left politics and Utopianism, as well as a variety of marxisms.

At the Chicago convention of the MLA in December of '71, a group of young radicals held a seminar on Marxist literary criticism which was so well attended that it had to be moved to a larger room. This unexpected success was the impulse for planning a forum on "Marxist Perspectives in Literary Scholarship and Teaching" under RC and MLA auspices for the following year. A small but representative group constituted itself as an editorial committee which undertook the work of organization, publicity, selection of papers, setting up workshops, etc., and arranged to meet periodically throughout 1972 to insure the success of the enterprise.

In the opinion of the *Chronicle of Higher Education* (January 8, 1973) we did a good job:

> Slowly but resolutely, Marxist criticism of literature is gaining currency as the most dramatic — if not the most cohesive — component of a general evolution of literary criticism in America. Marxist critics have in the past had little influence on the study and teaching of literature, but now they are beginning to make themselves heard with a force that may become difficult for the profession of English literature to ignore. . . Attendance at the session on Marxism at the MLA meeting indicated a broad interest. . . . The session turned out to be one of the largest gatherings of the week, some 400 people spilled out into the hallway.[2]

Indications are that this initial success has already sparked new activity in academia and in the literary field in general which will broaden public awareness of the Marxist Renaissance. Although the Marxist Forum of 1973 did not draw a big crowd, the workshops, which had been organized the previous year increased in size and number. These workshops, which bring together scholars interested in the application of Marxist literary theory in their own special fields — Shakespeare studies, French civilization, Latin American literature, theory of criticism, etc. — show signs of becoming a permanent feature of literary thought in American university life. In this volume we present the four papers read at the historic occasion of the first Marxist Forum, 1972.[3]

As word spread that a volume of Marxist literary criticism was taking shape, manuscripts began to arrive in surprising number and many of a very high quality. We may soon have enough for a second volume. Those included here were chosen as the most representative in several ways and in the first place, politically. It must be stressed that we quite consciously try to represent as broad a spectrum as possible of tendencies in Marxist literary thought. The only ideological criterion for publication was the recognition, explicit or implied, of this fundamental principle: that literature is a form of "social consciousness" which reflects real life, i.e. human activity, as the product and creator of history. These are Feminist, Maoist, Third World, and traditional Marxist.[4] Not only preoccupations, but points of view differ, and to bring them together in a single volume may be, under present conditions, one of the most important contributions we can make to a dialogue leading to greater unity on the Left. On the other hand the most glaring omission is a spokesman for black culture, but not for lack of a serious effort to include one or more.

The book is divided unequally into two parts, the first, the shorter, theoretical, the second, practical or applied criticism. This, too, is a significant reflection of the American situation. Serious theoretical work presupposes political and cultural development which, for reasons explained in the Introduction, had not sufficiently matured in the United States. Another reason, though an ambiguous one, is the strong influence of the Anglo-Saxon empirical tradition on American thought. We mistrust theories until they prove their usefulness in application, and we prefer to build thinking from particulars. Of course, this has its dangers, amply illustrated by the narrow pragmatism which has turned so many of us against philosophical and theoretical thinking of any kind, even in many departments of philosophy of our universities. We have sought to avoid such errors here.

The diversity of subject matter which marks the theoretical essays is proof enough of the range of problems engaging the thought of Marxist critics today: to define our stance vis-a-vis opposing schools (Jameson); to develop the aesthetic and historical categories which may enable us to structure a theoretical grasp of artistic production as a whole, in kind and in time (Finkelstein); to relate literary criticism and political action (LeRoy); to come to terms with black separatism and the politically ambiguous literary heritage which has been abused for reactionary ends (Stratman); to assimilate creatively the bourgeois heritage, including some of the Modernists (Baxandall); to understand the different ways works of literature are read by members of different classes, races, sexes, etc. (Robinson); to foster and encourage the new literatures arising side by side with struggles for national liberation in the Third World (San Juan). To varying degrees most of these writers are visibly influenced by developments in Marxism in other countries and are addressing themselves to an international audience; but all of them are speaking out of the matrix of the American experience. They are all aware that they are responding to an American political and cultural crisis whose outcome will affect the whole world.

Part Two, *Literature in History,* is arranged more or less chronologically from Shakespeare to Aime Cesaire. In such a collection our purpose goes further than convenience and simplicity. In all of these essays the authors are conscious of the historico-cultural moment of the works they study, both as reflections and responses to their times. Four take American subjects, four British, one French, one Caribbean, one German, and one a comparative study of an American and a Russian. This is quite understandable in simple statistical terms: the vast majority of our literary scholars specialize in English and American studies. It is probably also true that Marxist ideas have made slower progress among the learned in foreign languages and literature.

Some readers may learn here for the first time that Falstaff was a well-known social type with precise class origins (Siegel); that Pope understood very well the property relations involved in sexual inequality (Delany); that Blake had insight into the dialectic of creative and alienated labor in the building of modern civilization (Whitehead); that sense may be made out of the enigma of Coleridge's "Kubla Khan" when it is explained against the political background of its time (N. Rudich); that Balzac intuited a theory of value which may have crucially influenced Marx's own thought (L. Rudich); that Poe and Dostoevsky, as different and as distant as they were from one another, understood the phenomenon of alienation in terms of similar social coordinates (Harap); that Melville wrote from the point of view of the American working class, that he was against slavery, against imperialism, and against military oppression (Franklin); that James' frequent preference for depicting the problems of women was based on an understanding of the sexual division of labor and the special role of women as moral and cultural agents of civilization (Rubinstein); that Fitzgerald's class position deflected his social vision of the America of the 20's onto moral, psycho-analytic, and mythic explanations of the failure of the American dream (Zelnick); that Brecht revives and renews for modern use forms of symbolism characteristic of Christian medieval literature (Suvin); and that Aime Cesaire's heroic effort to dramatize a great social revolution ends up with the spotlight on the hero and on the playwright, while the revolutionary theme recedes into mere background (Fuyet and Levilain).

Of course the division into essays of theory and essays of practice has a measure of artificiality. Individual authors and works are discussed in Part One, and there are some notably interesting theoretical reflections to be found in Part Two. This is so much the case that we hesitated how to classify several of the essays. We hope, however, that readers will agree on the uniformly high quality of these essays, despite the fact that our contributors come from very different situations: we have a law student, two professors close to retirement, an independent scholar who can only work when family responsibilities allow, scholars on leave or sabbatical with full time for their task, etc.

Time and cash spare the Marxist less than most. A number of our young talents cannot find jobs in American universities and are being forced to abandon their chosen profession. Little wonder that this should be the case in humanistic studies, which have always been marginal in pragmatic America, when the stupid, senile capitalist system cannot even manage to employ thousands upon thousands of its trained scientific and technical workers. It is even less surprising that the first ones to be shut out from any field of intellectual work, but especially from ideologically sensitive areas such as the humanities and the social sciences, are those who have the courage, civic morality, and patriotism openly to oppose the Strangelove policies of the military-industrial complex.

The interest of American intellectuals is one with the national interest, that is with all those who create real, spiritual, and material values. We need a government which will reassert constitutional, civilian, and democratic control over the destinies of the country, and which will use the immense wealth of the richest society in the history of the world for the material and spiritual well-being of the people. The solution to the present "retrenchment" in American education is a massive federal funding of education at all levels. But in particular the federal government should finance the higher education of all men and women who are able and willing to attend colleges and universities.[5] The cost of such a program would not even approach the hundreds of billions engulfed in the military, moral, and political defeat we call Vietnam.

We have several times emphasized the diversity and the divergences of views held by our essayists. On one point, however, we all agree. The true interest of the artist, scholar, and critic who value the integrity of their work as creators of culture and producers of consciousness and knowledge is one with the workers in material production. No one has understood Marxism so long as he has not grasped the revolutionary significance of that fact. It is the seed of another great idea which will only be realized under a socialist democracy, the ultimate disappearance of that distinction, as old as class society itself, between physical and intellectual labor. These essays in Marxist literary criticism contain that idea as a necessary ideological pre-condition of their existence. They may help others to get the point. That is our contribution to the bi-centennial celebration of the founding of the Republic.

NOTES

1. Their authors are: Sidney Finkelstein, Gaylord LeRoy, Lee Baxandall, Fred Whitehead, Norman Rudich, Louis Harap, and Annette Rubinstein. Linda Rudich and Paul Siegel participated occasionally. Three members who deserve grateful mention, although they did not contribute to this volume are Richard Greenleaf, since deceased, Carol Remes, and Ted Norton.

2. French literature was represented in one of the workshops, and since then Latin American, German, Caribbean, and other modern literatures have been added.

3. Their authors are: Paul Siegel, Fredric Jameson, and David Stratman. Darko Suvin's essay was originally submitted as a paper to the Marxist Forum.

4. Sheila Delany, Lillian Robinson, Bruce Franklin, E. Sonny San Juan, Stephen Zelnick, Nicole and Herve Fuyet, and Mary and Guy Levilain.

5. Proposed by a group of concerned scholars to the delegate assembly of the MLA, December, 1973.

INTRODUCTION

I

Unfortunately this volume is unique. It is the first collection of *Marxist* literary criticism made up exclusively of essays by North American scholars and critics, i.e. citizens or adopted sons and daughters of Canada and the U.S.A. Other distinguished anthologies have made available some of the best Marxist literary thought from abroad[1] and radical anthologies have sometimes included Marxist writers.[2] All the contributors to this volume, despite the diversity of opinion, outlook, and interpretation herein revealed are trying to apply to the study of literature the fundamental categories of the Marxist analysis of society and culture, of material and spiritual production. That analysis seeks to account for ideological phenomena by relating them dialectically to the forces and relations of production of specific historically determined socio-economic formations. Marx writes:

> In order to examine the connection between spiritual production and material production it is above all necessary to grasp the latter itself not as a general category but in *definite historical form*. Thus for example different kinds of spiritual production correspond to the capitalist mode of production and to the mode of production of the Middle Ages. If material production itself is not conceived in its *specific historical form*, it is impossible to understand what is specific in the spiritual production corresponding to it and the reciprocal influence of one on the other. Otherwise one cannot get beyond inanities...Further: from the specific form of material production arises in the first place a specific structure of society, in the second place a specific relation of men to nature. Their State and their spiritual outlook is determined by both. Therefore also the kind of their spiritual production.[3]

The ideas and opinions expressed in this introduction are those of the editor.

Literary criticism is one mode among many of "spiritual production" and as such it reflects, responds to, and acts upon the society from which it emerges and in which it participates. If Marxist literary criticism is so rare in America, the causes are to be sought in the particular economic, political, cultural, and historical experience of American monopoly capitalism since World War II. Strengthened by an imperialist expansion unparalleled in history against victorious and defeated rivals exhausted by the war, the United States ruling class simultaneously launched at home an anti-labor, anti-communist, and anti-intellectual reign of terror, symbolized today as the McCarthy Era. If the techniques of purging the government, the schools, and the media of dissenters are more subtle and hypocritical today, the way was certainly made easier for the present generation of brain-washers by the swath cut by the Neanderthals of the Committee on Un-American Activities. But after all, they were acting according to their political nature. The intellectuals who aped them, those who turned informer, renounced the ideas they had defended all their lives, penned the apologies, brazen, shamefaced or stupid, of the corrupt, rapacious, and genocidal policies of the United States government denied thereby the integrity, the very essence of their vocation. Those were the days of Ike's theology, of the elevation of General Motors to the status of an ethical concept, of the "great debate" whether the islands Quemoy and Matsu were essential for the defense of the continental United States, of the agonizing moral doubt whether it was right to use firearms to keep improvident neighbors out of your family A-bomb shelter, of the blizzard of hoaxes: spies, "affluent society," "end of ideology," "bipartisan foreign policy," the Warren Commission Report, and the big unifying hoax, "the Communist menace."

Various branches of the thought police, protected by a secret budget (for reasons of national security, of course) invaded, bought and terrorized all the important institutions of communication: schools, media, the arts. The C.I.A. showed particular interest in cultural matters by funding the Congress for Cultural Freedom and *Encounter* magazine. Foundations, student organizations, agencies for travel and study abroad, the press piped thinking into safe channels in order to protect the American people against such pernicious ideas as peaceful coexistence, racial and sexual equality, and Marxism. The price for intellectuals went up with the demand for submissive technicians who narrowed the tasks of thought to that of eliminating the "dysfunctions" of state monopoly capitalism and its imperialist policies.

For awhile at least they apparently did a good job. Big business ate small business and grew bigger. Agro-business united with big business to eliminate those "dysfunctions" caused by small farmers; the military-industrial complex helped accelerate the processes of "rationalization" and "modernization" of the economy, and the monopolization of power to the cost of our social services, democratic institutions, and common welfare. By these means, plus two Asian wars waged with demented ferocity, the subversion of any government which failed to create "a favorable climate for investment," the subsidizing of military and fascist dictatorships, with their attendant favorable climates, the "American way of life" penetrated to the farthest reaches of the "Free World," while relishing the hope that its blessings would soon also be available to the socialist countries. Add to these disasters the effects of Stalinism before and after the Twentieth Congress of the C.P.S.U. at which Khrushchev denounced the "cult of personality," and the eclipse of Marxist thought, including literary thought, is not hard to explain.

At the same time the New Critics re-discovered in the wake of *l'art pour l'art* and modernist formalism that works of art are discreet, autonomous, self-referential, radically implicit artifacts without relation to any reality except perhaps our aesthetic sensibilities. In fact they never carried out these impossible theories; certain areas of meaning became the recurrent themes of the school, e.g. religious, psychoanalytic, mythic, primitivisitc symbols. It was "heresy" to talk about the social, political and historical dimensions of literature. When the New Critics glorified Donne, Neo-Classicism, and Symbolism, while attacking Shelley, Romanticism, and Realism, in the name of pure art and autonomous word-artifacts, they were taking an ideological stand, in which the conservative, political, and religious content was more than implicit.

But times have changed. The New Critics and their aristocratic pretentions, Southern agrarian nostalgia, anti-historical bias, and complex aesthetic ideals are distinctly passe. To argue the case for Marxist criticism in opposition to them would today be an antiquarian pastime. The New Critics literary approach denies all relevance of artistic production to real life, all ideological commitment, all cognitive value but especially the political significance of art. The military, economic, and political defeats of U.S. imperial policies at home and abroad which first became undeniable in the mid-60's and which today have reached the proportions of a generalized crisis throughout the capitalist world produced ideological repercussions in every domain of thought, revealing (inter alia) the anachronistic and reactionary content of the New Criticism. People of all strata began to ask questions about "the American way of life," questions about war and poverty, about political power and wealth, about social institutions and national priorities. In a time of economic and social crisis, question becomes protest, and protest reveals the growing incapacity of the governing classes of a sick society to respond with anything but brutal repression and base deceit to the needs of its citizens. The revival of an interest in Marxism in the United States in the teeth of every official refutation, denunciation, and ridicule of the last thirty years is one of the products of that crisis.

The vacuum left by the New Critics in the field of literary theory has not been replaced by any single body of literary doctrine capable of rallying the kind of spontaneous support which can constitute a "school" of criticism. Structuralist, Freudian, and archetypal currents are the main contenders, but their different emphases make it hard for them to join issue in any decisive way. The Marxist challenge to these and to all idealist theories of literature does not deny the importance of linguistic, psychological, or mythic elements in literature. It makes three claims: (1) that those are limited analytical approaches which do not and cannot constitute a general theory (cf. the parable of the six blind men and the elephant) (2) that the development of a general theory is an ideological and scientific necessity in the present state of national and international politics and culture, and (3) that progress already made by Marxist aesthetics, criticism, and literary history justifies our belief in the growing usefulness of the method. In brief, the relevance of Marxism to the creative preservation of the humanistic literary tradition for our generation and for the future is the assurance of its imminent strength.

II

A Marxist approach to literature implies more than studying a work against the historical, social, and biographical conditions of its creation. That much had been achieved by bourgeois literary historiography by the middle of the nineteenth century. Marx takes it for granted in a passage of the *Grundrisse* dealing with literary theory: "But the difficulty is not in grasping the idea that Greek art and Epos are bound-up with certain forms of social development. It rather lies in understanding why they still constitute with us a souce of aesthetic enjoyment and in certain respects prevail as the standard and model beyond attainment." To assure the survival of the great works of the past, to select them for transmission to the future is a value judgment. It is a claim that they serve the aesthetic needs of the present, and humanistic studies are in the last analysis an effort to adjudicate among the conflicting claims to "immortality" of the productions of past cultures. But present culture is also historical and our value judgements about the past imply a certain understanding of our times, an informing ideology in terms of which, more or less consciously, we elaborate the criteria governing our choices.

Relevance for Marxists is not merely a function of current topicality. The present, detached from the history which gave it shape and from the goals which are shaping the future, is an empty concept. The Marxist philosophy of culture insists on the historical continuum as a guide for action and sees the present as the historical crux which must be understood in terms of the future possibilities it affords. In a speech before the Proletcult Congress, Lenin defined the cultural tasks of the revolution:

> Marxism has won its historic significance as the ideology of the revolutionary proletariat because, far from rejecting the most valuable achievements of the bourgeois epoch, it has, on the contrary, assimilated and refashioned everything of value in the more than two thousand years of the development of human thought and culture. Only further work on this basis and in this direction, inspired by the practical experience of the proletarian dictatorship as the final stage in the struggle against every form of exploitation, can be recognized as the development of a genuine proletarian culture.[4]

Marxist theory provides a method for the critical preservation of those values which may contribute to the revolutionary transformation of class to classless society. The interpretation of literature is a political act because the present is history.

Professor Robert Weimann, in an important theoretical essay,[5] has tried to work out the methodological implications for literary history and criticism of the historicity of the present. He shows how the opposition of the New Critics, with their emphasis on the "present meaning" of past literature and the traditional, positivistic literary historians seeking its "past significance" — an opposition characteristic of a crisis in bourgeois thought — can only be resolved by nothing less than "an integration in method and purpose."[6] Historicity is an objective property of the work of art, and the conditions of its creation (*Entstehungsgeschichte*) are consubstantial with its mimetic structure and potential longevity; its trans-cultural, timeless moral character (*Wirkungsgeschichte*) must be understood dialectically as historical product:

> A dialectical approach, which is conscious of its own social function, will have to consider the problem of literary history from an angle where literature *is* history, and history is an element of literary structure and aesthetic experience. What is needed is not simply an act of combination between the literary historian's approach ("A is derived from X") and that of the critic ("A is better than Y")...One has to be contained in the other, and the historical sense of the critic needs to be quite indistinguishable from the critical sense of the historian.[7]

Thus it is that the critical evaluation of a work as "present experience" informs anew for each generation our evolving capacities to perceive meanings in the great works of the past, meanings which must remain latent and potential until changes in our own condition, in the material and spiritual relations of production and culture produce new dimensions of consciousness. The integration of history and criticism reunites past significance and present meaning so that art is seen as "not merely a product, but a 'producer' of its age; not merely a mirror of the past, but a lamp to the future."[8] And Weimann adds: "Incidentally it was Karl Marx who pointed out that art is one of the 'besondre Weisen der Produktion' — the 'special forms of production' — in the sense that the work of art can produce its audience, and influence their values and attitudes."[9]

This raises the question of the specific value of aesthetic production, appreciation, knowledge, and criticism in the Marxist outlook. What we have said up to now may apply in varying degrees to all modes of cultural (ideological) production. In his Preface to *A Contribution to the Critique of Political Economy*, Marx identifies the aesthetic as one of the forms of consciousness through which we apprehend and interpret the real world.[10] It follows that poetry, that art is not reducible to the political, religious, legal, philosophic, or any other form of consciousness, that its purposes and meanings, its values, must be understood in their own terms. Up to now we have emphasized its historical and political values in order to take position against the de-historicizing tendencies of the major bourgeois trends. We shall conclude this introduction with a tentative philosophical assessment of the place of the aesthetic in Marxist thought in relation to the economic, scientific, and political modes of consciousness.

III

In the *Economic and Philosophic Manuscripts of 1844*, Marx defines the pre-conditions for aesthetic production by contrasting human and animal labor:

> In creating a world of objects by his practical activity, in his work upon inorganic nature, man proves himself a conscious species being, i.e., as a being that treats the species as its own essential being, or that treats itself as a species being. Admittedly animals also produce. They build themselves nests, dwelling, like the bees, beavers, ants, etc. But an animal only produces what it immediately needs for itself or its young. It produces one-sidedly, whilst man produces universally. It produces only under the dominion of immediate physical need, whilst man produces even when he is free from physical need and only truly produces in freedom therefrom. An animal produces only itself, whilst man reproduces the whole of nature. An animal's product belongs immediately to its physical body, whilst man freely confronts his product. An animal forms things in accordance with the standard and the need of the species to which it belongs, whilst man knows how to produce in accordance with the standard of every species, and knows how to apply everywhere the inherent standard to the object. Man therefore also forms things in accordance with the laws of beauty.[11]

Universal, free, conscious, purposeful labor is exclusively the character of the human species. This means that human nature will be fully expressed only under conditions of labor which guarantee to the species through all its members the fullest control and enjoyment of the collective product of labor. Under capitalism the natural resources, productive forces, labor process, and final product are expropriated as private property for the control and enjoyment of the possessing classes. Labor which should express the joy of human self-realization is tranformed into the curse of humanity, into purposeless, mind-killing, self-alienating bondage. The universality of the species, its capacity to produce according to "the standard of every species" and to "apply everywhere the inherent standard to the object" is transformed into the crippling disfigurement of human standards, so that capitalist man is forced to produce the destruction of nature as a step to the destruction of man himself.

Art is that form of labor which best embodies human self-realization through the purposeful, conscious, free, and universal shaping of nature according to the measure and standard of human needs. Aesthetic production is the model of un-alienated labor, the quintessence of man's mastery over nature in accordance with his historically achieved freedom vis-a-vis his product. Our quotation from Marx continues:

> It is just in his work upon the objective world, therefore, that man first really proves himself to be a species being. This production is his active species life. Through and because of this production, nature appears as his work and his reality. The object of labor is, therefore, the objectification of man's species life: for he duplicates himself not only, as in consciousness, intellectually, but also actively, in reality, and therefore he contemplates himself in a world that he has created.[12]

We may thus distinguish three ways in which man's transformation of the world defines him generically as a natural species differentiating him from all others: (1) by his practical labor, which progressively shapes the raw materials of nature into the use values of human survival and supremacy, into the accumulated wealth of industry, culture, and civilization. Man's labor reflects his species essence as *power*; (2) by science and philosophy, ultimately based on the experience of the labor process but retained and accumulated in the form of consciousness of general natural laws which enable man to produce universally in accordance with the standards of all species. Man's science expresses his species essence as *knowledge*; (3) by art, creation according to the laws of beauty, creation in freedom from immediate physical need, universal creation which takes as its subject the universal creator, man himself, as he changes historically through the growth which science and technology impart to his labor power. Man's art expresses his species-essence as *freedom*.

Naturally, these three modalities of production are intricately interrelated in real life: the greater our productive forces, the greater also our knowledge and freedom. The common trait which is the unifying sign of human production is the exteriorization, objectification, and reproduction of the species-character in the outside world. The humanization of nature and society is achieved in different ways by labor, science, and art. In order to define the value of the aesthetic, we shall distinguish first art and science, then art and labor, and finally, art and politics.

Art is the sensuous representation of the direct, immediate, material, personal, and collective encounter between human beings and the social and natural field of their activities. But it is not enough to contrast the abstract sciences to the concrete arts because the arts have their own way of expressing meanings which go beyond the sensuously perceived forms through which they must express, represent, interpret, evaluate, and generalize a view of life. Wilhelm Girnus formulates this difference thoughtfully in his article "On the Problem of Ideology and Literature":

> Let it suffice to say that science compresses experience in the form of a general law, but that the human subject is always a personal subject and requires that his potentialities be articulated from the sensual-concrete standpoint of his personal existence. From this standpoint the subject projects for himself by means of imaginative literature his potentialities as generic subject in order to obtain possible coordinates for his self-positioning in the universe.[13]

In other words, the aesthetic can only be expressed through a subject who signifies more than his own individuality by objectifying himself in the social medium, in this case, of language, so as to allow others to see themselves and position themselves as generic subjects. Art is, par excellence, the social product of individuals, a form of labor which provides social man with the materially expressed, imaginative, therefore ideological, versions of his place in the world in specific historical times and places. Art is the valorization of the individual subject in his capacity to conceive and recreate himself generically, i.e., as human through the imaginative re-structuring of the natural world of things and processes and the social world of language and consciousness. Sidney Finkelstein emphasizes man's appropriation of the world through art in his formula: "The transformation of subject matter into subject." He writes: "A leap in the ability to command the outer world is a leap in the ability to respond to it. . . ." And later on, "The history of the arts can be called a record of the successive stages in the humanization of reality, revealing the constant change and expansion of the awareness of beauty to include ever new subject matter and ever new aspects of familiar subject matter."[14]

What, then differentiates the aesthetic from the economic? Practical labor makes a reshaped, humanized nature into the reflection of man's productive power. "Knowledge" is the name of man's intellectual self-doubling. Through labor and science he learns the inherent measures of animate and inanimate nature, its underlying necessities, regularities, laws. But nowhere more clearly than in art does man produce generically, that is, over and above physical need, according to his own measure, as master of nature and self-creative agent freely confronting his product. In other words, in art man takes himself as the subject matter which must be appropriated, transformed, into generic subject; it is a reshaping of the materials of nature, society, and consciousness into the representations, historically conditioned, of our emerging freedom vis-a-vis our products, nature, and society. Economic production learns to appropriate the world by the "inherent standard'" of each object; art appropriates for social consciousness our achieved humanity in the concrete process of overcoming itself generically. Art records our growing social power over nature as the freedom we gain through the recognition of necessity. In this sense art is the snythesis of labor and science, expressing our fullest capacity to create "according to the laws of beauty."

How does the art of the modern era interpret the state of human freedom under capitalism? How do we stand in relation to the natural and social world we have created? Do we confront our product freely? All the important art of the bourgeois era replies in the negative, and that negation is one of its main enduring values. The literature of the last two hundred years is a detailed documentation, in well-articulated stages, of the progressive dissolution of the human personality under bourgeois conditions of life. In this sense, all art is political, for the critique of unfreedom as the fundamental psychological, social, and moral condition of man is implicitly a demand and a preparation for freedom. Whether Balzac, Tolstoy, Kafka, or Mann defended in their conscious ideologies this or that inadequate political philosophy, the truth of their art has become a weapon of the modern aesthetic consciousness against the alienation of the late capitalist world. Their verdict thus confirms that of the revolutionary Marxist tradition which translates consciousness into action. That is why bourgeois aesthetics and criticism depoliticizes art, not only denying its social and ideological functions, but denouncing as propagandists those artists and critics who have the courage and common sense to call or ignore their bluff.

Politics, man's relations of power and authority to the state and to the community, is the central preoccupation of the Greeks, of most Elizabethan plays, and is crucial in the works of the great moderns from Stendhal and Balzac to Tolstoy, Mann, and Brecht. This is natural since the task of art is to propose generic images of man and since man is generically a social animal whose relations of freedom and necessity with nature are mediated through the socio-political structures which enable him to produce economically, intellectually, and artistically. The myth of that ahistorical, apolitical, asocial individual who haunts our metaphysical psycho-dramas as neurotic victim or symbol of the absurd is the product of a dying culture, a product whose ideological function it is to disparage human achievement.

The art of late capitalism does not and cannot depict man generically in the critical period of our revolutionary age, because to do so implies ineluctably to show him developing strategies to overcome alienation, to realize his freedom vis-a-vis his product as master of society and nature. In a word, bourgeois art and bourgeois criticism are not interested in the development of an historical aesthetic consciousness and therefore must feed on alienation raised to a metaphysical power. Up to now it has been good feeding: the alienation industry has boomed. Proust, Joyce, Kafka, and Mann were the great diagnosticians, analysts, and critics of the period of bourgeois decomposition. Their success spawned a bevy of self-satisfied epigones who passively reflect like disfiguring symptoms the myriad alienations of a dying culture.

But despite the rococo refinements of all the mini-Joyces, Proust-lettes, and *Kafkalekh*, a dull repetition has set in; it is beginning to cloy. It is on the contrary the politically committed writers — Brecht, Aragon, O'Casey, Neruda, etc. — whose horizons stretch beyond the turgid pollutions of our capitalist hell, who have most renewed the sources of creative life. These are the true innovators of modern literature and of modern poetics. The power and variety of their works are based on an ideological commitment which mobilizes imagination, skill, and thought on the realities of struggle, suffering, and will to live of our revolutionary era. Ours is, par excellence, a political reality, for it is in the domain of political struggle that the fundamental issues of human freedom will be decided.

We have argued that aesthetic creation displays a form of consciousness linked to labor on one hand by the concrete sensuousness of its product and to science on the other by its power to generalize experience. Man's conscious life in society and nature is art's characteristic concern even though it may take as subject matter the historically determined limits of that consciousness, of that freedom, as in tragedy. The value of the aesthetic is the transformation of lived experience "from subject matter into subject," of our "conscious life-process" into images embodying "the fundamental idea underlying the sum of a given reality,"[15] of praxis unaware of itself into an object of consciousness through aesthetic distance, of the mesh of historical contingency and necessity into resources of human freedom. No form of poetic insight, no form of spiritual invention may be proscribed. Creative fantasy has its place just as surely as the realistic novel and the factual documentary in "positioning" ourselves generically in terms of our historically realized freedom. Political, revolutionary experience is at the core of modern history; literature is not politics, but it cannot give us a true picture of our condition if it ignores politics, nor can a criticism which ignores or distorts the political content of literature achieve the status of an overall theory of the history and nature of artistic creation. Nothing human is alien to art, and man is inter alia a "political animal."

When the history of art is seen as the record of man's emerging freedom, the importance of the political dimension becomes clear. Labor and science have tipped the balance of nature in our favor. Modern technology has changed the ancient dream of abundance for all into an attainable possibility. The last obstacle is a social order which can only assure the power and privileges of the few by fostering misery and oppression on a global scale for the vast majority of the human race. That is why political consciousness and political struggle are becoming one of the touchstones of cultural significance in all domains of thought, including the arts and the theory of the arts. That is why formalist, psychological, and mythical modes of interpretation of literature, past and present, are inadequate to explain the facts of "spiritual production" today. The developing Marxist theories of literature, art, and culture in general are informed by the political and social realities which they actively strive to explain and shape, in order to make the transition from capitalism to socialism as humane as possible. That is why Marxism is the natural heir to the great humanistic tradition in which it discerns the stages of mankind's emerging freedom as expressed by its relations to nature, society, and the state. Marxism has given new meaning to the works of Aeschylus, Rabelais, Shakespeare, Goethe, Cervantes, Balzac, and Tolstoy, and all those artists who show men conquering something more of their humanity by struggling to change the world.

NOTES

1. See *Marxism and Art: Essays Classic and Contemporary*, ed. Maynard Solomon, Alfred A. Knopf, New York, 1973; *Marxism and Art: Writings in Aesthetics and Criticism*, ed. Berel Lang and Forrest Williams, David McKay Co., Inc., New York, 1972; *Preserve and Create: Essays in Marxist Literary Criticism*, ed. Gaylord LeRoy and Ursula Beitz, Humanities Press, New York, 1973. A few Americans are included in Maynard Solomon's anthology.

2. See *Radical Perspectives in the Arts*, ed. Lee Baxandall, Penguin Books, Baltimore, Maryland, 1972. This volume includes some American writers.

3. Karl Marx, *Theories of Surplus Value*, quoted in Solomon, *op. cit.*, p. 63.

4. V. I. Lenin, *On Literature and Art*, Progress Publishers, Moscow, 1967, p. 155. From a draft resolution presented to the Collegium of the People's Commissariat and the Proletcult Congress for endorsement.

5. "Past Significance and Present Meaning in Literary History" in LeRoy and Beitz, *op. cit.*, pp. 30-51.

6. *Ibid.*, p. 40.

7. *Ibid.*

8. *Ibid.*, p. 41.

9. *Ibid.*

10. From *Karl Marx and Frederick Engels: Selected Works*, International Publishers, New York, 1968: "In considering such transformations a distinction should always be made between the material transformation of the economic conditions of production, which can be determined with the precision of natural science, and the legal, political, religious, aesthetic, or philosophic — in short, ideological forms in which men become conscious of this conflict and fight it out." p. 183.

11. From *The Economic and Philosophic Manuscripts of 1844 by Karl Marx*, ed. Dirk J. Struik, International Publishers, New York, pp. 113-114.

12. *Ibid.*, p. 114.

13. From *New Literary History*, Vol. IV, Spring 1973, #3, pp. 483-500. The quote is taken from page 486 of the article.

14. See Sidney Finkelstein, "Beauty and Truth," pp. 54 and 60 of this volume.

15. Maxim Gorky, "Art and Myth," in Solomon, *op. cit.*, p. 244.

PART I

CRITICISM IN HISTORY

1

CRITICISM IN HISTORY

Fredric Jameson

If Marxism is a system among others, if Marxist literary criticism is a literary *method* among others, then, or so the objection runs, it ought to be possible to spell it out in a relatively straightforward way, without that complicated dialectical apparatus which, derived as much from Hegel as from Marx, seems to make such presentations into tortuous affairs of reflexivity and autoreference at every step of the way. Can we not simply talk about class and history, about ideology, and about the function of a given literary work in a given situation, with a polemic honesty that dispenses with the philosophical refinements? What about Brecht's and Benjamin's defense of *plumpes Denken* — crude thinking? Surely, as all real Marxists know, there is something intolerable about the use of the accusation of "vulgar Marxism" to frighten us away from the real issues and to encourage a kind of intellectual discourse more respectable and more acceptable in the university.

I think that the problem lies in this, that we are always *in situation* with respect to class and ideology and cultural history, that we are never able to be mere blank slates, and that truth can never exist as a static system, but always has to be part of a more general process of *demystification*. This, in its simplest form, is the justification and the essence of the dialectical method; and the proof is that even *plumpes Denken* takes its value from the intellectual positions which it corrects — the overcomplicated Hegelianism or philosophic Marxism for which it substitutes some hard truths and plain language. So *plumpes Denken* is not a position in its own right either, but the demystification of some prior position from which it derives its acquired momentum and of which it comes as a genuinely Hegelian *Aufhebung* or cancellation/transcendence.

This is why it seems to me at least as important to come to terms with the various critical methods practiced today, as to outline the method of the future. There is not only the evident fact that most of us have been formed in one or the other of those older "methods"; there is the far more basic presupposition that the Marxist point of view is secretly present in all those methods — if only as that reality which is repressed, or as that which is covertly opposed, that consciousness which is threatening and which the *mauvaise foi* of critical formalism then projects out of itself as its converse or its nightmare. So we do not have to be defensive about a Marxist literary criticism; that is more properly the stance of those who want to flee history. Nor do we need to suggest that Marxism is an *alternative* to those methods: rather, it is to be seen as their completion, and as the only method which can really finish what it is they all in their various ways set out to do.

Our hypothesis is, then, that all apparently formal statements about a work bear within them a concealed historical dimension of which the critic is not often aware; and it follows from this that we ought to be able to transform those statements about form and esthetic properties and the like into genuinely historical ones, if we could only find the right vantage point for doing so. The picture is then not one of turning away from the formalizing kinds of criticism to something else, but rather of going all the way through them so completely that we come out the other side, and that other side, for Marxists, is what is loosely known as history. Only to put it that way is to suggest all the wrong things too, and to convey the idea that it is simply a question of substituting one specialized discipline — that of the historian — for another — that of the literary critic. What I have in mind, however, is the point at which a specialized discipline is transcended towards reality itself; the point at which — and this under its own momentum, under its own inner logic — literary criticism abolishes itself as such, and yields a glimpse of consciousness momentarily at one with its social ground, of what Hegel calls the "concrete".

In what follows, I would like to give a sense of this momentary contact with the real, at least insofar as it takes place in the realm of literary studies; and in so doing, to touch on some of the critical methods which have seemed the most rewarding or at least the most prevalent in recent years, and also the most self-contained, and mutually exclusive. I would propose in particular to say something about stylistic analysis, about ethical criticism and myth criticism, about Freudian approaches, and about structuralism. No doubt what follows will be by way of a critique of these various methods; yet it is a critique which does not seek to dissolve their relative autonomy, or to abolish any of them as semi-independent methodologies. What I want to show is that none of these modes of interpretation are complete in themselves, and that their appearance of autonomy results from limits and boundaries arbitrarily fixed on the interpretative process. I would like to show that if you prolong any one of these methods even on its own terms — you always reemerge into the historical dimension itself, which thus comes as an implicit or explicit completion of all literary analysis or interpretation. I think in this connection of Serge Doubrovsky's striking description of the Marxist critical process, where he says, "you reach the heart of a text at the very moment you pass beyond it to its social context".[1] Such a formulation has the advantage of reminding us that the historical dimension does not come as a merely formal or academic type of completion — it reemerges with a kind of shock for the mind, as a kind of twist or a sudden propulsion of our being onto a different plane of reality. It involves what is properly a transformational process, conversion techniques, a shift in mental perspective which suddenly and powerfully enlarges our field of vision, releasing us from the limits of the various, purely literary methods, and permitting us to experience the profound historicity of their application, as indeed of all mental operations in general.

1

To begin with stylistics, it would seem that as generally practiced today, it tends to fall into two rather distinct and mutually exclusive types to investigation. In what we might call the classical or philological stylistics — that of Spitzer and Auerbach, or Jean-Pierre Richard — the various aspects of a syntax or of a style are understood as so many manifestations or externalizations of that more fundamental and indeed fictive entity which is the style of Rabelais or Faulkner, the spirit of the Baroque or of European realism, the genius of place, or whatever. The other stylistics — I take David Lodge's *Language of Fiction* as a convenient example — Riffaterre would be another — deliberately limits itself to the intrinsic effects of the individual work, enumerating the linguistic traits or features characteristic of that work — the vocabulary field, the predilection for certain types of sentence structure, and for certain types of verbal patterns over others — and attempts to show how each of these features — or the totality of them — contributes to the construction of that unique effect on the reader which is the aesthetic end or aim of the individual work in question. The distinction between these two antagonistic methods may become clearer if we characterize the second one as essentially a rhetorical analysis — dealing not with a corpus or a period but rather with the properties of discourse in general and of a single verbal object in particular — while the first is more properly *stylistic* in its emphasis on the uniquely personal, in the etymological sense of the *stilus*, the inimitable and wellnigh physiological specificity of my own handwriting. How to choose between these two methods, the one idealistic and speculative, the other empirical and analytic?

I would prefer to suggest that each in its own way corresponds to a different view of language and thereby to a distinct historical mode of the latter's development. Rhetoric is an older and essentially pre-capitalist mode of linguistic organization: it is a collective or class phenomenon, in that it serves as a means of assimilating the speech of individuals to some suprapersonal oratorical paradigm, to some non- or pre-individualistic standard of "beau parler", of high style and fine writing. A profound social value is here invested in spoken language, one which may be gauged by the primacy of such aristocratic form as the sermon and the verse tragedy, the salon witticism and the poetic epistle.

Style on the other hand is a middle-class phenomenon, and reflects the increasing atomization of middle-class life, and the sapping of the collective vitality of language itself, as the older collective and pre-capitalist social groupings are gradually undermined and dissolved. Style thus emerges, not from the social life of the group, but from the silence of the isolated individual: hence its rigorously personal, quasi-physical or physiological content, the very materiality of its verbal components.

We may put all this the other way around by reformulating it in terms of the literary public. Rhetoric would then reflect the existence of that relatively homogeneous public or class to which the speaker addresses himself, and may be detected by the predilection for standardized formulae and fixed forms, and by the continuing influence of the oratorical tradition as codified in classical Anitquity. Style is on the contrary always an individual and problematical solution to the dilemma of the absence of a public, and emerges against the background of that host of private languages into which the substance of the modern world has been shattered.

Such a distinction now permits us a more genuinely historical evaluation of the results achieved by both of the two stylistic or rhetorical methods I have been describing. It also permits us to understand such things as the relative disparity between the English and the French traditions of the novel (and incidentally between the types of literary criticism to which each has given rise). For if the English novel is modernized at a far later date than the French — around 1900, say? — this is surely to be accounted for by the vitality of the rhetorical strain in it. The English novel — all the way to Conrad and Ford and beyond — is irrepressibly spoken — elegant or chatty, Ciceronian or intimate — in a way which after the great letter novels, or at least after the death of Balzac, has no equivalent in the French tradition. Such narratives (I mean the English) have their readership vividly built into them; and one cannot read them without at once visualizing the drawing rooms and Victorian furniture in which they find their natural setting. The great English novels of the eighteenth and nineteenth centuries are thus forms of direct and quasi-immediate social communication and embody an aesthetic essentially oral in character: hence the linguistic priorities in them, which are those of the spoken rather than written composition, and where the sentences are not conceived as precious objects to be fashioned one by one, but rather emerge and disappear with all the permanent provisionality of spoken communication, telling, digressing, repeating, exclaiming, rambling, and apostrophizing. This is to say that in the English tradition, the individual prose sentence and the individual prose paragraph have not yet become dominant literary and stylistic categories in their own right: the spoken period, albeit on a familiar and intimate level, here clearly outweighs the later structures of a more modernistic aesthetic of the art sentence and of the visual text. The rhetorical dimension of the English novel thus only too clearly reflects the British class compromise, in which the older feudal aristocracy is able to maintain its control of the apparatus of the state to the very middle of the First World War by granting privileges to the bourgeoisie at the same time that it appropriates for itself the techniques of the latter's commercial and productive activity.

Whereas in France, rhetoric in the novel is at one stroke abolished in 1857, with the publication of *Madame Bovary*. Henceforth the novel is no longer the written prospectus of some essentially natural and quasi-oral storytelling, but rather the pretext for the forging of individual sentences, for the practice of style as such. And what was hitherto a cultural institution — the storytelling situation itself, with its narrator and class public — now fades into the silence and the solitude of the individual writer, confronted with the absence of a reading public as with some form of the absence of God. For in the development of France, which has so often seemed paradigmatic of modern political and class history in general, the July revolution of 1830 signals the definitive retirement of the aristocracy from the realm of governmental control, while the June massacre of 1848 confirms henceforth permanent antagonism between bourgeoisie and proletariat. After 1848 in France, therefore, the primacy of the middle classes announces the beginning of that process of social atomization and monadization of which the modern literary language — stylistic rather than rhetorical, profoundly subjectivistic rather than collective — is one ideological reflex among others. Under such circumstances, clearly enough, there can be no stylistic analysis which is not ultimately political or historical in character.

2

If we turn now to what may be called ethical or moral criticism, the Marxist position may well seem paradoxical, if not scandalous, to those trained in some Arnoldian tradition, and for whom it goes without saying that literature is always an ethical force, and always takes as its subject or has as its content ethical choices. And of course, if everything is a matter of ethics, then clearly enough so is literature. But the proposition that in our time politics and political questions have superceded ethics or moral ones implies a complete transformation of the status of the individual in society: it suggests that we would do better to limit the notion of ethical choices and ethical acts to those situations alone in which individuals face each other as conscious and responsible moral or rational agents; or in which such an autonomous individual or subject confronts his own Self or personal development. To put it this way is to realize that in the modern world, and therefore in modern literature as well, there are many experiences and situations which are far more complex than this, where an individual or a character is faced not with an interpersonal relationship, with an ethical choice, but rather with a relationship to some determining force vaster than himself or any individual, that is, with society itself, or with politics and the movement of history; and there are other situations in which he finds himself confronted by the influence of forces and instincts within himself which cannot be assimilated to consciousness in the older sense of autonomous reason. In both these cases, we have left ethical content, and ethical criticism, behind for a literature and a criticism of a more political or psychological cast; and it follows that a literature for which ethics or moral choices are the principle subject-matter will require a fairly stable class context for its development — you cannot explore sophisticated questions of interpersonal relationships in the midst of social upheaval or extreme psychic disintegration.

Thus the very project of an ethical literature is itself socially and historically symptomatic: to take an illustrious example of what no one doubts to be a work with ethical content, George Eliot's *Middlemarch,* we may briefly summarize that content under the form of a double lesson.

Middlemarch teaches us on the one hand that, as isolated as our individual lives are from each other, they nonetheless continue to exert a mysterious subterranean influence on each other of which we ourselves are scarcely aware: the network of such influences — George Eliot calls it a "stealthy convergence of human lots" — constitutes the very body and reality of the social fabric, hidden except in moments of unusual vision from our everyday awareness. "Dorothea's full nature, like that river of which Cyrus broke the strength, spent itself in channels which had no great name on the earth. But the effect of her being on those around her was incalculably diffusive: for the growing good of the world is partly dependent on unhistoric acts; and that things are not so ill with you and me as they might have been, is half owing to the number who lived faithfully a hidden life, and rest in unvisited tombs."[2]

The other lesson of *Middlemarch* has to do with the reliability of consciousness itself, and with the profound difference there is between ideas, concepts, and values which we understand in a purely intellectualized way, and those somehow concretely realized for us in our life experience. Only think, in this connection, of the comical disparity between Mr. Casaubon's universal key to mythology, with its hypothesis of an unbroken tradition from the earliest generations to our own time, and his shattering discovery of the imminence of his own death; think of Dorothea's initial vapid pietism and of her later, painfully won understanding of the realities to which those doctrines correspond. Here the novel triumphantly reassumes its function as a demystification of consciousness and as the guardian and the purifier of genuine ethical content.

From a historical point of view, however, such content is to be received with a certain methodological suspicion: or rather, like the interpretation of statutes and ordinances in the legal superstructure, it is first and foremost to be understood negatively. Just as you do not legislate against things nobody does, just as the existence of a given taboo at a certain period in history tends to suggest the prevalence of the crimes against which it is directed, so also no one needs to teach what everybody knows; and ethical doctrines are in this sense to be understood as symptoms of a social situation which calls out for the supplement or the corrective of the doctrine in question. So George Eliot's novelistic construction of a community or a *Gemeinschaft*, her doctrine of the secret interweaving of human existences, stands itself as a symptom of the increasing disintegration of community, of the increasing difficulty her contemporaries have in feeling their society to be an organic totality. This — rather than the overt political, or I should say anti-political attitudes expressed in the book — is the most basic way in which it reflects the realities of its social context.

As for the second major theme of the work, or what we might call the existential dimension of George Eliot, it expresses that distrust of the abstract to be found everywhere in modern middle-class culture, growing more and more pronounced in the present century and of which existentialism is itself of course one of the more striking manifestations. Such distrust — a kind of philosophical anti-intellectualism, a growing conviction of the gap between words and real meaning or real experience — arises from the increasing autonomy of culture in the middle-class world. It reflects the disintegration of the older codified social wisdom; a proliferation of private languages and private philosophies which is itself but the reflection of the increasing automization of private existence; the alienation of language by commercial uses and the commercial media; in short, the division of labor and the structural mystification of middle class man about his own social reality, a mystification more complex and of a far greater intensity than that obtaining in any previous kind of society. George ELiot's novel, as language, is obliged to work its way back up the current of a debased speech in order to find some original and unsullied content; yet not that content, but rather the process of linguistic reinvention itself, yields the surest clue to the concrete historical reality in question. So we cannot even understand *Middlemarch* in the fullest way without replacing its ethical concerns in their historical situation, without seeing them as a response to an essentially social dilemma, without indeed translating them into political terms of which George Eliot was not always herself aware; and the ethical categories — which are semi-autonomous to the degree to which George Eliot herself considered them ultimates or absolutes, a semi-autonomy of moral philosophy and religious problematics which has its source in the English situation, and of which a sociological analysis could be made in its own right — are least of all the final terms of our literary comprehension.

3

With myth criticism it is much the same, except that the myth critic is the prisoner, not of some concrete historical class or in-group situation, as rather of a utopian vision of his own devising. For myth is the imaginative consciousness of primitive social life, of the archaic or neolithic *Gemeinschaft*; it is a pre-individualistic storytelling which seals the unity of the tribe, confirms their common past through the celebration of the heroic founders of culture itself, and unites their individual minds through a shared symbolism and a shared ritual (Durkheim's description of religion). If, therefore, in the modern world we find or seem to find mythic patterns in our literature, this is surely not because the novelist in question has been able once again to tap archaic sources of the imagination or of the collective unconscious, but only because he has experienced the nostalgia for such sources and such origins. Northrop Frye knows this very well, as his insistence on the translation or degradation of myth into literature shows: "The structural principles of a mythology, built up from analogy and identity, become in due course the structural principles of literature. The absorption of the natural cycle into mythology provides myth with two of these structures; the rising movement that we find in myths of spring or the dawn, of birth, marriage and resurrrection, and the falling movement in myths of death, metamorphosis, or sacrifice. These movements reappear as the structural principles of comedy and tragedy in literature."[3] Or again: "Total literary history moves from the primitive to the sophisticated, and here we glimpse the possibility of seeing literature as a complication of a relatively restricted and simple group of formulas that can be studied in primitive culture. If so, then the search for archetypes is a kind of literary anthropology, concerned with the way that literature is informed by pre-literary categories such as ritual, myth and folk tale."[4] What we do not find in Frye, however, any more than we find it in Levi-Strauss, is some genuinely historical account of how history itself began, how the cold societies were transformed into hot societies, how the mythic storytelling of neolithic life gave way to the literature of the more complex social forms. (As for Frye's own recent statements about art and society, I would have to characterize them as making room for the *social* function of literature at the expense of it *historical* function. In Ricoeur's terminology, Frye offers us a positive hermeneutic not unlike that of Ernst Bloch, one which stresses the origins of art in the deepest and most primal longings of the collectivity. He does not betray, however, the slightest awareness that hermeneutic can serve another, equally vital, but negative purpose, namely that of demystification: what Ricoeur calls the hermeneutic of suspicion, that of the critique of ideology and of false consciousness. Yet it is precisely that negative hermeneutic which takes as its object historical man, and which is alone capable of dealing with and correcting the distortions of the utopian wish as the latter emerges into the repressive structure of a given concrete situation in history itself.)

Still, I don't mean by this to recommend that we jettison myth criticism, only that we invert its priorities. After all, in such works as those of

Bakhtin[5] we find something like a myth criticism whose sound has been turned back on, a myth criticism willing to account historically and socially for its own content, and to defend the position that the forms which come out of the older collectivities, the literature of festival and of the saturnalian celebration of a whole community, has precisely the value *for us today* of standing in accusation of our own social life, of constituting a condemnation of the market system as such from which, henceforth, all genuine popular elements have disappeared. So where Frye tries to mystify us, and, implying mythic elements still at work in our own society, uses his doctrine of the literary archetypes to reinforce our sense of the identity between the literary present and this distant mythical past, and to inspire some sense of the continuity between our psyches and those of primitive man, it seems to me equally feasible, and more realistic, to do the reverse, and to use the raw material shared by both myth and literature to stimulate our sense of historical difference, and to help us to an increasingly vivid apprehension of what happens when plot falls into history, so to speak, and enters the fields of force of the modern societies. So what myth criticism ought to be telling us is not that modern writers recreate myths, but rather that they wish they could; and it ought to be explaining the origins of such a compensatory wish in the very structure of modern social life itself.

4

We must however sharply distinguish this kind of archetypal or Jungian or religious myth criticism from the Freudian variety, which has a very different intent and very different implications. Genuine Freudianism is, like Marxism, a materialism: which is to say that it cannot really be assimilated to the ideal coherence and consistency of a purely philosophical system. It stresses, on the contrary, the contingency and lack of autonomy of consciousness, the scandalous and irrevocable dependency of the mind on something which irreconcilable with the latter's sense of order and meaning and the like, in the occurence, on human sexuality itself. It would no doubt be a mistake to speak of *a* Freudian criticism, as though there were only one, or worse yet, as though there existed a single authentic or fully accredited, orthodox variety. Just as Freud himself throughout his career evolved a series of distinct models or hypotheses about the psyche, models not always reintegrated into some definitive synthesis, so a literary criticism inspired by Freud's discoveries finds itself confronted with a very rich series of themes, around any one of which a distinctive interpretative practice might be organized. What I would like to suggest is that most of the methods thus inspired tend to result in literary interpretations which are essentially allegorical in character, the most representative being no doubt that which sees the various elements of the work as figures for the parts of the psyche, for the id, the ego and the superego. To say so, however, may appear at first glance to damn Freudian interpretation by association, and to burden it with the ignominy which has for so long clung to allegorical interpretation in general, as a kind of artificial refraction of the organic unity of a work into lifeless parts and mechanical personifications.

If you regard allegory in general, however, and Freudian allegory in particular, as a cultural and historical symptom rather than as one intellectual option among others, this is perhaps no longer quite the case. We may recall, in this context, Adorno's recommendation that we understand the Freudian psychic model as a new *event* rather than a new *theory*; that we understand the Freudian system as a sign of profound new changes and restructurations taking place in the consciousness of Western man in general. So, no doubt, for Freud himself, the Oedipus complex is a constant throughout history, along with the superego and the id, along with repression and sublimation; but in the present context it seems more useful, or at least more interesting, to understand the Freudian vision of the psyche as being itself a reflexion of the historic moment when the older autonomous rational consciousness begins to disintegrate, when the Subject can no longer be felt as an autonomous and intelligible whole in its own right, can no longer be seen as the responsible agent posited by ethical criticism, but rather begins to project an Other out of itself, and to feel itself surrounded with the dark and inaccessible, yet ultimately determinate realm of the unconscious. The Freudian psychic model is thus a kind of allegory of the mind, in which consciousness suddenly understands itself in relationship to other hidden absent zones of energy: such a discovery is tantamount to the realization by consciousness that it is not a complete thing in itself, not really autonomous, not wholly in control or wholly intelligible in its own terms. But this discovery is just as surely a social event as it is a scientific hypothesis.

Seen in this light, the works which call out for Freudian interpretation reflect through their allegorical structure some fundamental dispersal of the lived experience of consciousness, some fundamental disintegration of the psyche. Such works foretell the end of the age of individualism, and nothing is quite so comparable to the medieval practice of allegory in, say, *Le Roman de la rose*, as the great surrealist film of Buñuel and Dali, *An Andalusian Dog*, with its multiple levels, its looping temporal sequences and its use of doubles of the hero to represent the superego and the id. *Un chien andalou* shares with the poem of Guillaume de Lorris the conviction that to give a complete picture of the story of love — the central theme of both works — requires us to transcend the subjective point of view of the individual lover himself and indeed point of view in general as a literary category — and to present materials — in the one case cultural, in the other psychic — which are largely inaccessible to his own limited consciousness. Yet in spite of the peculiar stylization of such works, in spite of their depersonalized and wellnigh inhuman surface, they represent an attempt to construct a new and intelligible totality upon the ruins of the older individualistic one; they reflect psychic disintegration, to be sure, but at the same time they mark an effort at overcoming that state by the very fact of making it present to us as a complete process.

Freudian interpretation thus designates a fragmentation, but also a reunification of existence. In a situation in which consciousness is now but a minimal zone of our being, and a doubtful one, whose introspection and whose self-knowledge is no longer trustworthy, the Freudian schemes come as larger coordinates within which we may relocate the data of consciousness and correct their distortions. Allegorical criticism of this kind thus corresponds to the structure of a post-individualistic world, one in which neither the older unity of the *Gemeinschaft* nor the newer unity of the autonomous and individualistic bourgeois subject, is available.

At the same time such allegory has a political dimension of a far more specific import than the symptomatic character of its form. If indeed we remember the frequency with which, in Freud, the psyche is compared to a city or to a government, it will not be terribly surprising to find that all Freudian interpretation is in its very structure susceptible to expression in political terms, amounting, thus, to a political, as well as a psychic, allegory. Thus Buñuel's "passionate appeal to murder" is also an explosive document of modern anarchism and finds its explicit political expression in his next movie, *L'Age d'or*. Or to take another familiar illustration, Thomas Mann's *Death in Venice* is the story of the return of the repressed, the destruction of the psyche by its own rigid mechanisms of censorship — but it is also a prophetic allegory of the internal collapse of the authoritarian Prussian state, in that far closer to *Der Untertan* or *The Blue Angel* than, say, to Kafka or Hofmannsthal. So it is that the allegories revealed by the Freudian method prove to harbor a very explicit political content in their structures themselves, at the same time that by their existence as forms they stand as signs of the crippling effects of monopoly capitalism on the consiousness of modern man.

their structures themselves, at the same time that by their existence as forms they stand as signs of the crippling effects of monopoly capitalism on the consciousness of modern man.

5

When we turn, finally to Structuralism, we may find it equally difficult to isolate some official structural literary method. In actual practice, the literary criticism to which Structuralism has given rise tends to fall into two relatively distinct groups. On the one hand there is what we might call the apolitical branch or right wing of the structuralist movement, which through complicated descriptive analyses of individual forms, aims at the construction of a grammar and a taxonomy of narrative or plot structures, using surface oppositions or deeper quasi-syntactic structures to establish the essential movement of the narrative from contract broken to contract reestablished, from object lost to object restored, from contradiction through mediation to final synthesis.

On the other side of the political spectrum, we find a whole body of work — particularly centering around the literary review *Tel Quel* — which aims at making explicitly political correlations between the forms of discourse — the internal mechanisms of a text — the relative dosage of written and spoken — the reification or process-oriented character of a given style and attitude towards language — and forms of bourgeois or revolutionary consciousness.

Yet it should be understood that in reality both of these kinds of research are post-Marxist, and that even the relatively formalistic kinds of Structuralism tend to imply correlations between literary and extra-literary structures. Our task here is thus a little more complicated than it was with respect to the other methods we have touched on: for it is here a question, not so much of revealing some historical dimension implicit or concealed in the method, as rather of passing judgement on sociological conclusions already suggested by the critics themselves.

The vices of structural method are however not terribly difficult to localize: they arise almost exclusively from strategic and self-imposed methodological limits on the type of statements to be made, from a purely empirical attitude towards the individual text under study, and from a refusal, after the completion of the analytical procedure, to turn the attention back upon the structural method and categories themselves as part of the larger object of study. So what is at issue is not the technique of structural analysis as such: such techniques have permitted us to isolate the finest mechanisms of plot and narrative with something of that same microscopic precision which the New Criticism taught us to bring to bear on the verbal texture of poetry. What is at issue is rather the nature of the conclusions to be drawn from such research.

To illustrate this with a well-known and widely reprinted essay of the late Jacques Ehrmann, "The Structures of Exchange in Corneille's *Cinna*,"[6] no one can fail to be both impressed and convinced, I think, by the patterns there shown to be present in the very language of tragedy — patterns of giving and taking, receiving, buying and selling, pillage, heaping high with gifts or on the contrary the struggle to obtain a just recompense — such are some of the ways in which Corneille and his characters see the consequences of an act. It is clear that for them acts take place within a complex exchange system, in which every move commits your interlocutor to some reciprocal — immediate or mediated — obligation in return. With such an analysis, Ehrmann is of course in the very mainstream of the structuralist tradition: for his model derives from Marcel Mauss' *Essay on the Gift*, an essay whose seminal insights were adapted by Levi-Strauss to the marriage rules which govern the exchange of women in primitive societies in a study, *The Elementary Structures of Kinship*, which may be said to amount to the first great monument of Structuralism as an intellectual and philosophical movement.

What conclusions does Ehrmann go on to draw from the existence of these exchange patterns in the work of Corneille? It is only fair to observe that he refuses to be drawn beyond the limits of a purely literary study of a single isolated text. "A critic who enlarged his investigation to include all the works, or the major works, of an era," he tell us, "would see his goal metamorphosed. At that point, with the goal changed, the nature of his study would change. Instead of being literary, it would be either sociological or anthropological. The question is then raised of knowing at what moment the analysis of literary structures ceases to isolate the esthetic or literary aspects of an object and moves on to isolate its anthropological and sociological aspects."[7]

Unfortunately it is not quite so simple as all that, and the anthropological and sociological dimensions of which Ehrmann speaks are already included in his analysis in potential form in the very concept of exchange itself. A category like exchange comes to literary and structural analysis from the fields of anthropology and sociology and economics and is thus already profoundly comparative in nature. So at that point it does not really matter very much whether the analyst himself refuses, as does

Ehrmann here, to take the final step and to assimilate the verbal structures of *Cinna* to those deeper socio-economic ones — whether Mauss' potlatch, or the mechanisms of feudal hierarchy, or the market system of nascent capitalism — which are already latent in the concept of exchange itself. Such assimilation is already implicit in the analysis, and this seems to me indeed the fundamental contradiction of the structural method as such — the comparative nature of its conceptual instruments forces the reader to draw generalizing conclusions which can never be corroborated by the isolated object of a purely empirical type of study.

Even those conclusions are however historical in appearance only; for structural theory goes on to assimilate all these varied social forms — potlatch, feudal hierarchy, market system — to some more abstract linguistic or communicational relationship; and with this further development, we find ourselves in a wholly ahistorical realm for which categories such as exchange are seen as a priori and universal categories of the human mind and of human society in general.

Still, it is only fair to point out that — particularly in the most theoretically sophisticated specimens of structural plot analysis, those of Levi-Strauss himself — we are offered a somewhat different model of the relationship of literary to extraliterary structures. For Levi-Strauss, not content to isolate and describe the structures of a narrative, goes on to ask the *function* of such a narrative in the life of the tribe. It then emerges that primitive narrative or myth is yet another form of primitive thinking — *pensée sauvage* — or unconscious reasoning: the narrative is an attempt to reconcile irreconcilable contraries, to solve, through a kind of picture language, like a rebus or a dream, the conceptual antinomies or concrete contradictions which haunt the social life of the pimitive commune.[8] Thus narrative becomes once again an act — an act through which primitive man attempts, in the imaginary, to come to grips with his social context and to resolve its most crucial problems. So at length we glimpse a kind of literary analysis which, without even abandoning the purely formal specificity of the work of art itself, may immediately be reformulated in terms of an event in history; a kind of analysis for which the intrinsic and purely formal structures of the work are at one and the same time invested with all the value of a protopolitical act.

6

Such are then some of the ways in which literary analysis touches the ultimate ground of history itself. And perhaps it will have come to seem that in all this I have been systematically delivering literary criticism over into the hands of the historians, and subsuming literary study a little too hastily beneath the more all-embracing discipline of history itself. Yet the history I have in mind is not at all to be confused with the common ordinary garden-variety empirical history; to use an offensive but convenient phrase, it is indeed not bourgeois historiography at all, for the latter is not a genuine philosophy of history and does not posit a unified overall meaning to the stages of social development. It will be objected, no doubt, that the very notion of a philosophy of history has been discredited, and that the concept of a meaning in history as a whole has been shown to be the solution to a false problem. Yet just as Marxism is both the end and the completion of philosophy, so in much the same way it may be said to be both the end and the fulfillment of philosophies of history as well, and to demonstrate how the scattered and disparate events of history share common themes and common dilemmas, which link the toil and misery of Neolithic man to the most dramatic, as well as the most obscure, struggles of our own age.

A few years ago, it might have been necessary at this point to defend the Marxist vision of history, if not, indeed, to remind people what it was in the first place. Today I doubt if that is any longer really the case. In the past few years, we have witnessed the intellectual and political collapse of that liberal world-view which for so long served as an explanation as well as a justification of our economic development and of the aims of our foreign policy — I doubt if there are very many people left today who still believe either in the promise of the older American liberalism or in the theoretical accounts it used to give of the organization of American life. Now that we've come to understand counterinsurgency warfare and neo-colonialism, not as freely chosen options of good or evil political leaders, but rather as deeper and more ominous structural necessities of the American system; now that we have been able to observe what is left of the American way of life bombarded and pulverized by the twin corrosive forces of racism and commercialism and indeed to witness the beginnings of the deterioration of the American economic system as a whole, now that we have learned the facts about American responsibility for the beginnings of the Cold War, let alone more recent conflicts, Marxism has once again seemed to many to provide the only intellectually coherent and fully satisfying historical and economic explanation for the things that have been happening to us. It is a total explanation, and this is its formal superiority over all the other partial kinds of accounts — the culture critiques and existential diagnoses, the psychological analyses and the liberal and reformist types of ethical appeal — which use the amount of validity they do contain to obscure the sources of all those cultural sicknesses in the very economic structure of capitalism itself.

Still, to commit ourselves to a Marxist theory of history is not necessarily to identify the historical themes in terms of which our ultimate interpretation will be made. You will have observed, in particular, the use in the present essay of an interpretative code based on Tönnies' classic concept of the difference between *Gemeinschaft* and *Gesellschaft*, between the older organic societies and those fragmented and atomistic social agglomerations with which we are familiar in the modern world, with their profound subjectivization and their monadization of individual experience. Such an opposition is already implicit in Hegel and is quite consistent with socialist thought; but unfortunately it is just as consistent with conservative or fascist thought as well, which brandish a return to the older national or racial *Gemeinschaft*. The trouble with this particular theme as an ultimate description of social reality is that it amounts to a description of that reality from the point of view of the bourgeoisie alone, since it is in the forms of bourgeois life that such social disintegration is taking place. Yet the opposition between *Gemeinschaft* and *Gesellschaft* — one after all between two types of *society* — sometimes strikes me as being far more adequate and far less misleading than some of the psychological and existential concepts — such as that of alienation — which have come increasingly to be thought of as the principal Marxist contributions to modern sociological theory.

As far as alienation is concerned, it has always seemed to me ironic, if not downright comic, that a concept intended by the Marx of the *Economic and Philosophical Manuscripts* to apply to the way in which the labor power of working people was appropriated from them, along with their work satisfaction and the very products of their labor, should have been so enthusiastically adopted by the middle classes of the affluent society as a glamorous and pathetic way of characterizing their own subjective malaise and psychological complications.

The basic terms of any genuinely Marxist interpretation must surely remain those older and more familiar ones of commodity production and of class struggle; and if they tend to summon up spectres of the worst excesses of vulgar Marxism or of Soviet dogmatism, I can only point to that brilliant series of works in which only yesterday Adorno showed the commodity form to be at the very heart of twentieth century modernism.[9] As for the class struggle itself, its all-informing presence in our private lives as well as in the daily life of our society is the very first lesson which the Marxist textbook has to teach us; and in the absence of such an experience and such a concept there can be no Marxist theory worthy of the name.

Even granting these fundamental themes of Marxism, however, there remains the problem of the proper way of relating a literary analysis to them; and to characterize this very briefly in closing I would like to return for a moment to the essay of Jacques Ehrmann from which I quoted a moment ago. "I have said," he goes on to tell us there, "that I was not interested in looking upon literature as a form of economics. But that doesn't necessarily mean that the phenomenon of literature should be seen as unlike the phenomenon of economics. Using this perspective, it would be as much a question, with the one, of understanding the system established for the exchange of services, merchandise, and women which form the network of communications in ancient and modern collectivities, as it would be, for the other, a question of understanding the system of word and image exchange in literary and artistic communication. The latter system of exchange is, in effect, readily comparable to the former."[10]

In short, we have to do here with what Lucien Goldmann called homologies, or isomorphisms, or structural parallelisms between various types of social realities. This is indeed the principal sociological method of Structuralism, and the form which most structuralist versions of Marxism tend to take, involving analogies between the purely literary and verbal structures of the work and the various spheres of the legal system, the political ideology, the organization of the market, obtaining in the period in question.

To return to *Cinna* in this light, we find that for Ehrmann the various events of the tragedy — the gradual elaboration of the conspiracy against the Emperor, the doubts of Cinna himself, torn between his admiration for Augustus and his love for a woman who is the latter's mortal enemy, the Emperor's ultimate gesture of clemency with which the conspiracy is unravelled and the play concluded — all these events amount to so many stages along a "circuit of gift-giving" which can be buckled and fulfilled only by the supreme magnanimity of Augustus' pardon itself as a kind of absolute gift, self-founding and self-motivated. The play thus consitutes for Ehrmann a kind of narrative dramatization of the structural permutations inherent in the exchange mechanism current at the time of Corneille.

That there can be another and far less static way of relating a literary form to its underlying social reality I would like to demonstrate by reference to the literary sociology of Paul Bénichou in his seminal book *Les Morales du grand siècle*.[11] For Benichou the plays of Corneille are the literary and ideological expression of the rebellious feudal nobility of the

Fronde — a declining class, suffering increasingly from the centralizing absolutism, first of Richelieu and Mazarin, and then of Louis XIV, and increasingly edged out of positions of power by the parliamentary nobility (drawn from the upper bourgeoisie) as well as by the rising middle class itself. The politics of these great nobles are profoundly contradictory, for their revolt against the crown is born of a deep longing to return to the feudal license of an earlier era, while at the same time, insofar as the king is a *primus inter pares*, they cannot strike at his power without dealing a blow to their own pretensions as well and sapping the ideological bases of the feudal system as a whole. (And when, a century and a half later, the French Revolution itself began in precisely this way as a revolt of the nobles against the king, the consequences for those who set it in motion were appropriately disastrous.) In such a situation therefore, where no real solution is available, an imaginary one is born, a kind of ideological or political wish fulfillment, of which *Cinna* is one of the most striking manifestations. For the dilemma of the nobility could be resolved only if the monarch, maintaining his own legal authority, nonetheless in all his feudal generosity freely turned back to the nobles themselves all those privileges for which they had rebelled against him. Thus the theatrical gesture of Augustus is a little something more than a mere static reflexion of the thought patterns of the baroque *Weltanschaung*; it is an act charged with significance, which seems to suspend and appease for an instant all the deepest contradictions of the age. For such a point of view, Corneille's tragedy is not some mere document in the correlation between works and social classes, between forms of thought and forms of social life; it is first and foremost an event, one which can be shown to have a precise ideological function at a unique moment in history.

For me, therefore, the method of homologies, while not necessarily false in its results, is static and documentary, and derives ultimately from the history of ideas on the one hand, and from a non-Marxist sociology of literature on the other. I would call instead for a *functional* model of the relationship between a work and its social context, one capable of articulating the central paradox of a Marxist aesthetics: namely, that the force of a work of art is directly proportional to its historicity, that there is indeed no contradiction between our present-day appreciation of a work and its concrete historical content, that the greatness of Corneille is not atemporal, but springs immediately from the force with which his plays reflect the struggles of an event like the Fronde — itself apparently a mere historical curiosity for us today, the convulsion of an extinct class whose values mean nothing to us. Indeed, it will be recalled that it was precisely the Fronde which Lévi-Strauss chose as his example when, at the close of *The Savage Mind*, he undertook to discredit history itself as a mode of knowledge. He there implied that history was a matter of taking sides, and that, if such a relationship, which requires a delicate assessment of progressive and reactionary positions within a given historical situation, still makes sense for events of the middle-class era, in which we are still ourselves implicated, it becomes senseless when we return to an earlier period whose struggles no longer concern us. And of course, the ideals of the Fronde are both progressive and reactionary: reactionary in that they serve the ideological function of enlisting the people of Paris in support of an archaic feudal aristocracy, progressive insofar as they nonetheless foreshadow a revolt against the centralization of the feudal power itself. Yet the example of Corneille shows that such contradictions have a very special way of coexisting in the literary work, and that as a desperate and vital episode in the long class struggle of human history, it is precisely not in the history books that the Fronde lives on, but rather in the very bones and marrow of literary form itself. With such a vision of the work of art, the techniques of literary criticism find their ultimate ground in historical reality, and literature may be said once again to recover for us its value as a social act.

NOTES

1. Serge Doubrovsky, *Corneille et la dialectique du heros* (Paris, 1963), p. 15.

2. George Eliot, *Middlemarch* (Boston, 1956), p. 613

3. Northrop Frue, *Fables of Identity* (New York, 1963), pp. 33-34.

4. Ibid., p. 12.

5. See Mikhail Bakhtin, *Rabelais and his World* (Cambridge, 1968), and *Problems of Dostoevsky's Poetics* (Ann Arbor, 1973).

6. Jacques Ehrmann, ed., *Structuralism*, Yale French Studies #36-37 (Fall, 1966).

7. Ibid., p. 198.

8. See "The Structural Study of Myth", in *Structural Anthropology* (New York, 1967), pp. 202-228.

9. See, for example, his *Philosophy of New Music* (New York, 1974).

10. Ibid., p. 198.

11. Translated as *Man and Ethics: Studies in French Classicism* (New York, 1971).

2

BEAUTY AND TRUTH

Sidney Finkelstein

In the first half of the 19th century, two quite different thinkers asserted the interconnection of beauty and truth; John Keats and Karl Marx.

Keats, in his *Ode on a Grecian Urn*, speaks of a work of art as a moment of rapt life transmuted into a different form of existence, in which it is outside of time and change, and the cycle of life and death. In this transmutation, this moment is freed from the torments that have accompanied it, "a burning forehead and a parching tongue." No blood runs through it. It is a "cold pastoral." Yet so long as life goes on, and from death comes new birth, it is present to speak its friendly message, easing human woes; this is that truth and beauty are dialectically one, that truth, or a transitory moment of rapt life, is transmuted into beauty, as an object that unchanging, can yet affect and change new life. Thus "beauty is truth, truth beauty."

Marx, in his philosophical manuscripts of 1844 (*Estranged Labor*), states that man is different from the animals, in that as "conscious being," he has learned ways of labor beyond the satisfaction of his immediate needs for existence. In "working up" the world outside him, he has begun to see this world as an "object," something with its own qualities other than its ability to satisfy physical needs like hunger and thirst. Along with this confrontation of the world, he begins consciously to confront himself as an object. A new relationship rises between himself and this outer world. For in discovering this world's manifold qualities, or truth, he discovers his own potentialities beyond the satisfaction of physical needs, and thus can produce in freedom from such needs. And so, Marx says, man also creates "in accordance with the laws of beauty." Furthermore, what he has gained can be wrested away. For the human form of labor has its counterpart in the reverse process, or "estranged

51

labor," where his labor is degraded to become again a mere means to existence.

The phrase, "creation according to the laws of beauty," can serve, I suggest, as a good beginning definition of art. The question rises, then of just what these laws are. One that can be suggested is that beauty cannot be captured by direct aim. When an artist seeks to create something that is beautiful, and nothing else, all that he achieves is an academicism or imitation of another art work. We must look then to what has been suggested in the interpretation here of the poem by Keats and the passage from Marx; the integral connection between beauty and truth. And truth they say, as it relates to art and beauty, is not simply the immediate reflection of reality as it strikes the senses. It is the insight that comes when reality is put through a process, worked on and so rediscovered.

This coincides with what we know of the origins of art works themselves, in the earliest societies. The concept of "art as such,"of a work of art that has no other function than to be itself and give aesthetic delight, is a latecomer in the history of art creation. The creations of early societies that we now call art works were inseparable from other functions. There were immediate utilities such as tools, weapons, pottery, utensils. There were magical functions like picture and ritual to insure success in hunting, war, childbirth and agriculture. A central concept in early magic was that to imitate some object, animal, process or force of nature was to achieve power over it. Christopher Caudwell calls this creating "illusions" that at the same time can become real, by organizing a tribe about its collective tasks. And there is an element of the real in all these illusions, even if the real becomes symbol, like the imitation in primitive life of sexual acts as a magic ritual to ensure agricultural fertility in the spring. Indeed, tribal rituals also served to initiate the young into adulthood, and to impart to them the accumulated tribal knowledge and skills. Then there are functional works like lullabies and work songs. And for millennia, what we now call art was connected to functions like religion and historical chronicling.

Yet under these conditions, works appeared that we now recognize as fully realized and beautiful works of art, unified in form and content; pottery, baskets, weapons; cave paintings that imitate animals to be hunted or the process of hunting; masks and symbolic carvings to represent disembodied natural forces, spirits or nature gods; lullabies and work songs, combining music and poetry; mimed and chanted rituals that held the seeds of drama, and mythological histories that held the seeds of the epic poem and the novel. How, out of such functional service, did these works also attain the quality of art or beauty? Why do they appeal as such to us today, when we follow science, write documentary history, and no longer believe in magic, nature gods or mythologies?

A clue comes again from Karl Marx. It is frequently said today, with the widespread interest in the philosophical manuscripts of 1844, that the views of this early Marx were not those of the later Marx. This writer disagrees. It is true that Marx at the age of twenty-six was still making a heavy use of terminology derived from the previous German philosophical tradition. He was already, however, a philosophical materialist, and also aware of the exploitation of labor. He had not yet filled out his materialism with his profound studies of history, politics and the forces moving them, and with his development of the science of economics. When he did so, his terminology became different. Yet the insight that fills out the connection he drew in the manuscripts of 1844 between reality, labor and beauty can be found in his definition of the labor process, in Vol. I of *Capital*. After describing the labor process as the appropriation of nature's productions by man in a form adapted to his own wants, Marx adds, "By thus acting on the external world and changing it, he at the same time changes his own nature. He develops his slumbering powers and compels them to act in obedience to his sway."

Marx's definition of the labor process does not mean that every work act is an act of creation and human growth, just as when he says that the labor process is social, he does not mean that every work act is carried on collectively. What it does point out is that human labor in the aggregate has brought about permanent and continuous changes of nature and by the same process, has brought about permanent and continuous changes in man, the awakening of "slumbering powers," or the development of his skills and senses. The early adaptations of nature into tools or instruments could be simply appropriations or imitations, like a stone in the hand becoming a weapon, a piece of wood becoming a club or spear, a shaped container being an imitation of a gourd or eggshell. But as these adaptations took place, the qualities of nature were discovered with their laws, and these could be turned to human use. So it was discovered that flints could be chipped into sharp points, or that certain woods were better for bows and spears than others. Man's work with things awakened his skills and sensitivities of eye, ear, touch and the manipulation of his own body. The manifold sensuous qualities of the outer world, the shades of color, shapes, texture, movement and all the varied forms that nature takes, became embraced in his own perceptions. Or to put it differently, as man adapts nature to his own needs, nature in turn educates him. So, as he discovers more general laws of nature, whether the cycle of the seasons, or the arc of flight of a missile through the air, or the sprouting of seeds, or what is now the immense body of laws embraced in the sciences, the knowledge of these laws lends structure to his thought about the world. Thus Marx says in another context, "the formation of the five senses is the work of the entire history of the world up to now." And so, if art and beauty are rooted in the labor process, they are also developmental. On the one hand, there is the progressive discovery of reality, periodically disclosing new laws, new many-sided qualities, and new adaptibility to human growth. On the other hand, advancing with it, is the education of human perceptions by the real world. A leap in the ability to command the outer world is a leap in the ability to respond to it.

It is suggested here that the perception of beauty is one of the "slumbering powers" awakened by the labor process. The support for this belief lies in the fact that the creations of primitive society which we now find to be aesthetically beautiful , and which we call works of art, took the form of instruments of labor, in primitive society itself.

The term "instrument of labor" is here used in its broadest sense, to include not only tools, weapons and utensils, but also lullabies, work chants, "magical" paintings and "magic" rituals combining poetry, music, mask and dance. For these songs, magic paintings and rituals were also, like the physical instruments of labor, intermediaries between man and nature, in the process of attaining success in hunting, war, spring planting, giving birth to children. If the magical belief that to imitate some force of nature provided power over that force was an illusion, Sir James Fraser nonetheless points out that in this magical belief in the possibility of human control over the forces of nature lay the beginnings of science.

Developing hand in hand with these instruments of labor is language, along with other means of expression and communication, like drawing, modeling, music, dance. Let us call all of these, for simplicity, languages. And in fact it does not stretch the point too much, to refer to the craft, the accumulated skills and sensitivities that produced tools, weapons and utensils, also as a kind of language or means of expression.

In these "languages," even if we examine them in their routine use today as a common social possession, we can find a quality crucial to art. This is the interaction of outer and inner reality. Each imitates, reflects or appropriates the outer world in such a way that, in doing this, it also embodies the life process and mind of the human being.

Let us consider so commonplace a "utility" as the language of words.

The developing process of naming things enabled people to think about them without having to see, touch or handle them. It enabled people to exchange their perceptions and the products of their imagination. For the imagination, dealing with the intangible, rested on the grasp of the tangible. The English scholar, C. M. Bowra, in his book *Primitive Song,* cites an African Pygmy myth, referring to the sun and stars. It calls the Milky Way the "road of the sky," made up of the "dust of broken stars." The sun god, it says, travels along this road, and needing this "dust of broken stars" as fuel for the sun, gathers it up "like the woman who gathers locusts, and heaps them in the basket, and the basket is full and brims over." Thus this imaginative attempt to explain the forces of nature draws for its imagery on the real conditions of life of the people, and tells us graphically how they work and live. Again, in the most commonplace speech, the words form themselves into patterns of intonation, rhythm, inflection and accent, and this "music" of speech embodies the life-process of the human being speaking the words. A poet, of course, creates in his poetry a consciously refined word-music, but if there were no music of this sort in ordinary speech, there would be no music in the language of poetry. If we hear language used tonelessly, without accent or rhythm, we do not say that it lacks poetry. We say that it lacks a human quality.

So it is with drawing and modeling. No matter how exact a transcription of the outer world is sought, or how carefully the work is planned for a function, the eyes and hand combine, so that in the result we can see the rhythm of controlled movement, the various muscular pressures, the sensing and play with textures, which are transformed into concrete pictorial values. Music, in its "pure" form, does not present images of the external world. But from the earliest societies it has served to bring people together into common activity, to awaken common feelings among them, to expand the awareness of kinship. And of all the arts, it embodies most directly the life processes of the human beings, since it is shaped by the breath and by body tensions and movements. In music, also, there is the interrelation of "inner" and "outer"; on the one hand the evocation of states of feeling through the variations of pitch, and on the other, the evocation of physical and kinetic movement through rhythm.

What is the step from the habitual use of these socially created means of expression, or "languages," to the creation of an actual art work? There is no hard and fast line of demarcation, but rather the loose, shifting borderline always present when we deal with dialectical processes and qualitative leaps. A person may break into an excited narrative which, if written down, could be appreciated as an integral short story. What a child draws on paper simply to record, in terms of line and shape, what it has noticed, or examined, could be exhibited as a successful art work. And artists constantly find aesthetic material in ordinary speech, gestures and actions. But there is a decisive step which characterizes an art work. It is the achievement of an objective form which becomes self-contained, detached from the life processes of the creator, while embodying them in a transformed way. The art work exists as a social possession after the travail that created it is over, either as a physically concrete object like a drawing, utensil, painting, sculpture; or a conceptual object, like a written poem or story; or as a reproducible event, like a work of music or dance. The art work is now out of the hands of its creator. It has its own life; a bloodless, unchanging life, as Keats says, but nevertheless one that bears meaning, awakens responses, speaks of life by appearing to be the very life of which it is speaking.

What lies behind this attainment of an art form? The answer, I suggest, is that the outlines of this form rise from its origin as an instrument of production, in the broad sense used here to include physically shaped tools, weapons and utensils, and also work songs, lullabies, social rituals. This connection is glimpsed in the maxim that has been popular for a century, first in architecture and then in other arts; "Form follows Function." But this adage, when applied to art, oversimplifies the process. Let us take, for example, a utilitarian art that produced miracles of beauty in early society, that of pottery. It is conceivable that a jagged, misshapen pot or one produced merely by mechanical rote may perform its function as a container. What makes it a work of art, however, is that in the process of creating something to fill this function, a host of skills and sensitivities, of "slumbering powers," have awakened in the creator, including the imagination, and discoveries of what can be done with the material. When these imbue every part of the work and become crystallized in the final shape or structure, the result is a work of art. That is why we can be so moved by even a simple utensil from primitive society. It involves a moment of growth in a human being. It may be called a "human portrait," or at least can be said to embody a human presence, that of the creator who has grown an inch in stature in the process of producing it. It educates our own mind and senses, and response to the world. It has beauty, because of its truth.

Similarly the form of a magical cave painting or dance ritual might have risen from the imperative need to imitate the object as closely as possible. The imitation made it a magical instrument. Yet this could only be done with a man-created language through which the growth of human sensitivities and skills registered themselves in the final shape.

Thus the creation of an art work is a concrete and perceptible form of the basic process of humanizing nature described by Marx in his early manuscripts. He calls the change of nature which is at the same time an education of the human being, awakening slumbering powers, the creation of "the human sense corresponding to the entire wealth of human and natural substance," and "humanized nature" (*Private Property and Communism*).

To sum up, the perception of beauty is the awareness that an object crystallizes in its form not only its function, but also the awakening of the senses, the delight in discovery, engendered by working with the external world. The aesthetic emotion is the joy in learning, of a kind that transforms the human being and his entire response to reality. Beauty is not a measurable attribute of an object, like weight, size, or color. Nor is the perception of beauty purely arbitrary and subjective. The perception of beauty is an active relationship between the human being and the outer world, and it appears in early society in connection with instruments of labor, because these, too, stand for active exploratory relationships between the human being and the outer world. The quality of beauty in such works indicates that the creation of an instrument of labor has awakened powers far beyond those represented by the actual operation of the instrument. If we can take for granted that in primitive life the successful functioning of a tool, utensil or ritual was its paramount reason for being, the fact that these also attained beauty indicates that even this first step of creative labor engendered a freedom to produce outside of the satisfaction of immediate physical needs. Or in other words, we can say that other "functions" were born than those of meeting immediate physical needs.

Art is creation according to the laws of beauty, and the laws of beauty, if we follow early Marx, rise out of the process of humanizing reality. A work of art is a man-created structure, using language, shape-making, musical sounds, or any other socially created means for exploring inner and outer reality, which crystallizes a stage in the humanization of reality. As such it becomes a social possession and a means for educating and transforming people in their ability to respond to the world about them.

Art rose as a characteristic of human life in society long before there was a concept of "art as such" and "the artist," just as the search for ways to control and master nature rose long before there was the conscious scientific outlook and the scientist. "Art as such" could rise only after the division of society into social classes, exploiting and exploited, and the accompanying and subsequent rise of various divisions of labor, physical and intellectual. There also rose a division between "hand" and "head," between those whose forced labor produced the necessities of life and the relative few who appropriated for themselves the fruits of this labor, ruled the society, made its laws, took for themselves the accumulated knowledge and claimed to do the official "thinking." And so in history, the relation between the developments of productive labor and the accompanying achievements in knowledge and human sensitivity becomes an intricate matter to trace.

With the development of class-divided society, division of labor and the formation of the state, the relation dwindles between art form and the instrument of production. It continues largely in folk art. Otherwise for art creation, the instrument of production is replaced by the social institution whose function it is to create a social consciousness. This does not come into being specifically for the purposes of art, but it is a necessary part of the social structure, and it can serve under propitious conditions to bring creative minds before a public. To discuss these various social institutions and how they contribute their conventions to the forms of art is outside the scope of this essay. Some examples can be cited for illustration; the religious rituals in the amphitheaters of classical Greece, which, with the establishment of Greek democracy, gave form to the birth of drama; the use of temples and churches, East and West, for religious sculpture and painting that provided both vivid pictures of real life and deep insights into the internal yearnings of people; the combination of the printing press, book stores, newspapers, libraries and the rise of a broad literate audience, that became a framework for the rise of the novel to a major art form. Generally, such social institutions are not instruments of production, but they are links of great importance in the chain through which changes in productive forces and social relations become translated into changes of human psychology and social consciousness.

What the rise of art and beauty out of the labor process tells us, however, is why great artists, like scientists, have resisted any narrow specializations that would cut them off from social life and social consciousness; why, however lacerating labor can be under conditions of exploitation, productive labor can be and is one of the greatest sources of joy; why, if the arts have been encouraged by ruling classes to adorn their own lives and solidify their rule, the creators of great art works have only rarely been members of the ruling class, and have most often been people who had to work for a living; why great periods of art creation blossomed under conditions whereby "head" and "hand" could come together; why a folk artisan may sometimes produce a miracle of art and beauty, not thinking of it as art, while a highly learned specialist, master of the inherited techniques of an art, may produce a work of imposing deadness; why it has taken a succession of revolutions in society for the intellectual and aesthetic fruits of the social labor process to become the possession of an increasing number of those who do the labor.

THE PROGRESS OF HUMANIZATION OF REALITY

The humanization of reality means changing what is hostile, forbidding, and destructive, to what is an asset to and extension of human life, and a means through which human life can grow, externally and internally. It rests on the working-up of reality, but does not coincide with simply the physical changes brought about in the world. It is also a psychological change in human beings. This point needs to be stressed because some modern currents of thought draw upon Marx's theories of humanized reality to attack scientific materialism, or the concept that there is an objective world, whatever it consists of, outside of the mind. They claim that "man creates reality," and leap over the Marxist insistence that whatever freedom man attains to change the world rests on his grasp of "necessity." The humanization of nature is engendered by the labor process, which faces nature as "necessity" and so adapts nature to human needs. What humanization means as well, however, is that through this process the secrets of nature are progressively discovered, and its laws are revealed so that they can be consciously used as instruments of human progress, affording a step towards freedom. And along with this, the mind is enriched by the disclosure of nature's manifold sensuous qualities. Thus the primitive cave paintings of animals, with their sensitivity of line and detail, could come about only when animals were already being hunted, killed, and used for food, being no longer a purely strange and terrifying power looming above human beings. And so we must see these portrayals of animals as, so to speak, "human portraits"; disclosures of a stage in the growing mentality of the human being, disclosing new powers in himself with his mastery of outer reality. It is when every element in the painting plays a double role, evoking the object and the human presence, the perception and the perceiver, that it attains beauty and is a masterpiece of art.

There is also the humanization of human relations, so that people see others as kin to themselves. It is through cooperation that people can see another human being as both "object," or something outside them, and "subject," or something internally related to them. Thus they discover themselves in others, and learn from discovering in others what they themselves are. With the progressive changes, conflicts in and reorganizations of society, there is a progressive discovery, understanding, mastery and reshaping of the laws governing the organization of society. Human relations become more human in the sense that destructive antagonisms are increasingly replaced by cooperation; ignorance and fear are replaced by kinship and understanding; and through cooperation the individual is enabled to develop more freely,

And so humanized reality is not simply humanly changed reality, let alone "created reality," but a human relationship to reality. It is for this reason that, as we have seen, beauty is neither purely objective nor subjective, but an interrelation of the human mind with the real world. Each stage in the humanization of the external world, including both non-human nature and human relations, is a stage in the growth of the human being, an enlargement of the scope of individual life, a growth of the senses, and an awareness of a step taken to freedom. What happens is not a change in the physical basis of sense perceptions, but rather that with the new, more fruitful relationships of the individual to the outer world, the senses "open up" to it, so to speak. Each outer discovery is also an awareness of internal powers and riches, an enhanced consciousness of self. The aesthetic emotion, the recognition of beauty, is the consciousness of this leap in human powers. When we find that a work of art has the joy and excitement of beauty, this is another way of saying what we have learned from it, in a special way that makes us feel our own senses have grown, our powers have become heightened, the world is a little more understandable, and we can thereby live a little differently. The history of the arts can be called a record of the successive stages in the humanization of reality, revealing the constant change and expansion of the awareness of beauty to include ever new subject matter and ever new aspects of familiar subject matter.

The fact that art often seems to imitate life, but with a special intensity, has given rise to the mistake that art is simply a kind of adroit selection from the raw material provided by the world, just as the fact that the beauty of art cannot be detached from its form has given rise to the mistake that a work of art is simply a formal artifice with no necessary connection to outer reality. It is true that whether a work of art appears to imitate outer reality directly, as with much literature and visual art, or to shape materials about a function, as with architecture, or to deal with language and its implicitly human relationships, as with music, it does have a feeling of intense self-contained reality. This intensity of life comes however from the fact that in all of these various forms or methods, it embodies a human presence, perceiving, thinking and exploring.

Thus the beauty of art is different from that of nature, and it does not lie in the selection of seemingly "beautiful objects" from real life. Art does not substitute for nature or for life, either by reproducing nature or by behaving itself as a piece of environment. Works of art are man-created forms using socially-created methods or languages. No matter how faithful the subject-matter they present may seem to be to the world about us, their forms are not those of nature. A work of literature or painting is as much a unique structure, in this sense, as a work of music. Every element in a work of art, every word-phrase, image, line, stroke, color combination, succession of musical phrases, has been shaped by the human hands, skills, senses and mind. The reality or truth of a work of art is determined not by what facts we recognize in it, but by how much every part of it seems to be alive. Or put in another way, no matter what the work of art seems to be speaking of, what makes it art is that it is also speaking of us, enriching our responses to life.

The recognition of beauty is a response to something real, material and existing in the external world, but it is at the same time a peculiarly human response, and what it discovers is disclosed only by human activity. Just as the inner subjective growth of the artist is "objectivized" by the creation of the art work, or turned into an "object" so that it can enrich the subjective life of others, so art also establishes nature and people as "beautiful objects." In other words, when we discover beauty in the outer world, we are also discovering form in the outer world. This form is real. It is there. It exists. But to appreciate it means also to isolate and separate it from all the complicated detail of its surroundings, thus seeing it in a new relation to its surroundings. And for this process to take place, it is necessary for human beings to have developed a "sense of form": that is, to have created form themselves. Only by the difference between art — man-created work — and nature, can art serve its function, which is not to record natural beauties, but to be the great educator in the beautiful, transforming people to see it where it was not seen before. The word "camera" has become a catchword for the literal recording of reality. Yet a photographer, to make a beautiful portrait, does not need a subject who looks like a Hollywood idol, and he will forsake what are called "scenic beauties" to focus the eye on the rhythmic ripple of water or the play of sunlight over sand.

The subject-matter of a work of art has often been assigned to it by the customs and conventions of its times, just as the general outline and direction of its form have sprung, as we have seen, from the conventions of tools of production and social institutions whose ostensible aim was not art at all. So with the crafts, the subject-matter will be some utilitarian need that the work will satisfy. In religious or didactic art the subject-matter is some ideological lesson or generalization. And even in the period when art began to loosen its chains to official theology, its subject-matter was thought of as some factual truth. So Dante, who was, so to speak, his own theologian, was thought of for some time after he wrote, as one who had actually made the journey through hell and paradise. Many Elizabethan plays, including Shakespeare's, were offered as "true histories." But for the result to be art, the subject-matter must be transmuted into "subject," by which I mean that it must arouse the internal life of the artist and be made into a medium for thought about life.

Thus in the crafts, however serviceable a work may be, it does not have art or beauty unless some leap in human skills and senses is captured in the all-over form. With religious or didactic art, there is no art unless the subject-matter can arouse a host of real life memories and experiences in the artist, so that what the work discloses is a real pattern of life. To cite a modern religious work, T. S. Eliot's *Four Quartets* might be called a meditation on "time" as "life" and "timelessness" as both death and God. It takes on artistic depth through the graphic portrayal of Eliot's own loneliness and desolation, in the face of a God who is death;

> Or as, when an underground train in the tube stops too long
>   between stations
> And the conversaation rises and slowly fades into silence
> And you see behind every face the mental emptiness deepen
> Leaving only the growing terror of nothing to think about;

or through the flashes of humanized life,

> Sudden in a shaft of sunlight
> Even while the dust moves
> There rises the hidden laughter
> Of children in the foliage.

So it is with art which takes its subject-matter directly from nature, history or human and social experience. For art to result, the subject-matter must be turned into "subject," losing the transitory and ephemeral character it has in real life, and becoming a means through which the artist and art work can awaken people's minds to hitherto unrevealed patterns and movements of the real world. Thus let us take the subject-matter of a family torn by antagonisms, in which money plays a prominent role, the head of the family is murdered, and the criminal is at last detected. It has produced innumberable detective stories which are less art than literary, time-killing games, between the writer and reader. It has also produced *The Brothers Karamazov*.

This does not mean at all that subject-matter has no vital role to play. Such a belief is popular today, when instead of asking why so many artists find nature and their fellow human beings uninteresting and even repellent to them, theorists make this alienation into a universal law of art. The active, operative and organic relation between the objective or outer and the interior world is posited in Marx's view of humanized reality. What happens in art is that after the outer is put through an interior process, it is restored to the outer world: it is made again into an object. But this object, namely the subject-matter crystallized as a work of art, is different. It speaks. It has meaning.

This transformation of subject-matter can be illustrated by an analogy. A tree is perceived as an object of a certain size, shape and color. Let us say that the observer, drawing on his own experience and the generalizations of accumulated social experience, or science, gets to understand that this tree is one of a general body of things known as trees. Then studying the generality of tree, he discovers that it is alive and has a life history, that trees grow from seeds which are planted in the earth, that they divide into a trunk, branches and leaves, that they produce fruit, which dies, and more seeds, and that they themselves can decay and die. Following this, we can say that when he again sees the tree, he sees it quite differently. And in fact the trees in Jacob van Ruysdael's paintings and etchings, so different from the trees in medieval and Italian Renaissance paintings, indicate that the artist sees a tree as something alive, searching amid rocks for room that its roots may grow and anchor it in the earth, with trunks and branches that have been buffeted and bent by winds. Perhaps the artist has seen a Dutch farmer tear the stubborn roots out of the earth.

So we can say that Dostoevsky, taking his subject-matter from personages in the Russian life of his time, put them through a process, drawing upon all his knowledge, thought and experience, including his examination of himself, and his discovery of the rise of money power in Russian social life. He learned its corruption of both middle class and gentry, as well as the division rising between head and heart, between cold rationalism and human affection. He then reconstructed these personages as sharply delineated individuals, whose life stories now had profound meanings, revealing the inner life of the rapidly changing Russian society in which he lived. A novelist cannot portray "society," any more than a painter can portray the genus, "tree." He can portray only people. And by reconstructing them with the benefit of his social thought, insights and discoveries, he does not make them more abstract. On the contrary, their individuality is enhanced. As is often said, they become "more real than real."

The relation between life and art, opposites that interconnect, or that need each other, can be seen in the fact that life does not fall neatly into the patterns of tragic and comic that are common to art. Furthermore, the tragic in art evokes not despair, but the kind of exultation Aristotle refers to with his "catharsis," while the comic will leave an undertone of sadness. Both achieve artistic greatness and beauty with raw material that in real life would not at all be attractive or beautiful: the tragic with human catastrophes and the comic often with deliberate distortion, caricature, mock alienation.

Greek tragedy, for example, shows us, in addition to its supernatural elements, people carrying on suicide and murder, and torn apart by fear, anger, rage and frustration. Rembrandt's paintings and etchings, even when taking up Biblical subject-matter, show us how the poor of Holland live, and do not gloss over their poverty and misery. Beethoven in works like the "Eroica" symphony foregoes the writing of sweet, ornamental music to evoke dissonant clashes and tragic losses. But the real subject, or content, of Greek tragedy is neither the rule of the gods over human affairs nor human agony. It is human stature, for the revelation of which it was necessary to deal with human catastrophe. Oedipus will not bow to the gods even when they have trapped him. He dictates and carries out his own punishment. The subject of Rembrandt's art is not human poverty but human kinship, for the disclosure of which it was necessary to deal in a human way with those most impoverished in society, those whom Rembrandt's wealthy patrons would consider "nobodies." The subject of Beethoven's symphony, with its grand funeral march, is the need to struggle, to face the demands of life with its threats, catastrophes and conflicts, and the joy of conquering the forces of destruction.

So it is with the comic, which often presents familiar subject-matter deliberately distorted, stretched out of proportion, made grotesque, or turned upside down. This is done in so obvious a way that the audience is impelled to set it straight, return it to sense, put it back on its feet. But in setting it straight, an unsaid truth emerges, and the audience laughs in joy at its creative act. It has really walked into a trap. The artist has compelled it to think what he himself has not said. So the Fool in Lear tells the king, "I am better than thou art; I am a fool, thou art nothing." The audience sets this absurdity straight. It is the fool who is nothing, being the servant; the king is something; he is the better man; he is the master; he can whip the fool. But the bitter truth emerges that the king, by giving away his instruments of rule, has made himself vulnerable to be treated as a nothing, by those who now wield power. The king is not nothing, but he has acted foolishly, and the fool is the better man, in that he has the wisdom to see this. Or Daumier caricatures the Emperor Napoleon III as a seedy old rake. The audience sets this straight. The Emperor does not look like this bedraggled rake; he is a handsome man in a splendid uniform. But the truth emerges that spiritually the Emperor is a scurvy character.

So with the catastrophes of tragedy or the apparently mangled realities of comedy, the emotions which people carry away from the work are not the emotions which the subject-matter of the work of art would arouse in real life. The emotional travail that the human portraits in an art work seem to undergo, is the means through which the art work affirms its psychological truth, its kinship and parallel to the experiences of its audience. But these, as reflected through the special sensitivities and means of expression of the arts, are only elements in the construction of the art work. It is the work of art as an all-over unit, as an organic structure, that arouses the all-over emotion which the audience carries away from the work. This is the joy of learning and the sense of growth it brings, the heightened ability to confront reality while making this reality part of the workings of the mind itself. And it is the work of art grasped as such a unified, coherent form that arouses this feeling, because each step in shaping this structure is determined by the artist's thought about and insight into life, as aroused by his subject-matter. Thus the characterization or content of a Titian or Rembrandt portrait is a product not merely of the facial drawing and modeling but of the body, hands, costume, background, contours, color harmonies, spatial patterns, play of light, and in fact every element in the painting. Similarly, if the characters in *The Brothers Karamazov* stand out as profoundly significant and memorable individuals, this is a quality that has been given them by the novel as a whole, or by all the events, confrontations, conflicts and changes that make it up, not by any particular description Dostoevsky has given them. So, if form seems to be the determining factor in the success of a work of art, it nevertheless rests on content, or on subject-matter becoming subject, and then turned into object.

While anything can serve as subject-matter for art, even the artist's fascination with the materials of his craft, yet there are great achievements and petty ones, and there are certain demands laid upon greatness. For the forward movement of art rests on the part it plays in establishing humanized reality and making this humanization part of social consciousness; in other words, in its revelation of beauty where no beauty was known before, and in this respect, the artist collaborates with the movement of society. The giants of art have been those able to meet the challenge of the revolutionary demands of their age. The stature and grandeur of the human being conveyed by classic Greek drama and sculpture followed upon a revolutionary step in which democratic institutions were created that had been previously unknown in slave-holding society. In making their own laws, the citizenry took to themselves what had previously been humbly accepted as the prerogatives of the gods and their supposed kin and representatives on earth. By a similar historical process, it took the revolutionary developments in the city of Florence, when merchants and guilds broke the power of the landed aristocracy, to make the city the leading center for what can be called the humanization of religious art, turning the artist's eyes to the real life about them, and finally moving to break religious chains altogether, turning the artist's eyes directly on real life. It took the breakup of the feudal world in Europe to make possible the portraits that Titian created of popes and Shakespeare created of kings, discarding the aura of divinity and showing them as troubled, conflictful human beings. It took the revolutionary rise of the Dutch republic in the 17th century to make possible the beauty that Dutch art discloses in the poor people, the aged, the working folk, the common occupations of village life, and the labor of tilling the soil or fishing the sea, as well as the simple landscape itself seen through the villager's eyes. In 19th-century Russia it took the social ferment, the movements for freedom of the peasantry, the growing criticism of Tsardom and the old-line aristocracy even by members of the aristocracy themselves, to make possible the beauty of the portrayals of the peasantry that are found in the writings of Turgenev and the operas and songs of Mussorgsky.

The truth of art, then, is not factual or documentary truth, but human truth; not a record of the objective world but a disclosure of the ever-growing internal world, engendered by the human efforts to shape the outer world to human needs. It can speak effectively to people only by moving them, which means that people must recognize some aspect of their own internal or psychological life in it. It brings to social consciousness the new developments of human sensitivity and self-awareness made possible by the collective labor of changing the world. In society divided into antagonistic classes, it took revolutionary changes of society to make possible a new stage in humanized reality, and further revolutions to make this humanization something approaching a widespread social possession. But great art has always found its audiences, broadening with time. And once art has opened people's minds to the new qualities revealed in human beings and nature, this revelation can be permanently theirs. It becomes part of their thoughts and perceptions, and serves to create a new intimacy between themselves and the world they live in.

In the end, the revelations provided by art become a common possession. Society in the long run accepts only what serves it, only what is real and true, only what enables it to live and grow, for otherwise it perishes. And so with the passage of time, greatness in art, seemingly a capricious or subjective judgment, takes on the character of objective truth. The transformations which art has helped bring about in people cannot be turned back without destruction. Once a deeper, more liberating view of human beings becomes established, any statement of a less advanced view becomes grotesque, like a militarist today proclaiming the eternal necessity of wars, or a person mouthing racism, or one who asserts that those who work with their hands are lesser human beings, or those who deny the preciousness of human life, or those who make human estrangement a permanent or eternal truth of life.

ALIENATION AND ART

The humanization of reality, as I believe Marx conceived it and as I have tried to apply it to the arts, is a process that has developed, enlarged and made new conquests in the course of history. And so its opposite or "alienation" has also grown and developed in the course of history. This view differs from those which regard "alienation" as a kind of original sin, established with the first ability of the human being to survey himself as a conscious being, subject to mortality. Alienation in Marxist terms, which I believe to be the most fruitful terms, can only be properly understood in connection with the process of humanization, to which it stands as an opposite or reverse movement. Thus to Marx, estranged labor is possible only after a human form of labor has arisen. It does not refer simply to a social situation, like class exploitation, or the appropriation by one class of the products of another's labor. It is, like the human form of labor, a psychological situation resting on an objective reality. Under conditions of class exploitation, the worker is denied the development of his senses and powers engendered by human labor. The instrument of production, like the land, or the machine, has been turned into the private possession or property of the exploiting class, and instead of its being an extension of the laborer, he becomes a one-sided appendage to it. The work process demands that he deny or stifle his humanity, and the products of his labor become something not his, not controlled by his mind, but inimical and hostile to him. Thus he must work in order to live, but the more he works, the more the work lacerates his mind and body, and he even creates conditions that may throw him out of work. Today, in the age of great monopoly networks, such estranged labor has become a phenomenon of intellectual, scientific and professional work.

And alienation is more than estranged labor. It occurs among all classes of society, including the exploiters and rulers. It is not to be confused with class antagonisms and class struggles. It is a psychological or internal conflict, engendered by certain objective realities; a situation whereby people find themselves controlled by the very forces which they set in motion to bring them freedom and growth. So the free market-place, the arena for the growth in capitalist profit-making, turns into a brutal competitive world in which each capitalist is faced by others who are his would-be destroyers, precisely because of their identity of interests to his.

The freedom sought is false or illusory, for the freedom of one rests on the denial of freedom to another, and so the very search makes the searcher a slave to the combat he generates. The very bourgeois social network which seemed to expand the humanization of human relations — and in the period of bourgeois democratic, humanist struggle against feudalism it appeared to do this — has become a force for the disruption of human relations and the brutalization of life. The characteristic of alienation which makes it a social-psychological phenomenon is that the alienated person frustratedly sees himself as the engineer of his own destruction, with no escape.

I suggest that each form of alienation which appears after a new development of humanized life, reaches a higher pitch of intensity than any previous alienation. For example, Marx finds alienation under capitalism to be far more intense, all-pervading and far-reaching than alienation in feudal society. "Feudal landed property," Marx writes, "is already by its very nature huckstered land — the earth which is estranged from man and hence, confronts him in the shape of a few great lords." But there also is in feudal relations, he writes, "a human, intimate side." With the rise of capitalism, "the idle enjoyment of the products of the other people's blood and toil" turns into "a bustling commerce in the same commodity." Since this commerce is distinguished by an intense competition, "landed property in the form of capital manifests its dominion over both the working class and the proprietors themselves who are either being ruined or raised by the laws governing the movement of capital." It is at this point that Marx sees "the complete domination of dead matter over man." Later, in *Capital*, he develops this thought of the domination of dead matter over men, due to the operation of economic law, as the "fetishism of commodities," which also reaches its highest intensity under capitalism. But in the emergent bourgeois struggle against the feudal and monarchic institutions, the dominant demand was for individual rights, the scientific and humanist view of reality, and the democratization of political life. The competitiveness of the marketplace was secondary to the equality that the marketplace betokened, in contrast to feudal restrictions. At this point, as both Marx and Engels have pointed out, the rising class tries to represent the needs of all society. And this is magnificently reflected in the arts, in the painting, music, poetry, drama, story and novel from the Renaissance through most of the 19th century. I suggest that the very heights attained by the humanization of reality in the breakup of the feudal world and rise of bourgeois society, find their counterpart in the intensity of the alienation in the 20th century, with the crisis of capitalism, the world wars and depressions, the trustification of economic life, the apparition of fascism.

I think that we must examine periods of both history and art, not in terms of total humanization or total alienation, but in terms of conflict between these opposing trends, with one as the uppermost. And so it is with individual people, including artists. The most social human being suffers some alienation, due to the contradictions of society. And the most alienated struggles to find some area of activity in which he can restore his humanity.

In respect to art, I suggest that realism be considered a special stage in the progress of the humanization of reality. The term realism, of course, has been subjected to different views and definitions. The definition I suggest is an art which explores the internal change, new sensitivities and psychological conflicts in people, in a way that shows their organic connection to the social conflicts and struggles of new versus old in the external world. Realism rose as a concept along with the victory of bourgeois society and the emergence of "art as such." For when art broke the chains of theology and ceased to be merely the decoration of upper-class life, the task it took to itself was that of freely ranging over the entire expanse of outer social reality and human self-examination. I also suggest that realism in art is a broader concept than can be found in the use of any one work of art or any one artist as a model. It is more of a collective task, carried on by many artists in an age, each of whom stimulates the others.

If art is directly related to the humanization of reality, how does alienation show itself? The most obvious form is in the assault upon the arts; the onesidedness forced upon people, destroying their own latent creativity and making them insensitive to art, and the capitalist drive to turn the art process into a form of commodity production, even while it turns the art works of its own heritage into luxury commodities.

But artists also suffer from alienation, to a greater or lesser degree. I suggest that the effect of alienation may be seen in the European and American art of the Renaissance through the 19th century, in what could be called the deviation from this balance of inner and outer worlds. These deviations or offshoots have taken two directions. One is that of subjectivism, in which the emphasis is on the interior world, the internal conflict or anguish, with the connection weakened or obliterated to the movement of social relaity. The style tends to be that of dream fantasy or distorted reality, the distortions being the sign of an inner intensity which can find no adequate clothing in outer reality. The other is that of a formalism or super-objectivity, in which the polished handling of the means of expression of the arts is paramount, along with the attempt to create as lucid, rationally organized a structure as possible, standing as an objective entity. The inner life and turbulent conflicts of reality are allowed to enter only to the extent that they do not disrupt this controlled, rational order. Illustrations can be found in the art of the 17th and early 18th century. In painting, after the great humanist realism of the Italian Renaissance, there appears the subjectivism of El Greco, who also can paint with magnificent realism; the rationality of a Poussin, who however expresses a deeper interior life than appears on the surface of his finely organized classicism; the dream life of a Watteau, and his attraction to life as already put through the medium of art. In English literature, the great wave of Elizabethan lusty realistic humanism is followed by the interior torments and subjectivism, expressed in irony, of a John Donne; the mysticism of the metaphysical poets, who also use formalist methods to organize their work; the controlled rationalism of Alexander Pope. It should be said that these are all artists of great genius and accomplishment. But alienation has made some headway in their work, compared to their revolutionary predecessors. They search for the expression of their humanity in narrower or more limited arenas than those of the humanist realists; either in the concentration on their internal life, the conflicts of which now seem mysterious or spiritual in origin, or in the refinement of their craft, the perfection of which seems to give the work a concrete substance of its own. And from a high birds-eye view of the history of art during these centuries, they do not represent the main line of development. Rather the main line is restored by the reappearance of an art of inner and outer balance, of social and critical realism. And towards the end of the 19th century, there are far more intense subjectivist and formalist trends.

In the 20th century, bourgeois ideology has come to the end of its cycle. In its origin, it welcomed the exploration of reality, and saw the growth and freedom of the individual as linked to that of his fellow men in society. Now it proclaims the world to be chaotic, incomprehensible, alive with imminent and overwhelming disasters. Bourgeois ideology, once humanist, now tries to make alienation into eternal truth; once applauding advances in knowledge, it now proclaims the impossibility of knowing anything; once seeing itself as progress, it now proclaims that there is no such thing as progress. And the effect of alienation in the arts is seen in that what the 20th century called an artistic "revolution" leveled its main attack against the entire realistic humanist heritage. This heritage was considered a monstrous error. The subjective and formalistic reached extremes never know before, ranging from nightmarish subject-matter, and deliberately repellent, cruel and inhuman images of reality, to what apeared to be no subject-matter at all. The subjective and the formalist, at times hostile to one another, repeatedly joined each other; for example, in painting, abstract-expressionism; in literature, the wave of metaphysical poetry set off by T. S. Eliot, combining religious or philosophical mysticism with a concrete neo-classical rhetorical polish; in music, the embrace by Stravinsky, the super-objectivist, and his followers, of the Schoenberg subjectivist "twelve-tone" or "serial" system.

To call this an art reflecting alienation does not mean that this art lacks human qualities. There has appeared in the wake of this revolution, of course, all sorts of drab, dead pseudo art, products of modernistic academicisms, works designed to follow one fashion or another in a commercialism disguised as experiment. But in the work of the truly gifted creators there is still humanized reality. It operates within the constrictions imposed by alienation. The artist-rebel hates the world he is in, but sees no other possible. And so, ironically, he seeks his humanity in rejecting society, thus intensifying his loneliness and feeling of impotence. He can be human only by being inhuman. His "wisdom" is the conviction that there is nothing to know, that knowledge and progress are illusions. Even the "no subject-matter" art has some humanity, just as it also has subject-matter. This subject-matter is in some cases the artist's view of an irrational and hostile universe translated into his own individual desolation. In others, the subject-matter consists of the sheer physical materials of the art itself, with whatever unconscious or visceral feelings their manipulation aroused in the artist. The only reality of which he is certain is that which he can physically touch or handle. In either case the artist approaches the danger of an almost complete loss of his individuality.

To call this "revolutionary" art an art driven to the wall by alienation is not to denounce it for existing, or to deny that it may have explored certain sensitivities which will be part of the permanent arsenal of art. It is only to deny that this art is really an art of revolution, or of the future. It is really an art which sees no future for humanity.

To complicate the picture, it has to be said that there is another, very powerful current in the 20th century artistic "revolution" which consists of a mock or contrived alienation and inhumanity, used as a shield or cover for profound humanist feelings. The spirit is often that of the semi-secret communication of the class-conscious mountebank or jester; the deliberate creation of nonsense, or of an upside-down reality, so that the knowing auditor can set it right, or the assumption of inhumanity as a shield for feelings that are too vulnerable in the face of a hostile world. In Joyce's *Finnegan's Wake*, for instance, the comic is at least as important an element as the mythological, the dream psychology, and the anthropology. He may see the world as incomprehensible, but so long as he can laugh, he is undefeated. An outstanding example in literature of this mock alienation, or non-involvement, shielding deep human sympathies, is the style of Hemingway, whose heroes must harden themselves to face a world that is implacably hostile and powerful. In pictorial art, a prime example is that of Pablo Picasso, whose human sympathies and keen eye for the data of life are evident to those who look, and whose various styles of mock alienation could be a series of screens and shields to protect these feelings before a hostile "official audience." In music, the deliberate shock qualities may be cited of Bela Bartok, whose humanity is amply evident in his loving and creative use of the riches of folk music.

Another form of mock or contrived alienation may be cited; that of the plays of Bertolt Brecht. In his theory he renounces both humanist portraiture and the accompanying empathy. The effect must be, he says, to jolt the spectator, to make him think, to make him understand and hate the society that oppresses him. This is the form, he believes, that must be taken by a politically educative art.

Whether this is a path for the future of art can also be questioned. But it may be that Brecht is right, that this is the best form art can take if it is to teach political lessons.

But then the converse rises, that the business of art as humanized reality is not primarily to teach political lessons; that is a craft in itself. This does not mean that art as humanized reality cannot talk politics. What artist is more political than Sophocles or Shakespeare? But they dealt with people who were making politics, and whose humanity or loss of it was expressed in their political decisions. Not all art need deal with this kind of subject-matter. This does not mean however that the artist should not engage in politics, or ally himself with the working class and all the oppressed and exploited. This is the path which enables him to develop his individuality in terms of social humanity, and to face reaction with the confidence of knowing the most important things that it is possible to know in his time. But then the task rises, of translating the knowledge gathered from these experiences into terms of the innermost hopes, yearnings, strivings for growth and freedom, of the people of his time. This is a function that only art can perform.

LITERARY STUDY AND POLITICAL ACTIVISM: How to Heal the Split

Gaylord C. LeRoy

I shall attempt to offer some Marxist guidelines for literary study in the university, with the notion that they might help to heal the long-standing split between teaching and activism. Everyone has known teachers in the forefront of the activist movement (in regard to withdrawal of troops from Vietnam, the struggle against pre-fascist political repression, etc.) who often appear to teach as if literary study must necessarily be a sphere apart. The political struggles in which they are engaged appear not to have influenced what they taught, and conversely the theoretical and imaginative concerns of the teaching make no contribution to the activism. I have a friend who willingly offers himself to seve on all kinds of political committees. He supports amnesty for young draft-resisters, volunteers to do the uncongenial work of money-raising, joins the line of demonstrators when the police arrive with night-sticks and mace. But his approach to professional work in English is not different from that advanced by Northrop Frye in *The Anatomy of Criticism*. Like Frye, he examines literature in terms of a conceptual framework derivable entirely from literature itself. "The critic should be able to construct and dwell in a conceptual universe of his own," Frye says. The fact is, though, that Frye's "self-contained literary universe" logically cuts literary study off from an examined world view, and necessarily from activism.[1] Frye makes little attempt to explore the connection between his "modes" and the historical periods that gave rise to them. His approach to literature, it has been said, demands nothing in the way of historical understanding. Frye in the end makes literary study inconsequential. Literature for him becomes "an irrelevance".[2] So my colleague, who supports every kind of activism in the afternoon, adopts for his morning work in the classroom a premise that invalidates whatever connection one might try to make between literature and the demand for a change in national priorities.

The new activists have exhibited almost unlimited inventiveness and daring, but in spite of our admiration for what they have contributed to the revitalization of the American left, we should still recall that the revolutionary movement requires also ideological radicalization within the professions, and that this is an area, so far as literature is concerned at any rate, in which during a decade of revolt the advance has been imperceptible.

The split between activism and teaching has a parallel among creative writers. Young poets who took part in the Pentagon demonstration that Mailer describes in *Armies of the Night* returned to Philadelphia on the following Sunday to write poetry in which the dominant feeling was one of anguished helplessness. At the Pentagon, caught up in an experience for which there has been little precedent in this country for 25 years, they learned something about the enhanced sense of personal power that comes when one's purposes are shared by masses of men, so that the individual will merges with a seemingly irresistible collective purpose. They had been part of a demonstration that helped eventually to retire a president and, it seemed for a time, to end a war. The next day, in an act of regression, they fell back into the elitist despondency of T. S. Eliot.

We confront here a problem that we have not yet in the West been able to solve, though one gets the impression that the moment may now be at hand. What bliss it would be to belong to a society where the great role of interpreting works of the imagination could be seen as a concern only slightly less weighty than the effort to transform society — even as having something to do with that effort. Marxists can be of help here by bringing to bear the strength of a total theory, comprehensive and unified, which shows us that the literature and life of society are closely interrelated. Literature reflects and interprets the practical activities of man, it reports hints and foreshadowings of as yet unrealized experience as it first enters into the realm of consciousness. If you come to literature with the comprehensive world view of Marxism, it ought to be impossible to keep it fenced off from the rest of life, and especially from political activism.

RADICAL LITERATURE

I will say just a word or two about an approach to radical literature, mainly because this is not generally a sizable part of the teacher's concern in the classroom, but also because the subject has not yet been worked out in anything like the kind of detail we need.

We can begin by taking note of significant changes in thematic material between the two decades in which radical literature has flourished, the 30's and the 60's. In the 30's, depression phenomena were uppermost, with exploration of the realities of exploitation, as in James Farrell's study of middle-class deprivation (*Studs Lonigan*), Dos Passos' account of capitalist alienation in the previous decade (*USA*), Steinbeck's story of the ex-tenant farmers in *The Grapes of Wrath*, and James Agee's documentary dealing with poor whites in the South, *Let Us Now Praise Famous Men*. Today, possibly the corresponding phenomenon in radical literature is the account of the protest and resistance by relatively well-off middle-class people, as with Norman Mailer's report on the confrontation at the Pentagon in *Armies of the Night* (by no means a satisfactory radical document, of course, despite Mailer's enormous talent). In the 30's, the emergence of German-Italian fascism was an important theme for European radical literature, also for our own, as in a book like Hemingway's *For Whom the Bell Tolls*. In the 60's, the parallel theme was the menace of American imperialism at home and abroad. A forerunner of this trend was Joseph Heller's *Catch-22*; notable recent examples are Jonathan Schell's *The Military Half* and *The Village of Ben-Suc*.

Much radical literature of the 30's had to do with organizational struggles in the labor movement, Steinbeck's *In Dubious Battle* and *The Grapes of Wrath*, Cilfford Odets' *Waiting for Lefty*, and the important new genre of the proletarian novel, including works like Ruth McKenney's *Industrial Valley*, Jack Conroy's *The Disinherited*, Robert Cantwell's *The Land of Plenty*, and Josephine Herbst's *The Executioner Waits*. The 60's saw little radical literature on these themes, mainly because of the political inactivization of American workers in a period of rightist leadership by an aristocracy of labor. Uppermost themes instead were the emergence of the Third World, with Frantz Fanon's *The Wretched of the Earth*, the writings of Che Guevara, etc. Much more important than this was the theme of Black Liberation. This was forecast in the 30's in the work of Richard Wright and others, and was surely a foremost feature of radical literature in the 60's, with Malcolm X, Eldridge Cleaver, Leroi Jones, Julius Lester, and others.

One notes a change also in the relative importance of genres. The most important genre in the 30's was fiction; consider the work of Sherwood Anderson, Erskine Caldwell, John Dos Passos, James Farrell, Hemingway, Ruth MacKenney, John Steinbeck, Nathanael West, Thomas Wolfe, and

Richard Wright. To be sure, there was a significant development in the documentary also, as with James Agee, The Federal Writers Project, Sherwood Anderson, Josephine Herbst, Erskine Caldwell, Louis Adamic and Meridel LeSeuer. Nevertheless, it would seem that the relative importance was reversed in the 60's, with straight fiction a somewhat sub-dominant genre, and a great deal more attention being given to the documentary, autobiography, and other modes of non-fiction. Many think that James Baldwin is better in his non-fiction than his novels, and the documentary has been an important form for Eldridge Cleaver, Frantz Fanon, Norman Mailer, Malcolm X and Jonathan Schell. Erwin Pracht has suggested that at a time when people find their reality bewildering they will turn to the documentary rather than to fiction.[3] Is that what is happening now? In a time when the ruling class can command unprecedented technological media for influencing the mind, reality becomes increasingly mystifying, and we should perhaps expect that the documentary, in which the primary goal is to dispel illusions by a first-hand or researched account of what is really going on, will become a centrally important genre.

One contribution of Marxism to the study of radical literature will be to develop concepts to be used in critical analysis. East European critics have developed a significant body of theory that can be adapted for this purpose. As an example one might mention first the question of the writer's capacity to penetrate to the causal nexus of a society in revolutionary transition. This would imply an understanding of the roots of our troubles in the disintegration of capitalist society and of how the general condition of alienation is intensified by monopoly domination in almost every sphere of life. It would mean comprehension also of the unalienated existence within a human community which man has the power to bring into realization as part of a socialist society, once he succeeds in getting control of the social process. The radical model would include understanding of the program of revolutionary struggle, with attention to the central role of the working class and with recognition of the role of each of the important components of a revolutionary coalition — the coalition in which the Negro people, because of the special racist exploitation to which they are subject, have an incalculable role to play. The model would include also some grasp of the interdependence of different sectors in the world system of liberation in which, wherever you may be, you have a job to do (this in contrast to the notion, advanced in recent years by the *Monthly Review*, that we can look to other people, the exploited "proletariat" of the Third World for example, to liberate us). The model would include also a notion of rightist and leftist deviations from the main line of strategy, and the ability to distinguish between revolutionary and pseudo-revolutionary slogans. It would include some grasp of new developments in man's nature and new manifestations of human powers as we move toward a condition in which man becomes increasingly subject, instead of object, of history. Another feature would be new types (typical situations, typical characters).

A set of concepts like this would raise a variety of questions about specific literary works. In regard to plays that deal with the strategy of revolutionary struggle — *Dutchman* and *The Slave* by Leroi Jones, for example — one would want to consider, along with their literary merit in the conventional sense, the way the black rage in these works appears to push the writer in the direction of the kind of leftism we see in the earlier development of Malcolm X and Cleaver, a leftism these writers superseded. When it comes to a book like James Agee's *Let Us Now Praise Famous Men*, one's response might well be almost at the other extreme. There is some question as to whether this is a radical book at all. It is romantic and religious rather than political. It is full of an anger that wins our esteem — but more anger than insight, one sometimes feels. Nor do we get any conception of revolutionary strategy. The typification in the book is traditional, not radical. Yet this is a book of outstanding literary power. So with Agee, as with Jones, we will have to handle as best we can a tension between literary merit in the conventional sense and the book's relationship to a model of radical art.

To return to the question of the causal nexus, what would one say about such radical works as Richard Wright's *Native Son*, the *Autobiography of Malcolm X*, or Eldridge Cleaver's *Soul on Ice*? One notes a remarkable grasp of the causal nexus in *Native Son*, of course implied rather than stated. An important feature of the books by Malcolm X and Eldridge Cleaver is the account of how they fought their way through from a black nationalist position to some understanding of the socio-economic roots of our troubles (where previously they had looked only to race), and so came to understand the need for a black-white revolutionary coalition. In dealing with these books, then, one would want to consider their literary merits and also, when you look at them in relationship to the radical model, the degree of penetration to the causal nexus. The matter is more difficult with a writer like Norman Mailer, if you consider him in his evolution from hipsterism to the pseudo-radical art of *Armies of the Night* and *Miami and the Siege of Chicago*. There can hardly be any question that Mailer's legacy of hipsterism keeps him from a grasp of the causal nexus. No one who brushes aside ideology the way Mailer does in *Armies of the Night* is going to achieve an understanding in depth of the movement of this society. With Mailer you have the impression of enormous literary talent, much greater than that of the three writers just mentioned, but also of an almost fatal shortcoming when we consider his work in relationship to a theory of radical art.

In approaching the subject this way we could show that radical literature provides a significant record of a change in consciousness now taking place. The transformation in consciousness is an outcome of the struggle, by means of revolutionary activity, to become subject of history. It is an outcome of this struggle and at the same time (since we are dealing with a dialectical phenomenon) it is an indispensable weapon of this struggle.

While considering the features of radical literature that have been named here, one would always try — as has been said — to be aware of literary qualities in the restricted sense, command of diction and metaphor, capacity to create characters and handle dialogue, concern with innovations in technique, and so on. Often it will be necessary for the student to maintain a tension between the radical principles as outlined above and literary merits in this more conventional sense.

On occasion we will want to consider something Erwin Pracht has said about *form* in radical literature. When a writer is absorbed with the discovery of a new reality, Pracht says, form may for a time suffer, and this should not too much upset us.[4] It will be well to have this point in mind when we have to answer colleagues whose only concern is with formal excellence and who are always likely to underrate works of radical literature that may have enormous importance because of their contribution to the discovery of this new reality.

In the study of radical literature (as of traditional literature for that matter), basic Marxist theory will always supply the social context of one's thinking. In taking up radical literature in a college course, where only a small part of one's time can be devoted to basic theory and where at the same time many students will be either ignorant or misinformed or both, one is in a situation that might parallel that of a cleric among infidels who found himself restricted to six class-hours for religious cosmology, scholastic philosophy, and the scheme of salvation. The works I have found most useful for the necessarily curtailed yet indispensable introduction to Marxist social theory are Emile Burns' *Introduction to Marxism*, Engels' *Socialism: Utopian and Scientific*, and selections from Selsam and Martel's *Reader in Marxist Philosophy*. There may be some merit also in using a theoretical work of the 60's like David Cooper's *To Free a Generation: The Dialectics of Liberation*. The essays in this book belong to the last few years, they are heterogeneous in character (Freudian, existentialist, Marxist, structuralist, left sectarian, and so on), so the book gives one a good opportunity to consider the erratic varieties of radical theory that have been current in this decade.

CONTINUITY-DISCONTINUITY

An approach to radical literature of the kind outlined here would help to heal the split between literary study and social practice by demonstrating the relationship between literature and the goals and strategies of the left. In the present article, however, I want to deal primarily with the literature that constitutes the major portion of the academic curriculum. I'll speak of three ways in which Marxists can contribute something to the effort to restore unified inter-connection between this major portion of their professional work and radical activism. A possible approach to all past literature, in the first place, is to examine continuity and discontinuity between past and present, as Robert Weimann has done in his treatment of Shakespeare in "Past Significance and Present Meaning in Literary History."[5] Two common approaches to performances of Shakespeare are necssarily unsatisfactory, he says. The first is that of the scholar-antiquarian whose chief impulse is to defend the text against adaptations that might be suspected of infidelity to the Renaissance frame of reference. His mistake is to sacrifice present meaning to past significance. But equally unsatisfactory is the approach of the producer who stresses present meaning at the cost of past significance. In his work the modern tone will be certain to jar with a text "whose verbal and poetic structures are conditioned by a different system of reference." What is needed is to maintain the tension between the historical and the modern point of view. The producer must have both worlds as points of reference. He must make the play as Elizabethan as is possible without abandoning its meaning for us, and as full of meaning for us as is possible without abandoning its Elizabethan character. In short, his task is to combine in a new unity the maximum amount of historical and contemporary significance.

For illustration, Weimann gives an account of two performances of *Hamlet* in the G.D.R. In the Berlin production, he explains, stress was put upon a world out of joint and on Hamlet's realization that this world must be changed. Hamlet himself came forward as a representative of a new era, not lacking in capacity for action, but held up by the question of violence. His problem was how to use force which he had seen only in its abuse. He shrinks from this and searches for a bloodless solution.

Weimann's comment is that this interpretation had a great deal of present meaning but did not fit too well into the text of the Renaissance play. In the other performance at Karl Marx Stadt, Hamlet was presented as a representative of values that were utopian in his time but have remained relevant into our own day, and he was pitted against powers frightfully evil and dangerous, as was made clear even in the interpretation of Polonius, Osric, and Rosencrantz and Guildenstern. The play presented then the contradiction between an advanced view of man and mighty powers which stood in the way of implementing this view. Weimann's comment was that here the past significance turned out to have maximum meaning for today without doing violence to the text. If we compare these two performances with the absurdist rendering of Shakespeare, we see that the performances Weimann describes do in fact relate the Renaissance play to an interpretation of our time having a distinctively (though not necessarily exclusively) socialist character.

Weimann's critical method will apply to literature in any genre and any period of the past, coming for that matter right up to the past of last year — or we might almost say of last week, such is the speed of change in the modern world. One implicaton of the thesis is that the meaning of past literature will, to some extent, differ according to time and place with each succeeding generation. Each new performance of an historical work should have some element of discovery. To make this discovery, however, we must be equipped with a profound Marxist historical scholarship — more than an *historical* scholarship, for that matter. We must know the past and the present, and in addition we must have some sense of the kind of society man has the capacity to create; in this way we will be equipped to deal with three moments in time: past, present, and future. This approach to literary study would mean an inevitable break with currents in bourgeois scholarship, since the radical differs from the establishment scholar in his understanding of all three moments in time.

MODERNISM

A second way in which the cleavage between activism and teaching can be repaired is through the development of a comprehensive, socially-based and convincing interpretation of modernism. This would make clear the connections between literary study throughout the whole period of modernism (late 19th century to the present) and a radical view of our own time.

I am assuming that we must keep the term modernism for a variety of trends in literature and art initiated in the last third of the 19th century in England and the United States, somewhat earlier in France. The shift in temper, which lasts up to our own day, is of such vast importance that a name becomes indispensable, and in spite of all the objections to the term modernism, no better label has been found. We are dealing with a reversal of main trends that lasted from the Renaissance to the end of the 19th century.

In order to make my point with some degree of concreteness, I will speak of modernism in late 19th century England, where it emerges conspicuously with Walter Pater and his contemporaries. The contrast between Pater and Arnold is especially instructive. The new sensibility is to be traced in the later Victorian poets: Fitzgerald, Rossetti, Morris, Wilde, Swinburne, Lionel Johnson, and Ernest Dowson. The modernism of Walter Pater and the English decadent poets leads directly to the modernist features of writers like Joyce and Eliot in the 20th century. We are dealing with a dominant trend in Western art from the last third of the 19th century to the present.

The truth is that one encounters a kind of pre-modernism somewhat earlier in 19th-century England, as for example in poems by Matthew Arnold. They express bewilderment in the face of a universe without meaning ("Obermann", "The Scholar-Gipsy"), with resulting feelings of loss of identity and of the power to feel, something akin to the modern experience of alienation ("Empedocles", "Tristram and Iseult", "Memorial Verses", "A Summer Night", "The Buried Life"). The response to these feelings may take the form of suicidal anguish ("Empedocles"). Arnold gives voice also to feeings of man's irremediable isolation ("Yes, in the sea of life enisled") and expresses the impulse to withdraw into the self ("Obermann", "The Scholar-Gipsy"). An outstanding feature of Arnold's response to the modernist vision, when compared with that of Tennyson and Browning, is the way he refuses to have recourse to any dubious moral, philosophical, or religious props ("To A Friend", "In Utrumque Paratus", "In Harmony With Nature").

If the epoch of modernism begins in the 1870's, what do we make of the earlier pre-modernist vision in Arnold, as also in Tennyson and Browning? The answer is that what characterizes the sensibility of the later period is *surrender* to the modernist vision; in the pre-modernism of the earlier period this vision is confronted, but the poets struggle to withstand it. Arnold withdrew "Empedocles on Etna" from the second edition of his poems (see *Preface to the Poems, 1853*) because he was not willing to become a spokesman for the modernist sensibility. He struggles for poise and tranquillity partly as an alternative to these feelings ("Quiet Work", "To A Friend"), and as an alternative to them also he attempts various kinds of qualified affirmation ("Memorial Verses", "A Summer Night", "The Buried Life", "The Scholar-Gipsy", "The Grande Chartreuse", "Dover Beach", "Rugby Chapel").

One of the most important contributions of the Marxist scholar will be to make clear what generates modernism. The answer, so far as England is concerned, is to be sought in the dialectics of the social transition of (approximately) the 1870's. As with the shift in class structure at the time of the Reform Act of 1832, the later transformation was brought about by quantitative changes in the previous decades. To understand the transformation of the 1870's, we should go back to consider the nature of the equilibrium that preceded it, the chief feature of which was the alliance established in 1832 between landowners and the new industrial middle class. Considering the capacity of an unfettered industrial system to expand the forces of production, it appears clear that the coalition had at least a partially progressive character, so that social protest between 1832 and 1870 was largely predicated on the assumption that significant changes could take place *within the system*. Yet contradictions continued to assert themselves, and as a result the middle decades were marked by a series of quantitative changes which were to lead when the time was ripe to the second major qualitative change in our period, that of the 1870's. The quantitative changes manifest themselves in an increasing accumulation of evidence concerning the unworkability of the system and also of a continuing protest against the society in which the conflict betwen moral affirmations and a debased social reality became ever more palpable, as Ruskin never tired of pointing out.

It is possible that the quantitative change alone would have been sufficient to bring about a qualitative change, but the transition was accelerated by a major depression and the threat of imperialist war, both of which brought about a situation which we can best understand if, using the language of our own time, we say that it now became apparent that the ruling class could not deliver on its own promises of domestic prosperity within a stable international order.

The equilibrium brought about by this qualitative change in the 1870's resembled that which had preceded the Reform Act in that the ruling class now came once more to adopt a predominantly reactionary role. But the leading force in the ruling-class coalition before 1832 had been the landowning aristocracy, whereas the leading force now was industrial capitalism. Capitalism itself now goes on the defensive. Policies associated with the preservation of ruling-class privilege take the place of a program designed to solve the problems of society as a whole. Imperialist policies dictated by class interests but manifestly destructive of any intelligible conception of the general welfare become increasingly coercive. As a consequence of the transformation, the social criticism that in the middle decades of the century had operated within the confines of the established order now associates itself with a revolutionary program given political expression by the new socialist parties of the 70's and 80's. The 1870's thus initiated the unstable equilibrium that has marked the major capitalist countries from the late 19th century to the present.

Modernism may be thought of as a change of temper within the superstructure traceable ultimately to the qualitative change in the basic class structure of society that initiated the highly unstable equilibrium of late capitalism. The roots of modernism lie, in other words, in the emergence of a society of permanent crisis. The new temper is not to be understood except through reference to a ruling class that has outlived its usefulness and faces eventual extinction. Here lies the source of the irrationalism, mysticism, and pessimism in the modernist temper. The new attitudes are often accompanied by the illusion that the decline of the governing class constitutes the decline of an entire society. Modernism is to be thought of as a deformation of vision whose ultimate causes are traceable to a state of intensifying disorder in the structure of existing society. When the temper appears in people far removed from the ruling class, it is to be explained partly as a by-product of the class domination which expresses itself in the principle that the predominant ideas of any society are those of its ruling class. The profound despair and the sense of victimization that have marked the century from 1870 to 1970 can hardly be thought of except in terms of the domination of a class that is unwilling to accept the notion of any alternative to the existing structure of society. The media often appear to resemble an industry designed to eradicate the notion of a viable future. Any imagined alternative is made to seem even more fearful than what exists. (George Orwell spent the bulk of his career turning out books in support of this view.)

The new unstable equilibrium initiated two literary trends, modernism and socialist realism. Modernism may be thought of as a literary movement circumscribed by limits imposed by the established order and therefore in a sense as the cultural expression of the dominant class in a society that has lost its progressive potential. While modernist writers are disillusioned by the existing order (Pater, Wilde), they are not able to see an alternative. Socialist realism, on the other hand, may be thought of as the literary expression of a social philosophy which assumes that the contradictions between productive forces and the existing relations of ownership can be overcome in a new (socialist) society. This is a literature of social revolution. William Morris and George Bernard Shaw are its most imposing early representatives in England.

This interpretation of modernism will explain why the movement was initiated so much earlier in France than in England. Disillusion following the hopes of the French Revolution became strong in the 1830's in France, and it is from that decade that we can date the phenomena of modernism in France, whereas the new equilibrium in English society brought about by the Reform Bill had the result of delaying for four decades the moment of disillusion. This view of the genesis of modernism will also explain why in the United States modernism (with Henry Adams, Stephen Crane and others) — and also its dialectical opposite, socialist realism (with Howells, Bellamy and others) — appeared about the same time as in England. The principal distinction between the American and English experience in the 19th century, when examined in the light of the concepts employed in this essay, is that the English development of Victorian humanism has virtually no parallel in the United States (assuming, that is, that Emerson and Thoreau represent positive romanticism rather than Victorian humanism). The difference is surely traceable mainly to the disruption of the national life by the Civil War.

The explanation of the genesis of modernism offered here is on a high level of generality, and needless to say in dealing with a specific writer one would attempt to be more specific, to show how this social causation expressed itself through the writer's individual experience, and to make clear also how certain individual experiences having little to do with the transformations in society may also have helped foster the new attitudes. The main thing to insist upon is that the great movement of modernist art has a special relationship to the dead-end perspectives of the bourgeoisie.

The Marxist view of modernism becomes all the more convincing when we contrast it with interpretations advanced by bourgeois scholars. Here are four:

(1) The change is regarded as a nodal point in the decline of the West, with the implication that the humanist tradition cannot be restored (E. H. Carr,[6] Barbara Ward[7]).

(2) Scholars whose outlook shows the continuing influence of modernism sometimes look upon the change at the end of the 19th century as a kind

of advance toward a 20th-century (existentialist) sensibility that may even be regarded as a culminating breakthrough in the evolution of the West (William Madden,[8] Morse Peckham,[9] Martin Esslin,[10] William Barrett[11]).

(3) Modernism is looked upon primarily as a consequence of the breakdown of traditional religious faith. The Victorians themselves often thought of the matter this way. Both Tennyson and Browning, for example, shielded themselves against the assault of modernism by reaffirming traditional belief — belief in spite of the evidence, as it often seems, especially with Tennyson. Robert Penn Warren takes at face value the Victorians' own understanding of the situation and writes as if the collapse of religious faith were sufficient explanation for the onset of modernism.[12] In *The Disappearance of God in the Nineteenth Century*, Hillis Miller likewise assumes that the modernist sensibility was brought about primarily by the collapse of religious dogma. But one can think of other periods in which skepticism concerning religion has been associated with a confident world view; also those Victorians who abandoned traditional belief but at the same time looked forward with confidence to the possibility of social advance were immune to modernist attitudes. While the religious crisis often precipitated modernist attitudes, it cannot be thought of as the primary cause.

(4) Sometimes the interpretation is so eclectic as to yield no significant meaning for our time.[13]

All four interpretations blind us to the fact that the roots of the new temper lie in the contradictions of capitalism. In so doing they deny us an understanding of past and present that might equip us to solve the problems of today. We have an example here of how in current establishment scholarship a class-oriented view of the present leads to a class-oriented interpretation of the past, and then how the latter comes back to corroborate the former. We are confronted, that is, with a class view of both past and present in which each confirms the other. (The same may be said, of course, of the Marxist interpretation of the emergence of modernism; here also a class view of the present helps to make clear the nature of the historical crisis just behind us, and then this view of the past serves to reenforce our understanding of today. The difference between establishment and Marxist scholarship, then, boils down in a sense to a difference in class position. But we do not have to leave the matter there, for one class view is more in accord with objective reality than the other.)

One is tempted in dealing with modernism to adopt the wrong tone. The reason is that the literary phenomena are closely related to trends in modern life against which we must necessarily do battle. Modernist art presents a fearful picture of the tearing down of a traditional view of man, every item of which reflects the destructive influence of a class that is heading toward destruction and preparing to take the whole monumental achievement of civilization with it. A leading feature of the new temper is a qualitatively new sense of human powerlessness. Man comes to conceive of himself in modernist literature, as we have said, not as the creature who fashions history but as its victim. We see this emerging first in English literature in the work of late 19th-century writers like Edward Fitzgerald, Housman, Hardy, Henry Adams, and Mark Twain.

Another trend is a loss of perspective that manifests itself in depiction of life as chaotic and incomprehensible; chaos, as Miasnikov has said, comes to be pictured from within.[14] In general, we can say that the perspective in realism is sufficiently detached so that the writer is able to relate the torment of modern man to specific causes, to picture aberration *as* aberration (as Lukacs says), to grasp the element of modern nihilism without denial of the human, to confront the horrors of our time without paralysis of the spirit. In modernist art perspective of this kind is lost, a subjective view of the maladies of contemporary man is identified with universal human experience; conditions abstracted from their historical context are taken as an absolute. (It is significant that the skepticism concerning the reason implied in these features of the modernist temper — the skepticism that continues in the existentialist movement — pertains only to the reason that concerns itself with social structure and social change; the reason as it operates in the sphere of the natural sciences has not been called into question.)

Then again modernist literature often embodies a fragmented conception of man, with brutal or animal features magnified and traditional human features (sense of community, moral energy and sensitivity, etc.) residual only. This view of man may be associated with a new interest in the abnormal and perverse, but sometimes it is to be explained as a quest for meaning through sensation in a time when other kinds of meaning appear unavailable. (We are speaking here of trends only in literature circumscribed by the world view of the dominant class. In the revolutionary literature that develops concurrently with modernism, most of these traits are reversed; we get confidence, optimism and a revitalization of the humanist tradition as opposed to the modernist features just named.)

These features of the view of life in modernist literature all correspond to trends we deplore in the real world, and it is easy enough to transfer our distaste for the characteristics in life to their reflection in art. Sometimes there may be a certain justification for the tone that results, because literature of this kind has in fact tended to foster and perpetuate the attitudes in question. Still, the normative tone is to be avoided. The best argument for steering clear of it is that the phenomena of modernism are dialectical, and we have here reviewed only one side of the dialectic. If we turn to the other side, we see that modernism embodies also liberating and creative trends. The modernist sensibility will have no truck with bourgeois values; often it recoils from respectable society with the most intense revulsion, as with Wilde, Yeats, and Joyce. The revulsion is of course altogether unlike that of the socialist humanist since it is not connected with the perspective of an alternative organization of society, but nevertheless the modernist revulsion does frequently function as a way-station in an evolution from a bourgeois to a socialist world view. (You see something of this sort in the beatnik and hippie revulsion in our time, which sometimes marks a transition toward revolutionary activism.)

Modernist trends are often accompanied by a release from repression, especially the social-sexual repression of the Victorian middle class. In this release from repression we have a parallel to the affirmation of the spontaneous features of man's nature in romanticism. The new literature tends, in consequence, to have deep roots in the instinctual life. Modernist writers create without inhibition and are able to reveal depths in the self not previously available for artistic expression. We see this most clearly in Yeats and Joyce. To be sure, when we speak of finding an artistic outlet for the deeper regions of the self, we need to be reminded that this will often be a self marked by the bewilderment, anguish and nihilism of a society incapable of progressive initiative. Still, most excellent writing will require that the author express without hindrance the whole of what is in him, and we should not find it surprising therefore that so much first-rate literature of the last century has had strong modernist features.

Even when it comes to the purely artistic features of modernism, the dialectics of the phenomenon must be taken into account:

(1) Modernist art is marked by ceaseless experiment in technique. We see this in writers of the last third of the 19th century, and even more in the 20th — Pound, Eliot, Yeats, Joyce.

(2) On the other hand a marked feature of modernist literature is the separation of art from life. The center of concern shifts to literary technique. This may be explained partly by the search for new forms to serve as a vehicle for a deeper awareness of the self, but it may also

indicate that the interest in content has receded. Much modernist literature serves as aesthetic escape. This is especially true of the decadent
romanticism of Rossetti, the early Morris, and Wilde. (We have here a
second example of the affinity between the art of the modernist period
and romanticism; the first example was the release from repression, just
mentioned. (Are these trends related to the parallelism mentioned above
between the social equilibrium of the two periods, after 1870 and before
1830?)

The chief reason for avoiding the normative tone, then, is that it
associates itself with only one side of the dialectic. But there are other
reasons. The normative tone transfers attention from aesthetic to ethical
considerations. Ethical considerations are never irrelevant in art, but one
would not usually want to consider them in isolation from the aesthetic
character of the work. Even more important is the fact that for the
radical reader modernist art may well have a significance other than that
which the author intended. Provided that the teacher-critic can relate the
literary work to an examined world view, there may be as much instruction
in regard to the plight of man in our time in the dead-end nihilistic literature of modernism as in critical realism. We have an example of this in
Inge von Wangenheim's account of the light thrown on the nature of
capitalism by Beckett's *Waiting for Godot*, a play customarily described
as modernist.[15] In the article included in this volume on fascist, racist,
and elitist art, Lee Baxandall points out how the illusion and despair of
some modernist authors can be "demystified" by critics whose understanding of history and society will put the work in a different perspective.

And another thing, there can be little doubt that the positive features
of modernism — that is, the new candor, the reaching down to the
deepest caverns of the self, and of course the technical experiment — can
be taken over for a new, socially-oriented literature. This subject has been
explored in an initial way in Horst Redeker, *Abbilding und Aktion:
Versuch ueber die Dialektik des Realismus*.[16]

Yet another reason for avoiding the normative tone is that modernist
features in art scarcely ever come unalloyed. There is almost invariably an
intermesh of modernist and realist trends. The exception would be the
cheap mass art of a society in an advanced stage of decay, where the only
function appears to be to disable the mind, to degrade and brutalize.

The cue then is to engage in a partisan and committed struggle
against the corrupting influence of a ruling class that has outlived its
usefulness, but at the same time when we consider literature that indi-

rectly reflects this influence, to adopt a tone that is impersonal and analytical, rather than normative.

It should not be hard to learn how to avoid the normative tone. The main task is to deal with three areas of experience — basic social theory, required for an understanding of the root causes of modernism in society, then a mediating sphere of aesthetics between literature and social theory, and finally the literary work itself. If we can achieve sufficient knowledge of the materials of these three layers, we will find that whenever we touch this subject, we will be making some contribution to a radical understanding of literature and society, and this will be a contribution necessary to the goal of healing the split between teaching and activism.

CRITICAL REALISM — ITS PERSISTENT VITALITY

The third area in which Marxism has a contribution to make is the study of writers of recent times in whom the realist tradition is relatively strong — writers, say, like Hemingway, Dreiser, or Faulkner. Of course the principle of continuity-discontinuity will apply here, since we are still concerned with the usable past. But we need also a structure of concepts bearing upon the relationship between this kind of literature and the totality of the Marxist world view. We need, in a word, a theory of realism.

Again, the term. If "modernism" is unfortunate, "realism" is not much better, considering how different the American usage is. But what can we do? So far as I can see, simply go ahead and use the term, while at the same time taking pains to ward off the inevitable misunderstandings that arise in an intellectual climate in which two concepts of realism overlap, where one is familiar and the other unfamiliar, and where the unfamiliar one is the more complex and more deeply charged with philosophic implications. Realism in the Marxist sense, then, does not imply a direct relationship between art and reality. It does not imply immediate comprehensibility. It does not mean muckraking. It does not mean an art concerned primarily with externals. Ionesco had this misconception in mind when he wrote that "realism, socialist or not, never looks beyond reality. It narrows it down, diminishes it, falsifies it, and leaves out of account the obsessive truths that are most fundamental to us: love, death, and wonder. It presents man in a perspective that is narrow and alien; truth lies in our dreams, in our imagination: every moment of our lives confirms this statement."[17] The fact is that many works of realism will necessarily be concerned with the inner world of feeling, imagination and dream — and with Ionesco's trilogy of love, wonder and death.

The term realism in its Marxist use does not necessarily imply the presence or absence of any given quality of style. While there will necessarily be a relationship between style and realism, this must always be examined concretely. The concept of realism does not in itself exclude any style.

A major concern in the consideration of realism has to do with the degree of truth in the reflection of a given reality. Of course this involves a host of problems — but what critical system does not? What is truth? What is reality? What is the relationship between literature conceived as a model and what the model refers to? Many different kinds of relationship are possible, but the critic must determine which one applies in a given instance. Also, when it comes to truth, who is to be the judge?

Further misconceptions. The truthful relationship is not that of the photograph. The concept of realism allows plenty of room for the subjective sensibility of the writer. The reality that realistic art concerns itself with includes not only what *is* but what is possible. Realist art will function as an instrument of discovery.

The matter can be put in a useful light if we focus on the breakthrough from the false consciousness ("ideological" consciousness) of class rule — that false consciousness that partly develops automatically out of class contradictions and is partly also the product of manipulation. Questions about true and false consciousness are not to be asked normatively, any more than the questions concerning modernism discussed earlier. The questions are to be raised rather because they call attention to essential features of the work in its relationship to the world we all seek to comprehend and in its effect on readers who have their own work to do in this world. What we learn about this subject will be only one of many elements to be considered — but one of the most important.

Other major features of realism relate in one way or another to this question of true and false consciousness. For example, one could hardly imagine a more searching question than the one Lukacs proposes as central for the Marxist interpretation of literature and art, the question having to do with appearance and essence — a subject already mentioned in connection with radical literature.[18] The goal of art, Lukacs asserts, is neither a faithful presentation of surface phenomena nor the rendering of an essence independent of surface. The goal rather is an all-embracing interpretation of a complex totality in which surface and essence appear in different roles as insight deepens. One expects from art both a rendering of the surface phenomena of life and some degree of penetration to a reality having greater depth.

In his most recent work on aesthetics, Lukacs uses the term "to defetishize" in order to get at these issues.[19] He here extends the term Marx and Engels took over from primitive religion and used for social analysis when they talked about the attribution of magical qualities to inert objects — the fetishism of commodities or of money. Lukacs points out that in its appearance, as opposed to essence, society has in fact a fetishized character, and an art that does not go deeper than the surface embodies a "capitulation to fetishism." T. S. Eliot's poetry represents capitulation to the fetishized world of monopoly capitalism, Lukacs says, and he speaks of the nihilism, cynicism, dread, despair, *Angst*, and mystification that commonly result from capitulation of this kind. On the other hand, art may have the function of penetrating beyond the surface to essence and thus "defetishizing" reality. He speaks of Balzac and Tolstoy as writers whose main function throughout their work was to clarify and restore the integrity of man by stripping off appearances and making the reader aware of deeper levels of truth. Lukacs proposes that the question of whether an artistic work removes the cloak of fetishism or retains it may be thought of as a main criterion for distinguishing between progressive and reactionary art. He is here getting at something similar to what Brecht had in mind when he said an important function of art was to penetrate to the "causal nexus" in society.[20] It goes without saying that a grasp of how art relates to appearance and essence in society is at its beginnings. As Marxist theory and new investigation continue to develop, our understanding of these matters will become more adequate to the complexity of the subject.

The interpretation of appearance and essence will have a dialectical character — especially so since "essence" in any area is generally to be understood in terms of contradiction. For society in our time the chief contradiction is that between forces and relations, the forces being thought of as including the totality of movement toward a more productive and rationally ordered society, and the relations (in the sense of established social structure) denoting primarily the system of ownership and control which stands in the way of realization of these drives. The main contradiction in our time, in other words, is between the vast potential of contemporary society and the paralysis of that potential traceable to the obsolescent character of the existing system of ownership and control. Every variety of political protest, on campus and off, is to be understood within the context of the central contradiction.

When we make use of the concepts of appearance and essence, we are repeatedly reminded of how difficult it is for the writer in our time to penetrate to essence; the mass media and the entire weight of the dominant culture stand in the way. For it is a culture that seeks perpetually to persuade us that things are in fact what they appear to be; it cloaks the causal nexus and fosters an alienated consciousness unable to perceive the contradictions in terms of which surface phenomena can alone be comprehended. If the role of art is to defetishize, then the task of the artist becomes inordinately difficult in these circumstances.

These concepts help explain why the radical estimate of Dreiser has always been so high. Dreiser was in fact able to go far toward an understanding of the causal nexus in American society — much farther, for example, than a writer of greater literary talent like Fitzgerald. (This is not to say that Dreiser writes better novels than Fitzgerald. We are talking about one consideration that bears upon a literary work, one among many. Obviously a novel that goes far toward a grasp of the causal nexus may in theory have little other literary merit, just as books with other merits may fail when looked at from this point of view.) The concepts of appearance and essence will help us see also that an art like the absurdist theater expresses the very spirit of the times, for the plays in question present us with appearance detached from anything approximating serious struggle for comprehension of essence.

These concepts supply tools for the examination of literature that deals with such major phenomena of our time as depression or war. How many novels do in fact give us an understanding of war, including its causes? One doesn't ask for overt political analysis but rather that the lives of the fictional characters be presented in such a way as to make clear the deeper meaning of war, what caused it and what interests are involved, both apparent interests and those of which many participants may be unconscious. What is to be said of *The Naked and the Dead, The Young Lions, From Here to Eternity* and other war novels when we look at them this way? When it comes to the depression, the question again has to do with comprehension of the causal nexus. Are the misfortunes of the individual presented within a context that makes clear the causes in the malfunctioning of a social system? In the actual depression, the consciousness of many victims was in fact "fetishized", so that they imagined their misfortunes were somehow proof of *personal* inadequacy. Do we get this kind of fetishized consciousness or a deeper understanding of causation in novels like Farrell's *Studs Lonigan,* Dos Passos' *U. S. A.,* or Steinbeck's *The Grapes of Wrath*? Could one say, still using the principle of appearance and essence, or of fetishized and defetishized reality, that American writers have been somewhat more successful in dealing with the depression than with war?

The concept of appearance and essence explains some of the claims advanced on behalf of socialist literature. In the socialist countries, it is argued, at any rate in situations where the common citizen is increasingly drawn into the process of decision-making, he acquires an understanding of the nature of contradiction and is better able therefore to achieve insight into the relationship between appearance and essence. Such conditions are favorable, it is argued, for a literature that goes far toward perception of the true nature of the causal nexus and is able accordingly to throw light at one and the same time upon outer and inner meaning.

Another tool to be used in getting at the grasp of reality in literature is the concept of the "typical." This also has a bearing on the question of true and false consciousness, since a writer imprisoned by false consciousness would be obstructed in his effort to grasp the typical. The concept of the typical serves to focus attention on significant artistic insight, on varying levels of generalization and degrees of comprehension, and also on the art through which the writer communicates his understanding of these matters. The typical, like appearance and essence, will have meaning in proportion to one's understanding of the complexity of man's nature and society. The concept is close to that of the "historically significant."

The typical can be thought of as related to the general versus the particular (only in the typical in literature one expects both the general *and* the particular); it can be understood in terms of necessity as opposed to chance or accident (only again in literature one would expect a combination of the two as they appear in reality). We should be reminded here also of the Hegelian-Marxist notion that necessity does in fact realize itself through chance, and of Lenin's saying that the highest task of knowledge is to discover and disclose the logic of that historic and social necessity that expresses itself in an endless chain of seemingly chance happenings.

If the typical is related to the general, to necessity, and to the historically significant, then it obviously is related also to the subject that has just been discussed, namely, essence as opposed to appearance. It follows that one way to discover the typical is through an analysis of contradiction. A question to ask of contemporary novels, accordingly, would be how well does the writer grasp the typical contradictions of our time and to what extent does he succeed in portraying the typical within the context of this understanding. A quick response might be that the novels of several decades ago did the job more adequately than do those of this moment. Do Mailer, Malamud, and Bellow, for example, portray the typical contradictions of our time? They do and they don't. Does Updike? Perhaps the answer here is that he *did* and he doesn't. Maxwell Geismar asserts that James Jones is a major novelist of the moment. How successfully does James Jones describe the typical contradictions of this society? These are important questions to be asked of almost all writers — of Faulkner, of Salinger, of Nathanael West.

S. Petrov asserts that the typical should not be confused with the average.[21] Hamlet represents a grasp of the typical on the part of Shakespeare, in that the central forces of the epoch were brought into conflict in his person; we see in him the collision between the past and a new and different world that is coming into being. But it is not to be supposed that this conflict was articulated in the average man of Shakespeare's age. Similarly Don Quixote represents a penetration to the typical on the part of Cervantes. Here again we have the collision between two epochs in world history, the chivalric past and the utilitarian future. But again it is unlikely that the conflict appeared explicitly in many men of the age. Was it not rather the genius of Cervantes that enabled him to penetrate to the typical of which his contemporaries were unaware?

Petrov makes a contribution to understanding of the typical by exploring the concept of the "generally human." He traces the generally human to conditions that persist without marked change in different epochs. It manifests itself in the passions associated with class society, in positive traits (the struggle against exploitation, the Promethean drive, the striving for freedom and happiness) and also negative (servility, avarice, and so on). All such traits enter into the concept of the typical. Yet the generally human is not identical with the universal. For one thing, the universal is almost always associated with an abstract, unchanging human nature, whereas the generally human will be understood as always in dialectical connection with the historically specific. If we take the jealousy of Othello as an example, where another might take note of the "universal" pure and simple, the critic making use of Petrov's concept would attempt to isolate not only the generally human but also that which belongs peculiarly to Shakespear's age.

In Clyde Griffiths of *An American Tragedy* you have an appetite for material luxury that may perhaps be described as "generally human," but Clyde also belongs to the early decades of this century in a particular country. A dominant theme in *The Sun Also Rises* (vanity saith the preacher) also belongs to the generally human, but the talk and behavior of Lady Brett, Michael Campbell and others belongs specifically to Paris and Pamplona in the years following the First War. If we consider Joyce's *Dubliners* or the *Portrait of the Artist*, the severing of bonds by Stephen Dedalus perhaps represents a "generally human" phenomenon, but Stephen himself belongs to Ireland in the period following the aesthetic movement. The task of the critic who seeks to understand both the generally human and temporally conditioned is somewhat more complicated than that of his colleague whose concept of the universal can be used without reference to the special coloration imparted by a given time and place.

The "totality principle" may also function as part of the theory of realism. It raises questions about the extent to which a literary work advances toward a "total" view of its subject. For example, do we get an awareness of the causes of the condition that is portrayed? If the plague in Camus' novel is to be thought of as in part having reference to fascism, one might object that the reader is not given enough insight into the causes and the possible cure of the social disorder under examination. Something similar might be said of *All the King's Men*, for in the interpretation of Huey Long's brand of American fascism, Robert Penn Warren gives much attention to the psychology of his characters but shows little comprehension of economic and political realities. The totality principle may lead to considerations similar to those already discussed under the heading of appearance and essence. For example, Lukacs writes of war novels:

> From *All Quiet on the Western Front* to *The Naked and the Dead* many honest, realistic novels of great aesthetic and ethical merit have been written. But war can only be understood in its totality if the writer has a perspective which enables him to understand the forces that lead to war, as Arnold Zweig had in *Education at Verdun* or A. Beck in *The Road to Volokamsk*. These latter works, far from giving us monographs on war, elevate the personal fate of their characters to the level of the typical; they mirror the totality of war in concrete relationships between typical, but living human beings.[22]

The totality principle may lead to significant observations that one might otherwise have missed, but tact is needed. For example, one would expect a different degree of totality (the concept is always relative) in different genres, perhaps less in poetry than in the novel, and also, one would always want to consider the historical period in which the book was written. A treatment that might today seem inadequate from this point of view may have constituted a great step forward in its time. An example would be the exploration of unconscious motives in Dostoyevsky. And then of course one must always guard against the mistake of asking that the writer do something that was far afield from his intentions. The totality principle is also related to the issue of true and false consciousness, since failure to grasp "the whole" may well be associated with the latter.

The theory of realism requires attention to the question of the writer's command of the historically specific, his sense of how social relationships and man's very nature show the influence of a given time and place. In *The Historical Novel* Lukacs describes how this historical sense came into being in the 19th century. With the French Revolution and the Napoleonic wars, history for the first time became part of the consciousness of masses of men. He regards it as important that mass armies replaced mercenary armies, so that people who were drawn in this way into the events of the age came to think of their own experience as historically conditioned. In the 19th century also, capitalism came to be thought of as representing a definite historical era in human development. Lukacs speaks of the contribution of Condorcet and Hegel to the development of thinking in terms of historical process.

So here again we can say that — where other things are equal — one might well take account of the writer's awareness of his moment in history. The tendency to stress the timeless at the expense of the historically conditioned has an important source in the ideology of a class with a powerful interest in obstructing social change. Stress on the timeless is a major feature of myth criticism, Freudian criticism, and archetypal criticism, to name three current fashions.

Let me say a word or two about how the principles reviewed here might affect the critical estimates of three writers. A central question for each would be the extent to which he has been able to break his way through the false consciousness of our time and achieve a "defetishized" world view.

HEMINGWAY. Just what picture does Hemingway give us of the lost generation phenomena that he records with such power in his work of the 20's? There can hardly be any question that his great achievement was to depict the spiritual void, the death of love, the death of value. But it is not enough to describe the achievement as Mark Spilka does in "The Death of Love in *The Sun Also Rises*."[23] One would want also to ask about the depth of Hemingway's understanding of the lost-generation temper. Is there any sense of historical causation? Do we see the lost generation as constituting a phase in the transformation of Western society, as something to be understood in terms of what brought it into being and what eventually is to come after it — namely, the restitution of value in a different kind of society? A tentative answer might be that Hemingway has a rather limited sense of social causation in this period of his career. But when it comes to the 30's, we move from a relatively static view to a conception that takes into account the realities of social change. In *For Whom the Bell Tolls*, Hemingway is aware of an historical crisis in modern society and he does have some understanding of its causes and the way out. We can speak of an element of advance in the shift from Hemingway's temper of the 20's (when he appears as inactive spectator of collapse of value) to that of the 30's (when he becomes a participant in the struggle to comprehend and influence an historical situation whose roots are to some extent understood and whose outcome can to some extent be forecast).

To claim that there is an element of advance in this one feature of Hemingway's work does not require one to claim that his art benefited in every respect. Ivan Kashkeen, the Marxist critic of Hemingway, has much to say about failure in style in the later Hemingway, when his manner sometimes appeared almost to be a parody of himself. But Kashkeen demonstrates also that Hemingway's own point of view in the twenties was perilously close to the vision of *nada* he portrayed, and he analyzes the advance that came when Hemingway in the 30's moved toward identification with a progressive class, and even discovered that there was something important enough to die for.[24]

A radical critic could not adopt the view advanced by Ray B. West, who asserts that Hemingway could not handle affirmation — that he always failed when he tried — and then goes on to scoff at the notion that it was important for him to *attempt* the affirmations of the thirties.[25] The artist's responsibility is to his sensibility and not to an abstract view of the world, West says; affirmation may represent a *danger* to the novelist. We can take West as a representative of scholars of the 50's whose main effort was to bring Hemingway (and most literature for that matter) into the framework of a world view that claimed to be politically neutral but in fact constituted part of the ideological weaponry of an economic class fighting a defensive battle in a Cold War. But while breaking with Ray B. West, we might nevertheless come to the conclusion that Hemingway's work in the 30's, despite its greater comprehension of the historically specific, was artistically inferior to that of the 20's, because the writer could not put as much of himself into the affirmations of the later period as had gone into the depiction of anguish earlier.

DREISER. One would want to point out Dreiser's conquistador advance toward command of the historically specific, the capacity to penetrate to the causal nexus, the relentless examination of the debasement of the American dream. The achievement is the more impressive considering the opaqueness of modern society for most writers — for all of us. To see Dreiser this way does not mean that this is all we see — any more than in the case of Hemingway. Dreiser followed false leads when he tried to discover what was wrong with this society (social Darwinism, for example), and no one would want to be put in a position of having to defend Dreiser's style. Still, this interpretation breaks with the one that has remained dominant in the university since it was formulated by Lionel Trilling many years ago (in *The Liberal Imagination*). Trilling, who at the time was himself turning away from Marxist currents in criticism, passed a kind of Cold-War verdict on Dreiser by dismissing him as a bungler and a bore.

FAULKNER. One of the most attractive features of this kind of radical approach to literary study is that it opens up many problems that are not easily solved. With the giants of literature in recent times, one wants to know to what degree they were able to break through barriers of false consciousness. How much were they able to perceive concerning the special ways in which modern man is to be thought of as historically conditioned? It is significant, I think, that Marxist critics now writing about Faulkner are in disagreement on this. Some say that in representing the acquisitive drives of the Snopes clan as a perversity of human nature, without any apparent connection with capitalist compulsions, Faulkner was showing a certain inability to penetrate to the causal nexus.[26] Others are impressed, on the other hand, with the strength of Faulkner's exploration of the concrete force of circumstance in his study of morbid or perverse behavior, as in Joe Christmas in *Light in August*, Sutpen in *Absalom! Absalom!* or in *Sanctuary*.[27] When it comes to human potential, some argue that the backward pull toward traditional values in Faulkner and perhaps his preference for pathological or under-equipped characters suggests a view of man as fettered by his own nature.[28] Others argue that the entire corpus of Faulkner's fiction supports the "man will prevail" theme of the Nobel Prize speech, that man's capacity to fight it out against adverse circumstance is the very sound and fury of Faulkner's works — even that in picturing man this way Faulkner was rediscovering an aspect of the American national character.[29] In spite of the vast mass of Faulkner scholarship, the things the radical critic needs to know have not yet been elucidated. A job of research has to be done to relate the novels to their milieu and ours (as the radical understands both), to discover what we as radicals can use and what we cannot use, to determine the degree to which the novels symbolize unchanging man and the degree to which they present man within the frame of an alterable social structure.

What is to be said in summary concerning critical realism? In considering the relationship between the writer's "second reality" and the real world, a central queston is the extent to which he has been able to make a breakthrough from the false consciousness of our epoch and penetrate to the causal nexus. In focusing attention on this question, we necessarily relate the literary work to an awareness of our own reality as the radical understands it. Literary study is thus brought into connection in one more way with the radicalization of the student's consciousness, and we have a further means to heal the split between work in the classroom and political activism.

*

I have confined myself to four ways in which students of literature might relate what they are doing to their practical work in the radical movement. The first had to do with an approach to radical literature, and the next three were concerned with the examination of continuity and discontinuity between past and present, modernism, and critical realism.

Two final remarks are called for:

(1) NEED FOR RESEARCH. All the approaches suggested above require an advance in the kind of radical scholarship that would make use of the theory of historical materialism, including the Marxist generalizations concerning the driving forces of history, the relationship between superstructure and base, etc. A movement of scholarship of this kind would in turn require a series of revolutions in the graduate school, in the entire Ph. D. program, and not least in the Modern Language Association. In the meantime, we'll do what we can!

(2) THE PROBLEM OF THEORY. When we speak of the Marxist understanding of society, we run at once into a series of difficulties, not least of which is the absence in this country of regard for theory — both theory as such, and more specifically Marxist theory. It is not an accident that the existentialist craze found in this country a climate more favorable than in the countries where it originated. If existentialism may be regarded as the philosophic expression of the petty bourgeoisie in the period when paths toward the future have been blocked off by controlled

media and institutionalized terror, then we can see why hopelessness in regard to theory has been a central feature, and we are reminded at the same time of how congenial its American climate proved to be.

Norman Mailer voices a representative American attitude when he dismisses Marxist theory as reductionist, simple-minded, doctrinaire. He thinks of its proponents as men with an unbreakable logic that always gets broken by history. The leaders of the Pentagon March, he says, were quite right to rely on improvisation. For they had had enough experience with water-tight strategies of leftist groups, "all sure of themselves and all proved wrong by history."

> Well, Macdonald, Lowell, and Mailer...did not need to discuss the sound-as-brickwork-logic-of-the-next-step. The March tomorrow would more or less work or not work. If it didn't, the Left would always find a new step...if the March did more or less succeed, one knew it would be as a result of episodes one had never anticipated, and the results might lead you in directions altogether unforeseen. And indeed how could one measure success or failure in a venture so odd and unprecedented as this? One did not march on the Pentagon and look to get arrested as a link in a master scheme to take over the bastions of the Republic step by step, no, that sort of sound-as-brickwork-logic was left to the FBI. Rather, one marched on the Pentagon because...because...and here the reasons became so many and so curious and so vague, so political and so primitive, that there was no need, or perhaps no possibility to talk about it yet, one could only ruminate....[30]

Here we have an example of "spontaneity," the notion that it is better to improvise rather than to plan strategy in the light of examined theoretical premises.

Some of the sources of this scorn for theory are familiar enough — the American pragmatic frame of mind, for example. Then the counter-attack against the left in the McCarthy era created an atmosphere in which it has been almost impossible for many people to discover what Marxist theory is all about. Further, one can hardly exaggerate the disastrous consequences of the revelations concerning Stalin. The moral many people drew was that when you adopt a systematic political ideology, you court disaster. (In so far as they interpreted the calamities of the Stalin era in this way, instead of seeking to erect safeguards against a repetition of what happened then, we have another instance of the effect of an intellectual climate permeated by counterrevolution.)

In practical life the consequences of our poverty in theory are far-reaching. We have difficulty in comprehending the source of the violence-prone breakdown of civil society at home and of military aggression abroad, and we find ourselves at a loss for a strategy that would guide toward wresting control of the system from those who now hold power. Without theory protest leads to a revolt in the void (chanting and beads, vandalism, lives that stagger from fix to fix). So much for the consequences in practical life. For the approach to literature proposed in this paper, to be deprived of theory constitutes an almost fatal impediment.

If we are to move in the directions proposed here, then, a good deal more is required than for literary study in the conventional sense. We have to develop a critical apparatus suitable for this new kind of literary study and at the same time to master the social theory required to support this new aesthetic structure. In doing this we cannot absent ourselves from political activism, since both the aesthetic and social theory we are concerned with are of a kind that can be constructed only in the closest association with practice.

NOTES

1. Northrop Frye, *Anatomy of Criticism*, pp. 7-12.

2. Alvin Kibel, in *Partisan Review* (Summer 1965), Vol. 32, p. 466.

3. Erwin Pracht, "Socialist Realism," pp. 231-245. This essay, along with others by Robert Weimann, Georg Lukacs, Werner Mittenzwei, N. K. Gay, S. Petrov, B. G. Zhantieva, Elisabeth Simons, and Werner Neubert, appears in *Preserve and Create* (Humanities Press, New York, 1973), an anthology of contemporary critical essays from the Soviet Union, East Germany, and Hungary, edited by Ursula Beitz and myself. Other authors are cited from manuscript.

4. *Idem*

5. Robert Weimann, "Past Significance and Present Meaning in Literary History," *Preserve and Create*, pp. 32-51.

6. In *The Soviet Impact on the Western World*, New York, 1947, E. H. Carr describes the epoch from the Renaissance to the period we are discussing as a hiatus between two totalitarianisms, that of the Middle Ages and that of the twentieth century.

7. Barbara Ward describes our period as a lull before the emergence of "an inhuman order of society," a "social order...alien to human personality and human freedom." See "The Illusion of Power," *Atlantic Monthly*, December, 1952.

8. William A. Madden, "The Victorian Sensibility," *Victorian Studies*, September, 1963.

9. Morse Peckham, *Beyond the Tragic Vision: The Quest for Identity in the 19th Century*, New York, 1962.

10. Martin Esslin, *The Theater of the Absurd*, New York, 1961.

11. William Barrett, *Irrational Man: A Study in Existential Philosophy*, New York, 1962.

12. See Robert Penn Warren's essay on Hemingway in Morton D. Zabel, ed., *Literary Opinion in America*, New York, 1951.

13. This kind of eclectic treatment of the Victorian period is to be seen in Jerome Buckley's *The Victorian Temper*, Cambridge, Mass., 1951, and *The Triumph of Time*, Cambridge, Mass., 1966.

14. A. S. Miasnikov, "Modernism," in MS.

15. Inge von Wangenheim, "On *Waiting for Godot*," in MS.

16. Halle (Saale), 1966.

17. Eugene Ionesco, *Notes and Counter Notes: Writings on the Theater*, New York, 1964, p. 16.

18. Georg Lukacs, "Appearance and Essence," in *Preserve and Create*, pp. 17-21.

19. Lukacs, *Aesthetik*, Neuwied am Rhein, 1967.

20. Werner Mittenzwei, "The Brecht-Lukacs Debate," in *Preserve and Create*, pp. 199-299.

21. S. Petrov, "Realism — The Generally Human," in *Preserve and Create*, pp. 23-29.

22. Lukacs, *Realism in Our Time*, New York, 1962, p. 101.

23. Charles Shapiro, ed., *Twelve Original Essays on Great American Novels*, Detroit, 1958, pp. 238-256.

24. "Ernest Hemingway: A Tragedy of Craftsmanship," in John K. M. McCafferey, *Ernest Hemingway: The Man and His Work*, Cleveland, 1950; also "Alive in the Midst of Death: Ernest Hemingway," in Carlos Baker, *Hemingway and His Critics*, New York, 1951.

25. Ray B. West, Jr., "Ernest Hemingway: The Failure of Sensibility," in William V. O'Connor, ed., *Forms of Modern Fiction*, Minneapolis, 1948.

26. Boris Suchkov, "The Bourgeois Intellect in our Time," in MS.

27. T. Motyleva, "William Faulkner," and P. V. Palievsky, "Faulkner's Road to Realism," in MS.

28. Suchkov, *op. cit.*

29. Motyleva and Palievsky, *op. cit.*

30. Norman Mailer, *Armies of the Night*, New York, 1968, p. 102.

4

CULTURE AND THE TASKS OF CRITICISM

David G. Stratman

Literature is a real part of our experience. It says something about how we feel about ourselves and other people and about our relation to them, and it says something about our idea of the physical world around us and our relation to it. Furthermore, it has an effect on the way we see things — it informs our sense of self and of people and the world. An idea of human relationships — say, for example, of the relations possible between men and women — as it appears in a work of literature may either contradict or reinforce the idea we already have; but since literature is an aspect of our experience, it will to some extent shape the sum of our experience. A particular idea in a work of literature of man-woman relations might have considerable effect in reinforcing our own idea, especially if it seems to reflect our previous experience; our assent to this new literary experience comes more readily if it seems to reflect our previous experience in the context of the culture.

It is this aspect of the literary experience, its effect in shaping or reinforcing our ideas, particularly our ideas of our relations with other people, that I consider to be of especial importance, and it is this aspect of literature that an adequate Marxist criticism must deal with. In this paper I want to discuss what literature as an aspect of culture is and does, and what I think is the task of criticism consequent upon the nature of culture in society.

What I am saying about literature can be extended to culture in general. We generally use the word "culture" in two ways: to mean what a "cultured" person has — what he picked up in his "humanities" courses in college — and to refer to the whole of a society's economic, social, political, and cultural institutions, art, beliefs, etc., as in the phrase "feudal culture." The two senses of the word are of course related. The economic, social, political and cultural institutions of feudal society are both the expression and the instruments of class rule of the feudal ruling class, the landed aristocracy; the culture of feudal society expresses the values, the idea of social relations, the ideology of that class. Specific ideas that we refer to as feudal, for example, a late feudal idea of man-woman relations expressed in the concept of courtly love, we would not apply to peasants under feudal rule, any more than we would think that revolting peasants had the Great Chain of Being much in mind.

Let me state my propositions about literature in terms of this idea of culture. Literature expresses, conceptually and in terms of action, characters, etc., ideas about ourselves, other people, the world; and it affects, by change or reinforcement, those ideas we have. But the culture which characterizes a society is the culture of its ruling class. The culture reflects the whole pattern of human relations in society by which that class secures its rule, and whose institutions it controls — for instance, the universities, the schools, the publishing houses, the media. Expressed in class terms, my propositions about literature (culture) amount to this:
1. The culture of a ruling class expresses the ideological conditions (the necessary ideas) for the existence of that class as a ruling class;
2. The culture of a ruling class reinforces its class rule.

By the "ideological conditions" of class rule I mean those ideas of the individual and of human relations, and ideas about the material conditions of human existence, which the ruling class must enforce to stay in power. For instance, in capitalist society the ruling class needs to promote sexism and a distorted idea of man-woman relations both to divide the people it controls and to gain extra profits from the super-exploitation of women workers. Capitalism needs racism; without it the white worker could see the situation of the black worker in terms of the super-exploitation of his class brother, and thus ally with him to their mutual benefit. The institutions which the capitalist class controls attempt to persuade people that racist explanations, that blacks are the cause of their own problems, is correct, or the result of the cultural or genetic inferiority of blacks, as Professors Jensen and Herrnstein maintain. The ruling class must promote the idea that there is "nothing to be done," that its rule is simply a permanent fact of existence. The feudal class based the idea of the permanence of its rule on an idea of the will of God; the modern capitalist class bases its permanence on an idea of human nature — that the structure of society is an expression of the nature of man. From the bourgeois perspective, capitalist nature *is* human nature; thus we get books on "the naked ape" and "the territorial imperative."

Since the culture does reflect the human and productive relations in society by which the ruling class secures its rule, the ideas which serve that class may strike the people in society as simply a reflection of their cultural experience. The social position of women and black people or of the working class as a whole is difficult to change precisely because the inferior position seems to be evidence for the truth of the ideas which justify the position. The second of my propositions, that the culture of a ruling class reinforces its class rule, is another way of stating the fact that culture is, whether we like it or not, a weapon in the class struggle, and that capitalist culture — the culture of the university, of the media, of our literature — is a weapon in the hands of the capitalist class.

I would like to consider these two propositions in detail by discussing Leroi Jones' play *The Slave* in terms of class ideology. I have selected this play for several reasons. Since many people would say that in the relatively flexible and open society of modern America there is a flourishing or at least nascent revolutionary literature, it is only appropriate that I attempt to deal with a play that is put forward as being revolutionary. Two of Jones's (Imamu Baraka's) plays, *Dutchman* and *The Slave,* are perhaps the examples of contemporary black (and "revolutionary") drama most frequently used in college courses, and Jones himself is generally thought of as modern black drama's leading figure. I think it is important that we examine just what it is we are teaching when we teach Jones, or any literature that touches on the relations between black and white people. Furthermore, the play centers on a discussion of culture and its role in society, and expresses in very clear terms ideas about culture which I think it is important that we examine.

*

The Slave is written in the context of the tremendous pressures of racism in American society and culture — pressures which many teachers of literature, represented in the play by Bradford Easley, have attempted to counteract but with perhaps questionable effect. It is intended as an attack on that racism, and Jones struggles to draw into the sharpest light the racist attitudes and social passivity of the professedly enlightened sections of the middle class. But *The Slave* accepts certain important premises of capitalist culture, and inevitably develops into what is, I think, more an attack on black people than a weapon in their liberation, and which, far from being a "revolutionary" play or from expressing the needs or aspirations of most black people, militates against the very idea of revolution or even of substantive social change. The outlook which this

paper examines in the most detail, and which leads to the basic contradiction in the play, is elitism, a false estimation of the role of the working
class in society. An important aspect of the play which I do not examine,
but which is related to elitism, is its nationalism; that is, Jones envisions
the struggle for black liberation in the only terms in which it cannot
win — race war — under the leadership of black petty-bourgeois intellectuals. I would not like my remarks about *The Slave* to obscure the one
most important thing about it: the context from which it comes. Racism
is the most vicious aspect of American society; nationalism is an inevitable response to racism in white society. A further caution: for the
purposes of this paper, my interest in the play does not extend to obvious
questions of it relation to the personal aspects of Jones' internal struggles
at the time of its writing, or to his further development as the more
thoroughgoing cultural nationalist, Imamu Baraka, though I think I say
nothing about him inconsistent with his later development.

The setting of the play is the apartment of Bradford Easley, a white
forty-five-year-old professor of literature, and Grace Locke Vessels
Easley, the white former wife of Walker Vessels, who is a leader of the
black revolution taking place outside the apartment throughout the play.
The scene is punctuated by explosions. Walker Vessels has returned, he
says, to take back with him his two daughters by Grace.

Walker and Easley spend a remarkable amount of time discussing
"the death of Western idealism." Walker Vessels is a Yeats-quoting revolutionary, "the gaudiest example of Renaissance man," Easley says, "I've
heard of."[1] He affects an Irish accent and calls Easley "Faggy," just one
of many "ignorant vomiting faggot professors" — faggot because Easley
as a professor represents the impotence of a decadent white culture.
Walker has apparently, like Jones himself, had quite a bit to say about
that culture, and Easley throws it back up to him:

> I thought you meant yourself to be a fantastic idealist. All those
> speeches and essays and poems . . . the rebirth of idealism. That the
> Western white man had forfeited the most impressive characteristic of
> his culture . . . the idealism of rational liberalism . . . and that only the
> black man in the West could restore that quality to Western culture,
> because he still understood the necessity for it. Et cetera, et cetera. Oh,
> look, I remember your horseshit theories, friend. I remember. And now
> the great black Western idealist is talking about use. (p. 62)

The essence of Walker's attack on Western culture is not that it
expresses the cultural perspective of a class whose existence depends on

its exploitation of white and black peasant or working classes. The problem Walker sees in Western culture is that it has lost "its most impressive characteristic . . . the idealism of rational liberalism." "Idealism" is being used in two senses here: to refer to the attitude of humanitarianism and *noblesse oblige* which supposedly characterized precapitalist culture, and to refer to the philosophical idealism one associates with Plato or Hegel. In both senses idealism is an aspect of ruling class culture. *Noblesse oblige* obtains when the ruling elite feels threatened and fearful of the people's ability to act; philosophical idealism, with its lack of a sense of the material conditions of social life, is the expression of the separation of the culture of an exploiting class, either feudal or capitalist, from the life of the masses of people engaged in constant struggle to produce.

To try to put Walker and Easley's discussion in some perspective, let me recall another conversation about culture in a book about slavery. Augustine St. Clare, in a discussion with Miss Ophelia in *Uncle Tom's Cabin* of, among other things, the relation between slavery and capitalism, explains his brother Alfred's views on culture. Alfred, he says, is a born aristocrat, while he is a democrat. As an aristocrat Alfred believes, he says,

> that there can be no high civilization without enslavement of the masses, either nominal or real. There must, he says, be a lower class, given up to physical toil and confined to an animal nature; and a higher one thereby acquires leisure and wealth for a more expanded intelligence and improvement, and becomes the directing soul of the lower. So he reasons, because, as I said, he is born an aristocrat; — so I don't believe, because I was born a democrat.[2]

Alfred's aristocratic definition of "high civilization," or of culture, has two aspects: in the sense in which he intends it, as what *ought* to be the condition of society, his brother the democrat, whom Stowe presents as a sympathetic character, and who seems to present her viewpoint here, disagrees; but in the sense in which it is merely descriptive of the cultural level of the respective classes in quasi-feudal or capitalist society, it presents the picture which Stowe consistently develops in the book.

Though she has St. Clare raise the question of the condition of workers under capitalism, and has him suggest that "there is a *dies irae* coming on, sooner or later, [that] the same thing is working in Europe, in England, and in this country..." and that "the masses are to rise, and the under class become the upper one" (p. 274), this question is, of course, much beyond the slavery she means to deal with and she does not attempt much description of the "lower class, given up to physical toil" under capitalism. It is significant, however, that just as she color-codes individuals, so she also "class-codes" them; thus, if a character is described as "vulgar" or "common" or "low-class," we can be pretty sure he will be no good. But she does describe blacks in the condition of slavery, and she describes them consistently, with the exception of a super-Christian or aristocratic (and "white") slave elite, in Alfred's aristocratic terms. When Tom gets to Simon Legree's plantation, he sees:

> only sullen, scowling, imbruted men, and feeble, discouraged women, or women that were not women, — the strong pushing away the weak, — the gross, unrestricted animal selfishness of human beings, of whom nothing good was expected and desired; and who, treated in every way like brutes, had sunk as nearly to their level as it was possible for human beings to do. (p. 356)

In Stowe's view oppressed people — the "toiling masses" — are brutes; the most oppressed are the most brutal. Her problem in the book, to the extent that it is intended as an attack on slavery, is to find a force for change. She is writing out of what is often a very intensely-felt sympathy for the suffering of the slaves, and details that suffering in an immensely effective way. But her idea of the people suffering under slavery leads her to eliminate the masses of slaves in the fight against slavery and to rely on Northern and Southern ruling-class figures — the St. Clares, the Shelbys, the Senator Birds. The one slave she has escape to "do something for his people," George Harris, is so white he has to color his skin to pass for a Spanish gentleman; his intention is to help set up a republic in Africa, where people will "rise [i. e., get ahead] by [their] individual worth" (p. 443). To prepare for his task George goes to a university in Paris.

Stowe's separation from the developing Northern working class and the Southern slaves leads her into the trap of accepting the outlook of the Northern industrial capitalist class, and is the basis of a fundamental contradiction in the book. The vantage point that she enjoys, writing at the brink of the rapid transformation of American society by industrial capitalism, gives her a remarkable understanding of the forces newly unleashed in the society. She shows very clearly how productive forces affect the Shelbys and the Haleys, how the choices open to any of her characters are shaped and limited by the social situations in which they find themselves, and how only the destruction of slavery and even of capitalism as *systems* can end the misery of the masses whom these systems exploit. She consistently tries to show the extent to which the *ideas* which any individual has are products of the interaction of material and cultural forces. And yet her "solution" to the problem of slavery which she expresses in the epilogue is that "every individual can see to it that *they feel right*." What can you do? "You can *pray*" (p. 454; Stowe's emphasis). Her acceptance of the racism, elitism (most people are stupid and need to be controlled by a few exceptional figures), and individualism of the developing capitalist class has led her to reject as a force for change the only people who could have brought about the change she so desired — the oppressed people themselves.

It might be useful to describe here what an alternative set of values would consist of. Alfred St. Clare jokingly refers to his brother in one such conversation about slavery and capital as a "red republican," which was both the term used for communist workers at the time, and the name of the newspaper in which the *Communist Manifesto* first appeared, in 1851 — the year in which Stowe was writing and beginning to publish her book. Just three years before, Marx and Engels had presented the *Manifesto* to the founding congress of the Communist League. Against the whole gamut of capitalist ideas the international workers were posing their own class perspective: against racism, the class solidarity of the exploited; against elitism, reliance on workers as the leading force for change; against the pacifism Stowe recommends for blacks through the figure of Uncle Tom, struggle against the exploiting class; against the individualism which is the basis of Stowe's outlook, collectivism; and against the nationalist solution she suggests through George Harris, inter-nationalism — the international unity of the working class.

It is precisely those ideas which are a function of St. Clare's or of Harriet Stowe's class outlook, especially the idea of culture, which Jones' play in an obverse way reflects. Jones does not introduce a direct or unqualified statement of an idea of culture as Mrs. Stowe seems to; whatever the characters express tends to be modified and frequently undercut by the other characters. The problem in approaching the play critically is to distinguish between those ideas which constitute the largely ironic dramatic material of the play and which should be seen in terms of the development of the characters or the argument, and those ideas which constitute a kind of constant of perspective — which are, in fact, the ideological premises without which its particular dramatic development would not be possible. Walker Vessels *is* "the slave," and is to be seen ironically as still in bondage to what Jones identifies as simply the Western or "white" cultural tradition, even while he acts as a black revolutionary. But the central premise of the play is an important premise of capitalist culture — that there is a split between the mind and the body, between thought and action in the individual, and that this dichotomy finds its wider expression in society, split into an imbruted lower class without intelligence, and an elite of intellectuals who, while they are blessed with "high civilization" and a clear social intelligence, by the fact of their function as intellectuals are incapable of social action. That the play is based on this premise is of crucial importance for its development; the play necessarily takes a counterrevolutionary turn since the one social element which it presents as having the power to make a revolution — the masses of black people — are presented only in the terms in which Walker and Easley, bound by a rotting culture, can see them: that is, as being without the intelligence or the humanity to make a revolution worth having. The alternatives Jones presents are finally ugly and essentially meaningless change or no change at all.

Walker's role as a revolutionary is defined in the play by his idea of culture; and his idea of culture cuts him off from the masses of working class blacks who are making the revolution:

> in spite, despite, the resistance in the large cities and the small towns, where we have taken, yes, dragged piles of darkies out of their beds and shot them for being in Rheingold ads, despite the fact that all of my officers are ignorant motherfuckers who have never read any book in their lives, despite the fact that I would rather argue politics or literature, or boxing, or anything, with you, dear Easley, with you...

His men, he says, are even "lousy marksmen, and none of 'em worth shit" (p. 78). Walker's idea of his men is a measure of his bondage to bourgeois ideas.

Apparently what is so horrible about Walker and his ideas for Grace and Easley is not so much their content, but that he has acted on them. His actions have gone beyond the specific intellectual idealism of Easley who "thinks of life as a purely anarchic relationship between man and God . . . or man and his work . . . " (p. 75). In bringing his ideas to social reality he has changed, shaped, even destroyed people's lives — that is the horror. The old slave figure who introduces the play, and who becomes Walker as the play begins, defines in his first lines what Grace and Easley, and apparently Jones, see as the real ugliness of Walker's actions. "We invent death for others. . . . Stone possible lovers with heavy worlds we think are ideas . . . " (p. 43). And even if the ideas are "right, . . . [it] doesn't mean anything. The very rightness stinks a lotta times. The very rightness." (p. 44).

Walker is able to act not because he has resolved the bourgeois dichotomy between thought and action. He accepts the premise that to bring ideas to reality corrupts the ideas and destroys the reality. While he sees that Easley has "backed off from reality too many times," his only response to Easley's idealism is that "right is in the act! And the act itself has some place in the world . . . it makes some place for itself" (p. 75). For Easley to act against black oppression would have been "an intellectual compromise"; for Walker to act he has to involve himself with the black masses who are happily free from any of the sensitivity and intelligence that incapacitates Easley. They fight because they aren't "in their right minds. . . . The country twisted 'em. The country had twisted them for so long" (pp. 76-77).

Walker as "the slave" is split between what Jones calls the "white" culture he has ingested and his natural ties to black people, or as the play has it, between thought and action. The play never moves outside these alternatives, never holds out the possibility of fighting for a meaningful social justice for Walker the slave to reject. Walker's view of the masses of people who are excluded from the "high civilization" of ruling class culture is that they constitute, as Stowe implies, a "lower class, given up to physical toil and confined to an animal nature." When the black working class acts on the basis of its working-class values of solidarity and militant struggle against the ruling class, it is expressing its "animal nature." Walker's elitist viewpoint leaves him without any force in society for a vital, liberating revolution, so that he must finally concur with Easley's judgment: ". . . if the Western white man has proved one thing . . . it's the futility of modern society." The whole question, Walker says, "comes down to baser human endeavor than any social-political thinking. What does it matter if there's more love or beauty? Who the fuck cares? . . . The point is that you had your chance, darling, now these other folks have theirs." Easley says, "God, what an ugly idea," and Walker, head in hands, responds, "I know" (pp. 73-74). The final absurdity of Walker's bourgeois vision is that he apparently does not see the systemic nature of racist oppression: that capitalism needs the super-exploitation of black and Latin workers and the whole ideology of racism that enforces that exploitation, and that it will enforce that super-exploitation as long as it exists as a system. The ghettos, the misery of people in dirty, dangerous jobs or no jobs at all, the vicious prison systems are apparently the product of a few bad individuals at the top of the system. Walker says to Easley:

The cruelty of it, don't you understand now? The complete ugly horse-shit cruelty of it is that there doesn't have to be a change. It'll be up to individuals on that side, just as it was supposed to be up to individuals on this side. Ha! . . . Who failed! (p. 74)

The Slave is intended as an attack on bourgeois culture, and it shows what it leads to; but Jones does not see that culture in class terms, as generated by and serving an elite capitalist class, but simply as "white" or "Western" culture. In other words, Jones accepts the most important premise of ruling class culture: that its ideas are classless universals, beyond social relations and not generated by capitalist class needs and class position. The play is thus bound by its own irony. The source of the stifling sense of futility in the play, the source of the play's limitations, is *Jones's acceptance,* not merely Walker's, *of bourgeois ideology, even as he thinks he is rejecting it.* Bourgeois ideology creates a framework outside of which the play does not move. Jones does not present in his play the only class force which can break through this irony, because he does not understand its role in society. The sense the play finally leaves one with is like the line in the prologue: "Time is a dead thing really." Nothing changes or can be changed.

I am not suggesting that the essence of a Marxist critique of *The Slave* should be that it is not revolutionary. It is not. The question, however, is why is it not: what are the ideas of the individual, of human relationships under capitalism, of the majority of people — working people — who live in society, of culture and of the social process itself which Jones has brought to the play and which *The Slave* as a very effective piece of drama expresses? What cultural premises inform its development and make it what it is? And if we judge that it is effective in its expression of these ideas and in their realization in the interplay of characters and dramatic action, what is its effect? What view of people and of the world does it reinforce? Or to put the question in sharper political terms, what role do the assumptions that workers, especially black workers, are sub-rational, or that there is a fundamental dichotomy between thought and action, or that social change is neither possible nor necessary, play in the class struggle? Why is literature that expresses these ideas given such prominence in the university and the media?

The writer describes and the critic examines the world as he knows it. The world he knows has been thoroughly transformed by capitalist relations of production and by capitalist ideology; none of it is untouched. The world as it seems, all its rich possibilities trammeled in the contradictions of the system, impresses itself on one's mind as a world of intrinsic and ugly limitations. Furthermore, one knows this world from a point of view which resolves itself into a class perspective, a position in society relative to the material conditions of production and class struggle. Marx and Engels point out in the *Communist Manifesto* that what the bourgeoisie produce above all are their own gravediggers; that is, the operation in society of the forces of capital produces the counterforce of labor in a conflict which will be inevitably resolved in the transformation of capitalism into socialism. The contradictions inherent in capitalism produce an interplay also of class ideologies; the freedom which consists for the bourgeois in individualism and the freedom to exploit can exist for the working class only in collectivism and the struggle to oppose exploitation.

The world as it is can only be understood in terms of its contradictions and possibilities, the interplay of the class forces which shape it. The separation of intellectuals from the material conditions of production and class struggle is the material basis of a whole gamut of intellectualist illusions about society, and is of tremendous significance in our understanding of the social aspects of culture as well as the prospects for social change. We inevitably tend to abstract phenomena from their social matrix; these phenomena, abstracted from their real conditions in society, take on the character of universals. The violent, competitive, exploitative nature of human relationships in capitalist society mean "man" is aggressive, "man" is violent, "man" is greedy. The separation of bourgeois intellectuals from working class thought and action means thought and action are inherently divorced. Dialectical materialism holds that "if you want knowledge, you must take part in the practice of changing reality."[3] To have a clear grasp of the material conditions of human existence, one must engage in the struggle to shape those conditions to meet human needs; without that direct relation to the material basis of social life, one tends to lapse into the idealism of the teacher of literature or the mechanical materialism of the behavioral psychologist. To understand the dynamic that informs the relations of people in society, one must engage in the class struggle. Only the working class has the direct experience requisite for a clear, non-illusory social understanding. It is the only class in society with the power and the potential to smash capitalism and to end class exploitation. The alienation and sense of futility that characterize so much modern literature — and which are almost palpable in so many departments of literature — are expressions of the separation of the culture and teachers of culture from working-class experience. The sense that there is "Nothing to be done" is thoroughly debilitating; but it is perhaps the strongest feeling one gets from the literature of the last hundred years in America, and one hundred-seventy years in England.

A premise of the culture of our humanities courses is that the inges-tion of that culture somehow makes us better people, that it does in some indirect way "serve the people" by educating an element of the popula-tion to one extent or another in the exercise of "the free play of the imagi-nation," and by preserving and transmitting a tradition of imaginative achievement which is humanizing in its effects. I think though that this culture — the cultures in fact of a succession of exploiting classes — is not humanizing but destructive of the lives of most people in this society, and that what we see as the free play of imagination is an illusion. To the extent that the material and cultural bases of our own ideas or of a work of literature remain unexamined, our imagination or intelligence is not free but determined, and the effect of our work in the field of culture will be the opposite of what we intend it to be. To the extent that we have accepted not so much the specific ideas as the perspective of the econo-mics, sociology, philosophy, history, literature of the university, we unconsciously support a class the effects of whose rule over society most of us despise. We have to undertake an examination of the bases — in the material forces of society, in our relation to those forces, and in the vast accumulation of ideas that we bring to our literary experience — of the concepts of literature that we entertain in a conscious and articulate way and less self-consciously, in practice, and the real effect of that litera-ture on our lives and on the lives of the people of the world. Literature as an aspect of culture is neither a series of free imaginative acts nor a set of social documents, but a powerful force. We must understand the forces that are shaping our ideas and our lives, and we must understand the content of those ideas; without such understanding we cannot deal with these forces, and our role in the university will continue to be purveyors of a culture whose roots and effects we do not comprehend, and whose continuance means the continuance of the unfreedom of the vast majority of the world's people.

Bourgeois culture is an exceedingly complex and pervasive force. Our task is to bring that culture under examination in a clear, sharp, persuasive way. As critics and teachers we can make a considerable contribution to the anti-imperialist, anti-racist, pro-working class move-ment. A thoroughgoing critique of imperialist culture and of its role in the university, and of the university's role in society, is a tremendous undertaking that will necessarily depend on the participation of very many of us. As teachers we can work with our students in examining afresh not only the literature but our response to it and the cultural conditioning that has shaped that response. Above all this will require the de-mystifying of our attitude toward what we have tended to see as a separate world of literary values. These efforts will be the basis of a new vigor and significance in our work, as we establish the basis for a pro-working class culture.

NOTES

1. Leroi Jones, *Dutchman and The Slave: Two Plays by Leroi Jones* (New York, 1964), p. 50. The subsequent references are to this text.

2. Harriet Beecher Stowe, *Uncle Tom's Cabin* (Washington Square Press: New York, 1962), p. 235. Subsequent references are to this text.

3. Mao Tse-tung, "On Practice," *Four Essays in Philosophy*, (Peking, 1968), p. 8.

5

LITERATURE AND IDEOLOGY

Lee Baxandall

Q: Who likes racist, sexist, chauvinist, elitist,
    even fascist art?
A: Nearly everybody.

I began an earlier version of this essay with the above epigraph as the
actual title.* Some persons challenged the assertion, saying that the
"everybody" who likes Eliot, for example, is in reality a narrow white-
skinned cultural elite in the capitalist countries, while most of the popula-
tion in these lands, not to mention the Third World peoples, do *not* like
Eliot at all, and have their own rich and far more realistic cultural traditions which critics could far more usefully take as their object of interest.
Is this so? I think that the evidence of this essay will prove that the
question is much more complicated than a mere sociological relativism
can resolve. Moreover, the issue of ideology in relation to literature (and
the other arts) is many-sided; and the challenge to revolutionary smugness (or as Lenin phrased it, "Communist conceit") which my epigraph
provocatively impugns, is just a beginning if a decisive aspect to be
worked through, among the numerous aspects of the position and function of ideas in a context of artistic values. Not all aspects can be explored
in the space available here; but perhaps some of the obstacles to understanding can be cleared away.

Many works of art must puzzle us when we seek to describe and

---

* Written in 1965-66 for *Studies on the Left*. When *Studies* ceased publication the
essay was instead placed in the second issue of *100 Flowers*. It has been extensively
revised for the present appearance, and I wish to acknowledge the refinement of concepts
owed particularly to the work in this area by Stefan Morawski.

explain them. Their effect on our receptivity (aesthetic and otherwise) will be largely positive yet certain of their elements will be disturbing. For instance, the verse of Rudyard Kipling is exciting, boisterous and colorful, and imperialist in its implications when you place the plaintive sentiments in historical framework. Is it okay to be stirred then by Kipling's art? If one replies "no," is a genuine value of the Kipling verse being cast into oblivion (perhaps temporarily and with cause)? If one replies "yes, but," what is the articulation we shall bring to this ambiguity of the work of art and the equivocation of our repsonse? Shall we admit the ideological aspect without criticism, because the artistic value is significant? If we criticize the ideological element implied by Kipling's historical and class assumptions, how shall we do it without doing violence either to the wholeness of his verse or the integrity of historical progress and our role in that progress? These are some of the questions that are raised by the uneasy cohabitation of ideological with artistic values.

Kipling, of course, is but a convenient instance. Other examples abound — leading to the temptation, more often than is pleasant to contemplate, for revolutionary parties or regimes to arbitrarily circumscribe or nullify the role of artistic tradition in the current social and cultural development. A tradition which is ambiguous may well seem a dubious partner in the immediate tasks, which exact from the revolutionists an all-out and disciplined commitment. Why should the dead artist whose class allegiances and social values may demonstrably be tied to the dying way of life be allowed to sow confusion where there is already too much adversity to progress? So runs the argument for negating the influence of the artistic heritage; an attitude, I must add, which finds absolutely no support in the foremost classics of Marxist thought, Marx, Engels, and Lenin.

Still, the grounds for being troubled by the "decadent" or "reactionary" influences of literature and the other arts are significant. *Triumph of the Will*, that monumental tribute to Hitler and to Germany's past and future glory, filmed by Leni Riefenstahl with major footage taken at Nazi rallies, is found somehow moving by many persons who generally hate the principles of fascism — even Jews. Should such an insidious work of art be shown to an apparently vulnerable public at large? D. W. Griffith's *Birth of a Nation* is the great early movie epic, a milestone in the development of the medium. But the warmest human values in it are shared among its Ku Klux Klan protagonists — should *Birth of a Nation* be shown beyond a narrow audience of experts? The James Bond films of a few years ago, and more recently the Black superstud films in the tradition of *Shaft* and other organized-crime movies like *The Godfather* made in the U. S., are finding huge audiences with their ethnocentric power-tripping and denial of larger values combined with a sensationalism of sex, drugs and dominance. Do such films have nothing valid expressed in them, even if symptomatically; nothing which a progressive movement could put in context both with criticism and with its own superior ideology of artistic creation?

These are some few examples of racist, chauvinist, elitist, and fascist art which, to greater or lesser extent, make a claim on the attention of audiences in other historical situations. Moreover, if the issue of sexism is raised, nearly the whole of artistic tradition is found culpable to some extent when judged by present standards of consciousness, since most art reflects symptomatically the status of and attitudes toward women in male-dominated societies. Even the art created by women may glorify male sexist values; for instance, the Riefenstahl film *Triumph of the Will*.

In brief, much of the thought in representational art falls short of the standard of democratic ideology that has been reached in our time. The substantial progress of human equality of opportunity, both in idea and in fact, is scarcely to be doubted. The Socialist movement has since the nineteenth century carried the vanguard responsibility, causing the survivor capitalist countries to pay lip service to the rising democratic tide and, where compelled, to grant concessions. Since this is the evolved relation of past ideas in art to present expectations, it is not surprising that the explicit attitudes and situations represented in literature, poetry, drama, etc., have come under sometimes-intense rebuke from revolutionary parties in the throes of valuational and institutional upheaval. A key instance is the attack of the Chinese party leadership on the "old," i. e. pre-1949, conventions of Peking Opera, which often introduced supernatural protagonists and glorified the ruling classes while denigrating the poor and laboring classes. "New" Peking Opera (e. g., *The Women's Battalion*) offers exemplary tales of the oppressed defeating the privileged sectors of previous Chinese society. This reformed genre, drawing eclectically on Chinese and Western sources for its music, dance movements and story elements, has been assigned exclusive rights to the stage. At least one recent article in an authoritative Chinese party journal has rejected the music of Beethoven as "capitalistic", and similar attacks have been made on Shakespeare and other classics in the Western artistic heritage.

If works of art are perceived wholly and exclusively in terms of plausible evidences of the class-ideological ties exhibited by their authors — either immanently (within the works) or extrinsically (using secondary, biographical evidence) — then this intolerant attitude towards the artistic heritage might be strongly justified. The past works of art could be condemned for being no more than vehicles of racist, sexist, chauvinist, elitist or fascist values. They would possess no ambiguous dimension; that is to say, no compensatory or redeeming values. However, this description of works of art, whether of the past or present, seems at sharp variance with the characteristics of artistic creation. There is no way to compel party or government participants and functionaries to perceive and acknowledge the specific traits of aesthetic objects if they recognize only countervailing priorities. One may argue and struggle for this recognition of integral aesthetic priorities, however, and one should if they are in question. For if the integrity of artistic creation and experience is not noted in a social situation then the entire contribution of this crucial sector of human resource and further human achievement will be diminished and perhaps squandered in relatively fruitless propaganda efforts "embellished" by the shards and piecings of a former artistic integrity.

My argument, then, is not that the artistic tradition is free of ideological blemishes. It is rather that the remaining traces of outdated class-ideology are perhaps the least consequential and influential aspect, at any rate of what we call the "classical" art of the past. Where "reactionary" ideology does occur prominently — say, in Shakespeare's *Merchant of Venice* which the Marxist Morris Schappes has sought to keep from the stage, due to its blend of anti-Semitism with anti-capitalist attitudes — my response is if possible to avoid intolerance toward a significant and symptomatic dramatic work (except in a specific situation where *The Merchant of Venice* might directly inflame a pogrom atmosphere). In an historicist theatre such as rightly might be expected of socialists actively developing the uses of the stage, the repugnant ideological aspects of *The Merchant of Venice* might be "distanced" by devices ranging from program notes of excellent historical and ideological quality, to a vivid Prologue speech achieving the same result, or even to the extent of refashioning the Shakespeare text within an encompassing and "explanatory" framework as a play-within-a-play (but only if the adaptation is achieved by a skilled author, e.g., Brecht's adaptations of Goethe's *Faust*, Lenz's *The Tutor*, Farquhar's *The Recruiting Officer*, Sophocles' *Antigone* and Shakespeare's *Coriolanus*).

Dysfunctional ideology may thus be distanced or expunged or even substituted, if great care and skill are applied; but as I mentioned, it seems to me these ideological aspects are perhaps the least significant dimension of the classical heritage, and I wish now to stress the more important dimensions. These are two:

A. THE MIMETIC OR REALISTIC COGNITIVE CONTRIBUTION.

Not all works of art are mimetic of reality (or what at a more profound level of synthesizing typification we designate as realistic works). Architecture while functional is not mimetic in a basic and meaningful sense; most music is not; some painting is not; dance need not be mimetic. Where mimesis or realism occurs, however, it nearly always provides a far richer representation of the materials and composition of real personages, situations, and processes, than a purely "ideological" interpretation could describe and explain. This consideration was invoked by Marx and Engels in their famed discussion of the writings of Honore de Balzac. His ideological Royalism seemed a superficial trait to them, a mere overlay which was in fact contradicted by the realistic depictions of social processes in his novels and the ideas which could appropriately be derived from these depictions. In other words, the classics of the artistic heritage tend to provide richly human representations of the qualities and values of social life in various periods and even of human beings in general: the characters in Shakespeare's dramas, for instance, seemed to Marx to foretell the greatness of human passion and talents which might be widely realized under the more favorable, future conditions of communism. In this view (which was Marx's if not that of more "sociological," reductively-deterministic Marxists), the class-delimited dimension of the work of a major artist was certainly worth remarking and situating, but generally it did not decisively shape the evaluation of that work. The artist's *cognitive* perceptions (which might be at odds with his seeming class interests) frequently dominated whatever explicit socio-political ideas he might accept.

B. THE CONTRIBUTION OF FUNDAMENTAL, CONSTITUENT AESTHETIC VALUE

is the other chief dimension which in major art compensates or entirely overweighs the tendency of ideological aspects to prove out-of-date or reactionary in effect. Not all art is representational in the sense discussed above, which crystallizes the intensive if selective microcosm of an aspiring human world. But *all* art is, by definition, composed of certain fundamental or constituent values which distinguish it from non-art and which, of themselves (and distinguished from other possible dimensions of art), enrich the human potential. These values may be characterized broadly as formal and expressive. We shall see, in the next section of this essay, how the constituent aesthetic values interrelate with cognitive and ideological values.

The constituent aesthetic values are all the values there may be in the work of art (again, architecture — its material function apart — or music are prime examples). Or, cognitive and/or ideological values may be present. Consider the *Triumph of the Will*. It is a powerfully cognitive film. Its cognition is primarily of a national society whose class institutions are in the grip of an ascendant, mystified idea of "socialism" the condition of which is enthusiastic deliverance to a commonwealth ideal rather than the concrete transformation of socio-economic structures. With this cognition is comported an ideological point of view within the film, fully committed to the realization of this mystified ideal and mystified in accordance with it. Thus, one finds the cognitions rendered through the camera simplified deliberately to a few, yet overwhelmingly welcome, attitudes and emotions: solidarity with the nation, dedication to a leader and a goal, respect, even awe, for the group and the leader, self-respect, the sense that the national and the personal will can achieve its ends. The artistic choices solidify these ends. Long shots of the masses in dynamic, disciplined movement. Reverent close-ups of the leader. Close-ups of followers, cognizant of their determination yet awe for the leader. Personal idiosyncrasies are suppressed. Seldom-varying public attitudes, public emotions are presented. Overlaid on the human and the constituent artistic values are the speeches of the leaders, represented in accordance with the film director's ideology so as to prove convincing. Yet this ideological element (both cognized and implied) is secondary to the tremendous sight of a society in process of self-mobilization, and it is easily possible for persons destined to be harmed by the express ideology of the film to miss the future implications, so stirring is the immediate spectacle. And this precisely because the ideological aspect is not so realized as either the cognitive or the fundamental aesthetic dimensions. Immediately, the film appeals to and fictionally gratifies the wish ever more endemic to advanced capitalist society, to become profoundly integrated into a non-alienated group with a clear historical tradition and destiny. Who does not wish to see his will triumph?

The cognition of an apparently dynamic social group in the process of ridding itself of the characteristics of alienation is shrewdly controlled. The present diversities and miseries of the masses are not shown; only the expectation of deliverance in their eager faces and disciplined actions. We may take the cognitively restrictive yet monumental organization for what it is worth; and that much is not negligible. The film has the compressed, disciplined aesthetic strength of a military march on a grand scale; it is of Mahleresque dimension, yet never drops out of cadence. As such *Triumph of the Will* may instruct us profoundly in the characteristics of an ersatz Socialism and the constricted emotions and thought that accompany and enable it. Indeed, to go along with a tide of humanity may be satisfying, regardless of the historical corner it turns, or doesn't turn. The appeal in this experience may compatibly exist with any ideology, Communist, Fascist, whatever, so long as one does not *historicize* the ideology, and the cognitions, by introducing a larger knowledge of the present circumstances and the philosophical and ideological expectations that diverse socio-political groupings premise on it.

When one does, however, introduce this kind of knowledge (a consciousness-raising of the reception of the work of art), the ideological influence of the combined cognitive-ideological components will be exploded, although their symptomatic interest will survive. At this point even the tiniest discrepancy in an otherwise monumental artistic strategy may confirm the suspicions of a dawning skepticism. This moment notably occurs in *Triumph of the Will* near the end, as Hitler speaks to a rally in Berlin. The crowd responds rapturously to a debator's flourish, and Hitler steps back from the rostrum; glancing downward at his text his head and face describe a small yet unmistakeable gesture of delight over his rhetorical skill. This betrayal of a smug technician's elitism is the first and only intrusion of private and selfish motives in the film. No more is needed to confirm, in the film's own strategic terms, the refusal of the film director to portray the full range of human reality. This tiny contradiction "criticizes" every other element of ideological and cognitive value; it is the crack in the monumental conception. The effect is comparable to Charles Ives' use of marching-band motifs in his compositions. A dissonance is intruded on otherwise simple but humanly appealing effects gained by the mobilization of the human desire to get ahead in stride with an enthusiastically purposeful group. Those who are dulled by training to the complexity of modern society will probably overlook the dissonance. For other persons, the intrusive value will distance the basically simple effect; reasoning and broader knowledge will be released to pursue the dissonant perspective.

This historicism of audience response, I feel, is as important for social revolutionaries to cultivate in emergent socialist parties and societies as is a socialist-oriented dialogue with the artists sympathetic to the historical trend. The latter will help to bring about a more historically-informed cognition and ideology in the emergent art. The former will result in a far more "useful" artistic heritage and a better developed public consciousness nourishing the basis of all further development, with the aesthetic, cognitive, and ideological values of art reaching far beyond art.

It is important to note that other revolutionary situations will produce different films than that most characteristic of the Nazi era. If *Triumph of the Will* was the fitting cognition of Germany in the later 1930s, *Memories of Underdevelopment* and *Lucia* have been the characteristic films of the Cuban revolution. The first consists of the thoroughly skeptical yet Marxist biographical reflections of an alienated intellectual involved with administering the social transformation; nothing more different from the Riefenstahl mythical construct can be imagined. *Lucia* is a deeply historical study of Cuban women as shaped by three distinct epochs of the island's development, including the Castro era (which is played as comedy). The eras are contrasted and compared, yet shown as a continuous development. It is symptomatic that no major film of the key political events, parallel to *Triumph of the Will*, has been attempted by the Cubans. If it were, it would have to be devoid of the monumental simplicity — the discipline, the abnegation of individuality, the uncritical awe of leadership — accentuated by Riefenstahl. The hypocritical secret gloating of Hitler would not occur, for in the leadership of Castro there has not been this elitist compartmentalization. Leader and followers have comprised a highly contradictory social complex which admitted, and on the whole valued, complexity. A political "spectacle" of the Cuban revolution would necessarily be a complexly articulated achievement.

Where the public is not enough consciousness-raised in its reception of art, or where the artist is not able (perhaps due to his medium) to bring sufficient historical concreteness to his creation, the communication of the intentional work of art to the public may be distorted. A case is the appropriation of militant Communist songs by the Nazis for their own, differing ends, once Hitler had come to power. This step roused consternation among Marxist aesthetic thinkers who had unreasonably assumed that a kind of immaculate distinctiveness protected, say, the melodies of Hanns Eisler from barbarian applications. Yet the German cadres in brown shirts now put new words to the familiar tunes. The International League of Proletarian Composers responded with a demand on its members: write melodies which henceforward would be inalterably "Communist" so the embarrassment could never again occur. In fact it should be obvious that a simple adrenaline-stirring tune, easy to march to with faith in one's cause, does not pertain to any single philosophy or party; it is too bereft of complexity (which in turn has to be historically patterned and referential) and that is the general fate of the song medium, that time and again under varying circumstances, its aesthetically most popular examples are appropriated for diverse historical statements.

Even historically rich works may suffer this ideological expropriation; but in their case, the result is a sure loss of substance. One case is precisely the Riefenstahl film as cannibalized by the Allies for propaganda purposes during World War II. Luis Buñuel, the film director, told the story to Carlos Fuentes: "I was asked to edit Leni Riefenstahl's documentary on the Nazi rallies at Nuremburg. The purpose was to use the film as anti-Nazi propaganda. I showed the final result to Rene Clair and Charlie Chaplin. Chaplin rolled with laughter, pointed at Hitler and said the Fuhrer was a bad imitation of Charlot." So much for reduction through the alteration of purpose. However, Buñuel continued: "Clair had misgivings: Riefenstahl's images were so damned good and impressive, no matter how you edited them, that the effect would be the contrary of what we were aiming at, a real boomerang. Audiences would be overpowered and come out feeling that German might was irresistible. The matter was taken to the White House. President Roosevelt saw the film and agreed with Clair. So it was quietly sent to the archives." Notable here is the frustration by the knowing Buñuel of the historical myth intended by Riefenstahl and the Nazis, which, however, retained an intimation of its full substance even in the truncated images of the whole.

An even more telling instance of the effect of ideological interference with a work of historical substance is the story of how Sergei Eisenstein's 1927 film *Potemkin* was tampered with by civil authorities in Western Europe. The first showings had enormous impact on audiences, and much fear was expressed as to the example the film might set for the restless classes. One solution hit upon was to remove the sequence concerned with rotten dinner meat, which prepared and justified the sailor's uprising. Next, the sequence of the quelling and execution of certain rebellious sailors was removed from its position early in the film immediately following the meat episode, upon which had followed a broader and for a time successful seizure of power. The sequence was reinstated at film's end where it fitted, to all intents and purposes, as the fated punishment for all the disobedience of the film. The ideological meaning was thus sharply curbed for the rebellion ended in punishment rather than in the exciting escape and the innuendo of ultimate revolutionary victory. Yet with the historical substance of the film diminished and the story line aborted, the energy and optimism of the film (again, the "images") still impressed audiences. Even in its "counterrevolutionary" editing *Potemkin* presented cognitions of humanly appealing values which redounded to the credit of the director and the patron Soviet state.

The case with poetry, as exemplified in Rudyard Kipling, is rather different. Poetry may be narrative and creative of fictions; it may just as well, as in his "Processional," be declarative and homiletic. Where he is a storyteller Kipling evokes the vigor and communality of the English barracks and barroom or of the colonial setting. In either case his ideology is coordinated to British imperialism. But this has not kept his stories and verse from a huge audience whether in India, the English isles, or Soviet Russia! The reason is not far to seek. Kipling aids the oppressed and suffering in achievement of a sense of pity for their lot; at the same time, he assures the oppressed and oppressors alike that their lot in life is necessary and ordained. In this way the dread of change is relieved. The formula is keenly alive to experience and it is comforting, just so long as the values and durability of Empire are acceded to. The problem is again one of consciousness-raising. Here, the constituent aesthetic values are lively within the immanent context of the commonplace experiences they evoke, and the ideology is so blatant, once its perimeters are grasped at an historical distance, that it should be easy to take Kipling rather easily and instructively as an instance of consciousness conditioned and delimited by its period. Just so did Brecht appropriate Kipling's verses for his play *A Man's a Man*, adding the historical conditionality.

I began with taking T. S. Eliot as the example of the difficult case for social revolutionaries (at least while he was alive), and I want to return to fortify his challenge now. It is perhaps best stated by Emile de Antonio, eminent maker of documentary films (*Point of Order*, *Year of the Pig*, *Painters Painting*) in a 1973 interview with *Arts in Society* magazine:

> My biggest quandary when I was an undergraduate at Harvard — and this to me is the key to the whole thing — was related to the reason why I left the Young Communist League. I joined the Young Communist

League when I was sixteen years old and I was about nineteen when I left. And I left over the question of T. S. Eliot, which is a very perverse reason to leave a political party. But I was first reading Eliot at that time and it became instantaneously apparent to me that he was the finest poet I was reading in the English language — of that period. And the older people I knew said, well, he's nothing but a goddam Fascist. And curiously enough he would indeed conform to my idea of a Fascist. He was an anti-Semite, he supported a reactionary religious cause, he called himself a Monarchist, he spoke in favor of Franco — which to me was really the test. On every account he was a Fascist. And yet, something else was left — his poetry. There was no person on the Left whom I admired who was writing poetry like Eliot. And the whole problem was stated for me right then and there and I, to this day, you know, thirty-six years later, I still don't know the answer.

That's concisely put. The radical filmmaker who as a youth broke with the YCL over finding a key to Eliot's poetry that respected its integrity, was surely at the same time a part of the privileged white elite which, according to its detractors, is conditioned to appreciate Eliot. Yet it is clear from de Antonio's account that sociological relativism will not finally explain his stubborn stand. He had an appreciation of what he took to be authentic values in Eliot's poetry, which ideological arguments could not disperse. What are these possible values and how might they comport with the reactionary ideology acknowledged also by de Antonio?

Eliot's poetry has neither the monumental aesthetic simplicity of a march tune nor the vivid fraternalism of a Kipling. An apt comparison would be the sinuously dolorous and long line intoned on a single flute as an innovative expression of modern urban alienation, but with recollections of a primordial loneliness. Eliot's early verse, which won enduring status as art, is at first encounter not simple in character: it is erudite and oblique in allusion and cadence, the product of a complex mind and sensibility. With further acquaintance, however, this poetry becomes the perfect equivalent in aesthetic values of a minutely experienced modern sense of abandonment and isolation. Of the total range of our century's emotions and cognitions, the sense of alienation alone was realized by Eliot if in a linguistically complex artistic medium. Few great poets express a great range of emotion; many achieve their complexity in a limited mode as Eliot has done. It was his inglorious but seemingly necessary task to create a contemporary Lament of Jeremiah — shored up by a conservative ideology of most distasteful character, which however does not detract from the cognitive-expressive aesthetic achievements of the best of his poetry.

Eliot did socially generalize his sense of alienation onto examples drawn from lower and lower-middle-class life. We may usefully ask to what extent Eliot's verse, devoid of a larger sense of historical reason and primarily emerging from and directed to an elite stratum, is none the less a representation of experiences felt in classes other than his own. In other words: to what extent are his expressed values democratic in this sense? In the Prufrock poem Eliot invites "you and I" to visit the "muttering retreats of restless nights in one-night cheap hotels and sawdust restaurants with oyster-shells." In "The Waste Land" we hear snatches of folk song (in German); visit a working-class pub, where we hear of a woman named Lil who doesn't want to have a child; and we meet a typist home for tea and a tinned meal, who indifferently makes it with a real estate clerk. Alienation in fact is experienced by all classes under capitalism. Eliot's *malaise* to this extent has its correspondences. Intensely felt, it does awaken wide, and one may say plebeian, recognition. But (and this is equally important) wherever Eliot may look in, he does not grasp any sensibility but his own. He imagines with the eyes and ears of the man served tea and marmalade by a footman in a room where "the women come and go talking of Michelangelo." Thus where Whitman sought to contain multitudes, Eliot attributes his own, limited experience to the *demos*:

> A crowd flowed over London Bridge, so many,
> I had not thought death had undone so many,
> Sighs, short and infrequent, were exhaled,
> And each man fixed his eyes before his feet.

The complexly varied experiences and emotions of the mass of people are only thus encompassed.

For the same reason of class, this single theme of urban alienation is placed unflatteringly in a context of a more cultured past. Eliot comments on the sordid typist episode:

> (And I Tiresias have forsuffered all
> Enacted on the same divan or bed;
> I who have sat by Thebes below the wall
> And walked among the lowest of the dead.)

Eliot often depicts the lower orders through his prism of a "Shakespearean rag," which is of no complimentary import to the Sweeneys and Mrs. Porter of his microcosm. None the less, despite the limited empathy and cognition that Eliot brings to his chosen task, many who have experienced the requirements of industrial capitalism will respond to his subtlety in expressing this sense of alienation that is characteristic of our time and not only of Eliot's class and the personal modulation of his poetry.

This poetry of alienation is productive for ideological ends unsuspected by Eliot. He does not encompass modern reason and democratic initiative, but while a context of metaphysics and elitism creates correspondences in the early poems, his own ideology fails artistically to be realized. That explains our ability to enjoy this poetry from a qualifiedly democratic standpoint and despite the poet's ideology. Moreover, the cognitive-artistic values of his work help us to ascertain the modern historical condition in an experiential mode which only great poetry can crystallize: with the result that our resolve to combat that condition can only be enhanced. Or such at any rate seems to me the outcome of the dialectic of the historically-informed reader with literature which gives an authentic, cognitive-artistic account of its occasions. I think that this process moreover shows us that even ideologically reactionary works from the artistic heritage and by contemporary artists may be beneficial to the general activity of interpretation and change of the world.

Similarly, the British feminist author Juliet Mitchell in a recent conversation remarked that she disagreed with Kate Millett's condemning attitude in *Sexual Politics* towards D. H. Lawrence or Norman Mailer whom Mitchell continues to read with interest and pleasure. It isn't that these authors are not sexist, Mitchell notes. However, they succeed in *reflecting* the sexism of their society and they manage to do so in a way which puts it at a distance so you can look at it, not as a program but as a phenomenon. They depict the sexism as artists: in brief, the ideology of sexism is supplemented to a decisive degree by artistic cognition.

This suggestion is developed by Andrea Dworkin in her analysis of *The Story of O* (published in *Feminist Studies*, II i, 1974). Dworkin sees this fiction as a sado-masochistic male fantasy indulgence. Yet she confesses to taking strong pleasure and instruction from it. In *The Story of O*, she writes, "the sado-masochistic complexion of O is not trivial — it is formulated as a cosmic principle" and as such it provides "a logical scenario incorporating Judea-Christian values of service and self-sacrifice and universal notions of womanhood, a logical scenario demonstrating the psychology of submission and self-hatred found in all oppressed peoples. O is a book of astounding political significance" Here as in her larger study, *Woman Hating*, Dworkin explores the history of literature commencing with fairy tales in terms of "dual (polar) role definitions" whereby "O is wanton yet pure, Sir Stephen is cruel yet kind, Rene is brutal yet gentle, a wall is black yet white, everything is what it is, what is isn't, and its direct opposite. That technique, which is so skillfully executed, might help to account for the compelling irrationality of *Story of O*. For those women who are convinced yet doubtful, attracted yet repelled, there is this schema for self-protection: the double double think that the author engages in is very easy to deal with if we just realize that we only have to double double unthink it." On this basis, Dworkin asks: "If we do not accept dual role definition, what other assumptions can we use as a basis for community?"

Precisely. A major cognitive-artistic achievement seems nearly always to outweigh the declarations of shortsighted ideology. This functioning of art is what makes it valuable even to social revolutionaries who would otherwise have some reason to distrust its historically limited range of ideas. If the social revolutionary leadership places its confidence in the people, it if emphatically acts to historically inform the people, it need have no fear of the transparent shortcomings of out-of-date or reactionary ideology. Rather it can count on the strength and resources of the people being fortified by experience of the artistic-cognitive values.

As to the provocative question I raised at the outset — who likes racist, sexist, chauvinist, elitist, even fascist art? — the answer would be as follows. On the basis of distinctions made within the essay, we see that the *ideology* attached to a very great number of humanly appealing works of art may be fairly characterized as racist, sexist, chauvinist, elitist, even fascist. However, what lends these works their appeal is not their ideology as such, which is historically delimited in relevance. Rather, the appeal of the works lies fundamentally in their cognitive and artistic merits. This contribution, in turn, belongs to the general inheritance of all humanity. Even such works as the Riefenstahl film are testaments to the aspirations of humanity and their ideological aspect may be distanced while the documentary dimension is rightfully retained. Socialist revolutionaries should and will develop their own artistic traditions and new works. This should not become the rationale for a rejection of other resources. For fundamentally, literature and the other arts are not an epiphenomenon of narrow class interests. Instead, they are a primary mediation and aim of humanity — a "weapon" in this sense, if you will — for the struggle with and the overcoming of alienation in all its aspects, and the realization of full human potential.

6

CRITICISM — AND SELF-CRITICISM

Lillian S. Robinson

"What century are you in?" When I was at Columbia, the first question one asked a fellow graduate student in English or Comparative Literature was always about the person's sub-field, the literary period in which she or he was specializing. The verbal formula was as unvarying as the ritual question itself and, even when it was my own habitual conversation-starter, I noticed its peculiar ontological implications. What did it signify to *be in* a certain century? It would have been considered inexcusably flippant to reply that, along with one's interlocutor, one's classmates and one's teachers, and whether one liked it or not, one was "in" the twentieth century. Yet our education did little to shed light on what it might mean to be "in" any other period. This paper is an attempt to examine the meaning of that question, the correct answer to it, and the reasons why I think it is of such urgent importance for us, as humanists, to be aware of the historical situation of our work — to know what century we are in.

My initial method is anecdotal, but it develops into what I think is a more systematic attempt to connect the disparate pieces. The first anecdote concerns a rather mysterious experience I had in a museum some years ago. I was about to begin graduate study in the history of art, and I took my work and myself very seriously. At the Byzantine Museum in Athens, one afternoon, I stationed myself in front of a large triptych with a Madonna and Child in its central panel, and began taking notes to record my professional observations and responses. After a few minutes, a

This essay is a revised version of a paper presented at the English Institute at Harvard in September 1973, and published in *College English*. The generous efforts and pro-vocative suggestions of Ira Gerstein, Louis Kampf and Lise Vogel were invaluable in transforming the talk for publication.

woman I took to be a museum attendant approached me, speaking in Greek and pointing from the icon to me and back again. My Greek is very poor, but her words, the repeated gesture, and the frenetic signs of the Cross she was tracing in the air between us eventually got through to me. She was asking whether the icon was an object of veneration to me — that is, if I were a Christian. I said — or, rather, indicated — that I was not. Growing more excited, the woman grabbed my arm and led me across the room to a smaller icon depicting what was presumably an Old Testament scene. There was Hebrew writing in the background of this picture, and my self-appointed guide and persecutor went through her rapid gesticulations again, somewhat more sternly: was *that* what I was? The anti-Semitism evoked both pride and defensiveness and I agreed that, like the picture and the funny lettering, I, too, was Jewish. With as little irony as I could manage, I thanked the woman for showing me the icon and returned to the triptych that had first attracted my notice. But the damned woman wouldn't let me alone. She kept on talking and gesturing, trying to pull me away from the Madonna and back to the painting I "belonged" in front of. Finally — and most meretriciously — she told me that it was against the rules to write in the Museum and that I would have to put my notebook away. At this point, exasperated, I gave up on the triptych and moved on to take notes about an enormous Byzantine angel several rooms away.

My response to this incident has passed through several distinct phases over the years. At the time, I was mostly annoyed at the interruption of My Work and at the racism that prompted it. But I was also faintly amused at the naivete of this poor woman, who apparently thought that art had a meaning and a function, that those possessed social and ideological import, and that, if you couldn't relate to them on that level, you had no business in the place. As the incident receded in time and an elite graduate education — in art and later in literature — made further inroads into my good sense, the anger diminished and the amusement grew, for I was increasingly convinced that the critical approach implied by the old woman's actions was pathetically innocent. More recently, a vision of both art and criticism as political expressions has forced me to reevaluate the assumptions of the woman in the Byzantine Museum. Although I still believe I have the right to admire and analyze what I do not worship, I have begun to think that, on some level, at least, the woman knew a lot more than I was ever taught about the function of culture and criticism.

Another aspect of the problem is reflected in the experience a friend of mine has been having with an article he published in 1970. By way of illustrating some effects of humanist training on one's historical perspective, he began the essay with a two-paragraph discussion of what is had been like for him to be a successful graduate student "in" the eighteenth century, identifying intellectually with the literary culture of Alexander Pope, while remaining "ignorant of the larger culture . . . [surrounding] the masterpieces" he studied. Most graduate students, he wrote, suffer similar limitations:

> the Enlightenment is little more than a vague rumor to them, as is the industrial revolution and urbanization; the fact that there was a popular culture central to the lives of the vast majority of the population simply does not come within their field of professional concern. I began to feel uneasy about my work when it dawned on me that I really agreed with the objectives of the Enlightenment.[1]

The passage goes on to describe how the author came to understand that there was a disjunction between his imaginative life, rooted "in" the eighteenth century, and the constellation of political and cultural attitudes shaped by his own material and historical experience. The world his literary education had encouraged him to embrace was, of course, politely free of distinctions based on class, race or ideology, so it took him some time to realize that, since he was a Jew, neither Swift nor Pope would have received him socially. His mannered fantasy had been a grotesque anachronism: "the Jewish socialist from Washington Heights, sitting in his Chinese garden swapping epigrams with Dr. Arbuthnot!"

Reading these remarks in their original context — an article about the politically compromised nature of literary study — I considered them a wry and rather modest attempt to demystify and make sense of fragmented experience. My colleague was performing that act for which liberal education is supposed supremely to prepare us: he was attempting to know himself, he was asking that fundamental question, "What the fuck am I doing?" Some people read the passage very differently, however. For whatever motives, they see it as a pathologically subjective approach to "our" cultural tradition. Whenever a political attack is directed at the author from within the profession, these paragraphs are exhumed, paraphrased and cariactured. He is widely believed to have projected some kind of private paranoia onto the great writers of the eighteenth century, decided on the basis of that paranoia that these distinguished men would have snubbed him, and developed an implacable grudge against them. Having refused the invitation to a timeless and gracious world he'd ceased to believe in, he found himself in the classic position of the child who not only points out the Emperor's embarrassing nudity, but proceeds to inform the rest of the crowd how far *they'd* sold out by praising the softness of the insubstantial velvet, the shine on the non-existent cloth of gold. At my friend's own institution, a retired dean — an individual who had once managed to quote Montaigne in support of procedures leading to dismissal of my colleague and myself — wrote an appeal for gentlemanly values in humanities teaching. In this document, which was printed and distributed at university expense, he heaped scorn on an unnamed professor who, convinced that Pope and Swift would have disliked him personally, refused to teach their works in his own courses and prevented others from doing so in theirs!

I encountered the third bit of anecdotal evidence while reading the entertainment section of the Sunday *Times*. On the front page, the headline over an article by Walter Kerr posed the angry question: WILL WE EVER SEE THE BACCHAE AS EURIPIDES WROTE IT?[2] My immediate reaction was to answer "Of course not, *schmuck*," and move on to livelier reading. When I returned to the article, however, I discovered that the argument was somewhat more subtle than anticipated. Kerr was inveighing against a current London production of *The Bacchae*, which a director from the Third World had interpreted as anti-imperialist drama, with Dionysius representing the liberating energy that moves an oppressed people. Nor was this the only recent version of the play that distressed the reviewer, for he also dismissed *Dionysius in 69* as an "apologia for the [sic] counter-culture" and a "limp" one at that — surely a most un-Dionysian attribute!

Despite the headline, the critic was not calling on us to recreate the conditions under which *The Bacchae* was first produced. (What's the matter, Kerr, you want to go fight in the Peloponnesos? You want *slaves*?) All he asked was a faithful rendering of the text — the *English* text, of course — with, perhaps, a discreet adoption of some few techniques characteristic of Attic theater: the chorus, maybe the masks, but no men playing Maenads, I bet, and for heaven's sake not all that sitting around on hard stone benches. Kerr was not suggesting that we reproduce — or even consider — the social forces within which *The Bacchae* functioned when Euripides wrote it, forces that may well be obscured by translating the play into the terms of our own modern history. Rather, he wanted a denatured *Bacchae* that did not document Athenian experience or Athenian theater, but that remained unsullied by twentieth-century tensions. In such a play, the references to góds, wives, kings and servants, to wars, epidemics and power politics, do not represent social experience, but are transfigured onto a higher, asocial realm. They are seen as expressions of timeless, "universal" categories that are as stylized as wearing white robes or speaking in verse. The tragedy does not take place somewhere, but Everywhere; it is freed from having to be about something, in the interests of being about Everything. I think I understand the travesty Kerr wants to see in the theater because it is the same *Bacchae* I have encountered in the classroom, the one that was taught to me and that I was encouraged to present to my own students as the departmentally-sanctified Real Thing. (Fortunately, throughout Euripides' tragedy, Dionysius the Liberator wears a smiling mask.)

These three vignettes share a concern about our ability to recognize and respond to the distinction between subjective and objective categories of historical experience. In each of the *exempla*, some questions are raised about the proper relationship of individual experience to the apprehension of a work of art. Although Alienated Man — existentially isolated and despairing in a world of subjective forms — is the contemporary bourgeois hero, he is no one's idea of a good critic. Even the modernist critic, immersed in those same subjective forms, normally retains a certain responsibility to the social act of communicating insights and helping to render aesthetic experience intelligible. Given these assumptions, the only difficulty is to identify which are the subjective elements of consciousness, which the objective ones.

I would maintain that, as the products of social experience, the personal responses evinced by the people in my three anecdotes are by no means subjective. The ˉconsciousness informed by membership — especially what could be called active membership — in one's race, one's class, or one's sex is an objective phenomenon. The idea that "life is not determined by consciousness, but consciousness by life," is probably too familiar to require much elaboration. For my present purposes, however, it is worth looking at how Marx and Engels completed the paragraph in which they originally made that pronouncement: "In the first method of approach the starting-point is consciousness taken as the living individuals; in the second it is the real living individuals themselves, as they are in actual life, and consciousness is considered solely as *their* consciousness."[3] What the authors are trying to do here is to remove the clouds of abstraction that surround the notion of consciousness as long as it is understood as a force capable of either constituting or determining life. Although it adds a more rigorous note, the term "consciousness," thus idealized, has no more precision than the word "soul," and becomes its secular equivalent. This form of mystification can be avoided only if we remember that the vague polysyllable "consciousness" has to belong to real people, that it possesses no being or significance apart from people, and that its specific content must depend on the nature of real people's experience.

The historical materialism that *The German Ideology* begins to enunciate takes issue, then, with idealist theories — theological, philosophical, or psychological — that perceive consciousness as the determinant of experience. Yet, taken out of context, the initial statement of the position would still seem to leave room for the grossest and most self-indulgent solipsism, for, if *your* consciousness is determined by *your* life and *my* consciousness is determined by *my* life and we all have our own idiosyncrasies and our own suffering, then in the experessions of consciousness — in the arts and their interpretation, for example — pretty much anything is legitimate. The continuation of that paragraph suggests, however, that it is not personal history that Marxists regard as central to consciousness, but social history. And that when we talk about individuals producing their lives, and their lives, in turn, determining consciousness, we are talking about the *social* production of human life.

Of course, we all have individual histories and those histories constitute part of the psychic and intellectual baggage we bring with us to a new experience, including our first contact with a given work of art. If, say, a mysterious dark bird appeared one day and pecked out your grandfather's eyes, the incident is probably going to be relevant to your reading of certain poems by Edgar Allan Poe and Wallace Stevens. Indeed, the event might be of such overriding importance in your mental makeup that you can't get much out of "The Raven" or "Thirteen Ways of Looking at a Blackbird," and that's too bad. If I can't get much out of, say, "Prufrock," these days, because I read it as a woman, that is also too bad. But I refuse to believe that the two kinds of damn shame are in any sense equivalent.

A couple of years ago, I published an article in which it was freely acknowledged that members of oppressed groups often respond subjectively to the content of art. My co-author and I insisted, however, that such a response was no more subjective than that of the dominant culture — merely more overt. [4] My present position amounts to a reconsideration of even that qualified admission. It is founded on the view that, when there is a difference between personal and social experience, it is the latter, properly understood, that has the primary role in the understanding of art. Thus, my friend's Jewishness, the London director's

African origins, like my femaleness, are qualitatively different, in their effect on consciousness, from the multitude of personal eccentricities and private details that also mark our lives and that have a more limited, though quite genuine, social basis. And the opinions we advance — my socialist friend's belated support for the Enlightenment, my youthful preference for aesthetic form over the Christian god as an object of worship, Walter Kerr's yearning for a "pure" production of Euripides — do not reflect the accidental operation of casual tastes, but are ideological products of the same categories of class, race and sex, acting as historical forces. The *Times* does not "happen" to have a theater critic who wants to keep Dionysian energies in their place (Periclean Athens is about far enough, in space and time). And I am not a working-class misfit who was spontaneously convinced that art was made for art's sake and — quite incidentally — my own social mobility.

I have asserted rather categorically that social experience is not only different from private experience but that, acknowledged or not, it is the dominant force in the making of art or criticism. This assertion remains to be supported and justified. It seems to me that bourgeois criticism inverts the categories of objective and subjective and thereby distorts the kind of relationship that subsists between art and audience. That is, it behaves as if the work of art, which it perceives as a product of the artist's subjectivity, has a certain objective life, an autonomous reality, of its own; we, the critics, are subjective beings, and, though our mission is to apprehend the work in its full (objective) reality, the process is to some extent mediated by our own subjectivity. From this perspective, the interchange between the work of art and its interpreter appears as a relationship between a subjective being and an objective thing. And the sensitive, informed work of critical interpretation, itself apparently an autonomous and objective thing, seems to enter into a relation with that other thing, the work of art. The only language we have to describe the process makes all this seem like a right and natural and inevitable condition. (Witness my own near-personification of "bourgeois criticism" in the course of this very discussion.)[5]

But in fact we are not simply ambulant subjectivities; we are the products of human history and of certain material developments within it. And the work of art is a *work*, the product of human labor, socially (though in our culture not often collectively) produced. [6] It is made by an historical being using socially developed means to arrive at a social expression. Not only is the artist situated in history, but the art itself is. It is quite true, that is, that the artist's consciousness contains elements other than those determined by class, race and sex or the operation of those forces in particular conditions. The artist has a biography, a subjective history, and also a craft, a relation to the formal elements of the art. And she or he may be convinced that those elements are the whole point of any work of art. But the formal components — as well as matters of "style" — are social facts. In the twentieth century, new styles in the arts have frequently been received with questions about whether, for example, this thing that the orchestra was playing was really music or whether this object hung for exhibit was really to be regarded as a painting. Under the hegemony of modernism, the answer is always, "Yes, it is art." But the persistence of the question means that, even if the barriers are flexible, there remains an assumption that, at any *particular* moment, there is some commonly held view of what is and what is not a work of art. In a sense, the more flexible the boundaries of acceptable form, the greater our awareness that those boundaries exist.

If the creator and the means of art have an historical, a social existence, then there is something exceptionally peculiar about the critical mode I described earlier, wherein the reified interpretation, the work of criticism as thing, engages the work of art as thing in some kind of relationship. I believe that it is our present stage of material civilization that has confused the situation so that the world of art comes to resemble that of religion: "In that world the productions of the human brain appear as independent beings endowed with life and entering into relations both with one another and the human race." [7] A human relation, initially established between people as historical beings, thus comes to assume "the fantastic form of a relation between things." [8]

The source of these observations is Marx's chapter on Commodity Fetishism in the first volume of *Capital.* [9] This may suggest that I think an analogy exists between the situation in art and that of material production. In fact, I would go further and say that I think it is more than an analogy, for the work of art is not only a product of the brain but of the hand — that is, of a labor process. And it is a literal, not a metaphorical product. One aspect of this fact is that, in order for the artist to survive and for the work to have an impact on the social world, it has to enter the capitalist market, to be actually or potentially bought and sold.

Does my use of Marx's terms mean that the work of art is not only a thing but the specific kind of thing called a commodity? And does it matter for cultural theory whether it is a commodity or not? I think it does matter for an understanding of what critical fetishism means, and for that reason I wish the answer to my first question were simpler. Everything that can be placed on the market is not a commodity; as Marx points out, "in order to sell a thing, nothing more is required than its capacity to be monopolised and alienated." [10] He also makes it clear in a number of places that the kind of commodity he is discussing (and hence the kind that can be fetishized) may be reproduced in any quantity by the application of labor. [11]

I believe that the way modern art has responded to and made use of the technology of advanced capitalism shows the extent to which it is coming to fit this second definition, to share with conventional manufactured commodities the capacity of being reproduced by the application of labor. In the nineteenth century, works of art were not commodities in the analytic sense of the term; in the twentieth, they are still not the same as other objects, but they are somewhat less special.[12] What is more important, however, is the way they are pereceived, for our critical approach to them is increasingly conditioned by our participation in a culture where the autonomous life and mental processess of commodities is taken even more as a matter of course than when Marx first named the curious phenomenon.

If we are to be able to see the work of art for what it is, without critical fetishism, it is essential that we see it whole and within *its* history, from a vantage point informed by *ours*. Now, "the life-process of society, which is based on the process of material production, does not strip off its mystical veil until it is treated as production by freely associated men, and is consciously regulated by them in accordance with a settled plan. This, however, demands for society a certain material ground-work or set of conditions of existence which in their turn are the spontaneous product of a long and painful process of development." [13] If we take the making of art to be at once a kind of commodity-production, created for distribution under specific market conditions, and a kind of ideology-production, expressing and reinforcing those "specific market conditions," then what Marx says about historic process is particularly vital to the small corner of that process occupied by literary criticism. That is, only social experience eventuating in the free association he speaks of can fully demystify art in general or any work in particular. It seems a rather prolix and indirect sort of invitation to a revolution. Yet the most criticism can do in the meantime is to reveal and examine the mystification, the way in which the present mode of making and studying art is an extension of the system's characteristic "inversion of the relations between dead and living labor." [14]

An important part of this effort involves getting in touch with those elements of a critical response that are shaped by our own participation in history. It seems to me that the most positive steps in this direction — steps that have at least served to inject some vitality into departments of literature — have been made by Third World people and by women. In both cases, the existence of a movement for social liberation has made it possible for those of us still in the academy to recognize and express the consciousness informed by our condition. The flowering of black and feminist criticism — concentrating on writers and audiences that had previously been excluded from consideration, and reevaluating the monuments and attitudes of the dominant culture — is a welcome sign of life. But it has not always led to good criticism because, although it reflects that individual historic consciousness that I have been claiming is not purely subjective, it also reflects a very limited understanding of that consciousness as a part of history. As a result, critics who are struggling against the literary objectification their group has traditionally suffered participate in that objectification by talking about "black" and "woman" as if these were trans-historical categories.

In the area of feminist studies, where I feel best qualified to comment, a body of criticism has developed that is remote from the concerns of the movement for women's liberation and that is of limited usefulness to it.[15] I think this has occurred because of the isolation in criticism of the category "woman" from the other historical forces and events with which it interacts, forces that have made the meaning and experience of "woman" anything but static and absolute. Such criticism succeeds to the extent that it asserts — often angrily and, to my mind, always refreshingly — that criticism does indeed have a gender. And it fails to the extent that it proceeds from there as if gender functioned as a natural, rather than a social category. Of necessity, it begins by recognizing sexism as a social constraint, but then it fails to examine the forces in a particular society that made the constraint take certain forms.[16] Awareness of sexism provides a new way of looking at literature and at the conditions it reflects, but that awareness is too often inflexible and unmodulated. Thus, most feminist criticism does not help us use literature to understand an urgent issue that literature is uniquely fitted to illuminate — the peculiar forms sexism has assumed in *capitalist* society.

Although my primary concern is with making critical analysis available to a living movement, I believe that criticism whose historical insensitivity makes it impossible for the movement to use it is not professionally useful, either. It acquiesces in the peculiarly ahistorical approach of what is supposed to be literary history and, like bourgeois criticism in general, treats the encounter with a work of literature as a confrontation between the self and an objective thing.

A criticism whose point of departure was the awareness of *class* as historical determinant could not wander so far from history. Those of us who work this particular critical vein have a tendency to speak as if all the material forces with which we are concerned were equivalent and present similar problems; in our ideological shorthand, class, race and sex seem almost to fuse into a single concept. In fact, the kinds of issues they raise as they begin to operate in criticism are different from one another and call for an overall analysis that can show how they function together. The reason I think a stance that recognizes the class nature of art and criticism is most likely to be faithful to the exigencies of history is that one cannot admit the validity of "class" as a category without also seeing it historically, which may be why its validity is not often admitted and why the most massive and brutal attempts to deny the existence of an analytic category occur with respect to class. (I suspect, for example, that the majority of well-meaning academics who have been taught to consider proletarian culture and proletarian criticism as some doctrinaire aberration of the Depression era have no idea that there really is a proletariat and that it has an historic role as well as an historic definition.)

I called minority studies and women's studies sources of the first liberating energies within the profession. This priority is no accident, but is closely linked to the history of social movements in this country, and also to the masking of class distinctions and class struggle that characterizes American political mythology. I do not believe that this is by any means a permanent situation — in society or in criticism. But I will be very much suprised if the next stages of proletarian struggle are contained by the creation of chairs of Proletarian Studies in the bourgeois university.

What, then, do we do with the chairs we've already got and that some of us are sitting on? If human history really is the history of class conflict, and if that did not change just because Senator McCarthy or the Sociology Department said it did, what does that have to do with literary history, with me "in" the sixteenth century and my colleagues "in" the eighteenth, the fourteenth, or the nineteenth? I think it means, above all, learning to ask new kinds of questions and putting the answers to use. For our own period, it means taking mass culture seriously — examining the art addressed to working people, the forms it uses, the myths it creates, the influence it exerts, and seeking a new audience for criticism among those people who are the chief actors in history. For the past, it means looking at the recognized masterpieces as historically alive: conditioned by historical forces, produced in specific material circumstances, serving certain interests and ignoring, threatening or repressing others. And it means considering how popular culture coexisted and sometimes overlapped with those monuments.[17] Only in this way, I think, can we as interpreters of literature finally come to be *in* the twentieth century, rather than letting it roll over us as it moves forward to someplace much better.

NOTES

1. Louis Kampf, "The Trouble With Literature," *Change*, 2 (1970), 27.

2. *New York Times*, August 19, 1973, Section 2, 1.

3. Karl Marx and Frederick Engels, *The German Ideology* (1845-6; rpt. New York: New World-International, 1967), p. 15.

4. See Lillian S. Robinson and Lise Vogel, "Modernism and History," *New Literary History*, 3 (1971), 177-99. Vogel and I continue to build on this article. The present paper is my share of that development; hers is reflected in "Fine Arts and Feminism: The Awakening Consciousness," *Feminist Studies*, 2 (1974), 3-37.

5. I realize that some readers will be less distressed by the personification than by my characterizing some — indeed, most — criticism as "bourgeois." There is no other term, however, that is comprehensive enough to describe newspaper reviewers, New Critics, self-proclaimed "structuralists," and the run of literary historians. I imagine each of them would be the first to deny participation in the same "mainstream" as any of the others. If this is so, I prefer to use what I believe is the right term, and trust that my subsequent argument will demonstrate its appropriateness.

6. In this and what follows, I have been influenced by Christopher Caudwell's *Studies in a Dying Culture* (rpt., New York: Monthly Review Press, 1971), especially his essay "D.H. Lawrence: A Study of the Bourgeois Artist," pp. 44-72. As far as I know, however, Caudwell did not pursue his ideas to the conclusions I am advancing.

7. Karl Marx, "The Fetishism of Commodities and the Secret Thereof," *Capital*, Volume I (1867; rpt. Moscow: Progress Publishers, n.d.), 77.

8. *Ibid*.

9. For another application of the concept of commodity fetishism to culture, see Meredith Tax, "Culture is Not Neutral, Whom Does it Serve?" in *Radical Perspectives in the Arts*, ed. Lee Baxandall (Baltimore: Pelican-Penguin, 1972), pp. 15-29. Tax emphasizes the alienation inherent in the production and consumption of art

under capitalism and employs commodity fetishism as a way of explaining the elevation of that alienation into "an artistic creed, which becomes in its turn a critical dogma." (Page 23).

10. Karl Marx, "Transformation of Surplus-Profit into Ground-Rent: Introduction," *Capital*, Volume III (Moscow: Progress, 1971), 633.

11. See, for instance, *Capital*, III, 759, where he refers to "works of art, whose consideration by their very nature is excluded from our discussion."

12. This is a more controversial and complex issue than I can deal with here. It seems to me that one kind of evidence to pursue, aside from theoretical grounding and artistic evidence, is the history of copyright law and the culture surrounding *it*. Particularly suggestive is the recent movement, led by the pop-artist Robert Rauschenberg, for a "copyright" system in the visual arts. (Rauschenberg's action was inspired by seeing a picture he'd sold to Robert Scull a few years before auctioned off by the collector for an amount I believe was nearly 10,000% of its purchase price. From a Marxist standpoint, Rauschenberg's parting remark was most provocative: Leaving to consult an attorney, the painter told Scull, whose fortune comes from owning a fleet of taxi-cabs, that he owed every artist in the place free cab rides!)

13. Marx, *Capital*, I, 84.

14. Karl Marx, "Rate and Mass of Surplus-Value," *Capital*, I, 294.

15. I described some aspects of this problem in an article written rather early in the present stage of the women's movement and of feminist criticism: "Dwelling in Decencies: Radical Criticism and the Feminist Perspective," *College English*, 32 (1971), 879-89.

16. I have been forced to personify again — and to generalize. Although I do not mean to place an undue burden on a single article of this type, I think a good example of both the successes and failures I allude to is Elizabeth Hampsten's trenchant, witty, but essentially ahistorical piece, "A Woman's Map of Lyric Poetry," *College English*, 34 (1973).

17. This is not my "program." I hope the reader will recall that the "we" of my original audience meant the participants in the English Institute. For all of us, however, my recommendations amount to no more than enlightened empiricism unless the results are put into action by a revolutionary movement. Until there is a movement that can make use of cultural analysis, that work is futile. But unless certain work is done — particularly in the area of mass culture — that movement will not come into being.

7

ART AGAINST IMPERIALISM,
For the National Liberation Struggle
of Third World Peoples

E. San Juan, Jr.

For the majority of Third World peoples brutalized by the nightmare reality of a colonial past and a neocolonial present, art is literally a matter of life and death. It reflects in varied forms the ongoing class struggle. It reflects the sharpening contradictions between the oppressed masses in revolt and disintegrating monopoly capitalism with its feudal or comprador lackeys. Art thus cannot deny its social origin nor its historical destiny.

In the 1844 *Economic and Philosophic Manuscripts,* Marx pointed out how integrally commensurate, even identical, is the development of the aesthetic and creative faculty with social practice, i.e. work, productive transaction between man and nature in history:

> Only through the objectively unfolded richness of man's essential being is the richness of subjective *human* sensibility (a musical ear, an eye for beauty of form — in short, *senses* capable of human gratification, senses affirming themselves as essential power of *man*) either cultivated or brought into being. . . . *human* sense — the human nature of the senses — comes to be by virtue of its object, by virtue of *humanized* nature. The *forming* of the five senses is a labor of the entire history of the world down to the present. [NE ed., p. 141]

Whether they like it or not, artists in the "undeveloped" countries of Asia, Africa and Latin America serve as witness and participant to a complex but law-governed process in which a new configuration of human relations, both the antithesis and fulfillment of the present, is assuming integrity and substance in the womb of the old dying system. Depending on the artist's choice, aesthetics in the context of the class struggle may serve either as midwife or executioner. Like man himself, its ministry submits to Engel's maxim of freedom as "the recognition of necessity."

This conception of art's role, its import and efficacy in mediating consciousness and reality, is implicitly committed to the goal of radical social change. Either one decides to take a stand in full awareness or allows himself to yield to "blind necessity" — on the surface, a dualism which art as a king of human engagement seeks to resolve. But surely many aestheticians in the metropolis, scrupulously calculating the decorous mixture of pleasure (*dulce*) and usefulness (*utile*), would dissent. Those who believe art contains a self-sufficient or autonomous terminal value transcending contingent interests and needs, may be scandalized by what they call "vulgar instrumentalism." For them, the genuine artist takes the side of all humanity and universal truth in the creation of immortal beauty. His only responsibility is to his *metier*, his vocation.

Perhaps it is wiser to subsume this hackneyed theme of the bankruptcy of "art for art's sake," whether it disguises itself in Kantian categories, New Critical/Northrop Frye scholasticism, or structuralist metaphysics, in the far more challenging responses of the ultra-left, anarchist orthodoxy and of the "Right" opportunists who try to revise Marxism-Leninism to suit compromised subjective ends.[1]

The Third World countries right from the time when the emerging bourgeoisie of Europe proceeded to accumulate capital by plundering the colonies, have been systematically "underdeveloped." They have been reduced to the classic status of supplier of cheap raw materials and labor, and dumping ground for expensive industrial products and other manufactured commodities.[2] With the consolidation of bourgeois hegemony in the 19th century, finance capitalism intensified its exploitation through export of capital, territorial division, war and other insidious schemes first described by Lenin in *Imperialism, the Highest Stage of Capitalism.*

Imperialism, in effect, wrested from the Africans, Asians and Latin Americans the right to control their productive resources and to determine their lives, manipulating the ideological superstructure — cultural forms embodying value-systems, modes of self-interpretation, etc. — to maintain the natives in the bonds of self-hatred, impotence and awe at the slave-master. In the pit of colonial domination, the native's senses, no longer effective powers of worldly intervention, are mystified and estranged until he is finally deprived of any awareness of identity as producer, as the motive force of history.

Amilcar Cabral formulates the problematics of this experience succinctly:

> Both in colonialism and in neo-colonialism the essential characteristic of imperialist domination remains the same: the negation of the historical process of the dominated people by means of violent usurpation of the freedom of development of the national productive forces. On the basis of this, we can state that national liberation is the phenomenon in which a given socio-economic whole rejects the negation of its historical process. In other words, the national liberation of a people is the regaining of the historical personality of that people, its return to history through the destruction of the imperialist domination to which it was subjected.   [*Revolution in Guinea*, p. 102]

To effect the maximization of profit, imperialism disrupted the historic process of internal class struggle within the different societies it violated and subsequently instituted racial, chauvinistic discrimination. Co-opting a privileged stratum of the indigenous ruling class, it enforced alienation. This alienation, transmitted through the various media of communication, schools, etc., may be conceived as the over-all mystification of the forms of consciousness (values, habits, fashions, tastes, ideals) arising from, and affirmed by, the loss of vital decision-making powers. From this comes the African's Europeanized sensibility; the myth of French, British or American cultural/technological supremacy; the fetish of capitalist investment as the miraculous key to modernization; philosophy, art, literature, etc. as neutral, privately-disposable property and attribute of individuals freed from mundane concerns, receiving from the anarchy of the capitalist market the dividends of catharsis, self-actualization, and so forth.

Because art crystallizes man's way of perceiving reality in accordance with his generic, historically unfolding needs and potencies, we cannot ignore the concrete material situation, the uneven development of the socio-economic formation, in which the artist functions.

In other words, art cannot be divorced from praxis. Man makes himself, reproduces his own nature, in association with other men. To deny this is to fall into idealist mystification. If art is conceived not as an inert product for contemplation but as a mode of interpreting and changing reality, then the real motive force of the imagination exists not in the sphere of noumenal freedom, but in the actual tension of the class struggle. The much-vaunted freedom of the imagination acquires meaning only within the limitations of the artist's sensory world, a world located within the historical domain. His sensibility registers the pressures of material forces and acts on them to the degree that his reason (theory realized in practice) succeeds in grasping the dialectical movement of the historical experience he inhabits. This is why a class analysis of the intellectual's role and the cultural differentiation in Third World societies should precede any attempt to understand the significance of art there for the masses, the agents of production and progress.

The historical experience of Third World societies in general shows that the pettybourgeois intelligentsia, the university-trained elite which includes writers, painters, teachers, scientists, etc., constitute a privileged segment (perhaps the "weak link" in the State apparatus) removed from the peasants and workers by their role in the production process. [3] On the whole, they tend to rationalize and justify what exists, the status quo of imperialist domination. They are the "whores" of appearance. Tutored in France, England, the United States, etc., the native intellectual, while enjoying his marginal share of the surplus-value stolen from the laboring masses, is nevertheless still exposed to the humiliating paternalism of his Western employers and the cunning suspicion of his countrymen.

Two alternatives are open to him. He can deny the objective inequality in his mind and exalt the supra-class, supra-racial status of the artist. A disembodied spirit, he ironically enacts a naturalistic and empirical transcription of everyday reality, surrendering to the illusion of the statistical average. He is happy, his conscience is at rest. His benevolent impartiality is rewarded with cash and sinecure. This is what we may call "Right" opportunism.

Or he can get rid of his petty bourgeois hang-ups, the egotistic lifestyle encrusted on him by the decadent and parasitic milieu of Paris, London, or New York, and "go native" again, this time extolling a mystical essence like "Negritude" or an authentic Oriental (Gandhian?) spirit. This we may call "Left" opportunism. Kim Il Sung repudiated this trend of "restorationism." He stressed self-critical discrimination, endorsing the immediate priority of Lenin's thesis on the dialectical growth of the cultural tradition:

> Restorationism is an anti-Marxist ideological trend which restores and glorifies the things of the past uncritically, in disregard of the demands of the times and the class principle. If restorationism is allowed in the field of cultural development, all the unsound aspects of the culture of the past will be revived, and reactionary bourgeois and feudalistic Confucian ideas, as well as other outmoded ideas, will grow in the minds of the people.
> A relentless struggle should be waged against the tendency to copy

blindly the antiquated, reactionary things of the past, idealizing and embellishing them on the pretext of taking over the heritage of national culture. We must discard backward and reactionary elements in the cultural heritage, and critically inherit and develop progressive and popular elements in conformity with the realities of socialism today.

[*Revolution and Socialist Construction in Korea*, p. 199]

One example of the first alternative is the Filipino poet Jose Garcia Villa. Born of the landed gentry class and reared in the dominant capitalist ethos of competitive individualism, conspicuous consumption and bohemian elitism, Villa damned his countrymen, migrated to Greenwich Village, aped the techniques of Gertrude Stein, until he was finally glorified by the Edith Sitwell clique of modern-day aesthetes. Asked why his poetry was abstract, Villa revealed the kernel of his reactionary apriorist and a-historical outlook in his reply:

The reason for it must be that I am not at all interested in description or outward appearance, nor in the contemporary scene, but in *essence*. A single motive underlies all my work and defines my intention as a serious artist: The search for the metaphysical meaning of man's life in the Universe — the finding of man's selfhood and identity in the mystery of Creation. I use the term *metaphysical* to denote the ethico-philosophic force behind all essential living. The development and unification of the human personality I consider the highest achievement a man can do.

This is a paradigmatic statement, instances of which one can multiply: e.g., Jorge Luis Borges' metaphysical puzzles, Lewis Nkosi's or John Nogenda's image of the artist as the Elect, Kamala Markandaya's self-indulgence in grotesque pathos and sentimental voyeurism. One can cite a dozen Third World artists whose expertise in the banality of the Absurd wins them kudos in the cocktail circuits of the "Free World."

Of the second alternative, the most instructive case is Leopold Senghor.[4] To achieve decolonization in a mechanical fashion, Senghor proposes a mystical affirmation of "Negritude" as a distinctly African essence which cuts across class boundaries. Contrast this with Aime Cesaire's idea of "Negritude" as a weapon of resistance to the assimilation/acculturation strategy of neocolonialism. It turns out that Senghor's "Negritude" is a kind of escapist narcissism which obscures the class contradictions between the African comprador bourgeoisie and African workers, peasants, and other exploited sectors. As an a-historical idea, "Negritude" negates art as social praxis. It is untimately counter-revolutionary. Such a sectarian reaction to the imperialist technique of monopolizing all history, relegating the past of the colonized and his memory to the inert realm of prehistoric barbarism, may justify such misleading phenomena like a unique "African socialism" more realizable by legislative fiat than by class struggle.

Given the national dimension of the class struggle in the Third World countries, with the masses except the comprador minority being oppressed by alien rulers, there exists a tremendous revolutionary potential in the emergence of a consciousness of national culture, the birth of national self-esteem. This is a necessary first stage in the liberation struggle against imperialist aggression. It has been voiced by Che Guevara in his category of the innovative "New Man," by the recent discovery and revitalization of Afro-Cuban culture, by the collective endeavors of Nicolas Guillen, Pablo Neruda, Carlos Fuentes, Luis Valdez's Chicano guerilla theater, the Ramona Parra Brigade in Chile, etc. It characterizes the cultural nostalgia of Tagore and other Asian intellectuals.

In *The Wretched of the Earth*, Frantz Fanon eloquently articulated the need to destroy the colonial system, its base and superstructure, which broke the historical continuum of the colonized, deluding the native that he can only be the passive consumer while the alien intruder is the sole creator of commodities and spiritual goods. But it is also Fanon who emphasized the primacy of the national struggle: "To fight for national culture means in the first place to fight for the liberation of the nation, that material keystone which makes the building of a culture possible... The nation is not only the condition of culture, its fruitfulness, its continuous renewal, and its deepening. It is also a necessity." [pp. 233, 244]

But what Fanon failed to point out, and what others who reject a Marxist-Leninist framework (like Paulo Freyre the Brazilian pedagogue) ignore, is that the concept "nation" in this moment of world-history cannot be a homogeneous, reified totality. In fact the national struggle today can only be a triumphant anti-imperialist transformation of a colonized or neocolonized country if the working class, in broad alliance with the peasantry and other democratic forces, leads the struggle. Proletarian politics implemented by the vanguard party comprised of the most advanced elements of the toiling masses must command any cultural revolution aimed not only to recover national pride but also to change permanently the alienating social relations of individuals by abolishing the exploitative material conditions: private ownership or control of the means of production, tryanny of exchange-value (profit) over use-value, devaluation of work, etc. Hence the spirit of proletarian internationalism orients the culture of "new democracy."

In the Third World, only the leadership of the working class in the liberation struggle can release the productive forces and thereby adjust the form and quality of human association with the content of productive life.

In their obsession with Form and the "independent" subjectivity of the artist, theoreticians of the New Left have sometimes forgotten the cardinal premise of radical thought: ideas spring from social praxis, ideas become a material force when consciously grasped by the masses in revolutionary action. Art then begins to function as a sensory manifold of values and qualities that heightens our cognition of the world, its limitations and possibilities for collective action. It ceases to be simply an autonomous mode of self-realization. Compelled by his attack against "repressive de-sublimation" and his passion for utopian extrapolations, Marcuse defines the aesthetic sense as "the capacity of receiving the impression of Form: beautiful and pleasurable Form as the possible mode of existence of men and things." [5] This may be fine Hegelian philosophizing, but not historical-materialist or class-oriented elucidation of art's humane service. The medium is not the only message. Even for the "engineer of the soul," technique is not everything. What is required is an intelligent concern with the meaning being formed which is needed to raise political consciousness, awaken the spectator of fate to become an actor, and intensify the people's commitment to revolution.

Could we salvage from the fictitious ethical objectivity of corporate liberalism any poetics to promote the all-round development of all men? In what sense can Third World cultural workers be mentally equipped and mobilized for destroying feudal/bourgeois culture by contemplating the constellation of symbols and archetypes in Nabokov, Samuel Beckett, in the artifacts of the much advertised exponents of Angst-ridden, modernist sophistication?

To enable us to appreciate the differences in aesthetic criteria due to underlying ideological premises and milieux, it may be worthwhile to juxtapose a remark made by the well-known novelist Jerzy Kosinski, president of American P.E.N. (Poets, Essayists, Novelists) apropos of the topic "Literature and Revolution — Can a Writer be Uncommitted?" with convictions of Third World artists. Kosinski observes that

> While a writer's primary commitment does not seem to have changed, his audience's receptivity has diminished. The majority of contemporary society, trained by the mass media to expect the simplest situations and emotions, can no longer digest the novel, whose intent is the expansion

of individual consciousness. The 'normal' readership is continually bombarded by visual images, and has been trained by television to observe without becoming engaged, to experience 'art' as passive reception. Ironically, the only truly unaffected audience now is the blind, whose access to literature is wholly through the imagination. Thus at a time when so much of the mass media — both visual and verbal — tends to retard individual and social awareness, the writer's ability to counteract fragmentation and isolation is particularly valuable. In the absence of any religious sustenance, the creation of an internal imaginative world is the only remaining means to emotional integration. [*American PEN Newsletter*, Summer 1973]

In the "atomized society" Kosinski refers to, the artist grapples with "the unknown, his own existence." Skeptical despair, cynicism, withdrawal into an abstract subjectivism open to irrational (fascist) machinations, the metaphysical dilettantism of artistic experiments divorced from the mass struggles of working people — these characterize the self-appraisals of bourgeois writers published in *Partisan Review, New York Review of Books, Encounter,* etc.

On the other hand, we have the intransigent principles of Third World writers:

The poet does not have a different personality when he writes than when he talks or fights. A poet is not a degenerate dreaming that he is flying in the clouds, he is a citizen engaged in life, organizing life.
— Nazim Hikmet (Turkey)

Today, for the first time, the writer's valid words prove that the words of Power are invalid. . . . The fact is that the head of the most powerful nation in the world was run out of his post by the students, intellectuals, journalists, writers, by men with no other weapon than words. . . . Nobody can remember the Alamo, the *Maine*, the *Lusitania* or Pearl Harbor to justify daily murder and destruction in Vietnam. No "manifest destiny" convinces us that in order to insure the doubtful democracy of South Vietnam's oligarchs a country must be erased from the map with napalm and phosphorus. Similarly, nobody can be content with simply asking for proper legislation to resolve the black problem, which is not a legal problem but one of alienation and which is not a conflict of feelings but of being. In those conditions, words become rhetoric on the side of power and heresy on the side of dissent: words deny the orthodox position assigned to them by the Founding Fathers.
—Carlos Fuentes (Mexico)

The days are over when the artist was a new Narcissus who, before the mirror of the stream, marvelled and adored the shadow of his own self. The artist is now a witness and part of the immediate present. . . . The artist is directly involved, as participant and member of society, in the lot of men with whom he has been destined to live. He knows that he is part of society, a part that contributes to the whole but also receives from the whole. Like Antaeus in mythology who fought with Hercules, the artist must needs stand always on solid earth, his feet on the soil, because from the heat and power of the soil spring the life and strength of his body.

— Amado V. Hernandez (Philippines)

I would be quite satisfied if my novels (especially the ones I set in the past) did no more than teach my readers that their past — with all its imperfections — was not one long night of savagery from which the first Europeans acting on God's behalf delivered them. Perhaps what I write is applied art as distinct from pure. But who cares? Art is important but so is education of the kind I have in mind. And I don't see that the two need be mutually exclusive.

— Chinua Achebe (Nigeria)

In the uneven development of social forces in the Third World, the central task of the artist is to demystify the class-distorted picture of the world established by imperialist domination. His vocation is to undermine, not reinforce, the predominant interest of the ruling class. In order to dismantle the sacrosanct engines of repression, one must reform public opinion and restore to the masses their self-confidence, their long-suppressed tradition of resourcefulness and creativity. The principal task, namely, to transform the people as an object (in-itself) to a subject (for-itself), also presupposes and entails converting the deracinated native intellectuals into revolutionary cadres serving the people. That is what, I believe, the May 4th Movement in China essentially accomplished. It is the task the National Democratic Cultural Revolution in the Philippines pursued when the pettybourgeois writers and artists committed "class suicide" (to use Cabral's phrase) and intergrated with the masses in militant practice. Art followed the principle of the mass line: "from the masses, to the masses" (Mao Tsetung).

Literary critics and aestheticians in monopoly capitalist society react violently and often ignorantly to the radical conception of art as an ideological weapon in the class struggle. Rejecting art as a coherent mode of apprehending the contradictions of society, they define art as an autotelic structure of qualities expressing non-class attitudes and values.

They reject art's function of mediating between class consciousness and the historical situation, not simply mirroring but revealing in typical synthesis the interconnected trends and tendencies of the whole historical process: what is coming into being, what is passing away. They deny the mimetic process and its educational impact because they accept exclusively, perhaps with some nuanced qualifications, the organic-expressive-formalistic notion of art. What they really want is to refute the bourgeois concept of "economic determinism" in striving to denounce the tendentious, didactic theory of art. In doing so, they betray utter contempt for art as a social performance, a powerful instrument for shaping men's minds and therefore their collective vision of the good life.

Meanwhile, for the Third World peoples confronted daily with degrading poverty, hunger, disease, racist bigotry and genocidal weapons, art spells life or death.

Unquestionably there are moral and material incentives to combat art propagating imperialist domination. Should not the partisans of "socialist realism," the followers of Plekhanov, Lukacs, Gramsci, Sartre, Althusser, Brecht, etc. try to link up the proletarian cultural revolution in the metropolis with the Third World's anti-imperialist struggle in the ideological realm — as Lenin exhorted time and again? Should we welcome the transitional third way of "critical realism" to afford liberal reformist writers room to exercise their subtle wit, their moralizing paradoxes, their ironic satire which often leads to cosmic nihilism if not to perverse postures of self-pitying ego trips? Should artists in Asia, Africa and Latin America overthrow the stranglehold of U.S. corporations and the Hollywood-Madison Avenue apparatus by expropriating the techniques of John Cage, Le Corbusier, Norman Mailer, Robbe-Grillet, Pop Art, and Happenings?

To repeat a commonplace: Marxism is a method of analysis, a critique, a guide to action, not a set of metaphysical dogmas. Consequently, one cannot legislate on what artistic method or style revolutionary artists participating in the national liberation struggle should adopt. Moreover, there is a combined unity-struggle of opposites in every conjuncture of events, at every stage of the total revolutionary process.

At the same time, however, one cannot be so eclectic that in trying to avoid the fixation on a doctrinaire mystique of the "proletariat" regardless of prevailing class alignments, especially in Third World societies, he succumbs to the futile notion that since the bourgeoisie (according to the *Communist Manifesto*) was once historically progressive, therefore Third World artists should assiduously cultivate their knowledge of Shakespeare, Milton, Dante, Goethe, Cervantes, etc. Recall that these names, representing the great Western dispensation, have been used by the colonial administrators to justify bludgeoning to death millions of Africans, Asians, Arabs, and Latin Americans.

We are surely not accusing Shakespeare and company, but this only proves that we cannot measure the humane worth of art and literature apart from the unified structure of values or world-outlook, the ideological motivations and judgments, the resolutions and programmes for action incorporated in them. This is not to say that art is equivalent to agit-prop. In his "Talks at the Yenan Forum on Literature and Art," Mao Tsetung suggests that for the revolutionary artist, the question "For whom?" is a fundamental question of principle. Mao asserts and elaborates:

> In the world today all culture, all literature and art belong to definite classes and are geared to definite political lines. . . .
>
> Although man's social life is the only source of literature and art and is incomparably livelier and richer in content, the people are not satisfied with life alone and demand literature and art as well. Why? Because, while both are beautiful, life as reflected in works of literature and art can and ought to be on a higher plane, more intense, more concentrated, more typical, nearer the ideal, and therefore more universal than actual everyday life. Revolutionary literature and art should create a variety of characters out of real life and help the masses to propel history forward. For example, there is suffering from hunger, cold and oppression on the one hand, and exploitation and oppression of man by man on the other. These facts exist everywhere and people look upon them as commonplace. Writers and artists concentrate such everyday phenomena, typify the contradictions and struggles within them and produce works which awaken the masses, fire them with enthusiasm and impel them to unite and struggle to transform their environment. [*Selected Readings from the Works of Mao Tsetung*, p. 266]

Of course, Mao's thought should not be regarded as absolute dogma. His talk does not deal, and is not meant to deal, with the intricate criteria for judging the efficacy of certain modes, techniques, idioms, in achieving a socialist goal. But Mao's summing up — "the raising of standards is based on popularization, while popularization [N.B. not to be confused with "vulgarization"] is guided by the raising of standards" — precisely states in dialectical form the Party policy for doing artistic work among the masses. (Note that Mao is not at all preoccupied with the "liberated psyche" of the artist, self-confrontation, etc.)

We can illustrate how Mao's principle is applied by the Palestinian poets of the Resistance (e.g., Mahmoud Darweesh) in their unrelenting project of demystifying their exile, exposing its historical alterability, and thus energizing their audience into directed political action. But that will require another essay in its own right.

Suffice it here to demonstrate in brief how false consciousness evolves to class consciousness, how social practice vindicates the viably humane function of art, by quoting at length the words of two Vietnamese authors recorded in Peter Weiss's inspiring testimony and tribute to the genuine avant-garde, the people's artists, *Notes on the Cultural Life of the Democratic Republic of Vietnam*:

BUI HIEN —
> We wrote out of hate and out of sympathy. We wrote about the lives of oppressed people. At the beginning our class point of view was not clear. For the most part we writers came from the *petite bourgeoisie*. We had little education. Yet the *petite bourgeoisie* in colonial conditions is close to the have-nots. To their misery and also to their stubbornness. Still, we had not as yet become aware of the root causes of want and impoverishment. Not until the revolution did we grasp the full extent of the crime that had been perpetrated on our country.
>
> We lived in the midst of the masses, who were demanding their rights. This much is common to all of us: we took our themes from the daily existence of the peasants, the industrial workers, the fishermen, and the soldiers in combat.
>
> At first we simply transcribed events. In their raw, unorganized form. We kept to the surface of things. We still did not know enough about the thoughts of the people with whom we were living. That was our childhood sickness. We were blinded by the light of the revolution. But one night I saw the true face of my fellow man:
>
> We were in a heavily contested area. The enemy was sending up flares. The road and the shell-cratered fields were bathed in white light. Then I saw the faces. Faces of soldiers, of women, girls, children. They all stood there heavily laden, weighted down, carrying weapons, ammunition, and heavy loads of food carried on yokes. They held their heads high. These faces burned themselves into my gaze. They are imperishable.
>
> Formerly we reproduced our impressions in brief sketches. Today we go beyond the immediate event. We describe the struggle in its basic outlines. Behind the uplifted radiant faces we see the goal, the objective of the war. [pages 62-63]

NGUYEN DINH THI —

These peasants and soldiers, these self-taught people, are not trying to change literature by experimenting with the use of language. What they want to do is change the reader, their own world. For us a book is a weapon. . . .

With us everything has to do with realistic action. At the present time we need, above all, descriptions of the situation as it exists. We try to analyze events. Insofar as we make clear what is happening within people, show how they are holding firm, what they are accomplishing, we contribute to a strengthening of the power to resist. It is natural that from time to time the toil, the pain of losing some member of the family, the never-ending pressure of destruction, should overshadow hope. It would be inhuman to suppose that deprivations continuing year after year would leave no mark. Our consciousness for the time being is satisfied with a clear presentation of the perspectives of the people's war. We remind people of the indignities of colonialism, of the gigantic efforts which led to revolution, of the successes achieved during the years of construction. Our literature holds fast, it affirms. It assimilates the difficult experiences since the bombing attacks. Literature absorbs what the people have accumulated by way of thinking power and self-control. . . . We use a mode of expression understood by all . . . Aesthetics interests us only as a means of advancing elucidation. Our literature is intended to be political, to have a practical application. [pages 70-71]

NOTES

1. Vestiges of this abstract mode of thinking inhere in Fidel Castro's formula of "Within the Revolution, everything; against the Revolution, nothing" as guideline for Cuban artists; see his "Words to the Intellectuals" in Lee Baxandall, *Radical Perspectives in the Arts*, 1972, pp. 267-300. For recent developments, see Roberta Salper, "Literature and Revolution in Cuba," *Monthly Review* (October 1970), 15-30.

2. The literature on imperialism is enormous. The most useful are: Harry Magdoff, *The Age of Imperialism*, 1969; Paul Baran, *The Political Economy of Growth*, 1957; Jack Woddis, *Introduction to Neo-Colonialism*, 1972; K.T. Fann and D.C. Hodges, *Readings in U.S. Imperialism*, 1971; Andre Gunder Frank, *Capitalism and Underdevelopment in Latin America*, 1967.

3. The lessons of China's Cultural Revolution should highlight the crucial role of the intelligentsia in revolutionizing the superstructure as well as the total social

relations. In his article "Marxism and Mao," *Partisan Review*, XL, 1973, sociology professor Alvin W. Gouldner comments on the unique Chinese policy undergirding the educational reforms brought about by the Cultural Revolution, especially the changing of the traditional nature and function of the intelligentsia: "In the self-understanding of Maoism, the aim is to debourgeoisify the intellectual, to eliminate the rift between intellectuals and masses, to change the class character of intellectuals predominantly from workers or peasants, and themselves have an extensive personal experience of laboring as peasants or workers. This, to repeat, is Maoism's self-understanding of its policy toward the intelligentsia."

4. I am deeply indebted to Professor Omafume F. Onoge's unpublished essay "The Crisis of Consciousness in Modern African Literature: A Survey" for many valuable insights into the African cultural scene.

5. From "Art in the One-Dimensional Society" in *Radical Perspectives in the Arts*, edited by Lee Baxandall, Pelican Books, 1972, p. 58.

PART II

LITERATURE IN HISTORY

8

FALSTAFF AND HIS SOCIAL MILIEU

Paul N. Siegel

The theoretical groundwork of Marxist literary criticism may be said to be most succinctly expressed in this statement of Engels: "Political, juridical, philosophical, religious, literary, artistic, etc., development is based on economic development. But all these react upon one another and also upon the economic base. It is not that the economic position is the *cause and alone active*, while everything else only has a passive effect. There is, rather, interaction on the basis of the economic necessity, which *ultimately* always asserts itself." There are interactions within and between the various intellectual systems that are put together by the ideologists of the ruling class — the "ruling ideas of each age" being, as Marx said, "the ideas of its ruling class" — and there are also reactions upon the economic base. Economic development, however, changing men's social relations and consequently men's ways of looking upon life, is the stronger force in the interaction between what Marxists call the economic base and the ideological superstructure.

Marxists hold that the fields of intellectual activity worked in by scholars have only a relative autonomy. They will, for instance, recognize as a great work of scholarship Lovejoy's tracing of the development of the idea of the great chain of being, but they will ask how the different world pictures making use of this idea in the medieval, the Renaissance, and the neo-classical periods were rationalizations of the social position of the ruling class in each case. They will pose similar questions in considering the work of the literary historian who traces the development of a literary movement, asking what are the new social stimuli which caused a literary movement to take the course it did or what caused a new literary movement to break away from the old one. In short, Marxists seek to analyze the relation of literature to the other elements of the cultural superstructure and to the economic base upon which the superstructure is ultimately dependent. In so doing, they may make use of the results of the different kinds of literary scholarship — the study of the development of literary form and of the relation of the development of literature to the history of ideas, the history of science, the history of religion, and so forth — in which the spheres of ideological activity are seen as independent entities, come from God knows where and each an "influence" on the others, instead of being the different manifestations of a unified process of social development which Marxism finds them to be.

This is the method which I sought to apply to the study of Shakespeare in two books, *Shakespearean Tragedy and the Elizabethan Compromise* and *Shakespeare in His Time and Ours,* where I developed the thesis that Shakespeare's drama is an expression of the Christian humanist ideology of the new Tudor aristocracy. In an essay in the second book, "Shakespeare and the Neo-chivalric Cult of Honor," I showed that Hotspur is representative of feudal chivalry at its best, but with its characteristic defects, and that he recalls the powerful Elizabethan nobles of northern England, which remained half feudal up to the civil war of the next century. At the time of the Northern Rebellion early in Elizabeth's reign the members of the great Percy family, of which Hotspur was one of its well known ancestors, proclaimed that they only wanted to protect themselves against the newly made peers of the queen, who were plotting to suppress the ancient nobility. Hotspur's concept of honor is not that of the new Tudor aristocracy but that of the old aristocracy with strong feudal traditions, who argued that for the sake of one's honor it was proper even to fight against one's own country. In killing Hotspur, Hal, who has "a truant been to chivalry," takes over Hotspur's chivalric values, in accordance with the new aristocratic ideal of the courtier in which the virtues of the medieval knight are amalgamated with those of the humanistic scholar, but he purges them of their accompanying faults. In assuming the chivalric virtues in modified form, Hal gives up the frivolous irresponsibility of the tavern knight Falstaff, the degenerate descendant of the feudal gentry, as Hotspur is the best representative of feudal chivalry.

In the remainder of this paper I wish to expand on this observation about Falstaff, to explore more fully his place in Elizabethan society, and to discuss how this may enable us better to understand his character and the plays in which he appears. Bourgeois scholars have found that entering into Falstaff's making were such literary traditions as the braggart soldier and the clever parasite of classical comedy, the Vice of the morality play, the Devil of the miracle play, the Riot of the interlude, the Lord of Misrule, and the privileged court jester. The Marxist critic does not deny the existence of such traditions that enter into the shaping of literary works, for he is aware that the writer must, in writing the literature of his time, use the material bequeathed him by the past. All of these traditions did indeed enter into Shakespeare's rich comic creation, but Falstaff is something different than any of them or the sum total of them. He is drawn from the life of Shakespeare's London. John W. Draper, Lily B. Campbell, and Paul Jorgensen have shown him to follow the corrupt practices of accepting bribes for not pressing men into service and of padding the muster-rolls to receive more money, which went into his pocket, practices of which Elizabethan army officers were frequently accused. They conclude that Falstaff is a representation of an Elizabethan army officer. But while Falstaff's occupation after Hal has got for him the command of an infantry company is that of an army officer — he is not, however, an army officer in *The Merry Wives of Windsor* — he is not merely the member of an occupation but of a class.

Engels, writing in 1859 to Ferdinand Lassalle concerning Lassalle's historical drama *Franz von Sickingen,* said: "What wonderfully distinctive character portraits are to be found during this period of the breakdown of feudalism — penniless ruling kings, impoverished hireling soldiers and adventurers of all sorts — a Falstaffian background. . ." Without seeming to know this passage in Engels, which he does not cite, the British Marxist T.A. Jackson developed this idea in a fine essay published in 1936 in *International Literature* that has been overlooked by Shakespearean scholars, in which he wrote of Falstaff as follows:

> Shakespeare, in depicting Falstaff and his crew, depicted from life, in vivid truth, the phenomena of *decadence*, the degeneration and decomposition of an absolute class — that of the dependants upon the feudal order. . . . In form Falstaff's company is a quasi-feudal military company headed by a knight. In substance and in fact they are a crew of degenerate thieves, parasites, and spongers, foot-pads, tavern bullies, souteneurs and tricksters. Their lives and their ends follow closely the line followed in actual fact by Francois Villon in Paris, a century before Shakespeare's birth, while as more or less amusing scoundrels they form one of the earliest examples of the *picaresque* — the line. . . which is, as Maxim Gorki has pointed out, the nearest to an *heroic* line, persisting all through bourgeois literature from its beginnings.

By the end of the sixteenth century, London, the leading commercial city of Europe and the center of wealth in England, had swelled to twice the size it had been in the time of Henry VIII. It sucked into itself from all parts of the country a motley crew of fortune-seekers, including impoverished feudalistic gentry, whose fixed rents were reduced in value during this time of capitalistic expansion and inflation, feudal retainers and serving men who had been laid off, and professional soldiers, drawn in large part from these classes, who were out of service between foreign wars. But it was not only these who constituted the lively underworld of London. Jackson's reference to Villon came close to Elizabethan reality in ways of which he seemed unaware. The graduates of the expanded universities were, as an academic dramatic trilogy, *The Pilgrimage to Parnassus*, makes clear, unable to find jobs sufficient for their numbers. Literary patronage was also partly breaking down, and the literary market-place accommodated only penurious hacks. Representative of these hacks was Robert Greene, a Bohemian like Villon, although, unlike him, untrue to his Bohemianism, he produced on his death-bed (perhaps for money, perhaps for salvation), not a mocking self-epitaph but a fervent, even fevered, pamphlet proclaiming his repentance. The sensational manner in which Greene regaled his readers with the sins of thought and action he had committed shows how shocked citizens regarded these dangerous elements in their midst.

Down-and-out university men, down-and-out former soldiers, down-and-out cast-outs of the declining feudal sector of society, assorted riff-raff pretending to be soldiers returned from the wars, travellers returned from abroad, and gentlemen of ancient lineage—all of these were the declassed members of the London underworld. The way of life of Falstaff and his crew is theirs. As Jackson points out, Pistol's "Base is the soul that pays!" expresses "the innermost soul of 'Bohemianism' from Francois Villon, jesting before the gallows, down to this day." But it is not only in his way of life that Falstaff resembles Greene, but in his rejection of conventional belief. Falstaff, to be sure, parades his religion, although it is only lip-service, amusingly contrasted with his actions, while Greene, as well as Marlowe, the great Elizabethan rebel who had his being in this Bohemian milieu, were charged with privately flouting it, but Falstaff in his catechism on honor rejects conventional belief as they do. So Robert Louis Stevenson with an artist's perception has Villon contemptuously refute the notion of aristocratic honor in his "A Lodging for the Night."

Of all of the Elizabethan descriptions of the members of the underworld the closest in a number of ways to Falstaff is the burlesque description of another tavern knight, "The Melancholy Knight," by the

Elizabethan versifier, Samuel Rowlands. The melancholy knight, speaking in the tavern which is his haunt, tells of how his wife spends more than the rents he receives from his estate. His melancholy is very definitely connected with his economic situation:

> The Golden Age and Silver is decayed:
> Oh, now comes on a melancholy fit,
> To write of gold and not possess a whit.

He bewails the fact that a cobbler can buy more for cash than he for credit, and, while proudly proclaiming his knightliness, will not fight even if this means permitting others to call him a liar, "knowing I often lie when none perceives it."

So too Falstaff, full of comic exuberance and enormous vitality though he be, is vain of his knighthood and sometimes mournfully deplores his come-down and his way of life. The waiters at the tavern think of him as a "proud Jack," Mistress Quickly tells of how, on promising her marriage, he advised her to leave off her familiarity with her friends, for before long they would call her "madam," and Poins, reading Falstaff's impudent letter to the Prince, exclaims at the first words: 'John Falstaff, knight,' — every man must know that, as oft as he has occasion to name himself; even like those that are kin to the King, for they never prick their finger but they say, 'There's some of the King's blood spilt.' " In *Henry IV, Part I* he is continually voicing repentance for living in a manner unbecoming a gentleman. "If I do grow great," he says, having claimed the reward for valor in having "killed" Hotspur, "I'll grow less; for I'll purge, and leave sack, and live cleanly as a nobleman should do."

Repentance and melancholy go together: "The devil was sick, the devil a monk would be." " 'Sblood," sighs Falstaff, put in mind of the gallows which awaits highwaymen by the Prince's persistent jokes, "I am as melancholy as a gib cat or a lugg'd bear," and goes on, "Hal, I prithee, trouble me no more with vanity." His melancholy, like that of Rowlands' melancholy knight, is partly affectation, for melancholy was the Byronic pose of disaffected gentlemen or pretended gentlemen of the time, but Falstaff's melancholy is his very own. It is as deep and long-lived as his repentance: he bounds from it with his characteristic resilience. It serves his humor, however, to reverse the truth by speaking of himself as a melancholiac, just as it does to speak of himself as an innocent misled by a wicked Prince of Wales: "A plague of sighing and grief! It blows a man up like a bladder." Like Villon, although he engages in lamentation, he is really distinguished by his vitality.

In *Henry IV, Part II,* however, having, like so many other Elizabethan sham soldiers, acquired a bogus military reputation on which for a time he can get credit, he speaks no longer of repenting. He has given up the dangerous profession of highwayman for swindling. He continues, however, to maintain his pretence as a young blood. Whereas before he had valiantly assaulted the peaceful travellers on the highway with the cry, "What, ye knaves! Young men must live," he now inveighs against the age which cannot appreciate and make use of such gallants as he: "You that are old consider not the capacities of us that are young." For in "these costermongers' times," in this commercial age of successful tradesmen, all that valiant men can find to do is the ignominious taking charge of the bears used in bear-baiting and all that clever men can find to do is adding up the bills for drinks in acting as waiters in taverns. Why, things are come to such a sorry pass that merchants lead gentlemen on into debt and then demand security before giving them more credit.

Thus in his disdain for the commercialism and the degeneracy of the age, in his pride in his lineage, in his sometimes assumed melancholy, and in his lying and cowardice (I regard as settled the famous controversy about Falstaff's cowardice) — Falstaff resembles Rowlands' melancholy knight. This is probably not because Rowlands, who wrote his poem after the Falstaff plays, recalled Falstaff. It is because both Falstaff and the melancholy knight are representative of the same social class.

The Falstaff of *The Merry Wives of Windsor* is often said to be another fat knight with the same name. This is, however, rather exaggerated. The Falstaff of *The Merry Wives of Windsor* remains his old self in his referring to himself as a young blood, in his talking about repenting, and in his continuing to make use of his ingenious and blustering form of argumentation in speaking to Pistol. He has degenerated more than ever, but this degeneration is a logical progression, a progression which had already been exhibited in *Henry V*, where Shakespeare, with relentless artistic honesty, had had Bardolph die on the gallows for robbing French churches, where Pistol had become a pimp and a cut-purse, and where Dame Quickly had died of syphilis. In Falstaff's first appearance in *The Merry Wives of Windsor* he is turning away his retainers, Bardolph, Pistol, and Nym, whom he can no longer keep up, and announcing his need to live by the worst kind of thievery and trickery. Whereas in *Henry IV, Part I* he had followed the tradition of the robber barons in robbing travellers on the highway and in *Henry IV, Part II* he had followed the custom of the impoverished gallant of not paying his debts to the tradesmen, he now accepts a share of the petty loot of his followers, who have degenerated into pickpockets, swearing in their behalf that they are honest, soldierly servingmen. More than this, he thinks to be paid by Mrs. Ford and Mrs. Page for honoring them with his love and plays the part of a pimp toward the supposed Master Brook, although this is only the game of a confidence man who does not plan to come across with the goods.

It is true, however, that in *The Merry Wives of Windsor* Falstaff is an easy butt, having lost the mental agility which had enabled him to escape from his predicaments, although not without some laughter at his expense. The quick-witted old scoundrel has become a ridiculous old lecher at the mercy of the clever middle-class wives. Karl Kautsky in his *Thomas More and His Utopia* says that *The Merry Wives of Windsor*, which pictures the "struggle between decrepit knighthood and the upward striving capitalist class," is "the exuberant shout of joy of the advancing bourgeoisie." However, the tradition dating from the eighteenth century that *The Merry Wives of Windsor* is a court play gains strong evidence, as has been pointed out by William Green in his *Shakespeare's Merry Wives of Windsor*, from the allusions in the play to Queen Elizabeth, Windsor Castle, and the Order of the Garter. The mishaps in love and the final exposure of the degenerate old knight, so proud of his lineage and so unknightly in his behavior, who had stooped to two citizens' wives and stumbled as he stooped, would have tickled a court audience, as had the ludicrous love for a country wench and the final exposure of the pretender to gentility, Don Armado, in *Love's Labors Lost*. Falstaff's flattery is unable to turn the heads of the merry but honest wives, who in their bourgeois country-town milieu know their place in society, scoffing at the notion that they were meant to be court ladies. So too Page objects to his daughter marrying Master Fenton not only because that gentleman had squandered his fortune but because Page is suspicious about marrying outside of one's class: "He is of too high a region." These bourgeois are from a conservative sector of the bourgeoisie, not at all upward striving.

"If it were not for one trifling respect," says Mrs. Ford ironically, "I could come to such honour! . . . If I would but go to hell for an eternal moment or so, I could be knighted." For Falstaff, however, "honour," here as in *Henry IV, Part I*, is but an empty word, and, since it is that for a knight such as he, it must, he thinks, be so for every one. When Pistol demurs at acting as Falstaff's pander, Falstaff indignantly asks him how dare he speak of his honor when Sir John Falstaff himself is at times constrained to forget about his.

What is the secret of the power and attraction of this old scoundrel, especially in the Henry plays? One answer, I should say, lies in his questioning of conventional values, even though that questioning springs from an absence of all values except for those of mere egoism. It reminds us that the conventional call to duty may be destructive if unthinkingly obeyed. If Falstaff's rejection of honor, a rationalization for his cowardice, is amusingly contemptible, in addition to being amusingly adroit, Hotspur's devotion to honor causes him to be manipulated by the crafty politician Worcester and to bring havoc to England, just as appeals to national honor were used to justify the worst crimes against humanity in Vietnam. The juxtaposition of Hotspur's comments on honor and Falstaff's comments on it is, as has been frequently pointed out, certainly significant.

But it is not only Hotspur and the feudal nobility whose values are questioned by Falstaff. The language in which he addresses the travellers whom he and his companions rob questions the values of another class. The travellers consist of a group of franklins. Franklins were prosperous landowners below the gentry in social position, who, as we can see from the description of Chaucer's franklin, had a reputation for good living off the fat of the land. Falstaff, as he and his companions dash out at them, cries out: "Strike! Down with them! Cut the villains' throats! Ah, whoreson caterpillars! Bacon-fed knaves! They hate us youth. Down with them! Fleece them!" The travellers exclaim in fear, "O, we are undone, both we and ours for ever!" and Falstaff responds, "Hang ye, gorbellied knaves, are ye undone? No, ye fat chuffs; I would your store were here!"

Of course, part of the humor lies in the fact that Falstaff, the greatest of parasites, calls the franklins "caterpillars," the current term for parasites, that he, who is by his own admission close to sixty, presents himself as youth confronting age, that he, whose girth undoubtedly surpasses theirs, great as theirs undoubtedly is, calls them "gorbellied." Part of the humor also lies, however, in the suggestion that they are fat rogues of another kind and that in some sense there is little to choose between Falstaff and them as they stand quaking in fear before the hectoring of one who, unknown to them, is as great a coward as they. For commercial farmers had long been denounced for applying the screws to the peasantry, accumulating the pelf which Falstaff wishes were there so that he might deprive them of it and really ruin them. Handy-dandy, which is the thief?

In denouncing the franklins, Falstaff is obviously not speaking as a moralist or a reformer. He is associating himself with Bohemian youth against the fat, comfortable bourgeois. The confrontation between philistine father and Bohemian son has taken place since the early days of capitalism. Today, during the period of late capitalism, with its alienated labor and its frantic consumerism, the disaffection of youth in the United States, although not as acute as it was during the war in Vietnam, is far wider and deeper than it ever had been in previous periods. "They hate us youth" can stand as emblem for the feeling of many in our time.

Even more important than Falstaff as a questioner of conventional values in explaining his enduring attraction is Falstaff as the possessor of a zest for life that is unaffected by his circumstances. Robert Burns in his "The Jolly Beggars" drew an unforgettable picture of humanity in the midst of misery and degradation snatching some gayety from existence. Falstaff and his crew do the same in their tavern. They are a tribute to the thirst for life and the human solidarity that persists in despite of squalor. "Would I were with him," says the much abused Bardolph of the dead Falstaff, "wheresom'er he is, either in heaven or in hell!"

Falstaff, subtly drawn though he be, is based on the tradition of the clown or buffoon, the comic figure who throughout theatrical history has acted as the expression of man's irrepressible spirit. "The buffoon," says Susanne K. Langer in *Feeling and Form*, "is essentially a folk character, that has persisted through the more sophisticated and literary stages of comedy as Harlequin, Pierrot, the Persian Karaguez, the Elizabethan jester or fool, the *Vidusaka* of Sanskrit drama; but in the humbler theatrical forms that entertained the poor and especially the peasantry before the movies came, the buffoon had a more vigorous existence as Hans Wurst, as Punch of the puppet show, the clown of pantomime, the Turkish Karagoz (borrowed from Persian tradition) who belongs to the shadow play. These anciently popular personages show what the buffoon really is: the indomitable living creature fending for itself, tumbling and stumbling (as the clown physically illustrates) from one situation into another, getting into scrape after scrape and getting out again, with or without a thrashing." The great clown of today, of course, is Charlie Chaplin's tramp, always being chased away by the cop, but always returning after the cop has gone, and always maintaining his shabby elegance through everything.

So Falstaff too is a comic figure outside of the confines of the regular social order. Combining the highest reaches of wit and the horseplay of farce, he always finds ways of talking himself out of uncomfortable situations, even though he often has to endure some twitting, and, on being physically attacked by Hal and Poins, manages to run away, roaring as the clown does in his mishaps, and pricked on by a thrust at his rear. That the fat knight, heavy of body but nimble of mind, old in years but youthful in elan, is thus representative of the enduring spirit of ordinary humanity coping through the ages with the knocks of a rough world is his final triumphant paradox.

9

SEX AND POLITICS
in Pope's "Rape of the Lock"

Sheila Delany

Although Pope's *Rape of the Lock* is not an openly partisan piece, it has nonetheless a politics which differs little from that of Pope's other work. The politics of the *Rape of the Lock* is expressed in two major ways: in the sexual attitudes of its characters, and in the narrator's comments. Sexual behavior functions in the poem as an analogue to political behavior. In Belinda and the Baron we observe attitudes which, limited to themselves, have only private consequences, but which, practiced generally, have important public meaning as well. In criticizing Belinda and the Baron, Pope criticizes the social class which behaves politically as they do personally. That larger perspective appears in various passages of commentary, scattered through the poem and ranging in tone from solemn sincerity to sharpest irony. Through these passages the poem achieves its fullest meaning, for in them Pope expands his canvas from "high society" to society at large.

It will be the purpose of my paper to define the politics of the *Rape of the Lock*. I want to begin by placing the poem in its social context, and here I use "social" to mean both the larger political situation and the more immediate personal dispute which called forth the *Rape of the Lock*. A reading of the poem will follow, which I hope will show that Pope's version of sexual politics both reflects his general political attitude, and shares its limitations. While my conclusions will not suprise, they do represent a critical approach which has not been fully exercised on this best-known and most engaging of Pope's works.

I

The subject of the *Rape of the Lock* is love among the nobility. The poem was commissioned in 1711 by Pope's friend John Caryll, a wealthy squire. Its purpose was to reconcile two great Catholic land-owning families whose quarrel began when Robert, 7th Lord Petre, a relative of Caryll, snipped a lock of Miss Arabella Fermor's hair.

Pope himself had by this time become part of the high society he wrote about, though he was the son of a Catholic linen-merchant and inherited only a modest legacy from his father. Yet the poet's combination of literary genius and political tact won him the appreciation of noble patrons of both political parties, while the fortune he earned from his writing enabled him to remain financially independent of them. Pope cultivated the acquaintance of the rich and famous, and among his friends counted some of the most powerful and distinguished figures of the age. They included George Granville, Baron Lansdowne, the Tory electoral manager who requested that Pope revise his pastoral *Windsor Forest* into a celebration of the Tory Peace of Utrecht and the glories of Anne's regime; John Arbuthnot, Queen Anne's physician; Henry St. John, Viscount Bolingbroke, secretary of state to Queen Anne and Pope's lifelong friend to whom the *Essay on Man* is addressed; James Craggs, secretary at war and secretary of state under George I; Bishop William Warburton, preacher to Lincoln's Inn, Chaplain to King George II and Pope's literary executor. Pope was all his life distinguished by what his biographer Samuel Johnson called "voracity of fame," and lived to have his desire amply fulfilled.

What can we learn about the *Rape of the Lock* from Pope's personal response to the central figure in the aristocratic feud he had been asked to mediate? The question seems to violate the most sacred precept of criticism, in disregarding the distinction between Pope's personal opinions and his poetry, or between life and art in general. Yet in the case of the *Rape of the Lock*, the connection between life and art is unusually close, and few of Pope's contemporaries failed to make that connection. Moreover, there is no fixed esthetic distance between the artist and his art. With Chaucer it is often a mistake to confuse narrator with poet, whereas with Pope that identification is rarely wrong, and with a poet like Sylvia Plath, personal and poetic voices are virtually identical. Given the special circumstances in which the *Rape of the Lock* was composed, and given the usual particularity of Pope's poetry, an acquaintance with Pope's real opinions can only illuminate the work of art in which he explores at leisure the moral and social questions raised by an apparently trivial event.

In a famous essay[1] Cleanth Brooks has argued that Pope felt quite fully his heroine's charm, and that we are intended to feel it too. In emphasizing what he considers to be the ambivalence of Belinda's character and of Pope's attitude toward her, Brooks inflates the psychological dimension of the poem at the expense of its prominent social themes. I shall argue that Pope is far from being ambivalent about his heroine or her real model, and that his attitude toward both is more hostile than the polite critic might wish it to be. The complexity of tone in the poem comes, in my view, not from the character of Belinda, then, but from the nature of the society she inhabits.

In the autumn of 1714, Pope wrote a congratulatory letter to Miss Fermor after her marriage. The letter is a model of stiffly elegant courtesy, far different in tone from what Pope was capable of writing to women he liked. But let us hear Pope when he is writing to one such woman, his intimate friend Martha Blount, on the subject of Miss Fermor's marriage:

> My Acquaintance runs so much in an Anti-Catholic channel, that it was but tother day I heard of Mrs Fermor's being Actually, directly, and consummatively, married. I wonder how the guilty Couple and their Accessories at Whiteknights look, stare, or simper, since that grand Secret came out which they so well concealed before. They concealed it as well as a Barber does his Utensils when he goes to trim upon a Sunday and his Towels hang out all the way: Or as well as a Fryer concealed a little Wench, whom he was carrying under his Habit to Mr Collingwood's Convent: Pray Father (Sayd one in the street to him) what's that under your Arm. A saddle for one of the Brothers to ride with, quoth the Fryer. Then Father (cryd he) take care and shorten the stirrups — For the Girls Legs hung out — [2]

This letter suggests that Arabella Fermor had good reason to fear the gossip to which the *Rape of the Lock* exposed her, and that Pope's attitude toward her, when he was not writing for the public, consisted of a somewhat prurient contempt.

That the Fermors were not wholly pleased with Pope's effort is hardly suprising, and in a letter to Caryll (8 November, 1712), Pope disingenuously remarks that "the celebrated lady herself is offended, and, which is stranger, not at herself, but me." Pope managed to appease the lady and clear her name by attaching to the 1714 edition of the poem an unctuously flattering dedication, in which he assures Arabella that "the character of Belinda . . . resembles you in nothing but in Beauty." Yet such flattery rings hollow next to Pope's patronizing explanation of the machinery of the poem: "I know how disagreeable it is," he begins, "to make use of hard words before a Lady . . ." One is reminded of the portrait of Atticus in the *Epistle* to Doctor Arbuthnot; for the *Rape of the Lock*, with its prefatory letter, shows how well Pope himself could

> Damn with faint praise, assent with civil leer,
> And without sneering, teach the rest to sneer.

Pope's letter to Martha Blount shows him well-armed against the charm of even such a famous beauty as Arabella Fermor. His additions to the *Rape of the Lock* beyond its original 334 lines confirm the harshness of his judgment of Belinda. The additions include the machinery of the Sylphs, through which the deficiencies in Belinda's character are more fully exposed. They also include some of the most cuttingly ironical and damaging lines in the poem, many sexual innuendoes, and the important "touchstone" speech of Clarissa, whose "good sense" Belinda rejects.

All this suggests, then, that the complexity of the *Rape of the Lock* is not located in character. The source of complexity in the work is rather to be located in those passages which deal with Belinda's social world; here Pope's attitude is necessarily ambiguous, for his attitude toward the ruling class he wrote about was as divided as that class itself.

Competition among different ruling-class interests is a constant feature of social history. In Pope's time it was expressed in the contest of the Whig and Tory parties to control national policy. As the party representing mainly land-owning interests, the Tories disliked the War of the Spanish Succession, which had dragged on since 1702. They preferred in general a policy of peaceful isolation, for the cost of expansion and war fell most heavily on them. The Whigs, composed mainly of merchants, financiers, army men, lawyers and other professionals, stood for an aggressive foreign policy: it was they who lent money to the government, supplied war materials, and would profit from the total defeat of England's commercial rivals. The period 1710-1714 was the peak of Tory power, for in the general elections of 1710 the Tories on a peace platform had gained control of Commons. They concluded the Peace of Utrecht in 1713, which — despite compromises to which the Whigs were opposed — established Britain as a major colonial and commercial empire. Although the House of Lords, dominated by Whigs, opposed the treaty, Queen Anne obligingly created twelve new peers to provide the necessary Tory majority.

It was always Pope's boast, particularly in his letters, to have remained independent of both parties. Indeed his dislike of party politics was shared by others, even by Queen Anne, who in 1705 wrote to her treasurer Godolphin, "I dread falling into the hands of either party . . . Do all you can to keep me out of the power of the merciless men of both parties." It was shared too by Lord Halifax, who astutely remarked that any party is a conspiracy against the rest of the nation. Yet neither Anne's fear nor Halifax's disdain prevented their playing a political role; and Pope's financial independence should not be confused with neutrality. *Windsor Forest* was a service to the Tories; so was the later satirical campaign against the Whig gentry and the ministry of Walpole. As a Catholic, moreover, Pope would naturally incline more toward the high-church (and sometimes Jacobite) Tories than toward the Protestant Whigs under whose anti-Papist laws Pope and his family had been deprived of civil rights.[3]

I hope to show in what follows that *Rape of the Lock* presents, on one hand, Pope's general commitment to aristocratic and repressive values; and on the other, his distaste for the crude profiteering, the blatant display, and the moral superficiality of an increasingly influential part of England's ruling class. Belinda and the Baron are at fault, in Pope's view, in failing to maintain an aristocratic code of conduct, and in holding their sexual attitudes up to criticism Pope exposes the social attitudes of the upper bourgeoisie. Of course Pope's political criticism must remain limited by his acceptance of an aristocratic norm, for the aristocracy had an economic base quite as crudely exploitative as that of the commercial bourgeoisie. Because of this the poem can offer no serious alternative to the false sexual values it exposes, or to the political attitudes to which they correspond.

II

Belinda's foremost trait is self-centeredness. This quality Pope conveys partly through narrative action, partly through rhetoric. Ironic hyperbole is obvious from the start: Belinda is said to inspire the poem, like a Muse; in her soft bosom, as in Juno's (Aeneid I, 11) "dwells such mighty Rage;" her eyes, more than suns, "must eclipse the Day." These phrases parody the conventions of epic and of Petrarchan love-poetry; they also parody Belinda's sense of her own importance.

We first see Belinda asleep and dreaming: an appropriate intro-duction to a woman whose entire life has the narcissistic quality of dream, and whose consciousness is so limited that even awake she seems asleep. The content of Belinda's dream is no different from that of her waking life: flirtation and egotism. She dreams of "A youth more glittering than a birth-night beau" who whispers in her ear — not words of love, but of self-love:

> Fairest of Mortals, thou distinguish'd Care
> Of thousand bright Inhabitants of Air!
> If e'er one Vision touch'd thy infant Thought,
> Of all the Nurse and all the Priest have taught,
> Of airy Elves by Moonlight Shadows seen,
> The silver Token, and the circled Green,
> Or Virgins visited by Angel-pow'rs,
> With Golden Crowns and Wreaths of heav'nly Flow'rs,
> Hear and believe! thy own Importance know,
> Nor bound thy narrow Views to Things below.[4]
>   [I, 27-36]

Does "thy infant Thought" mean "your mind when you were a child," or "your innocent mind," or "your immature mind"? The reference to nurse's fairy tales implies the first, that to religious instruction the second, and the argument itself the third; for we find that the long conditional clause supports the naive conviction of self-importance. The startling juxtaposition of elves and the Annunciation ("Virgins visited by Angel-pow'rs") further suggests the limitations of a mind in which fairy tale and theological mystery are scrambled without discrimination.

The young man in Belinda's dream reveals himself to be none other than Ariel, her guardian Sylph. It is his special duty to protect Belinda, for

> Whoever fair and chaste,
> Rejects Mankind, is by some *Sylph* embrac'd.
>   [I, 67-68]

The condition will prove Belinda's undoing, for later, at the moment when the Baron prepares to snip her lock, the Sylphs perceive that Belinda's mind is on a man, and their protection is suspended. That moment need occasion no suprise, for we have already seen that Belinda's thoughts are not wholly chaste. Some thought or impulse "ev'n in Slumber caus'd her Cheek to glow" [24], and on waking she receives a billet-doux which is "no sooner read,/ But all the Vision vanish'd from thy Head" [119-20].

The narcissistic dream is soon translated into action when we see
Belinda at her dressing-table, at once priestess and goddess in "The sacred
Rites of Pride" [128]. The attack on pride and vanity was a common
topic in eighteenth-century literature, and one to which Pope, drawing on
the Catholic tradition of the seven deadly sins, could contribute with
special fervor. It is a constant theme in his own work as well. In May,
1711, just before Pope began work on the *Rape of the Lock*, the *Essay
on Criticism* appeared; there Pope had castigated pride as the main cause
of "erring judgment," as the "never-failing vice of fools," as the enemy
of wit, sense and reason [II, 201-14]. He meant, of course, literary
judgment and literary sense; but he meant a good deal more, and his
strictures on pride are not likely to have been forgotten so soon either by
the poet or by his audience.

At her dressing-table, Belinda is surrounded by exotic ornaments,
the result of Britain's booming commercial expansion:

> Unnumber'd Treasures ope at once, and here
> The various Off'rings of the World appear;
> From each she nicely culls with curious Toil,
> And decks the Goddess with the glitt'ring Spoil.
> This casket *India's* glowing Gems unlocks,
> And all *Arabia* breathes from yonder Box.
> The Tortoise here and Elephant unite,
> Transform'd to *Combs*, the speckled and the white.
>
> [I, 129-136]

It is as if England's luxury trade existed to bedeck Belinda with its
"glitt'ring Spoil." Indeed at this moment Belinda is the very symbol of
commercial Britannia, her self-absorption the image of the colonial
nation's will to absorb into itself the world's wealth. Pope himself
suggests an analogy between Belinda and Britannia in Ariel's second
description of the Sylphs and their work. Some, says Ariel, guide the
planets, others watch over nature and human affairs:

> Others on Earth o'er human Race preside,
> Watch all their Ways, and all their Actions guide:
> Of these the Chief the Care of Nations own,
> And guard with Arms Divine the *British Throne*.
>
> [II, 87-90]

To gloss these lines, as Warburton did, as "a mere piece of raillery" would be to ignore the complexity of Pope's political attitudes. Brittania, like Belinda, is "hedged round with divinity." For Belinda it is, as the poem shows, rather an unreliable divinity. For Britannia, though, Pope had recently found such divinity a useful rhetorical device. In *Windsor Forest*, Pan, Pomona and Ceres lavish gifts upon England, and Queen Anne is "As bright a Goddess, and as chaste a Queen" as Diana. Pope was far from being as critical of the British throne as he was of Belinda's dressing-table, even though he could scarcely avoid perceiving certain similarities.

A similar ambivalence appears if we compare the dressing-table scene with Father Thames' speech to the assembled rivers in *Windsor Forest*. Anticipating the commercial advantages of the Tory peace, Thames says,

> For me the balm shall bleed, and amber flow,
> The coral redden and the ruby glow,
> The pearly shell its lucid glove infold,
> And Phoebus warm the ripening ore to gold.
>
> [393-96]

It is as self-serving a vision as Belinda's, yet it can hardly be interpreted ironically unless we see *Windsor Forest* as an exercise in pure servility. More likely, I think, is that Pope was not in principle opposed to colonial expansion or to the profit accruing from it — indeed he invested in the Tory South Seas Company — but that he despised the profit motive in its cruder manifestations, along with the less discriminating taste he tended to associate with the mercantile Whigs. We may see Belinda, then, as an aristocrat whose main fault is that she behaves like a bourgeoisie. She is a silly aristocrat who, like Arabella Fermor, needs to be laughed into a serious aristocrat.

Having seen Belinda in private, we see her next, in Canto II, in public: a powerful figure and the object of general admiration:

> Not with more Glories, in th'Etherial Plain,
> The Sun first rises o'er the purpled Main,
> Than issuing forth, the Rival of his Beams
> Lanch'd on the Bosom of the Silver *Thames*.
> Fair Nymphs, and well-drest Youths around her shone,
> But ev'ry Eye was fix'd on her alone.

> On her white Breast a sparkling *Cross* she wore,
> Which *Jews* might kiss, and Infidels adore.
> Her lively Looks a sprightly Mind disclose,
> Quick as her Eyes, and as unfix'd as those:
> Favours to none, to all she Smiles extends,
> Oft she rejects, but never once offends.
> Bright as the Sun, her Eyes the Gazers strike,
> And, like the Sun, they shine on all alike.
>
> [II, 1-14]

Purple and silver, imperial colors, are associated with Belinda here; her jewelled cross and impartial gaze intensify the impression of power. The devotion revealed by the cross is of course to Belinda's own public image rather than to more orthodox objects of worship; perhaps that is why Jews and infidels might so readily kiss and adore it.

> Yet graceful Ease, and Sweetness void of Pride,
> Might hide her Faults, if *Belles* had Faults to hide:
> If to her share some Female Errors fall,
> Look on her Face, and you'll forget 'em all.
>
> [II, 15-18]

So Pope concludes his description, with cutting irony. His letter to Martha Blount hinted strongly that Belle Fermor did have faults to hide, and we have already seen Belinda busy with the "Rites of Pride." The equivocal "might" and "if" help to make the point that ease and sweetness may serve the same purpose as rouge. Equally ironic is the advice in the last two lines, for to respond to Belinda solely on the basis of her appearance would be to commit another "female error" of superficiality, of the sort already judged in Canto I.

Belinda's lock is now described in a passage whose imagery suggests the predatory element in her self-presentation:

> This Nymph, to the destruction of Mankind,
> Nourish'd two Locks, which graceful hung behind
> In equal Curls, and well conspir'd to deck
> With shining Ringlets the smooth Iv'ry Neck.
> Love in these Labyrinths his Slaves detains,
> And mighty Hearts are held in slender Chains.
> With hairy Sprindges we the Birds betray,

> Slight Lines of Hair surprise the Finny Prey,
> Fair Tresses Man's Imperial Race insnare,
> And Beauty draws us with a single Hair.
>
> [II, 19-28]

She has got herself up to hunt, to prey, to capture, and her object is not love itself but the social status that comes from being admired. We begin, then, to see susceptible mankind more as victim than aggressor; or, more accurately, we are invited to see the Baron, like Belinda herself, as aggressor and victim at once.

At this point Pope introduces the Baron, whose response to Belinda's beauty can be no suprise:

> Th'adventrous *Baron* the bright Locks admir'd;
> He saw, he wish'd, and to the Prize aspir'd.
>
> [II, 29-30]

Belinda expects him, after all, to see and to wish, perhaps even to aspire. That the Baron acts on his wish is only a consequence, then, of the false values to which both are committed. The Baron, like Belinda, commits the fault of behaving like a bourgeois. His motive is acquisition and profit, though not of money: he hopes to get the symbols of sexual victory however he can, and to flaunt them to increase his status among competitors. His altar is as much a monument to masculine self-importance as Belinda's was to feminine narcissism, and on it lie the obsolete sacrifices to his image of self-respecting virility:

> There lay three Garters, half a Pair of Gloves;
> And all the Trophies of his former Loves.
>
> [II, 39-40]

Determined to add another trophy to his collection, the ruthless Baron will use any means to augment his status:

> Resolv'd to win, he meditates the way,
> By Force to ravish, or by Fraud betray;
> For when Success a Lover's Toil attends,
> Few ask, if Fraud or Force attain'd his Ends.
>
> [II, 31-34]

That the Baron and Belinda so readily reduce themselves and each other to objects or tools — that their game is one which dehumanizes — is a facet of their consciousness which Pope can duplicate in his rhetoric. The animal and hunt imagery already cited helps to do this, and the poet further expresses the reductive consciousness of his characters in the brilliant use of such devices as zeugma and parallel construction. Ariel, for example, anticipating disaster, does not know

> Whether the Nymph shall break *Diana's* Law,
> Or some frail *China* Jar receive a Flaw;
> Or stain her Honour, or her new Brocade;
> Forget her Pray'rs, or miss a Masquerade;
> Or lose her Heart, or Necklace, at a Ball,
> Or whether Heav'n has doom'd that *Shock* must fall.
>
> [II, 105-110]

Later, when the lock has been cut,

> Not louder Shrieks to pitying Heav'n are cast,
> When Husbands, or when Lap-dogs breathe their last . . .
>
> [III, 157-58]

"But now secure the painted Vessel glides" — Belinda's barge, to be sure, and Belinda herself. So in temporary confidence she moves, while her Sylphs tremble "for the Birth of Fate."

The third and central canto of the poem, in which the climactic "rape" occurs, is the most explicitly political of all. Its opening lines set the scene at Hampton Court Palace, establish the real grandeur of the place, and delicately expose the very diminished grandeur of its current personnel:

> Close by those meads, for ever crown'd with Flow'rs,
> Where *Thames* with Pride surveys his rising Tow'rs,
> There stand a Structure of Majestic Frame,
> Which from the neighb'ring *Hampton* takes its Name.
> Here *Britain's* Statesmen oft the Fall foredoom
> Of Foreign Tyrants, and of Nymphs at home;
> Here Thou, great *Anna*! whom three Realms obey,
> Dost sometimes Counsel take — and sometimes *Tea* . . . .
> One speaks the Glory of the *British Queen*,

And one describes a charming *Indian Screen*;
A third interprets Motions, Looks, and Eyes;
At ev'ry Word a Reputation dies.

[III, 1-16]

The target here is not, of course, Queen Anne or the institutional aspect of government. The first four lines convey a genuine solemnity, and "for ever crown'd with flowers" suggests a permanence transcending that of the public gardens at Hampton Court. England's past and future, the history that has been made and will be made on those meads and in that structure: surely this is the source of Thames' pride and Pope's seriousness here. His tone changes abruptly, though, when he speaks of the present inhabitants of the court. (It is not entirely irrelevant to note that Anne was rarely at Hampton — she preferred Windsor and Kensington — but that it was a favorite gathering place for noblemen and wits.) The damaging zeugma and rhyme aim instead at the warped consciousness of courtiers: a consciousness which permits them to discuss queens and screens in the same tone, as it permits Belinda's friends to bewail the death of husbands and lapdogs with the same loud shrieks.

Place has been specified; now time is specified as well, and it is defined in terms of the larger social world:

Mean while declining from the Noon of Day,
The Sun obliquely shoots his burning Ray;
The hungry Judges soon the Sentence sign,
And Wretches hang that Jury-men may Dine;
The Merchant from th' *Exchange* returns in Peace,
And the long Labours of the *Toilette* cease . . . .

[III, 19-24]

Not surprisingly, the inhabitants of this larger world exhibit the same irresponsibility as do those of the court. Society at large is not merely a backdrop against which the trivial and not-so-trivial dramas of court life are played, nor is the sole purpose of the passage to remind us that girls like Belinda are as carefully shielded from social reality as they are from the sun's "burning Ray." The work of judges, jurymen and merchants is precisely that on which court life depends, and Pope shows us here — as he has shown us all along, whether directly or by allusion — the social fabric to which a serious aristocrat must acknowledge responsibility. Yet this does not exhaust the complexity of the passage either. Why does

Pope offer such an unflattering view of a social order in which he does believe? And just how unflattering a view is it?

Pope shows us a social order whose members at various levels have abandoned their obligations to it. In doing this he suggests the graver consequences of such abdication, for while the Baron and Belinda can do no lasting harm in their limited circle, their selfishness writ large can do a great deal of harm indeed. No doubt Pope would deplore the miscarriages of justice which resulted from the irresponsibility of judges and jurymen. What he seems not to see is that wretches hung not only so that jurymen could dine, but so that they could exist as a class, along with the wealthy landlords, financiers and merchants who in Parliament made capital offenses of housebreaking, robbery, vagrancy and coining of base metal. Such property laws increased in savagery until by 1740, "for stealing a handkerchief worth one shilling, so long as it was removed privily from the person, children could be hanged by the neck until dead."[5] These are the laws which an aristocracy made and which jurymen only enforced; they represent the habitual response of a ruling class to the protests of those whom it exploits. Pope has little to say abut the multitudinous poor, except to criticize a too-open contempt for them (in *Moral Essay* III, 99-106), and to note, in *An Essay on Man*, that

> The rich is happy in the plenty giv'n,
> The poor contents him with the care of Heav'n.
> [Epistle II, 265-66]

Social criticism in the passage cited is limited, then, to an obvious and superficial form of injustice, and, moreover, to injustice committed by members of the middle class. Once again the aristocracy is left, as a class, intact, its legal crimes unmentioned and its brutality ignored.

Nor is the passage on society without implications for the theme of sexual attitudes. We begin to see that Belinda's presentation of herself as an object originates in her society's reduction of all value to money value, all life to commodity. Indeed we can hardly avoid concluding that the reductive consciousness which Pope parodies originates in the economic process by which that society exists. The wretches who hang, being numerous and easily reproduced, have little commodity value. Belinda, like any wealthy young girl, has commodity value in cash and land settlements on her marriage, and in influential family connections. Her beauty, like that of an estate or a Chinese vase, makes her a more valuable acquisition. The effect of economic reality is observable in contemporary poems written on belles of the day, for these poems have more in them of appraisal than of praise. Noteworthy in the following "compliment" to Arabella Fermor are real-estate imagery and an attitude of cool scrutiny which belie the poet's purely verbal raptures:

> Thus Farmer's [Fermor's] Neck with easie Motion turns;
> The Purpling Flood in Circling Currents runs:
> Her Snowey Breasts those lovely Mounts arise,
> And with suprizing Pleasure seize our Eyes.
> Between these Hills flows Heliconian Dew,
> Which makes the Poet's Raptures ever new . . .[6]

So that Belinda has learned to see herself as society sees her, and to compete for the rewards which society grants. Only in *Moral Essay II* does Pope glance at the social causes of feminine self-display. Women, he writes, are ruled by two passions: "The Love of Pleasure, and the Love of Sway." The first is given by nature, the second by experience, and

> by Man's oppression curst,
> They seek the second not to lose the first.

> [213-14]

The relation of means to ends here is disputable, and it is reversed a few lines later. But the tantalizing glimpse of social reality disappears, "man's oppression" plays no further role in Pope's treatment of women in the *Moral Essay*, and we are left with a parade of power-hungry, pleasure-hungry caricatures. I do not find, then, that the passage cited above displays any such "totality of view" as Cleanth Brooks claims for it. On the contrary, Pope's loyalty to the ruling class he wrote for must limit his social criticism quite narrowly, just as his sexist assumptions preclude any real alternative to Belinda's mode of existence.

Belinda now sits down to a game of ombre (Spanish, *hombre*) with the Baron and another young lady. The politics of sex is advanced here through the pervasive sexual and military images of the episode, which allow us to see the card-game as a symbol of more complicated and important contests. It represents first the war of sexes in which Belinda habitually participates, and which will shortly erupt into armed skirmish. It also represents the "Spanish game" recently settled to Britain's advantage in the Peace of Utrecht. Belinda wins the game of cards, but her exultation is brief. Clarissa offers the Baron a pair of sewing scissors, and

> The Peer now spreads the glitt'ring *Forfex* wide,
> T'inclose the Lock; now joins it, to divide. . . .
> The meeting Points the sacred Hair dissever
> From the fair Head, for ever and for ever!
>
> [III, 147-154]

At this point the two meanings of "rape" come into play, for *raptus* is first the theft of property and second the abduction and violation of a woman. The rapacious Baron has taken from Belinda what is most intimately her own property. Pope would have us see that Belinda encouraged such a violation by displaying herself as nothing more than a desirable piece of property; he does not suggest that women display themselves as objects when society makes it worth their while to do so.

The Baron's theft constitutes, in Pope's view, a double offense, for in showing the acquisitive fervor of a bourgeois, he stoops to stealing from a fellow-aristocrat. Minor as it is, the theft is a breach of class trust, and the Baron requires, like Belinda, to be laughed to good sense. But the modern critic may inquire whether the Baron does not behave, after all, like an aristocrat. His class existed, in a sense, by theft. Their wealth — the rents, fines and taxes produced and paid by the laborers of England — was the fruit of theft on a national scale, and the development of British colonialism only expanded that *raptus* world-wide. The rape of the lock is the smallest possible theft in a society founded on legal theft, and Pope's acceptance of the latter will always provide a *terminus ad quem* for his criticism of wayward aristocrats.

Canto IV describes Belinda's sulking spell, and takes us through the fantastic landscape of the Cave of Spleen. Spleen is a fashionable aristocratic malaise and a specifically feminine complaint, for Spleen "rule[s] the Sex to Fifty from Fifteen." Pope suggests through the imagery of Spleen's Cave that the complaint may well be due to sexual frustration; there "Maids turn'd Bottles call aloud for Corks." Belinda's friend Thalestris only increases her despondency with a vision of shameful gossip and isolation. Belinda is no longer a marketable commodity; thought to be unchaste, she will attract neither wealthy admirers nor friends. The superficiality of Belinda's concern with the appearance of honor is devastatingly exposed in the sexual innuendo of the last couplet of the canto:

> "Oh hadst thou, Cruel! been content to seize
> Hairs less in sight, or any Hairs but these!"

Canto V opens with the speech of Clarissa, sole representative of good sense in the poem. There is no doubt that her speech — imitated from that of Sarpedon in the *Iliad* (xii, 371 ff.) and specially added in 1717 — offers a fairly reliable version of Pope's opinion in the matter. Pope's own note to the 1736 edition describes Clarissa as "a new Character introduced . . . to open more clearly the MORAL of the Poem." Unlike Belinda and Thalestris, Clarissa does not speak to the adamant and unrepentant Baron, "For who can move when fair Belinda fails?" Instead Clarissa addresses Belinda, much as Pope himself had done when, in his dedicatory letter to *Rape of the Lock*, he urged Arabella Fermor, along with other young ladies, to self-knowledge and to "good sense and good humor enough to laugh not only at their sex's little unguarded follies, but at their own." Like Pope, Clarissa does not dispute the whole process of self-presentation which is at the core of Belinda's character. Neither does she question the importance which society attaches to physical beauty, nor the luxurious life-style in which belles are "deck'd with all that Land and Sea afford." She merely asks, without answering, why all this is done, and advises the addition of good sense to physical beauty, for:

> "How vain are all these Glories, all our Pains,
> Unless good Sense preserve what Beauty gains."

In what does this good sense consist? Clarissa urges Belinda to make a virtue of necessity:

> But since, alas! frail Beauty must decay,
> Curl'd or uncurl'd, since Locks will turn to grey,
> Since painted, or not painted, all shall fade,
> And she who scorns a Man, must die a Maid;
> What then remains, but well our Pow'r to use,
> And keep good Humour still whate'er we lose?
>
> [V, 25-30]

The substance of Clarissa's speech is repeated in *Moral Essay II*, in Pope's portrait of the woman of sense. There, in a passage which recalls the imagery of the *Rape of the Lock*, Pope describes the woman who

> Charms by accepting, by submitting sways,
> Yet has her humour most, when she obeys;
> Let Fops or Fortune fly which way they will;
> Disdains all loss of Tickets, or Codille;
> Spleen, Vapours, or Smallpox, above them all,
> And Mistress of herself, though China fall.
>
> [263-68]

Clarissa's sentiments also anticipate in small the advice Pope would later give, on a metaphysical scale, in the *Essay on Man*:

> Submit — In this, or any other sphere,
> Secure to be as blest as thou canst bear . . .

It is useful advice for a ruling class to offer those whom it exploits. It is equally useful to the chauvinized Clarissa, for she counsels good humor in a theft to which she was accessory (III, 127-130). The opportunism of Clarissa's position becomes even clearer when she remarks that "she who scorns a man, must die a maid." This, we discover, is the answer to the questions posed earlier: the right use of beauty is not to tease a man, but to catch a man; a husband is "what Beauty gains." So that while Clarissa rightly deplores Belinda's "airs, and flights, and screams, and scolding," she, with Pope, is unable to address herself to the larger situation which calls forth such mannerisms.

Clarissa's advice is rejected, though for other reasons (one hopes) than it would be rejected now. The battle of sexes begins in earnest, with Belinda's attempt to get back her lock. But the lock,

> obtain'd with Guilt, and kept with Pain,
> In ev'ry place is sought, but sought in vain . . .
>
> [V, 109-110]

The lock is translated to heaven in the shape of a comet (*comes*, hair) which will serve, according to the ironical prediction, to foretell historical events:

> This *Partridge* soon shall view in cloudless Skies,
> When next he looks thro' *Galileo's* eyes;
> And hence th'Egregious Wizard shall foredoom
> The Fate of *Louis*, and the Fall of *Rome*.
>
> [V, 137-140]

"John Partridge," reads Pope's note to these lines, "was a ridiculous Stargazer, who in his almanacs every year never failed to predict the downfall of the Pope, and the King of France . . ." Had Partridge lived two generations later, part at least of his prediction would have come true when in 1789 the grandson of Louis XIV was deposed and later beheaded by the new national assembly of citizens. Perhaps the events of the French Revolution could have been foretold, though not from comets, and not by one who believed, as Pope did, that the existing social order duplicated a cosmic order and that both were "RIGHT!" But to some in the eighteenth century, the bourgeois revolutions of America and France were as welcome[7] as the socialist revolutions of Russia and China have been to many in our own time. For modern revolutionary movements, the target is precisely the cluster of values represented in the *Rape of the Lock*: sexism, together with the economic structure that creates it.[8]

NOTES

1. "The Case of Miss Arabella Fermor," in *The Well-Wrought Urn*, New York, 1947.

2. Pope's letters are quoted from the *Correspondence*, ed. George Sherburn (Oxford, 1956), vol. i. There is some possibility that the congratulatory letter to Miss Fermor was contrived especially for Pope's edition of his own letters (1737) in which it first appeared. The letter is not dated; there is no authority for it besides Pope's own edition; and other incidents show that Pope was never above such conscious manipulation of his public image. Although it is beyond the scope of this article to discuss the psychoanalytic aspects of Pope's attitude toward women, the paragraph quoted offers rich material for such discussion.

3. For a summary of these laws and their effect on Pope and his family, see Alexandre Beljame, *Men of Letters and the English Public in the Eighteenth Century* (London, 1948), pp. 373-75.

4. The text of the *Rape of the Lock* is quoted from the Twickenham Edition, vol. II, ed. Geoffry Tillotson, London, 1940; third ed. 1962.

5. J. H. Plumb, *England in the Eighteenth Century* (Baltimore, 1950), p. 17.

6. This excerpt from the anonymous *The Mall: or, the Reigning Beauties* (1709) appears in the Twickenham Edition of the *Rape of the Lock*, Appendix A.

7. For discussion of the radical attitude toward these events, see Carl B. Cone, *The English Jacobins: Reformers in Late 18th Century England* (New York, 1968), and J. H. Plumb, "Political Man," in *Man versus Society in 18th-Century Britain*, ed. James L. Clifford (Cambridge, 1968).

8. This is not, of course, to imply that sexism is unique to capitalist economy; rather that sexism in any society is an attitude which helps to preserve both the exploitive economy and its political institutions.

10

WILLIAM BLAKE AND
RADICAL TRADITION

Fred Whitehead

The dead brood over Europe...
  —Blake, *The French Revolution* [1]
The tradition of all the dead generations weighs like a nightmare on the brain of the living.
  —Marx, *The Eighteenth Brumaire* [2]

Since the end of the nineteenth century, numerous critics, interpreters, mystics and commentators have sought a "key" to William Blake's prophetic works. Indeed, as Northrop Frye has pointed out, Blake himself appears to invite attempts to discover a "key" by having Los state "I must Create a System, or be enslvd by another Mans." [3] Though in the last few years many critics have given up the attempt to find a system in Blake, being content to analyze or explicate in piecemeal fashion, the task as I see it is to strive "to seize the inmost Form" of his works, to understand and appreciate the total structure which makes them at once so fascinating and so perplexing.

The concern of this essay is with Blake's works rather than with his critics, but it would seem advisable to make clear at least the direction and main outlines of my own critical evaluations and assumptions. For the last twenty-five years or so there has been evident a kind of split among the critics, which in fact reflects a split in the literary criticism of Western Europe and the United States. This is the division between the social-economic critics on one hand, and the mythic-psychological critics on the other. Critics of the first kind, among whom I would include Jacob Bronowski, David Erdman and A. L. Morton, have been less numerous than the latter, such as Northrop Frye, Harold Bloom, Kathleen Raine, and George M. Harper. To be sure, both "sides" recognize the synthesizing character of Blake's works, and so at times there are points of contact; further, the differences of emphasis and approach have not been exacerbated to the point of personal enmity.[4] Happily, all seem to have accepted Blake's advice: "Mutual Forgiveness of each Vice/ Such are the Gates of Paradise" (E256).

In this critical division of labor, the social and economic critics have concentrated on Blake's relationship to events of his own time, while the psychological critics have been far more interested in Blake and European literature as a whole, in myths and archetypes such as the Oedipus complex. Professor Erdman has acknowledged the limitation of the first kind of criticism in his essay, "Blake: The Historical Approach": "This method may be described as the reduction of Blake's fourfold vision to single vision. This is what I do when I say Rintrah 'is' William Pitt, or Albion 'is' the people of England."[5] Professor Frye indicates the limitation of the second: "Blake obviously hopes for a very considerable response to vision in or soon after his lifetime. But even if everybody responded completely and at once, the City of God would not become immediately visible: if it did, it would simply be one more objective environment. The real 'heaven' is not a glittering city, but the power of bringing such cities into existence."[6] Elsewhere Frye has advanced similar notions: "The idea of the free society implied in culture can never be formulated, much less established as a society."[7] On the one hand we have the elucidation of "single vision," and on the other, a criticism which emphasizes the intuitive and the imaginative at the expense of the "objective."

Both approaches are of course valid and necessary, though neither is alone sufficient for a complete understanding of Blake. A Blake criticism which practically and concretely synthesizes the two is possible only after much more careful and perceptive work, such as that of Frye and Erdman, has been produced and assimilated. This essay is an attempt to draw together the mythic-psychological and the social-economic approaches and to show how they correspond to the interrelated levels of meaning in Blake's great prophetic epics. Blake's myths, like all myths, have social and economic dimensions.

A question which perplexed me when I first began to read Blake several years ago was why, in *The Book of Urizen* for example, Urizen splits off from the Eternals; why should the whole catastrophe have occurred in the first place? Blake's evident dissatisfaction with any theology (at least in the 1790's) left me discontented with ontological explanations such as, "That's what happened when the world was created." Later study of comparative anthropology and the literature and art of non-Western cultures convinced me that this aspect of Blake's myth was somehow connected with the peculiar character of European culture; further reading of economics and economic history persuaded me that purely mentalist and psychological explanations were inadequate. It was only when I happened to read some Marxist interpretative histories of the ancient world that a "firm and bounding line" began to appear; of particular interest and importance were V. Gordon Childe's *Prehistory of European Society* and *What Happened in History,* Benjamin Farrington's *Greek Science*, George Thomson's *Studies in Ancient Greek Society*, and Archibald Robertson's *Origins of Christianity*. Marx said that one of his own distinctive achievements was to link economic developments with the development of particular social classes.[8] The authors I have named elaborated the psychological changes accompanying social and economic development. Avoiding reductionist fallacies, they demonstrated that it is possible to achieve a total history. I have suggested that Blake is an artist who demands a total understanding, and such an understanding must encompass the origins of our basic myths and their transformations, taking into account their social and economic dimensions. Blake thought that most historical writing up to his own time consisted of superficial rationalizations, whereas history's proper function was the depiction of lived concrete reality. He cried out angrily in his *Descriptive Catalogue*: "Tell me the Acts, O historian, and leave me to reason upon them as I please; away with your reasoning and your rubbish. All that is not action is not worth reading" (E534).

It is my thesis that the main structure of Blake's prophecies is the representation of the entire history of European man, delineating the specific forms of psycho-social distortion and achievement to be found in his culture. Blake attempted the elucidation of a historical system spanning six millennia and two continents by correlating its basic features: conceptions of psychological faculties (which he called the Four Zoas); myths of creation, the origin of evil and suffering, sacrifice and hopes of resurrection; sexual customs and attitudes; technological developments; growth of urban society and class stratifications. All these elements are interrelated in something like the following way: the Eternals were man's faculties in the primitive consciousness of pre-class society; the "fall" was the destruction of primeval psychological equality during the rise of urban societies in the ancient Near East about 4000 B.c. brought about by such dramatic and profound changes as the accumulation of an economic surplus, the use of metals such as bronze and later iron, division of society into ruling and working classes, establishment of the state, organized religions and legal systems, and so forth. The division of society into different classes entailed at the same time a psychological division; as Marx put it, "the *division of labor* implies the possibility, nay the fact that intellectual and material activity — enjoyment and labor, production and consumption — devolve on different individuals."[9] Thus did the ruling, reasoning and directive faculty, Urizen, in the kings and priests, become dominant over the intuitive and imaginative faculty, Los, in the artisans who actually constructed the new society and economy. As Blake wrote in his annotations to Bacon, "A Tyrant is the Worst disease & the Cause of all others" (E614).

This revolution, which Childe called the Urban Revolution, informs the entire history of the ancient world, and was probably the most important development in Near Eastern and subsequent European history before the Industrial Revolution that began in Blake's own time; and while this second great revolution clearly reflected the ancient social and psychological divisions, it was eventually to provide the means for resolving them.[10] Indeed, Blake's prophetic works of the early and mid-1790's group themselves about either of the two revolutions: in the first group are *The Book of Urizen*, *The Book of Los*, *The Book of Ahania*, and the "Africa" section of *The Song of Los*; in the second are *America*, *The Marriage of Heaven and Hell*, *The French Revolution*, *Europe*, and the "Asia" section of *The Song of Los*. Historical man had a continuing dialectical relation to Eternal Man — "Eternity is in love with the productions of time" (E35) — a statement perfectly compatible with Blake's claim to have "given the historical fact in its poetical vigour" (E534). This is the simplest and most schematic formulation of Blake's "system," which becomes enormously complex, especially in the later great epics. I intend to devote a longer study to analyzing these complexities and placing them within the context of his artistic development, but here I would like to limit the discussion to a consideration of crucial themes and passages in the prophecies: the time limits of history, the Four Zoas, the problem of materialism, the links between technology and social class in his plots and characters, and some modern analogues.

The conception of the time limits of history as six thousand years is remarkably consistent in Blake's works. Its first appearance is in *The French Revolution*, in a speech by the Duke of Burgundy:

> Shall this marble built heaven become a clay cottage,
>   this earth an oak stool, and these mowers
> From the Atlantic mountains, mow down all this great
>   starry harvest of six thousand years?
>
> (ll. 89-90; E286)

It also occurs in the roughly contemporary *Marriage of Heaven and Hell*, where Blake writes: "The ancient tradition that the world will be consumed in fire at the end of six thousand years is true, as I have heard from Hell" (E38). References continue throughout the later epics, frequently in important passages, such as pl. 75 of *Jerusalem*:

> ...Los in Six Thousand Years walks up & down continually
> That not one Moment of Time be lost & every revolution
> Of Space he makes permanent...
>
> (E228)

S. Foster Damon suggested the relevance of II Peter 3:8: "But, beloved, be not ignorant of this one thing, that one day is with the Lord as a thousand years, and a thousand years as one day."[11] Chiliastic interpretation linked this passage with the original six days of creation and seventh day of rest in Genesis, further connected with the binding of Satan and the resurrection of the just in Revelation 20; after the whole seven thousand years the New Jerusalem would begin.

Behind this typology lies a social and psychological conception of the developing form of culture in history. The beginning of the time-scheme was, of course, the 4004 B. C. date for Creation as worked out by Ussher in the seventeenth century; the fifth and sixth millennia are the first two of the Christian era. Blake was not particularly interested in the exact chronology of the actual Biblical history, as is evident in the Watson annotations. The conception of six thousand years as a unit is not important to him for any mystical reasons, but rather, because it is an attempt to grasp the scope of civilized history.[12] In Blake's view, the Bible contains the entire history of the ancient world, from its archaic beginnings to its collapse in the fall of the Roman empire. Writing in the radical chiliastic tradition, he believed that the Bible provided important clues concerning the historical origins of ancient man, as well as indications of the kind of revolutionary transformation needed to overcome the tragic paradigms of class society.

An explication of Blake must take into account his view that man's psyche is as complicated as his society, his economics, or his history; Blake considered man to be a totality, and believed that all the structures of his being were related to one another. Furthermore, Blake thought that if man becomes divided, disjointed, or schizophrenic, the reasons for it are to be sought in the human totality, in man's biology, his mind, and his society. Blake's concern is with the psychological structures of European man, though of course more or less parallel structures are to be found in other cultures.[13] He believed that the psyche was fourfold, and furthermore, that the evidence for this went back to the beginnings of the culture. The emphasis on the number four is, again, not for mystical reasons, but for the same cultural reasons previously cited as the basis for Blake's conception of the history of his culture as of six thousand years' duration. The development of the Zoas in Blake's entire career cannot be fully detailed here, but the dynamics of the basic structure, as well as the major historical antecedents, may be briefly analyzed. As Frye has indicated in his chart of the attributes of the Zoas, their biblical origins are the four rivers in Eden, Ezekiel's four living creatures, the four parts of the great image of Nebuchadnezzar's dream in Daniel, and the four beasts in Revelation.[14] Nowhere in the Bible, however, are the Zoas functionally differentiated, as they were to be in Greek philosophy.

Blake's early interest in ancient philosophy is evident from the "three Philosophers" of *An Island in the Moon* (E440), and the amusing reference to "Aristotles Analytics" in *The Marriage of Heaven and Hell* (E41). In fact, he defines himself as a philosopher in the Lavater annotations (E590). As Blake developed the concept of the Zoas, each of the four is linked with one of the four elements of Greek philosophy: Tharmas with water, Urizen with air, Luvah with fire, and Urthona with earth. For example, in *The Gates of Paradise* the four Zoas as elements are depicted in pls. 2-5 (E258-259); they also appear on pl. 24 of *The Book of Urizen*.[15] As Benjamin Farrington has brilliantly demonstrated, the early Greek philosophers, the so-called pre-Socratics, stood at a crucial vantage point in the history of European civilization; coming from a society somewhat more primitive than the ancient Oriental empires, and also remote enough from their sphere of political control, they were in the position of being able to assimilate the achievements of those cultures without sanctioning their authoritarian practices, such as highly abstracted imperial states and heavy dependence on slave labor.[16] Aristotle, who suggested the limitations of his predecessors by noting that they restricted themselves to describing only two of four causes, the material and the formal, with Love in Socrates and Plato, for example, an approach to the third cause, the efficient. The fourth cause was the final, or the teleological.[17] We might explain the operation of these four causes in something like the following way: the material is the clay of a pot; the formal is the shape it takes; the efficient is the energy used to make it, as in the potter's wheel; the final is the use to which the pot is put, such as cooking or drinking. The causes are meant to explain the dynamics of the widest range of phenomena — psychological, physical, ethical, and metaphysical. However, Aristotle's heavy emphasis on metaphysics, related to his acceptance of an authoritarian state and slavery, ensured again that the Greeks would not escape the fate of their predecessors; nor did the Romans avoid it, being notably unoriginal in such matters.

We find the same notion of four causes operative in Dante, 1600 years after Aristotle, in his idea of the four levels of meaning in literature: literal, allegorical, moral, and anagogical.[18] In our own century, Jung's notion of the fourfold nature of the psyche depends on the same cultural tradition; his formulation is sensation, thought, feeling and intuition, and the relevance of Jung's psychological scheme to Blake's Zoas has already been demonstrated at length, though erratically, by W. P. Witcutt.[19]

The following supplement to Frye's chart may be provided on the basis of the preceding:

1. Bible	Eagle	Lion	Bull	Man
2. Pre-Socratics	Water	Air	Fire	Earth
3. Aristotle	material	formal	efficient	final
4. Dante	literal	allegorical	moral	anagogical
5. Blake	Tharmas	Urizen	Luvah (Orc)	Urthona (Los)
6. Jung	sensation	thought	feeling	intuition

It must be insisted once again that these correlations are propsed not for their numerological, mystical, or even archetypal significance, though this last is closest to what is intended; by grasping such relationships we are better able to realize just how profound Blake's cultural and historical knowledge was, and to appreciate the enormous synthesizing scope and energy of the prophetic works. I am not suggesting that such a structural scheme explains European psychological history sufficiently; that is the

error of the Chicago and Thomist schools, as well as many of the varieties
of occult and mythic criticism. Rather, when this scheme is linked with
the economic and social developments which condition its psychological
structures, we begin to get a total Blake criticism.

There is one complication of the proposed correlation, which is a
striking achievement for Blake, but which has frequently been a stumbling block for his critics, and that concerns the material cause and the
four elements. Many critics have asserted that Blake is not a materialist,
that he is spiritualist, and so on. One of the latest to do so is Kathleen
Raine, who writes: "To suggest that Blake could ever have been a
supporter of Marxist materialism or any of the other forms of materialism
that are all but world-wide today is either foolish or dishonest."[20] However, if this is so, why would Blake have linked each of the Zoas with one
of the four physical and material elements? The early Greek philosophers
were definitely and rigorously materialist, concerned with the concrete
and physical elements of the world. In my opinion, Blake is trying to
bridge the gap between a materialist notion of the world based on the
four elements, and a more complete philosophical conception such as that
advanced by Aristotle, which includes the final cause, the intuitive, the
purpose to which something is put. This would help to account for the
quality of concreteness and tangibility in the Zoas which we sense in the
prophecies.

Blake consistently stated that ideas, forms and images are dependent
upon the senses. He remarks in the Lavater annotations (1788), ". . .it is
impossible to think without images of somewhat on earth" (E590). Another
example of Blake's problematic attitude towards matter is in the
prefatory poem to *Europe*, where he asks a Fairy he has caught, "Then
tell me, what is the material world, and is it dead?" and the Fairy
answers, "I'll sing to you to this soft lute; and shew you all alive/The
world, where every particle of dust breathes forth its joy" (E59). In the
later Blake, the universal rejoicing of the Minute Particulars occurs at the
conclusion of both *The Four Zoas* and *Jerusalem*, just as the Fairy says
in *Europe*. Finally, in the annotations to Berkeley (about 1820), we find
a concept of the relationship of mind and matter very similar to that
advanced in the Lavater annotations thirty years earlier. Berkeley writes:
". . .Whence, according to Themistius. . .it may be inferred that all
beings are in the soul. For, saith he, the forms are the beings. By the
form every thing is what it is. And, he adds, it is the soul that imparteth
forms to matter"; Blake responds: "This is my Opinion but Forms must
be apprehended by Sense or the Eye of Imagination Man is All Imagina-

tion God is Man & exists in us & we in him" (E654). Sense, the earth, matter, were all necessary but not sufficient to a complete man, who must be guided by intuition and imagination which direct the use of the material product.

It is surprising that the technological aspects of Blake's prophecies have been so neglected in recent criticism. In a pioneering work, Bronowski stressed the importance of the imagery of the Industrial Revolution.[21] Erdman suggested that the imagery, in particular the image of the mill, was military rather than industrial, though he definitely links Los with contemporary artisans in iron and steel work.[22] Thus we have excellent studies of Blake and the technology of his own time, that is, of the second, Industrial revolution; but aside from a few passages in Frye and Morton (which shall be considered below), we have little concerning the very long range historical economic and industrial developments which are so fundamental to the prophecies. With these exceptions, Blake critics have been content to regard the recurrent image of Los and his hammer, to take one example, as simply metaphorical, as a symbol of the creative process, which of course it is, but that is only one level of meaning. Most critics have insufficiently emphasized the specific and concrete historical meaning of Los and the hammer, and have consequently given us an overly mentalized and psychologized Blake, or a "phenomenological" Blake, as presented in one recent discussion.[23]

To demonstrate the critical method to be employed here we may briefly consider John Ball's couplet:

> When Adam delved and Eve span,
> Who was then the gentleman?

These two lines, famous all over England during the Peasant Revolt of 1381, link sexuality, technology and social class together: sexually, the man digging and forcing and the woman spinning, i.e., nurturing and growing the child within her; technologically, delving and spinning being agriculture and weaving, the two main occupations of Neolithic man according to one of the first divisions of labor, that by sex; socially, the situation being prior to the appearance of ruling classes, of the "gentleman."[24]

Blake's prophecies must be read in the same way, for the same dense texture and correlated levels of meaning are evident throughout. In *The Four Zoas*, for example, Frye has suggested that the first four Nights follow the pattern of the four classical Ages, Golden, Silver, Brazen, and Iron, and that Tharmas, Luvah, and Urizen are associated with the first three respectively.[25] This scheme is somewhat simplified, as will be seen later, but it rightly stresses a definite sequence of historical events. Furthermore, we may observe that each of the Zoas has an occupation, and an economic role: Tharmas as a Shepherd represents animal husbandry, Urizen as a Plowman is agriculture, Luvah is associated with viticulture, and Urthona, in Los and Enitharmon, is metallurgy and weaving. In the First Night of *The Four Zoas*, Los and Enitharmon are born from the Spectre of Tharmas and Enion (the emanation, or female counterpart, of Tharmas); metallurgy and weaving are the result of progress from the stage of simple animal husbandry. A detailed examination of all such sequences in Blake's prophecies would require a whole book in itself; their tremendous panoramas show the cataclysmic social and economic transformations of the ancient Near Eastern and subsequent European historical cultures, and their accompanying psychological traumata. Here I would like to consider in some detail Los and Enitharmon, who became increasingly central in *Milton* and *Jerusalem*, as well as the binding of Urizen by Los, which was a crucial sequence in several of the prophetic works.

Figure Ia   Los.   *Jerusalem*, pl. 73

When Blake depicts Los working with his hammer at the anvil [see Plate Ia], he is giving us an image that has a definite and specific meaning in the history of ancient man: the beginnings of metallurgy, which as we remarked earlier, were part of a profound revolutionary development in the ancient Near East. As most scholars have agreed, Blake's sources for Los were Hephaistos, Vulcan, Thor, Plato's demiurge ("worker for the people" as Frye notes), and Tubalcain, "an instructor of every artificer in brass and iron" in Genesis 4:22. The resounding clangor and sooty atmosphere of many of the Los sections of the prophecies is the labor of 6000 years' building up of Golgonooza, Blake's term for the material structure of the great urban civilizations of his culture.

In *The Book of Urizen* and *The Book of Los*, when Los hammers and rivets Urizen's body with brass and iron, giving him a form, Blake is reconstructing the process in ancient history by which the artisans themselves gave form to the ruling classes who were to oppress them. They themselves constructed the authoritarian states, building the ornate palaces and temples in which their masters lived; they forged the bronze and iron weapons which led to their own deaths. Thus on pl. 10 of *The Book of Urizen*, Blake describes the labors of Los:

> The Eternal Prophet heavd the dark bellows,
> And turn'd restless the tongs; and the hammer
> Incessant beat; forging chains new & new
> Numb'ring with links. hours, days & years
>
> The eternal mind bounded began to roll
> (E74)

Blake includes the "fall" of Los in Chapter II of *The Book of Los* as well as that of Urizen earlier, patterning it after the fall of Hephaistos in Greek myth. There is an intended coalescence of internal and external events here, which is paralleled in the twentieth century by the surrealists. Blake correlates social and economic developments with psychological, inner history; the complex of historical events Blake describes led not only to political tyranny but to psycholgical trauma as well.[26] Not only were cities divided between rich and poor, between the palaces of Urizen and the dens of Urthona; man's rational and intuitive faculties were divided from one another. The society's organizing ability was split from its sense of direction and use. Finally, this pattern informs the whole subsequent development of the European cultures, and continues even today in the profoundly tragic division between ruling and working classes.

Drawing on probable references to contemporary events in the prophecies, Professor Erdman has convincingly associated Los with the workers of Europe in Blake's own time. In fact, Blake was part of a whole movement in European art which began including artisans within the proper subject matter of art, for their own value and interest, without the trappings of neo-classicism. F. D. Klingender suggested that Joseph Wright of Derby was one of the first artists to depict the operation of a forge without false Vulcanic overtones, such as setting the scene among classical ruins.[27] Goya's painting "The Forge," in the Frick Collection, is clearly in the same movement.[28] This new emphasis on the worker in industrial production is related to the rise of the labor theory of value in

the sphere of economic theory, accompanying the Industrial Revolution of
the eighteenth and nineteenth centuries; in this context we may recall
Damon's explanation of Urthona as "earth-owner."[29]

In the modern period, the figure of the grimy and muscular metal-
worker with a hammer becomes central in the iconography of working-
class socialist art. In fact, in the early years of the Russian Soviet
Republic, there was an entire school of Soviet poets, called the "smithy
group," which concentrated on describing the conditions of life of iron
and steel workers and the crucial contribution they were making to the
buildng of the new socialist society. One of their characteristic poems is
Alexey Gastev's "We Grow Out of Iron":

> Look! I stand among work-benches, hammers, furnaces,
>   forges, and among hundreds of comrades.
> Overhead — hammered iron space.
> On either side — beams and girders.
> They rise to a height of seventy feet.
> They arch right and left.
> They meet in the cupola and with giant shoulders
>   support the whole iron structure.
> They thrust upward, they are sturdy, they are strong.
> They demand yet greater strength.
> I look at them and grow straight.
> Fresh iron blood pours into my veins.
> I have grown taller.
> I am growing shoulders of steel and arms
>   immeasurably strong.

Figure Ib   Daughters of Los. *Jerusalem*, pl. 59

I am one with the iron building.
I have risen.
My shoulders are forcing the rafters, the upper
  beams, the roof.
My feet remain on the ground, but my head is above
  the building.
I choke with inhuman effort, but already I am shouting:
"Let me speak, comrades, let me speak!"
An iron echo drowns my words, the whole structure
  shakes with impatience. And I have risen yet
  higher, I am on a level with the chimneys.
I shall not tell a story or make a speech, I shall
  only shout my iron word:
"We will conquer!"[30]

The speaker is a Los-like iron-worker, who is building with tremendous effort and energy a structure like Blake's Golgonooza, within which he struggles to express himself, until he bursts out with his head in the sky, like Los on pl. 100 of *Jerusalem* [Plate II here]. The actual details of the building, the tools such as hammers, forges, etc. are similar to the description of Golgonooza in *Jerusalem* (10: 62-65, E152; 73: 8-15, E226).

    Closely related to the "smithy group" from the standpoint of graphic art is an illustration by Fred Ellis in the *Workers Montly,* May 1926 [reproduced here as Plate III]. The stance of the smith leaning over his anvil with the sun in the background is most strikingly similar to Los' in *Jerusalem,* pl. 73 [Plate Ia here]. In both cases the grimy and sooty nature of the smith's work is emphasized, as is the strenuous labor in which he is engaged. The sun promises a new day, "the opening morn,/ Image of truth new born" ("The Voice of the Ancient Bard," ll.2-3; E31). Thus from Maccabees to Molotov (both names mean "hammer"), from Tubal-cain to Stalin ("man of steel"), from Hephaistos to John Henry, we observe the continuity of a developing archetype, Blake's Los walking up and down his bright halls of 6000 years.

    Enitharmon's connection with the loom does not appear explicitly in the prophecies until *The Four Zoas*, and it is developed fully only in *Milton* and *Jerusalem*. Weaving, of course, was an important part of the archaic economy, and George Thomson and R. B. Onians have drawn together much interesting material from different cultures concerning the mythology and folklore of spinning.[31] For example, the Fates in Greek

Figure II

TOILERS-SMASH THE
CHAINS OF SLAVERY!
BEFORE YOU RISES
A DAWN OF FREE-
DOM!

LENIN

Figure III   Illustration by Fred Ellis, *Workers Monthly*, May 1926

folklore (and Norns in the North) spin the thread of man's life, and each has a different role in the process directly based on the ancient technique of spinning. The weaving industry of Europe Blake called Cathedron, and the bitter harshness of its operation throughout history is well expressed on pl. 59 of *Jerusalem* [Plate Ib]:

> And one Daughter of Los sat at the fiery Reel & another
> Sat at the shining Loom with Sisters attending round
> Terrible their distress & their sorrow cannot be utterd
> And another Daughter of Los sat at the Spinning Wheel
> Endless their labour, with bitter food. void of sleep,
> Tho hungry they labour: they rouze themselves anxious
> Hour after hour labouring at the whirling Wheel
> Many Wheels & as many lovely Daughters sit weeping.
>   (E207)

The three Fates themselves appear on pl. 57, as does Enitharmon with spindle and distaff on pl. 100 [Plate II]. Enitharmon, then, is not only Los' psychological and sexual counterpart, she is his economic partner as well. Their frequent antagonistic relationships derive more from the division of labor and the harshness and drudgery of their work than from innate or biological differences.

By now it should be clear that an adequate Blake criticism must have Frye's historical range and psychological insight, without his usual idealist limitations. In fact, if we accept the importance of Blake criticism for criticism in general, as Frye has suggested, then the Marxist critics must be prepared to deal more adequately with such subjects as archetypes, psychology, and iconography. In Blake's painting, "The spiritual form of Nelson guiding Leviathan, in whose wreathings are infolded the Nations of the Earth" [Plate IV], Christ, though half swallowed by the monster, is poised to strike Nelson down with a sword. In an illuminating discussion of this painting, Erdman explains that Christ is the type of Orc, or passion, antagonistic to tyranny even as France was struggling in the madness of the current continental wars.[32] There is a remarkable modern analogue in a Soviet poster of the civil war period [Plate V], where a horseman (bright red in the original) is similarly poised to kill with his sword an enormous white dragon whose tail and body encircle a blackened factory in the background. Both Christ and the horseman are examples of the Orc archetype, revolutionary human passion, in mortal struggle with the non-human, the bestial forms which have civilization by

Figure IV   The Spiritual form of Nelson guiding Leviathan, in whose wreathings are infolded the Nations of the Earth, 1809

1917 ОКТЯБРЬ 1920

Товарищ! Утроив энергию свою,
Сквозь строй орудий, штыков щетину
Радостно встретим в кровавом бою
Октябрьской Революции Третью годовщину!

Она—залог нашей близкой победы,
Рабами нам больше не быть никогда!
Чрез временные неудачи и беды
Мы шествуем в светлое царство Труда.

Мечем пролетарским сражен издыхая
Дракон империализма разинул пасть...
Советская, федеративная, социалистическая, мировая
Республика да здравствует ея власть!

Figure V   **October 1917-1920 — Soviet Poster**

the throat. The dragon, of course, is an ancient symbol of non-human tyranny, probably going back to the time when man actually had to contend with such creatures for physical survival; we need only recall Leviathan and Behemoth in the Bible, and Beowulf's tragic struggle with the dragon or "worm" in the second part of the Beowulf epic.[33] We might note, finally, that the Soviet horseman appears to have a much better chance of slaying the dragon than Blake's Christ does!

Northrop Frye has written that "during the last hundred years, most serious fiction has tended increasingly to be ironic in mode."[34] In practical terms, this means that, like most other Western critics, Frye focuses on such writers as Eliot, Yeats, and Beckett, and dismisses the literature of socialist countries as not being literature at all, but didactic writing or propaganda. Marxists have naturally been critical of this trend, but to my knowledge, little has been produced showing how inadequate the theory of Western criticism is as a result. Frye's own theory of archetypes has suffered from this selectivity. To take just one type, we might note the continuity, both imaginative and social, of the Plowman in literature: Frye has traced it from Hesiod through Chaucer and Langland, but he neglects it in more modern times.[35] In *The Four Zoas*, Blake closely patterns Urizen after the original biblical plowman, Cain. In the apocalyptic Night the Ninth, Urizen becomes once more a Plowman, rather than a tyrant King:

> The Sons of Urizen Shout Their father rose The Eternal horses
> Harnessd They calld to Urizen the heavens moved at their call
> The limbs of Urizen shone with ardor. He laid his hand on the Plow
> Thro dismal darkness drave the Plow of ages over Cities
> And all their Villages over Mountains & all their Vallies
> Over the graves & caverns of the dead Over the Planets
> And over the void Spaces over Sun & moon & star & constellation.
>
> (E378-379)

Urizen goes on to sow the souls of the dead, and all the warriors and the "Kings & Princes of the Earth" flee away to the sea shores and the deserts. In another Soviet poster [Plate VI], Blake's Plowman reappears, in the titanic proportions of a regenerated Zoa, plowing sceptres, crowns, bags of money and swords into the earth, to ready his field for the planting of a new day. Blake's archetypes thus have their analogues not only in medieval and Renaissance literature, but in the modern period as well.

Figure VI   The Red Plowman — Soviet Poster

The process of linking images and symbols could of course be continued, and that is part of what a lengthier study demands. It remains here to point out and emphasize the scale of Blake's artistic ambition. In the *Descriptive Catalogue* accompanying his exhibition of 1809, Blake said that he had been "taken in vision into the ancient republics, monarchies, and patriarchates of Asia," and had seen "those wonderful originals called in the Sacred Scriptures the Cherubim, which were sculptured and painted on walls of Temples, Towers, Cities, Palaces, and erected in the highly cultivated states of Egypt, Moab, Edom, Aram, among the Rivers of Paradise" (E521-522). He continued, "Those wonderful originals seen in my visions, were some of them one hundred feet in height... The Artist wishes it was now the fashion to make such monuments, and then he should not doubt of having a national commission to execute these two Pictures [the paintings of Pitt and Nelson] on a scale that is suitable to the grandeur of the nation, who is the parent of his heroes, in high finished fresco, where the colours would be as pure and as permanent as precious stones though the figures were one hundred feet in height." However, Blake was considered a madman by the dandies of Regency England; his exhibition was a failure, and he never executed the great frescoes of his proposal.

It is only in our own day that Blake's artistic proposal has begun to see fulfillment, in the splendid Mexican murals, for example, or certain Soviet monumental sculptures. Thus we may see Blake not only as the last antinomian (in Morton's phrase), but as part of a living and thriving culture, the maturity of which is coming in our own day. Its psychological dimensions were hinted at by Freud: "These ever-active and, as it were, immortal wishes of our unconscious recall the legendary Titans who, from time immemorial, have been buried under the mountains which were once hurled upon them by the victorious gods, and even now quiver from time to time at the convulsions of their mighty limbs."[36] The conclusion of F. A. Ridley's study of the revolutionary tradition in England indicates the social scope: "Gigantic battles lie ahead, vast vistas unfold, a new world in process of creation out of the crumbling ruins of the old. The English Revolutionary Tradition emerging from the reformist mists, will assert itself once more in its glorious integrity... We recall therewith the memory of the great revolutionary giants of our race, from John Ball and the Lollards to Thomas Paine and the Chartists. Great figures loom up from the forgotten past, mighty deeds renew their youth."[37]

In *Jerusalem*, Blake wrote:

> In my Exchanges every Land
> Shall walk, & mine in every Land,
> Mutual shall build Jerusalem;
> Both heart in heart & hand in hand.
>   (27:85-88; E172)

After the world of Stock Exchanges had disappeared, man could live in internal and external harmony, in the triumphant and peaceful unity of psyche and society, even striving toward the stars, as on pl. 100 of *Jerusalem* [Plate II]. This is what Blake foresaw in the conclusions of his two great epics, *The Four Zoas* and *Jerusalem*, and it is the ultimate meaning of his life and art.

NOTES

1. All quotations from Blake's works are from *The Poetry and Prose of William Blake*, ed. David V. Erdman, commentary by Harold Bloom (Garden City: Doubleday, 1965), which preserves Blake's eccentric spelling and punctuation. This edition is here abbreviated as E. E282.

2. Marx and Engels, *Selected Works* (Moscow: Foreign Languages Publishing House, 1958), I, 247.

3. Quoted in "The Keys to the Gates," in *Some British Romantics*, ed. James V. Logan et al. (Columbus: Ohio State University Press, 1966), p. 4. Los's statement is from *Jerusalem*, pl. 10, E151.

4. David V. Erdman, *Blake: Prophet Against Empire*, rev. ed. (Garden City: Doubleday, 1969), pp. 255-258; Frye, op. cit., p. 11; Bloom, E813, 815.

5. *Discussions of William Blake*, ed. John E. Grant (Boston: Heath, 1961), p. 22.

6. "Keys," p. 38.

7. *Anatomy of Criticism* (Princeton: Princeton University Press, 1957), p. 348.

8. Letter to J. Weydemeyer, March 5, 1852, in Marx and Engels, *Selected Correspondence* (Moscow: Foreign Languages Publishing House, 1953), p. 86.

9. Marx and Engels, *The German Ideology* (Moscow: Progress Publishers, 1968), p. 44.

10. On the Urban Revolution, see Childe, *What Happened in History*, rev. ed., with a new foreword by Grahame Clark (Baltimore: Penguin, 1964), chapter 5. For the ultimate, long-range effects of the Industrial Revolution, see E. J. Hobsbawm, *The Age of Revolution 1789-1848* (New York: Mentor, 1964), pp. 45-46; and Martin Nicolaus, "The Unknown Marx," *New Left Review*, No. 48 (March-April, 1968), 41-61.

11. *William Blake: His Philosophy and Symbols* (1924; rpt. Gloucester, Mass.: Peter Smith, 1958), p. 323. Blake is placed in the chiliastic tradition of seventeenth-century radicalism by A. L. Morton, in his essay, "The Everlasting Gospel," first pub. in 1958 and rpt. in *The Matter of Britain* (London: Lawrence & Wishart, 1966), pp. 83-121; see also M. H. Abrams, *Natural Supernaturalism: Tradition and Revolution in Romantic Literature* (New York: Norton, 1971).

12. It is striking how often the rough approximation of six thousand years as the duration of civilization is accepted in modern anthropological and historical disucssions, as if confirming the intuitive truth of tradition. See, for example, Fritz M. Heichelheim, *An Ancient Economic History*, I (Leiden: A. W. Sijthoff, 1958), 46, 51-52; and Marvin Harris, *The Rise of Anthropological Theory* (New York: Crowell, 1968), p. 147.

13. For an interesting discussion of early Chinese philosophy, see Joseph Needham, *Science and Civilization in China*, II (Cambridge: Cambridge University Press, 1962), 232-246.

14. *Fearful Symmetry* (1947; rpt. Boston: Beacon, 1962), pp. 277-278.

15. The plate from *The Book of Urizen* is without text, and is assigned no. 24 by Keynes and Wolf in their *Census* (New York: Grolier Club, 1953), p. 71.

16. *Greek Science*, rev. ed. (Baltimore: Penguin, 1961), Part One, esp. chapter 9.

17. *Physics*, II, 2; *Metaphysics*, I.

18. *Convivio*, II, i. The relevance of this passage to Blake is suggested by Frye, *Fearful Symmetry*, p. 10.

19. *Blake: A Psychological Study* (London: Hollis & Carter, 1946).

20. *Blake and Tradition* (Princeton: Princeton University Press, 1968), II, 275.

21. Jacob Bronowski, *William Blake: A Man Without a Mask* (London: Secker & Warburg, 1943), pp. 85-86.

22. *Prophet*, pp. 395-399; "Historical Approach," pp. 25-26.

23. Hazard Adams, "Blake and the Postmodern," in *William Blake: Essays for S. Foster Damon*, ed. Alvin H. Rosenfeld (Providence: Brown University Press, 1969), pp. 3-17, esp. p. 8.

24. I owe this interpretation of Ball's couplet to the poet David Cumberland. The relevance of the couplet to Blake's tradition is also suggested by Carl Woodring, *Politics in English Romantic Poetry* (Cambridge, Mass.: Harvard University Press, 1970), p. 9.

25. *Fearful Symmetry*, p. 278.

26. Morton's "Everlasting Gospel," esp. p. 92, is brilliant on these points; my discussion is merely adding to the foundation he laid. Concerning metal-workers in antiquity, the following works have been helpful: Heichelheim, op. cit., passim, but esp. I, 447-450; R. J. Forbes, *Studies in Ancient Technology* (Leiden: E. J.

Brill, 1955-1964); and Mircea Eliade, *The Forge and the Crucible* (London: Rider 1962).

27. *Art and the Industrial Revolution*, ed. and rev. Arthur Elton (New York: Kelley, 1968), pp. 55-61.

28. The painting is reproduced in Edgar Munhall, *Masterpieces of the Frick Collection* (New York: Frick Collection, 1970), p. 83.

29. *William Blake*, p. 326. On the development of the labor theory of value, cf. Hannah R. Sewall, *The Theory of Value Before Adam Smith* (1901; rpt. New York: Kelley, 1968), pp. 9-10, 70-71, 73-75; Edgar Stephenson Furniss, *The Position of the Laborer in a System of Nationalism* (1920; rpt. New York: Kelley & Millman, 1957), pp. 13, 16-25; Ronald L. Meek, *Studies in the Labour Theory of Value* (London: Lawrence & Wishart, 1956), chapters 1-2; and Charles Wilson, *England's Apprenticeship 1603-1763* (New York: St. Martin's Press, 1965), pp. 231-232.

30. *Russian Literature Since the Revolution*, ed. Joshua Kunitz (New York: Boni and Gaer, 1948), pp. 34-35. On the "smithy group," cf. George Z. Patrick, *Popular Poetry in Soviet Russia* (Berkeley: University of California Press, 1929), chapter 10 ("The Iron Messiah"); and Alexander Kaun, *Soviet Poets and Poetry* (Berkeley: University of California Press, 1943), pp. 127-143.

31. George Thomson, *Studies in Ancient Greek Society*, rev. ed. (London: Lawrence & Wishart, 1961), I, 334-339; R. B. Onians, *The Origins of European Thought*, 2nd ed. (Cambridge: Cambridge University Press, 1954), Part III.

32. *Prophet*, pp. 448-455. Sir Anthony Blunt has disputed the identification of the figure with the sword as Christ, in *The Art of William Blake* (New York: Columbia University Press, 1959), pp. 102-103; but see Erdman's rejoinder, *Prophet*, p. 451, n. 50.

33. For a fascinating discussion of Beowulf and similar dragon-fighters in the Middle Ages, see Walter Abell, *The Collective Dream in Art* (1957; rpt. New York: Schocken, 1966), chapter 10.

34. *Anatomy of Criticism*, pp. 34-35.

35. *Fearful Symmetry*, p. 335.

36. *The Interpretation of Dreams*, in *Basic Writings*, ed. and trans. A. A. Brill (New York: Modern Library, 1938), p. 500.

37. *The Revolutionary Tradition in England* (London: National Labour Press, 1947), p. 309.

11

COLERIDGE'S "KUBLA KHAN":
His Anti-Political Vision

Norman Rudich

1

In Xanadu did Kubla Khan
A stately pleasure-dome decree:
Where Alph, the sacred river, ran
Through caverns measureless to man
    Down to a sunless sea.
So twice five miles of fertile ground
With walls and towers were girdled round:
And there were gardens bright with sinuous rills,
Where blossomed many an incense-bearing tree;
And here were forests ancient as the hills,
Enfolding sunny spots of greenery.

2

But oh! that deep romantic chasm which slanted
Down the green hill athwart a cedarn cover!
A savage place! as holy and enchanted
As e'er beneath a waning moon was haunted
By woman wailing for her demon-lover!
And from this chasm, with ceaseless turmoil seething,
As if this earth in fast thick pants were breathing,
A mighty fountain momently was forced;
Amid whose swift half-intermitted burst
Huge fragments vaulted like rebounding hail,
Or chaffy grain beneath the thresher's flail:

And 'mid these dancing rocks at once and ever
It flung up momently the sacred river.
Five miles meandering with a mazy motion
Through wood and dale the sacred river ran,
Then reached the caverns measureless to man,
And sank in tumult to a lifeless ocean:
And 'mid this tumult Kubla heard from far
Ancestral voices prophesying war![1]

3

The shadow of the dome of pleasure
Floated midway on the waves;
Where was heard the mingled measure
From the fountain and the caves.
It was a miracle of rare device,
A sunny pleasure-dome with caves of ice!
    A damsel with a dulcimer
    In a vision once I saw:
    It was an Abyssinian maid,
    And on her dulcimer she played,
    Singing of Mount Abora.
    Could I revive within me
    Her symphony and song,
    To such a deep delight 'twould win me,
That with music loud and long,
I would build that dome in air,
That sunny dome! those caves of ice!
And all who heard should see them there,
And all should cry, Beware! Beware!
His flashing eyes, his floating hair!
Weave a circle round him thrice
And close your eyes with holy dread,
For he on honey-dew hath fed,
And drunk the milk of Paradise.

I

In these pages I shall try to show that "Kubla Khan" is a political poem
in the sense that its basic structure contrasts the political power of the
State with the creative power of the Poet. It is an anti-political poem in

that it decries the blindness of the state to the profoundest truths of human nature, the state's pretentious arrogance, unbounded hubris, pagan hedonism and ultimate failure to represent mankind's aspiration to happiness. On the other hand, the Poet is presented as the divine vessel through whose vision of nature and man, political alienation can be overcome and paradise regained. If Coleridge wrote "Kubla Khan" between the summer of 1798 and 1800, it crowns a political and philosophical evolution which can be traced through his writings in verse and prose from at least 1795 and, dramatically, from 1796. Renunciation of political action in favor of philosophical, religious and mystical probings of first causes is a major theme in such writings. At the same time he was losing his early enthusiasm for the French Revolution and more and more uneasily opposed Pitt's policy of alliance and military intervention with the continental powers for the purpose of restoring the Bourbons to the French throne. Napoleon's invasion of Switzerland in January 1798 marks the decisive turn from hesitations and doubts to total disillusionment, and that was the point of departure for the conservatism which shaded into the reactionary views of his later years. "Kubla Khan" was also the last fully inspired poetic expression of his career.

Coleridge was a political journalist and pamphleteer, who seriously considered a career in public life up to 1796. "Kubla Khan" is no pamphlet. The aesthetic is not reducible to the political, the religious, or to any other "form of consciousness"; nor does it exclude any particular content. The aesthetic is a specific mode of ideology, which simultaneously reflects, interprets, evaluates and generalizes through mimetic structures of discourse, the real world of concrete human activity; the artist shapes an imaginative version of human action out of a particular form of matter; he creates objects which embody and reveal in their contours typical situations of life, particular actions endowed with visible and potential meanings which transcend their particularity. In art, as in real life, the various forms of consciousness do not appear as isolated entities but as complexly interrelated products of the mind which surface in a thousand combinations as required by our different activities, at work or play, in our private or public lives. The critic separates and displays analytically what the poet feels and expresses as a synthetic whole; of course the critic is accountable for his own synthesis, an overall interpretation and judgment of the poem, but it is no longer that of the poet. Coleridge's anti-political vision is the ideological organizing principle of "Kubla Khan" and therefore an essential key to the moral, religious and mystical meanings implicit in its dense texture.

The basic lines of my interpretation of "Kubla Khan" were worked out independently of J. B. Beer's *Coleridge the Visionary,* [2] which presents by far the most coherent and scholarly analysis to date. He demonstrates convincingly that the poem is no mere collection of flamboyant images inspired by an opium dream and held together by word-music. On the contrary, it may be criticized because it tries to mean too much on too many levels; its overburdened symbols obscure the association of ideas and images which should reveal its aesthetic and logical progression toward a statement of doctrine. Beer reconstructs that doctrine by emphasizing the cabalistic, biblical and other mythological sources of Coleridge's imagery and by relating them to the entire range of Coleridge's intellectual preoccupations throughout his youth, but especially in 1797 and 1798. Isis and Osiris, Alpheus and Arethusa, Apollo and Dionysos, The Song of Songs, the story of Moses, and the whole mythic tradition of earthly paradises from Genesis to Milton and beyond are so fruitfully brought to bear on this classical enigma, Beer so effectively absorbs into his interpretation the best of the scholarship and criticism[3] devoted to "Kubla Khan," that he has achieved a new critical point of departure. Beer even has a peripheral awareness that Coleridge's political thought was at play in the poem. It is because he does not fully grasp the political dimension of the problem that the present study may be useful. I shall state after my discussion of the poem the points at which this political reading modifies his interpretation.

Writers on Coleridge's politics generally ignore "Kubla Khan".[4] Carl Woodring in his *Politics in the Poetry of Coleridge*[5] cautiously suggests that it may have contemporary political references. Two years earlier, he wrote the best single political interpretation of the poem I have run across.[6] Whereas Beer emphasized the priestly and artistic connotations of "Khan", Woodring links it to oriental despotism and more particularly to Catherine the Great whose orgiastic and bloody reign received Coleridge's horrified curse in the "Ode to the Departing Year." He accepts "Kubla Khan" as a fragment but a coherent one, when read as a contrast between the "impercipient Khan" and a potentially vatic Coleridge.

But it would be hopelessly confusing to attempt a point-by-point comparison of these interpretations with my own. The method followed here will be an *explication de texte* synthesizing those points of interpretation and documentation most useful to my reading, while emphasizing departures in interpretation resulting from the point of view adopted. This will be followed by a discussion of the high points in Coleridge's ideological development leading up to the composition of "Kubla Khan" and a conclusion dealing with its relevance to us. Space prevents me from completing this *explication de texte* with the formal analysis which would show that the various poetic techniques — metric, phonetic, and rhetorical — re-enforce and are elucidated by this reading. Perhaps the several formal indications interspersed throughout the body of the thematic material will suffice to make the point.

II

For the purpose of an overall interpretation the poem divides into two parts, each containing two stanzas which I shall call *The Emperor* (lines 1-30) and *The Poet* (lines 31-54) respectively. Subtitles for the separate stanzas are (1) The Decree, (2) The Chasm, (3) The Poet's Judgment, (4) The Poet's Vision and Mission.

The Emperor

1. The Decree

The first stanza tells how Kubla Khan, the Tartar conquerer of China whose absolute rule stretched from Korea to eastern Poland and from Mongolia to the Arabian desert, decreed the construction of a stately pleasure-dome, that is to say a monumental palace expressive of the grandeur of the state and empire he alone embodies, situated in Xanadu, an exotic site far away from human care and strife, a place of retirement and perfect sensuous enjoyment, an unequaled conquest of nature by the peaceful arts of civilization. His grandiose conception corresponds not only to his absolute power but to attributes of mind associated with his divine descent from the sun and their attendant functions — those of magician, artist, priest. He gave specific instructions that it should be located near a point where Alph, a sacred river, cascaded down through the underground caves into a sea of absolute cold and darkness. Nowhere is it said that the decree mentions a chasm or fountain, nor is there any indication that Kubla is conscious of their existence.

No sooner said than done. The Emperor's word is law, but it is also the word magically become flesh, become art. The iambic tetrameter of lines 7 and 8 suggests the rapid completion of the work on the walls. "Twice five miles"[7] are immediately walled off and topped with protective towers, a prodigious task even for the hordes of slaves at Kubla's command. Within, the man-made beauty of perfumed gardens and the natural majesty of ancient forests are brought together to serve the pleasure of the Emperor and of those he permits to cross the barrier of fortifications. The imperial state decree has measured off this ground, appropriating its sacred character, its fertility and timeless nature to the uses of the state and the person of the emperor. Throughout these lines the precision of law and geometry stand in contrast both in sense and metered sound to the measureless darkness of the caverns and the frozen sea below.

This contrast between the finite artifice of human reason and the infinite mystery of spirit and nature was explicitly stated years later in the *Statesman's Manual.* What makes the passage particularly apt is the linking of death to finite reason, divorced from all organic process, as if it were the self-sufficient absolute of true knowledge:

> The leading differences between the mechanic and the vital philosophy may all be drawn from one point; namely, that the former demanding for every mode and act of existence real or possible visibility, knows only of distance and nearness, composition (or rather juxtaposition) and decomposition, in short, the relations of unproductive particles to each other; so that in every instance the result is the exact sum of the component quantities, as in arithmetical addition. This is the philosophy of death . . . In life, much more in spirit, and in a living and spiritual philosophy, the two component counterpowers actually interpenetrate each other, and generate a higher third, including both the former . . . [8]

The pleasure-dome is the creation of human reason united to the absolute power of a single will, and sanctified by its location on the sacred river. But the fortifications indicate clearly enough that Kubla does not believe in the security of his utopia and prepares us for the tumultuous caves and ancestral prophecies of war in lines 27 through 30. From the very beginning Kubla's walled-in paradise is associated with war and with death, a frozen geometric death reminiscent of the lowest depths of Dante's *Inferno* where Satan's desperate wings eternally harden the ice prison from which he senselessly struggles to escape. The demonic reference is re-enforced by association with Milton's Satan building the glorious palace of Pandemonium in *Paradise Lost,* a pleasure-dome for fallen angels in place of their forfeited bliss.

2. The Chasm

Kubla's conception of the reconciliation of nature and civilization is the "arithmetical juxtaposition" of gardened palace and forests protected by walls. His concept of religion combines the sacred character of the river

and the terrors of the measureless caverns it feeds. Those dark depths
are the dead end of his imagination; the idea of immortality is beyond
his reach, except in the pagan form of an ancestral cult as we shall
learn at the end of the stanza. Kubla is a pagan priest-king.

The sense of the opening lines of the stanza beginning with the cry
of amazement, "But Oh!" may be construed in this manner: Kubla,
without realizing it, built his earthly paradise around or near a "deep
romantic chasm", the source of a fountain of tremendous force. It is a
"savage place", holy rather than sacred, a place of mystery and enchantment, not subject to geometric arrangement and "haunted by woman
wailing for her demon-lover". This evocation of the preternatural in
contrast with the aspects of nature subjected by Kubla's rational architecture brings with it a whole series of associated contrasts which make
up the symbolic fabric of the poem: "sunny dome", "waning moon",
day and night, reason and instinct, the civilized discipline of the state
and the demonic fury of unknown chaotic forces. But above all it is the
separation, revealed through Kubla's unawareness of the chasm, of male
and female. The State is associated with the male principles of reason,
conquest, and death; the chasm with the female principles of instinct,
desire, and birth. Kubla is the active builder who forces his will on man
and nature alike. The woman wails but must passively await her absent
lover. Reason encompasses the sacred; instinct is the source of the holy.
But one without the other remains incomplete: reason narrow in its
range, instinct blind with passion.

In lines 17 through 30 the movement from the fountain coming to
birth in the matrix of the chasm through the winding flow of the sacred
river to its final collapse in the caverns is described as a continuous
process. The passage combines the imagery of the volcanic fury of a
huge geyser with spasmodic, orgasmic release and excruciating birth
pangs to express the poet's religious awe before the unfathomable creative power of nature. This frightening but life giving chaos of wild
nature is the holy source of the sacred river to which Kubla is deaf and
blind. The fountain is the proof that the caverns do not end in a "sunless sea". The waters move through underground passages unknown to
man and reveal their immortality in the rebirth of fountains.

"Alph" is, in the first instance, derived from alpha and aleph, the
beginning, i.e., the river gets its name from the fountain; it is the river
of life, although Kubla conceives of it only as the omega of death. But
"Alph" is also Alpheus, the river-god who loved the nymph Arethusa,
sworn to virginity by the moon-goddess Artemis. To escape his pursuit

Arethusa was changed into a fountain. The waters of Alpheus still seek to join Arethusa underground. They move, according to ancient legends from the Near East, through Greece and Italy, to the head waters of the Nile, another sacred river. The river Alph is thus associated with the male deprived of his female counterpart. His incompletion corresponds to that of the wailing woman.

Born in turmoil, the "sacred river" runs its determined course "through wood and dale", forests and gardens, irrigating both and fertilizing them with the dross thrown up by the fountain — "the dancing rocks". Its time in the sun is brief, no longer than the five ages of man. Life meanders through an apparently incomprehensible maze to the mysterious finality of death. The arithmetic juxtaposition of fountain, river and caves, i.e. birth, life, death, produces no totalizing significance, no sense of the organic continuity or moral meaning of natural process. From turmoil to tumult through a maze, Kubla has done his best.

The point is that this ground belongs to the emperor, that the pleasure-dome was built for him and to the glory of his state and according to his decree. Lines 29 and 30 sum up his failure to bequeath to mankind an image of the earthly paradise. He remains cut-off from the holy sources of life whose eternity and power escape his wisdom. He accepts the "lifeless ocean", tumultuous meaningless death, death without redemption, without immortality as the image of man's fate. Contrary to his intention to achieve a higher synthesis, he sunders civilization and nature, reason and instinct, man and woman, in the name of his power and world empire. Between the two infinite mysteries of our origin and destiny he has measured out the sacred in the five short miles of life's determined and apparently meaningless course through the maze of "sinuous rills" which nourish the gardens of his pleasures. With blasphemous arrogance he has made Xanadu into the shrine of his own divinity.

But the ancestral prophecies of war rise to haunt him from the tomb and spoil his pleasure. The fortified pleasure-dome, like the paradise of the gods of Epicurus, was supposed to protect Kubla from all the cares of mortal men and to secure to him and all his successors an eternal and unalloyed sensuous delight. But the walls and towers which exclude mankind necessarily reveal Kubla's unavowed misgivings and fears. "The stately pleasure-dome" i.e. the conception of paradise generated by the state, is doomed to destruction by war. That is why lines 1 through 30 are consistently written in the past tense. Xanadu exists no more than the empires of Kubla or Ozymandias.

The Poet

3. His Judgment

Enter Coleridge, summarizing the essentials of Kubla's creation, summarizing and passing judgment. Kubla, descendant of the sun, worships the sun as part of the cult of ancestor worship. The pleasure palace is also a temple. Of course, the sun also symbolizes reason, the source of all enlightenment, the arts and sciences of civilization. Sun worship is an ambiguous business: ancestral ghosts and reason do not mix to a consistent theology; their juxtaposition in the unperceiving mind of the Khan denotes superstition. The Ancestral voices predicting doom from beyond the cavernous grave of the sacred river are a mournful reminder of the lifeless, sunless ocean on which the "sunny pleasure dome" has its ultimate foundations. The only "miracle" that can hold them together has to be a "device", an artificial and mechanical piece of human ingenuity, brilliant in a sense, an impressive achievement, but like Kubla's empire, destined to disintegrate. Coleridge's admiration is real, but knows bounds.

So much for the relation of dome and caves; again there is no sign that Kubla is aware of the fountain. Within the shadow of the dome cast upon the river by the sun, equidistant between the fountain and the caves, in the blindspot of reason, so to speak, the harmonious reconciliation of all the previously named contradictions is prefigured.

At that mid-point, neither deafened by the "tumult" of the caves nor overwhelmed by the "turmoil" of the fountain stands the poet. It is the perfect vantage point for perceiving the wholeness of Kubla's ephemeral "miracle." Four short irregular lines with a rhythm like dance or laughter, followed by a perfect heroic couplet, catch both his irony and wonderment. They prepare the way for the shift to the first person of the fourth stanza. Kubla's miracle was but is no more; the rest of the poem replaces state power with poetic vision.

4. The Poet's Vision and Mission

In lines 37 to 41 Coleridge enters fully into the poem as "I." From here to the end poetic vision is counterposed to imperial decree. The "damsel with a dulcimer" arises from an inner vision which he has lost. On the other hand, the woman of the chasm lies outside the range of Kubla's thought and decree. The damsel sings and plays a stringed instrument; her civilized music is opposed to the demonic wailing of the first. The Mount Abora of her song is the most complicated enigma of this most enigmatic poem.

In the Crewe manuscript Coleridge changed "Amara" to "Abora." "Amara" was Milton's name for a legendary earthly paradise near the headwaters of the sacred river Nile:

> . . . where *Abassin* Kings their issue Guard,
> Mount *Amara,* though this by some suppos'd
> True Paradise under the *Ethiop* Line
> By *Nilus* head, enclos'd with shining Rock,
> A whole day's journey high, . . . [9]

Why the change? In the first place, the association of "Amara" with a prison contradicts the entire purpose of the closing stanza which is to oppose systematically and point by point the works of the Poet to those of the Emperor already judged to be inadequate. The top of "Mount Amara" was walled-in by an impenetrable fortification of natural rock in which the Abyssinian Kings imprisoned their disobedient offspring. J. B. Beer explains why "Abora" solves the problem positively, adding new and rich associations to Coleridge's idea and maintaining the basic sense of the stanza in relation to the rest of the poem.

Two reasons may be suggested. The first is that the word 'abor' appears on the second page of Holwell's mythological dictionary with the comment that 'the Sun was called Abor, the parent of light.'[10] The second is that Beth-Abara was the place where Christ was baptized in Jordan by John the Baptist, and where the spirit descended upon him 'like a dove.' Milton used it in *Paradise Regained,* and Coleridge used it as a symbol for the place where Truth is revealed to man.[11]

The gain is considerable. The Poet, like Kubla, is a descendant of the sun, but it is the spiritual sun of inner illumination, a Christian, not a pagan sun. The biblical connotations of "Abara" confer on the Poet a sacerdotal mission sanctified by the Christian religion, rendering conquest and appropriation unnecessary. Poetic creation is a self-ordaining act through which the inspired Poet becomes the instrument of divine truth.

The damsel's evocation of paradise through song responds to Kubla's creation by decree. In poetic vision, man and woman, the passive and active mind, the unconscious and the conscious, combine to create poetry, a music of the imagination objectified in symbols depicting nature as a vast harmony, in which all oppositions are resolved and reconciled. Recalled from the depths of the poetic unconscious, the maid becomes one with the Poet, imbues his inchoate feelings and longings with articulate sound and speech, and brings to life the inanimate strings of the dulcimer. That is why Coleridge does not sing of Mount Abora in his own name. The rest of the poem asserts, shouts in a frenzied enthusiasm, god-possession, that if he could rediscover within himself the lost music of her inspiration, he would achieve in poetry and bequeath to all a paradisiac delight to pale Kubla's monument.[12]

The superiority of music to decree, of imagination to reason, of the woman-vision to masculine power is suggested as early as 1795, when Coleridge wrote "The Eolian Harp" apparently inspired by hearing the breeze play through the strings of a lute in the idyllic setting of his cottage in Somersetshire and in the tender company of his wife, Sarah. I cite the passage because it throws further light on the meaning of the dulcimer.

> Full many a thought uncall'd and undetain'd,
> And many idle flitting phantasies,
> Traverse my indolent and passive brain,
> As wild and various as the random gales
> That swell and flutter on this subject Lute!
>   And what if all of animated nature
> Be but organic Harps diversely fram'd,
> That tremble into thought, as o'er them sweeps
> Plastic and vast, one intellectual breeze,
> At once the soul of each, and God of all?[13]

The dulcimer symbolizes living nature whose hidden symphonic harmonies come to expression through poetic intuition of the spiritual oneness of the world. The same "intellectual breeze" which stirs all things lives in the poet. The "Abyssinian maid" symbolizes that spirit and is the sole hope that mankind will ever regain paradise.

Again it is J. B. Beer who gives the best explanation of Coleridge's preference for the dulcimer over the harp, lyre or lute. Coleridge had read in Burney's *History of Music* that the Sambuca (Dulcimer) gave a more feminine sound than any of the others. Beer suggests:

> The lyre is the traditional instrument of Apollo and the bards: and I do not think it fanciful to suppose that Coleridge had seen in the sambuca a symbol of the feminine complement for which he was

seeking — of the passive, delicate music which would sustain his own, stronger music and turn it into the mingled measure of his ideal vision.[14]

The distance between the poet and the emperor cannot be measured; they are not of the same world. Lines 42 to 54 proclaim the poet's mission in opposition to the Khan's; not to conquer but to seek within, not pleasure but delight, not law but music, not on behalf of the poet alone, but of all mankind. In the realm of the poetic imagination there are neither walls nor towers, neither war nor the dead hand of the past. The mission of the poet is to "build that dome in air, that sunny dome! those caves of ice!" That is, to achieve the synthesis of birth and death, civilization and nature, man and woman, thought and feeling.

But this is metonymy: the dome and the caves stand for the entirety of the earthly paradise which the poet carries within the chasm of his creative imagination. "And from this chasm" the fountain of poetry gushes, not with the volcanic chaos of nature in its most frenzied violence, but with the order and beauty of inspired prophetic truth. The lost vision of the damsel lies somewhere in those spiritual depths, the source of harmonious music as against "ceaseless turmoil." Her song and play represent the wholeness of the mind which enables the poet to see and capture the creative principle of nature as a single unity.

It is for the poet to assume the great task which the state could not and cannot fulfill: to keep alive in the human soul the image of a joyous humanity reconciled with itself, with nature, with God. The poet must assume this mission although men, awe-struck and frightened by his vision will close their eyes and circumscribe, build a psychological, a spiritual wall around the inspired prophet. But in his isolation the poet prefigures in his creative ecstasy the joy of a regenerate humanity. He is the sign of the future. Through him the infinite, immortal and universal spirit overcomes the perishable masonry of vain empires. Hope for the future lies with the poet, the true but unacknowledged legislator of mankind, the awesome carrier of a holy mission, a messiah proclaiming a new dispensation, a new Christianity which may supplant the idolatrous worship of the profane state.

III

There is general agreement that between 1796 and '98 or '99 Coleridge was, through characteristic metaphysical and mystical meanderings, and with "mazy motion," moving away, then turning away from his youthful radical enthusiasms, never to return. That turning set him on the course toward the reactionary caverns of clerisy and related Tory twaddle in which he buried the divine genius of his erring youth.

The best dating of "Kubla Khan" is that between 1798 and 1800. For my purposes, summer 1798 will do as well as a later dating, although Coleridge specialists, pursuing other purposes, will no doubt go on trying to establish it exactly. Colmer says: "After the death of the *Watchman*", (Coleridge's own political journal which ceased publication in May of 1796) "and until he became a leader-writer on the *Morning Post* in November of 1799, he relied wholly on verse for the communication of his political views."[15] With the *Watchman* he gave up the idea of a political career, retired to the country to read and muse on the deepest issues of religion and morality, metaphysics and mysticism. His growing dislike for atheism parallels his increasing doubts about the French Revolution as it decayed its way through the Directory and towards Napoleon. He was still a staunch opponent of the war in which England, under the hated Pitt ministry, allied itself with the worst of European tyrants, even Catherine of Russia, to crush the infant French Republic. ("Ode to the Departing Year," Dec. 1796).

He still excoriated private property as the source of all evil[16] and the beastly bourgeois (Whig merchants) who worship the golden calf forged from the coin of the laboring poor and from war profits. From his idyllic retreat he defended and praised the upholders of free expression in word and print against the witch-hunting anti-sedition laws of the government. But his immediate political concern was on the wane as his full poetic powers came to fruition in the "Rime of the Ancient Mariner" and "Christable" (1797). Thus Woodring: "If 'Christable,' 'Kubla Khan,' and 'The Ancient Mariner' are poems of escape, politics form a large part of what they escape from."[17]

Escape from politics or not, "Kubla Khan" is sufficiently different from the other two to warrant attention to the distinctive fact that here a depoliticized Coleridge invokes the despot of one of the greatest empires on human record in the title and theme of his poem. Between the Khan and the Mariner, Kubla and Christabel lies a political crisis. In January, 1798, Napoleon's armies marched into Switzerland and Coleridge's last flickering hopes that the revolution in France would be a great dawn of liberty for all of mankind turned into the indignant "palinodia" of his "France: An Ode", February, 1798.

It is indeed a full-fledged recantation, passionate with conviction, of the trembling fervor with which he greeted the great revolution in

France and rejoiced in its victories over "the dire array" of invading tyrants.

> With what a joy my lofty gratulation
> Unawed I sang, amid a slavish band:[18]

He calls upon all the elements of nature, "Yea, everything that is and will be free!" to bear witness how he was "inspired beyond the guess of folly" by the thought of liberty during his moonlit wanderings in the depths of the solitary woods. Clouds, sky and sea become the very image of freedom which filled him with an exaltation inseparable from his revolutionary hopes. But now:

> Forgive me, Freedom! O forgive those dreams!
> I hear thy voice, I hear thy loud lament,
> From bleak Helvetia's icy caverns sent — [19]

The France of Bonaparte now joins forces with oppressive kings in wars of conquest and enslavement. The French people,[20] by accepting this policy of aggression, show that their revolt had *dark* and *sensual* motives. They burst their chains for heavier chains and call it liberty:

> O Liberty! with profitless endeavour
> Have I pursued thee, many a weary hour;
> But thou nor swell'st the victor's strain, nor ever
> Didst breathe thy soul in forms of human power.[21]

Here in a nutshell is the first moral of the recantation. Coleridge admits to the mistake of having believed that the state, any state, could establish liberty among men. He was misled because he saw the revolution as a revolt of human nature against oppressive institutions. He confounded free nature and free nation in his worship of "Liberty." He understands now that Liberty shuns "factious Blasphemy's obscener slave", — the atheistic French Revolution — as well as conquerors and priests.

> And there I felt thee! — on that sea-cliff's verge,
> Whose pines, scarce travelled by the breeze above,
> Had made one murmur with the distant surge!
> Yes, while I stood and gazed, my temples bare,
> And shot my being through earth, sea and air,
> Possessing all things with intensest love,
> O Liberty! my spirit felt thee there.[22]

Clearly this goes further than a political recantation of former beliefs or a disgust with politics in general. He is confessing to a fundamental philosophical error, and for a worshiper of liberty, to a religious heresy. He was wrong about the nature of liberty which resides in a communion of love between man and the totality of nature.

"France: An Ode," ends like "Kubla Khan" with an image of the poet discovering in nature and in a kind of ecstasy the great Romantic truth that man's oneness with the universe is the secret of his freedom and happiness; and in both cases the discovery is counterposed to political figures — Napoleon and Kubla. The analogy is, to be sure, only formal: the "Ode" is a direct political response to contemporary events; "Kubla Khan" is a mythopoeic vision about the essence of the political. The movement from politics to political vision is described by Coleridge himself in a letter written to his clergyman-brother George.[23]

This palinodia in prose is meant to prove to his orthodox Tory and Anglican family that "our opinions and feelings on political subjects are more nearly alike than you imagine them to be." He denies any taint of "French Metaphysics, French Politics, French Ethics, and French Theology." Nothing distinguishes the contemporary rulers of France from "other animals of the same species."

> History has taught me that Rulers are much the same in all ages and under all forms of government: they are as bad as they dare to be. The Vanity of Ruin and the curse of Blindness have clung to them, like an hereditary Leprosy. Of the French Revolution I can give my thoughts the most adequately in the words of Scripture — 'A great and strong wind rent the mountains and brake in pieces the rocks before the Lord; but the Lord was not in the wind; and after the wind an earthquake; but the Lord was not in the earthquake: and after the earthquake a fire — and the Lord was not in the fire:' and now (believing that no calamities are permitted but as the means of Good) I wrap my face in my mantle and wait with a subdued and patient thought, expecting to hear 'the still small Voice', which is of God.

And news from America describing the decline of public and private morality confirms this lesson and reveals to him once again the basic illusion which makes it so hard to teach: "the error of attributing to Governments a talismanic influence over our virtues and our happiness — as if Governments were not rather effects than causes." Government is a necessary evil, a natural product of "original sin" for which "the Spirit of the Gospel is the sole cure."

"I am of no party. . . . I am no Whig, no Reformist, no Republican." Denouncing all such fiery and undisciplined spirits, he blames their increase on the unprincipled ministry. "I have snapped my squeaking baby-trumpet of Sedition and the fragments lie scattered in the lumber room of Penitence."

Then the decisive passage, the transition from Napoleon to Kubla, from politics to poetry, from combat to vision, is stated as a conscious program of life:

> I have for some time past withdrawn myself almost totally from the consideration of *immediate* causes, which are infinitely complex and uncertain, to muse on fundamental and general causes — the causae causarum — I devote myself to such works as encroach not on the antisocial passions — in poetry, to elevate the imagination and set the affections in right tune by the beauty of the inanimate impregnated, as with a living soul, by the presence of Life — in prose, to the seeking with patience and a slow, very slow mind, "Quid sumus, et quidnam victuri gignimur" — What our faculties are and what they are capable of becoming.

His love for nature has brought him tranquillity of mind which he desires to communicate to his fellow man, thus "to destroy the bad passions not by combating them, but by keeping them in inaction." He quotes his good angel, Wordsworth, who praises the lover of nature as the true lover of mankind:

> Accordingly, he by degrees perceives
> His feelings of aversion softened down,
> A holy tenderness pervade his frame!
> His sanity of reason not impair'd
> Say rather that his thoughts now flowing clear
> From a clear fountain flowing, he looks round —
> He seeks for Good and finds the Good he seeks.[24]

And so, as in "Kubla Khan," we move in this letter from the rockshattering violence of nature to the inner fountain of inspiration which is "the still small Voice" of God. Political recantation has become religious repentance, moral reform, philosophical apostasy. Moreover, the political issues have been superseded by all-embracing metaphysical abstractions which leave Coleridge safe within the bounds of his reverend brother's discourse. In the name of that necessitarian, pantheistic Christianity, which is more a personal faith than a theology, he denounces the atheistic radicals who side with the French and who stir the people to seditious acts against the public peace. He had contempt for their personal immorality which made a mockery of their abstract philanthropic intentions. But above all he feared them as demagogues who could unleash the same blind mob chaos in England that had brought disaster to France. Coleridge could sympathize with the sufferings of the exploited poor but he feared them.

In April rumors of an impending French invasion swept England. "Fears In Solitude" is more than a sad reflection on the horrors of war; it is a summary of Coleridge's political and philosophical feelings at that time. It restates the themes and attitudes of "France: An Ode," then being published, and the letter to his brother. Again he recants the follies of his youth, denounces the atheistic French and communes with nature. But several ideas pertinent to this study are more explicitly related than before and acquire a more precise sense.

Alone, in a silent, misty dell near Stowey he finds "Religious meanings in the forms of Nature!"[25] "In a half sleep, he dreams of better worlds", [26] and his heart is heavy with the thought that men who are brothers under God may soon be killing one another amid these peaceful fields, "beneath this blessed sun!"[27] He confesses England's wrongs abroad and at home, which have made her enemies among oppressed multitudes all around the world: slavery and disease brought to primitive peoples, corrupt institutions, money-lust, and exploitation of the poor:

> We have drunk up, demure as at a grace,
> Pollutions from the brimming cup of wealth;
> Contemptuous of all honourable rule,
> Yet bartering freedom and the poor man's life
> For gold, as at a market[28]

Religion is reduced to a mechanical, hypocritical, mindless mummery, so that "faith doth reel"[29] and atheism stalks the land. Britain, which has never suffered foreign invasion, sends its armies to devastate other lands, blasphemously invoking God in its cause and mouthing the abstractions of military strategy without an inkling of the cost in human blood and misery:

> We send our mandates for the certain death
> Of thousands and ten thousands! Boys and girls,
> And women, that would groan to see a child
> Pull off an insect's leg, all read of war
> The best amusement for our morning meal![30]

On such an England the coming French invasion appears as God's just retribution. Coleridge understood the moral dynamics of imperialism, brutalizing the conqueror as he brutalizes the conquered. But the invasion must be repulsed; the French, "impious and false, a light yet cruel race",[31] cannot act as God's scourge. A victorious and repentant England should soberly and honestly face the bitter truths of her past sins and work to amend. And then, versifying a passage from his letter to George, he discloses the heart of the error which has misled too many of his countrymen!

> We have been too long
> Dupes of a deep delusion! Some, belike,
> Groaning with restless enmity, expect
> All change from change of constituted power;
> As if a Government had been a robe,
> On which our vice and wretchedness were tagged
> Like fancy-points and fringes, with the robe
> Pulled off at pleasure. Fondly these attach
> A radical causation to a few
> Poor drudges of chastising Providence,
> Who borrow all their hues and qualities
> From our own folly and rank wickedness,
> Which gave them birth and nursed them. Others, meanwhile
> Dote with a mad idolatry; and all
> Who will not fall before their images,
> And yield them worship, they are enemies
> Even of their country!
> Such have I been deemed.[32]

With this plague on the houses of revolutionaries and reactionaries alike, Coleridge once again bows out of politics. His patriotism is based on more solid stuff than his views on constituted government or his opinions of the "poor drudges" called by God to be chastizing ministers. His love for country is as deep as family bonds and friendships, as the nature which inspired his noblest thoughts and poetic feelings, as his religious and moral beliefs. These are not political abstractions but a deeply felt oneness with England in her time of need. As evening falls and he leaves the dell for home, he is startled at the crest of a hill by an imposingly beautiful prospect of land and sea, church steeples, his friend's house and his family cottage beyond, in a single picture, by everything that makes him a patriot.

> This burst of prospect . . .
> . . . seems like society —
> Conversing with the mind, and giving it
> A livelier impulse and a dance of thought![33]

The love of nature has taught him the love of men which is true patriotism, the politics of the heart which no "Courts, Committees, Institutions, Associations and Societies"[34] can encompass. Nature becomes society, i.e., the true doctrine of society can only be the true doctrine of nature. The poet becomes a seer when he has turned his back on the state and seeks wisdom in the "religious meanings in the forms of nature!"[35] That, too, is the underlying idea of "Kubla Khan."

IV

Whether Coleridge wrote "Kubla Khan" sometime between May and September 1798, or as Elisabeth Schneider cogently argues, after his return from Germany in 1799 or later, it marks the climax of a complex ideological transformation in which politics plays as prime mover. Whether or not the businessman from Porlock ever really interrupted the glorious opium dream "in which all the images rose up before him as things, with a parallel production of the correspondent expressions, without any sensation or consciousness of effort",[36] attitudes, ideas, images and words which inform the structure and diction of "Kubla Khan" are central in the prose and verse of 1798 as conscious thought. In that language he is trying to come to terms with the overriding issues of the time, issues ineluctably thrust upon thinking men by the French Revolution and its consequences. Napoleon's invasion of Switzerland is for Coleridge much more than a political crisis; it forced him to rethink his entire philosophy of life and to fight it out with foes, friends and family, man, God and nature. We may now be in a position to complete our analysis of "Kubla Khan" as anti-political vision and to raise some fundamental questions concerning its value to us.

If Coleridge ever felt unqualified enthusiasm for the French Revolution, it did not last long. In so far as we can speak of any consistency in his attitude, it was directed against Pitt's policy of alliance with continental tyrants for the purpose of intervening in the internal affairs of France in favor of a Bourbon restoration. He continued to oppose that policy and to demand peace with France even after Napoleon had shattered his last illusions and hopes about the French Revolution, judging that its major result was to drive the revolutionaries to insane extremes of terror at home and war abroad. That is one of the morals of his satiric poem "Recantation: Illustrated in the Story of the Mad Ox", first written in the summer of 1798 around the time of the supposed composition of "Kubla Khan."

Coleridge deserves credit for having understood that the character of the revolution was in part a result of the foreign interventions and that its decay was the price it had to pay for self-preservation. What he did not and could not see was the historic significance of the unprecedented rising of the masses. He feared and hated the sedition of the mob and believed in the mission of the enlightened few. His utopian scheme for a Pantisocracy of select virtuous spirits who were to found without violence the reign of true liberty was conceived as an alternative to the French Revolution. But with Southey's apostasy and the failure of his journalistic plans he was left high and dry in the real world with the problem of finding a new escape. Fortunately this was poetry, and 1797-98 saw his best. It was also a period of intense religious and philosophical meditation, a deeply refreshing experience as compared to politics. He writes to Estlin in July, 1797:

> . . . I am wearied with politics, even to soreness — I never knew a passion for politics exist for a long time without swallowing up, or absolutely excluding, a passion for Religion — .[37]

By the time he writes to his brother in March of the following year, his political "soreness" has become a programmatic withdrawal from politics, buttressed by philosophic and religious reasonings. Governments, all governments, are original sin made visible, necessary evils brought on by man's depravity which they merely express, God's appointed scourges. Between the two letters fell Napoleon's invasion of Switzerland.

J. B. Beer shows that Coleridge had more than a passing knowledge of the Tartar Empire of the Khans. In *The Friend*, he spoke of Napoleon's attempts to "transform Europe into a Tartar Empire and elsewhere of Timur Khan as being, like Napoleon, an agent of God's wrath."[38] He saw both Napoleon and the Khan as types of Commanding Genius whose ambiguous role in history was that of fallen angels, preserving something of their divine origin most apparently in times of peace but demonically destructive during great historic upheavals. Thus, Kubla can build a magnificent pleasure-dome but cannot make it last because the "destructive element" he carries within him finds its way like a snake into his earthly paradise. The idea of the unity of opposites was not strange to Coleridge.

He liked to quote Tom Paine's dictum: "Government, like dress, is the badge of lost innocence; the palaces of kings are built on the ruins of the bowers of paradise." Beer shows the pertinence of this idea in discussing the second stanza of "Kubla Khan". The horrendous fountain is not a glorified image of creative energy in its highest manifestations: "I take such imagery to represent the 'Typhonic' element in the poem."[39] He shows by comparing the stanza to passages from other poems and political writings of Coleridge, that he linked the State to images of senseless violence. But Beer does not make an adequate distinction between two kinds of violence: that which imposes rigid rational forms on natural processes they cannot contain, and the explosive fury which reduces them to dust. In antiquity, Typho, the thousand-handed monster, laid low by Zeus's thunderbolt beneath Mount Aetna, was the image of popular uprising, and mob violence. Kubla's "stately pleasure-dome" is of the first kind, and the fountain is the opposite it contains. Civilization and nature stand to one another in a dialectic of repression precariously hemming in unfathomable forces. In "Religious Musings" we get both terms of this dialectic as specific and interrelated forces. The Whore of Babylon who represents the Roman Empire in the *Book of Revelation* is footnoted by E. H. Coleridge, Samuel Taylor's grandson: "I am convinced that the Babylon of the Apocalypse does not apply to Rome exclusively; but to the union of Religion with Power and Wealth, wherever it is found."[40] She gives birth among other ghastly shapes to "Moon-blasted Madness when he yells at midnight!"[41] Kubla is the supreme example of the "union of Religion with Power and Wealth." The wailing woman "beneath a waning moon" haunts the source of the "Typhonic" fountain which imperils Kubla's creation. Again, in "Religious Musings," we see the same dialectical movement, but from the other side. Coleridge is describing mob violence in the French Revolution:

> . . . for lo! the Giant Frenzy
> Uprooting empires with his whirlwind arm
> Mocketh high Heaven; burst hideous from the cell
> Where the old Hag, unconquerable, huge,
> Creation's eyeless drudge, black Ruin, sits
> Nursing the impatient earthquake.[42]

Thus does the "half-intermitted burst" of the volcanic fountain constantly threaten an ultimate catastrophe. Beer concludes;

> All this has its place in the second stanza and its imagery. Kubla
> Khan, the man of commanding genius, has temporarily imposed his
> will upon nature, but untamed forces still exist which can in a moment
> destroy the fragile pattern of order, security, and pleasure which he
> has set up. In consequence, the imagery here brings out and develops the
> theme which was foreshadowed in the sacred river and the sunless sea:
> the theme of a *natura naturata* out of harmony with *natura naturans.* [43]

And yet the fact, recognized by Beer, that these and others he cites are
specifically political references and images hardly influences his interpretation of the poem as a contrast of commanding and absolute genius.
In his most general statement about the poem, Beer completely avoids
its specifically political content: " 'Kubla Khan,'to sum up, is a poem
with two major themes: genius and the lost paradise." [44] His interpretation falls short of the full significance of his scholarship. This results
from Beer's failure to see Kubla in the first place as a political figure,
the conquering empire-builder, who made the name of Khan the dread
of two continents. Beer describes him as, "nearer to the ancient Eastern
priests," [45] who combined the functions of kings, theologians, judges,
astronomers, surveyors, physicians, and artists. The emperor Kubla is
absorbed into the type of commanding genius; thus the most concrete
meaning of the poem, its critique of the institution of the State, is made
to appear as a by-product of Coleridgean metaphysics. By emphasizing
Kubla's relation to Napoleon and the French Revolution, I do not
overthrow Beer's interpretation. On the contrary, it has been of invaluable service in uncovering the ideological sources which reveal "Kubla
Khan" to be the adequate expression of Coleridge's estimate of his
relationship to his times.

I am not claiming that Kubla is Napoleon; indeed such a view
would contradict the basic point of this paper, namely, that the poem
deals with the nature or essence of the State, Washington's and Pitt's,
as well as Bonaparte's. I do believe, however, that Napoleon provided
the occasion and the model for Coleridge's anti-political vision. Why,
then, did he write about Kubla and not Napoleon? Precisely because he
was after the abstract principle and not the immediate political issue;
because the legendary and exotic character of Kubla allowed for a
general statement, a philosophical absolute, which a contemporary reference, even to the great Napoleon, would have reduced to a mere
political diatribe; because to oppose the apotheosis of S. T. Coleridge to
the ephemeral Bonaparte would appear ridiculous as well as immodest,

whereas the victory of the vatic Poet, the messianic spokesman for all animate nature over the Power Principle embodied in the Khan transcends time, place, and personality as do all Eternal Truths. That is why mythopoeic trance, opium dream, prophetic revelation is his chosen mode of poetic discourse. The mythic symbol gives at once concrete image and depth of meaning, sensation and hidden truth.

Mythopoeia has another function, an aesthetic one, to raise the poet's vision to sublime heights, heroic grandeur. Miltonic diction was for Coleridge the unsurpassed model of epic style and particularly fitting in a poem about paradises artificial, real, lost and to be found. If Kubla's "sunless sea" and "caves of ice" may recall Dante's self-imprisoned Devil, Coleridge later in life associated Napoleon and Milton's Satan "as creatures who glory in the proud assertion of the self-sufficient human will."[46] The overthrow in men's minds of the idolatrous worship of the false gods of the State is the sacred mission of the poet. Thus is Coleridge's flight from the political realities of his day metamorphosed into an heroic assault on the bastions of human prejudice and delusion, with the inspired poet leading the vanguard of enlightened spirits into the fray despite the rejection of the fearful multitude. The truth of history is that political revolution betrayed by tyrants come and go, a bloody, repetitive succession of disappointments. The poet alone can truly lead mankind out of the infernal cycle and to the happiness of spiritual peace in harmonious reconciliation with himself and God's nature.

"Kubla Khan" has all the markings of Coleridge's reactionary politics. Although it is directed against the two Tartar despots, Kubla and Napoleon, Coleridge links Bonapartist imperialism and the French Revolution in a single anathema. The poem is an exhortation to abandon political struggle for the sake of the higher cultivation of the aesthetic, moral, and religious qualities of the soul. It is an attack on eighteenth-century Enlightenment caricatured as an age of dehumanized rationalism. It glorifies the poet as a prophetic spokesman for "clerisy" and as the carrier of ancient religious wisdom which it pits against the blindness and folly of modernity. It separates poetry from history, sublimating its meaning into the theological realms of absolute Truth and eternal categories of Good and Evil. Humanity will be happy in the future only if it restores Coleridge's mythical version of an idealized Christian past. Politically speaking, it is the opium dream of an avid reader of old books.

But "Kubla Khan" is a great poem. It has been in and out of

fashion, but I am convinced that it will live despite the basically reactionary political ideology which informs its structure. It is not enough to justify this opinion by insisting on the beauty and power of its language; such beauty and power have to be explained in their turn. Coleridge is here defending positive values of humanity and civilization despite his politics. If the history of the State oscillates between the blind violence of the mob and retributive tyrannical oppression of heartless rulers, all is not lost. The creative spirit of mankind, symbolized by the poet, will outlive, because it is eternal, all the Khans and Napoleons of this world. This creative power is associated with a struggle against the alienating impersonality of state power with man's oneness with *natura naturans* for his regeneration and harmonious self-realization, humanization. The poet as creator of beauty is the *avant-guard* of this process and must accept the burden of suffering which arises from the general incomprehension of his role. Coleridge's image of the inspired artist living under conditions of bourgeois society has become a commonplace; it is perhaps his most impressive prophecy. But the ring of total conviction which enlivens his verse is based on a deep belief that man's need for a better life, his desire to overcome alienation, will lead him to understand the liberating power of poetic prophecy. No matter how unfounded this belief has proved itself in the bourgeois era and despite the obfuscating mythopoeia, he hits upon a basic truth well-known to Marx: that the structure of bourgeois life is inherently hostile to art, to beauty, and to the free expression of man's creative powers. These are values well worth defending, although they can no longer be understood in the same way in our times. We are in sight of the day when not only this or that tyrant will be overthrown, not only this or that empire disintegrate, but when tyranny and empire will be no more. We can no longer draw hope from the vision of utopian Arcadia; we can use the past only in so far as it enlightens and inspires our work and thought toward new goals. But in the absence of any clear historical understanding of his situation, Coleridge could only draw poetic inspiration from the mystico-Christian pantheism and utopianism which were his personal creed. Coleridge's anti-political, religious ideology provided the only form available to him in which to defend aesthetic and moral values seen as requisite for human dignity and radically incompatible with any conceivable form of state power. *Kubla Khan* is at one and the same time the most enigmatic and the most complete statement of his faith in humanity, a faith which transcends historical time and class struggle: a humanism that must be changed in order to be renewed.[47]

NOTES

1. In departing from the practice of the standard editions which print the poem in three stanzas (1-6, 7-36, 37-54), I am following J.B. Beer who detaches lines 31-36 as a separate stanza in accordance with the printing of the first edition of the poem in 1816. See J.B. Beer, *Coleridge the Visionary*, Chatto and Windus, London, 1959, p. 206. All references in this essay to Coleridge's poems are based on *The Complete Poetical Works of Samuel Taylor Coleridge*, Clarendon Press, Oxford, 1912, edited by Ernest Hartley Coleridge.

2. *Ibid.*. I have frequently taught the poem to classes at Wesleyan University and lectured on it to groups on and off campus.

3. Cf. John L. Lowes, *The Road to Xanadu*, Houghton Mifflin Co., Boston, 1927; G. Wilson Knight, *The Starlit Dome*, Oxford University Press, 1941; Maud Bodkin, *Archetypal Patterns in Poetry*, London, 1948; Norman Fruman, in *Coleridge the Damaged Archangel*, New York, 1971, unfortunately shows no appreciation for Beer's work.

4. Cf. John Colmer, *Coleridge: Critic of Society*, Oxford University Press, 1959; David P. Calleo, *Coleridge and the Idea of the Modern State*, Yale Univ. Press, 1966; Albert E. Hancock, *The French Revolution and the English Poets*, Henry Holt and Co., New York, 1899. Kenneth Burke in "Language as Symbolic Action: Essays on Life, Literature and Method," Berkeley, 1966, senses political feeling in the poem.

5. See Carl Woodring, *Politics in the Poetry of Coleridge*, Univ. of Wisconsin Press, Madison, 1961.

6. See Carl Woodring, "Coleridge and the Khan" in *Essays in Criticism*, Vol. 9, October 1959, pp. 361-368.

7. Taken literally, this can be seen as a 5 by 2 rectangle with the fountain and the caves at either end, either just inside or outside the walls. There are various maps of Xanadu and Coleridge has been criticized for vagueness; but I like this one because the 5 by 2 reminds me of a casket.

8. *Statesman's Manual*, Appendix C, p. 353, in: S.T. Coleridge, *Biographia Literaria*, London, 1817.

9. Milton, *Paradise Lost*, Book IV, lines 280-284.

10. Ab-ora, Hebrew root.

11. Beer, *op. cit.*, p. 256.

12. My colleague, Paul Schwaber, speaking from a psychoanalytic view, commented as follows on this part of my essay:

> In section three you expound Coleridge's presentation of a vatic poet, bearing within his moment of inspiration the dialectical fusion of natural and human possibilities unavailable to Kubla and other political, object-subject, male-female types. But the vision of the damsel with a dulcimer, for all its hope and apparent preferability to the woman wailing for her demon lover, is itself a controlling vision: it is a wish about women: that they be emotionally passive and

delicate, make sweet music, but have none of that pulsating, angry, holy, uncontrollable creative energy associated with the fountain and caverns. The poetic vision that Coleridge celebrates in stanza three is a tractable one, even if it has certain social costs — like isolation for the poet himself. *That*, I think, accounts for the greater force (for me, at least) of the first two stanzas of the poem. For Coleridge's poetic accomplishment and his poetic vision are not synonymous. Could it be that he no longer wrote inspired poetry, though this poem would seem to hold out exactly that promise for him, because actual poetic inspiration for him put him in touch with those wild frenzies of natural force, personally perceived, of which he wanted no further part? To write more Ancient Mariners, Kublas, or Cristabels would be to re-experience, to breathe new life into, imaginative identifications with murder and guilt, omnipotent control, ungovernable energies, nightmarishly perverse sexual desires and failed patterns of control, fit symbols of those "bad passions" he wanted to destroy not by combatting them but by keeping them inactive. I think, in other words, that you have hit upon a solution to the problem of why Coleridge, after 1799, seemed to give up not only politics, but poetry too.

13. *The Eolian Harp*, lines 39-48.

14. J.B. Beer, *op. cit.*, pp. 253-254.

15. John Colmer, *op. cit.*, p. 51.

16. See Griggs, *Letters of S.T. Coleridge*, Oxford, 1956 (Letter to John Thewall, May 13th 1796), p. 212 ff.

17. Woodring, *op. cit.*, p. 223.

18. "France: An Ode," lines 26 and 27. This heroic self-portrait is somewhat of an exaggeration according to most estimates; but it should not be forgotten that it took some courage to speak for France in the 1790's in England. People were being jailed for less, and Coleridge publicly took their side against the government.

19. *Ibid.*, Stanza IV, lines 64-66. The lament of the icy caverns recalls the tumult of Kubla's "caves of ice." There is no space here to show numerous other parallels with "Kubla Khan."

20. Coleridge hoped briefly for a popular uprising which would overthrow Napoleon and restore the tarnished glory of the revolution.

21. "France: An Ode," Stanza V, lines 89-92.

22. *Ibid.*, Stanza V, lines 99-105.

23. Cf. Griggs, *op. cit.*, Vol. I, p. 394 ff. On March 10, 1798 about a month after the composition of his "France: An Ode." Elisabeth Schneider dates this letter from April 1798. Cf. *Coleridge, Opium and "Kubla Khan"*, University of Chicago Press, Chicago, 1953, p. 318. In the following few pages I shall be quoting at length from this letter.

24. Wordsworth. "These lines originally formed part of the conclusion to 'The Ruined Cottage.' See *Poetical Works of William Wordsworth*, ed. by E. de Selincourt and Helen Darbishire, 5 vols., 1940-49, v. 400-1." quoted in: Griggs, *op.cit.*, Vol. I (Letter to George Coleridge #238, March 10, 1798), p. 398.

25. "Fears in Solitude," line 24.

26. *Ibid.*, line 26.

27. *Ibid.*, line 40

28. *Ibid.*, lines 59-63.

29. *Ibid.*, line 79.

30. *Ibid.*, lines 103-107.

31. *Ibid.*, line 40.

32. *Ibid.*, lines 159-175.

33. *Ibid.*, lines 215-220.

34. *Ibid.*,lines 55-56.

35. In section IV, I have gone over the same ground covered by Albert E. Hancock, *op. cit.*, confirming his general conclusion that Coleridge was moving toward political conservatism between 1796 and 1798. I make, however, the additional point that the ideological form of this shift is the escape from and rejection of politics in the name of poetry and nature.

36. Elisabeth Schneider's book, *op. cit.*, convincingly discredits the Porlock story. My analysis corroborates hers. My tentativeness is meant to make the point that a poem is a form of consciousness even if elaborated in the unconscious workings of the mind.

37. Griggs, *op. cit.*, Vol. I, (Letter #198, 23 July 1797), p. 338.

38. Quoted by J.B. Beer, *op. cit.*, p. 215.

39. *Ibid.*, p. 232.

40. E.H. Coleridge, *op. cit.*, p. 121.

41. "Religious Musings," line 338.

42. *Ibid.*, lines 317-322.

43. J.B. Beer, *op. cit.*, p. 233.

44. *Ibid.*, p. 266.

45. *Ibid.*, p. 226.

46. J. Colmer, *op.cit.*, p. 178. Here again the Khan and the Emperor are birds of a feather.

47. This essay was published in the journal *Romantisme*, Paris Vol. 8, 1974 pp.34-53.

12

BALZAC AND MARX:
Theory of Value

Linda Rudich

"With the *increasing value* of the world of things proceeds in direct proportion the *devaluation* of the world of men."
[Karl Marx, *Economic and Philosophical Manuscripts of 1844*]

"Le Moyen Age, le siècle de Louis XIV, celui de Louis XV, la Révolution et bientôt l'Empire, donneront naissance à une archéologie particulière. Les ruines de l'Eglise et de la Noblesse, celles de la Féodalité, du Moyen Age, sont sublimes et frappent aujourd'hui d'admiration les vainqueurs étonnés, ébahis; mais celles de la Bourgeoisie seront un ignoble détritus de cartonpierre, de plâtres, de coloriages. Cette immense fabrique de petites choses, d'effloresences capricieuses à bon marche, ne donnera rien, pas même de la poussière."
[Balzac from *Ceux qui Disparaissent a Paris*, 1846]

Few would contest that Marx and Balzac had similar views on the effect of bourgeois relations and power in the course of human history. In fact, it would not be out of place to read certain famous passages from Marx as a resume of the content of the *Comédie Humaine*. The following from the Manifesto is an example:

The bourgeoisie, where it has got the upper hand, has put an end to all feudal, patriarchal, idyllic relations. It has piteously torn asunder the motley feudal ties that bound man to his 'natural superiors' and has left

243

no other nexus between man and man than naked self-interest, than callous "cash-payment." It has drowned the most heavenly ecstasies of religious fervor, of chivalrous enthusiasm, of philistine sentimentalism, in the icy water of egotistical calculation. It has resolved personal wealth into exchange-value, and in place of the numberless indefensible chartered freedoms, has set up that single unconscionable freedom — Free Trade. In one word, for exploitation, veiled by religious and political illusions, it has substituted naked, shameless, direct, brutal exploitation. It has converted the physician, the lawyer, the priest, the poet, the man of science, into its paid wage-laborers...

The bourgeoisie has torn away from the family its sentimental veil, and has reduced the family relation to a mere money relation.

I would like to suggest that the harmony in their viewpoints with regard to capitalism, a harmony which extends even to the material substratum of their separate visions, i.e. the language and concepts used in their respective works,[1] has at its source a common point of departure for the analysis of nineteenth-century social reality.

Both Marx and Balzac, with equal scientific fervor, take as the starting point of their social anatomies, the problems of the vital economy (économie vitale) of capitalism. In other words, the key to Balzac's prodigious and powerful realism, is that like Marx, he discovered the unity of the conflicting and seemingly unrelated aspects of social movement in the contradictory nature of all forms of production and reproduction in capitalist society. Again, like Marx, he chose as the most revealing element of this process the necessary transformation of all values into the commodity-form of value as part of the social metabolism of bourgeois society.[2]

My thesis is that Balzac, as a novelist, felt and observed the principal quality of post-revolutionary bourgeois society to be the contradiction between its unrivaled capacity to release and produce new sources of energy and wealth, both material and spiritual, and its inherent incapacity, on the other hand, to create this wealth without destroying all former qualitative relationships, without altering man's relationship to his own nature and creations, without sacrificing man's natural existence to his economic existence; in brief, without paying for the human aspiration towards creation and achievement at the criminal and unnatural cost of self-exploitation and/or the exploitation of others. I think that it is this insight which, as for Marx, was reflected and revealed in the *totality* of the processes and relationships of social existence, that explains why Balzac's work unites in such a special way both a relentless critical attitude and a deep human optimism.

In this paper I propose to examine briefly how the above reading of Balzac sheds light on some recurrent themes in the *Comédie Humaine*.

As we know, the problem of understanding and mastering the formula for the maximum use of human energy and forces ("les problèmes de l'énérgie ou de l'économie vitale") preoccupied Balzac throughout his life. From the beginning (*La Peau de chagrin*),[3] this concern expresses itself in a language borrowed both from ordinary life and political economy. The energy of life is conceived primarily as "capital-vital," and the laws of its movement are those of "capital-argent." "Capital-vital" can be "thésaurisé," "dépensé," "investi," "amorti," "concentré," "dissipé," etc. The first question about the dilemma of existence, which is conceptually the same in Balzac as that of the optimal use of human energy, is thus why a new science or "art de vivre" is necessary; in fact, the need to formulate a theory of "forces humaines" and human equilibrium imposes itself, because the so-called natural laws of human existence are no longer "natural" at all. The terms offered by the "peau" to Raphael de Valentin create an insurmountable problem because they are the limits prescribed for human life, conceived as belonging to the sphere of nature, i. e. the avoidance of excess and the tendency towards equilibrium as commensurate with the natural instinct for self-preservation and self-realization. This ideal of the "juste-milieu," however, though valid for a natural economy (the peasants living close to nature, for example) loses its conservative force, becomes fatal in contemporary society where "le vouloir nous brule et le pouvoir nous détruit." A new equilibrium which is in reality a disequilibrium must be found if one is to maintain oneself in a field of forces where the natural powers of man are inadequate to sustain desire and where his ever-expanding capacities and needs render self-fulfillment inseparable from depravation. Thus the reason that the powers conferred by the talisman not only do not suffice but also become antithetical ("le désir doit étendre...") is that the former natural metabolism they embody no longer sustains life in a social body animated by the unnatural rhythm and demands of capitalist reproduction.

The dilemma of modern existence,[4] poetically symbolized in the "peau de chagrin," originates therefore in the discrepancy between the specific properties of our social "second nature"[5] and those of our internal vital economy. If the traditional philosophies of existence incarnated in the magic skin and the antique dealer are out-moded, it is because a social organism functioning according to the laws of surplus-value has ruptured the unity between our natural balance and our productive powers. In these new circumstances, the avoidance of excess, just as much as its opposite, are extremes. The one reduces man to a minimal, sterile life, to the under-use of his true potentialities; the other, though robbing him prematurely of existence itself, at least permits a factitious self-realization in a momentary happiness. From the beginning, then, this theme coincides with the critique of a social order which cannot unify man's natural impulse to expand his powers over nature, with his equally natural desire for self-conservation and social integration.[6]

The "pathology of social life" is its incapacity to impart life and value to any individual or social resource in its natural form. In a world where money has become the blood of the "corps social," where quantitative exchange-value, not human worth, regulates the social metabolism, all human life which still functions according to nature is doomed to sterility, death, or a vegetative existence. "La vie, n'est-elle pas une machine à laquelle l'argent imprime le mouvement?" says Gobseck, the deformed precursor of all those Balzacian monomaniacs who will live as monuments of capitalism's capacity to reify the human personality, as incarnations of what Marx called "l'individu, devenu capital." It is only by grasping the full metaphorical weight of such fundamental Balzacian observations as "l'or représente toutes les forces humaines," "l'argent, c'est la vie," in brief, the central image of money replacing blood as the vital fluid of the social metabolism, that the depth of Balzac's critique of bourgeois relations can be understood. As always, his attitude is complex. On the one hand, money has the magic powers for its possessor so well-summed up by Marx in his *Economic and Philosophical Manuscripts of 1844*:

> That which I am unable to do as a *man*, and of which therefore all my individual essential powers are incapable, I am able to do by means of *money*. Money thus turns each of these powers into something which in itself it is not — turns it, that is, into its *contrary*...Being the external, common *medium* and *faculty* for turning an *image* into *reality* and *reality* into a mere *image*...*money* transforms the *real essential powers of man and nature* into what are merely abstract conceits and therefore imperfections — into tormenting chimeras — just as it transforms *real imperfections and chimeras* — essential powers which are really impotent, which exist only in the imagination of the individual — into *real powers and faculties*...Money then appears as this *overturning power* both against the individual and against the bonds of society, etc., which claim to be *essences* in themselves. It turns fidelitiy into infidelity, love into hate, hate into love, virtue into vice, etc....

Unfortunately many critics have mistakenly confused Balzac's awareness and fascination with this aspect of the role of money with his approval of it; and this, in spite of his explicit statements to the contrary. In this respect, Raphael's experience is again typical. His desire for wealth as the end-all of human happiness turns out to be an illusion because money "without the knowledge of how to manage it is meaningless." Money is *indispensable* to the full realization of one's internal resources in bourgeois society — but as *means*, not as an *end*. I mention this because all too often Balzac's empirical realism on this point has been misinterpreted.

Much more fundamental however is the ideological meaning attached to the new role money occupies in the social system. As I hope will be clear in this paper, Balzac's observation that money is its life-blood is not merely descriptive. It is the sign, the symptom, the proof that the political economy vaunted by bourgeois liberalism as "rational," "democratic," in conformity with "natural rights," etc. is in truth the opposite. The real significance of this metaphor is that it contains within itself *literarily* Balzac's central view that capitalism is an unnatural, non-organic, inhuman way of organizing social life. Thus the bourgeois' equation of money with life, his substitution of an inorganic principle for the natural principle of life-blood, must be seen as the paradigmatic expression of the reification, quantification, and deformation affecting all human and social relations in bourgeois society.

In this modern "hell" where virtues and true sentiments only survive to the extent that they transform themselves into exchange-values, how can natural intrinsic values ("valeurs-en-soi") and true human qualities preserve themselves?

The problem of the "forces vitales" is central, not because Balzac is preoccupied with personal or metaphysical longevity; his pursuit of a stable equilibrium or organic explanation of human and social metabolism, responds, I think, in the deepest sense, to his alarm and sadness at the human price paid for increased wealth and productivity.[7] The problem of "civilization," of society, is never that it is *a priori* unnatural. On the contrary, it is that the laws of movement of this "second nature," instead of reinforcing man's essential qualities have ruptured the unity of the organism, thus turning passions which were once life-sustaining into "éléments déstructeurs," thought, dissociated from sentiment into a "dissolvant moral," intelligence, deprived of social praxis, into illusory fantasy or paralysing retreat,[8] etc. The disequilibrium characteristic of modern bourgeois man, magnificently summed up in the formula "mourir pour vivre," is that in order to realize himself, to create, to valorize his personal and social wealth of potentialities, he must destroy and deform his internal harmony (between the heart, the body, and the brain) and his external harmony with his own work and society.

Throughout the *Comédie Humaine*, the impasse of this unnatural but inescapable dialectic expresses itself parallel to an equally passionate concern with creation and the new potential, material and spiritual, available to man. In my opinion it is the omnipresence of this nexus of contradictions which permits Balzac to apply his philosophical ideas so fruitfully to the observation of social movement. The longing for a unified explanation of social and mental phenomena which eventually develops into a comprehensive theory of social dynamics represents, as many critics have demonstrated, a major methodological breakthrough in literature, but the theory of interrelatedness alone would have been inadequate, had not the visionary Balzac located the specific and most characteristic contradictions of bourgeois society ("Tout se tient ici-bas" — Balzac).

The hypothesis that the reproduction of individual destinies is at the same time the reproduction of social relationships succeeds precisely because the dilemma of the "forces vitales" has its analogue in the "forces vives" (the forces which impart motion) of the social organism. What we might call Balzac's *enérgetique* underlies not only the physiology of private existence; it also characterizes the vital economy of a "civilisation dont la physionomie sous-entend la germination du bien et du mal" (*La Fille aux yeux d'or*).[9] Not surprisingly modern "drama" for the individual begins psychologically and chronologically at that moment when internal desire or aspiration comes into contact with the "forces réelles" of modern bourgeois society, i.e. in Paris where their contradictory nature is revealed most essentially and in advance of the provinces. Simultaneously a "hell" and a "paradise," "tete du globe, un cerveau qui crève de génie et conduit la civilisation humaine..." and "cadaverous city where people don't have faces but masks," Paris is vitalized, activated morally by its passionate pursuit of gold and pleasure and physically by a vast whirlwind of self-devouring energy. "La, tout fume, tout brûle,...se rallume, étincelle, pétille et se consume." At the core of this "monstrous" city, the epitome of civilisation" generating its eccentric, exorbitant, suicidal motion is a combustible matter, which like modern man's "organisation combustible" is caught up in this terrible dialectic of "mourir pour vivre."

Internal economy and external social economy share the same pathological defect; self-actualization is inseparable from self-consumption; productive activity exacts an excessive interest, an exorbitant expense of vital energy. Thus the unity of the human predicament throughout the *Comédie Humaine*. The money which has become the "vital fluid" of the contemporary social organism, the unnatural circulatory and reproductive system of bourgeois relations obliges all who want to survive and "se faire valoir" to deform their own vital economy. The particularity of the "forces vives," the laws of value of the capitalist marketplace is that they only confer life and motion to value insofar as it is posited as exchange-value. That is, modern drama proceeds from the tragic but ineluctable acknowledgment that there is no life outside of exchange-value.

The tragedies of all the pure characters (Eugénie Grandet, Mme de Mortsauf, Mme de Beauséant, etc.) as well as those of the young idealistic men who must undergo an education to survive in the hell of bourgeois society is that the values by which they live (all of which are pre-capitalist in that they profess a dependence on people, as opposed to things, devotion to non-mediated values such as religion, friendship, family or class, honor, etc.) have no currency in bourgeois society. Goodness, honor, loyalty, genuine love, family feeling, etc., are "noble" and "sublime" virutes in themselves, "vertues intrinsèques." But like the ironic properties of the "peau de chagrin," the natural ideal of harmonious and measured existence that these ideologies incarnate results in melancholy, suffering, victimization, impotence for their possessors the moment they interact with the "forces vives" of the bourgeois ethic. It is essential to understand that such characters are not condemned to martyrdom or retreat because of ill-fortune. Their destinies are directly determined by the laws of the transformation of value in the capitalist marketplace.[10] Vis-a-vis the "forces réelles" of the times, the intrinsic values espoused by these people suffer the fate of all use-values in bourgeois political economy, i. e. they have no value as such.[11] Outside of social circulation, they consume themselves in their use, and in order to circulate in the sphere of social movement, they must sacrifice their integrity, metamorphose themselves from "valeurs naturelles" or "valeurs-en-soi" into "valeurs réelles" or commodity values. That is why the essential drama of all those who represent authentic, inherent, natural values and virtues is double. Isolated and deprived of social worth, their very force becomes a weakness, because as implicit or intrinsic values they have no way of *reproducing themselves integrally*. In other words, prohibited by their status as repositories of natural value from valorizing themselves as such in the sphere of social circulation, they are obliged to consume themselves unproductively, "vivre de leur propre substance." On the other hand, in order to resist the movement of selfdevalorization, to turn "valeurs idéales" or "mortes" into productive, self-generating principles of life, one must obey the laws of the game — become something one is not, "se dédoubler," assume a mask, cast off one's natural self for an unnatural, artificial one, etc. Idealism, illusion, self-mortification, sterility, waste, suicide, affect or become the ultimate fate of all those characters who are unable either to metamorphose themselves or to ally themselves with a mediator, someone who will be the vehicle through which "une nouvelle et seconde vie" is possible, i. e. someone capable of exploiting their natural values and intrinsic worth as the material basis for his or her own life in society as a commodity. Rastignac, the model of a successful and conscious transformation uses the "treasure of his family's devotion" as a "discount" against his future, as a source of primitive accumulation for his existence as "viveur" and tool of Nucingen. His natural qualities, sincerity, ardor, good looks, etc., all the genuine "forces réelles" of youth, constitute as such a sort of capital for the future, but as we know, retained in that form, as "valeurs idéales," they are illusions. To survive and "se faire valoir," Rastignac must convert these "valeurs idéales" into "valeurs réelles."[12] "L'individu n'a d'existence productive q'ua travers la valeur d'échange, ce qui implique déja la négation de son existence naturelle."[13] The emotions themselves must obey the laws of capital and turn into commodities. True sentiments must be transformed into calculation and hypocrisy, love into an investment; people into objects to manipulate for personal advantage, etc. "Le coeur est un tresor des sentiments..." which in its natural state (a unity of "sentiment" and "intérêt") cannot survive in a world where "la fortune est la vertu." (*Le Père Goriot*)

Education is thus a "sentimental education," a conquest of the natural spontaneous self. The great crime of modern bourgeois society, Father Goriot's, for example, is to "give all of yourself, all at once." To live, "il faut toujours se faire valoir,"[14] know how to capitalize one's energy and passions so that they will pay off.

The core of the moral problem: the choice between struggle or obedience, between crime or retreat is thus based on the unnatural victimization of all who live according to natural sentiments and noble ambitions. How can one live ethically, when on the one side, self-realization involves the necessary acceptance of the world of reification and alienation, and on the other, non-participation, remaining on the fringes, leads to sterility, waste and/or death? "All or nothing" becomes the inevitable morality of a world in which complicity is universal[15] and exploitation of the self and others inevitable.

Should one then live in order to die (vivre pour mourir) or die in order to live (mourir pour vivre)? To choose the latter in good conscience one must above all be lucid, rid of one's illusions, honest with oneself about the fact that achievement and creation can only be obtained at the price of dehumanization and deformation — by deviation from the course of nature (either by super-concentration, or hoarding of life-energy, or its opposite, retail attrition or wholesale waste). That is why the bourgeois psychological problem becomes that of developing the force of character and bodily strength necessary to endure an unnatural existence. Monomania and monstrosity are therfore the result of the concentration of all energy and passion: in its bourgeois form, for the pursuit of money; while the opposite form of concentration, the consecration of one's life to a unique goal such as art, science, social regeneration, etc., appears as the anti-bourgeois path of resistance. Similarly, since both of these paths involve self and social alienation, "la volonté," the will, transforms itself from a natural human "quality," a psychological and moral attribute of human nature into a "force," a sort of "intérmédiare étranger" between man and his alienated powers.[16]

To live in purity, on the other hand, is to expend one's life-forces unproductively, and to retain one's integrity at the price of non-life. One need only think of the half-alive, melancholy, cloistral atmosphere which surrounds Eugenie, the mummies of *Le Cabinet des Antiques*, the vegetable existence of Raphael de Valentin, the mystical, purely cerebral end of Louis Lambert, etc. to realize how much duration, survival alone represents living death for Balzac. And, more than that, the retreat into self and isolation from the "forces vives" distorts the nature of an organism so violated, making it all the more unadaptable to life as it is.

"In our times the methods of struggle must be in harmony with the real forces and not with historical souvenirs," repeats a Balzac increasingly convinced that the struggle in, and in opposition to "le désordre actuel" must be lucid and realistic, if the values of human community and goodness are to survive. It seems to me that the maturity and consolidation of literary techniques, accorded unanimously by the critics to the Balzac of 1833-34 must be understood also in terms of the different proportions assumed by this dialectic of "mourir pour vivre." Generally speaking, as the causes and consequences ("effets") of this dialectic reveal themselves to be directly attributable to the malfunctioning physiology of the bourgeois order,[17] the former more philosophical emphasis on internal disequilibrium changes into a greater preoccupation with the disequilibrium inherent in the social organism itself. More and more as we shall see, the problem of a world governed by the laws of exchange and mediation,[18] its antagonistic nature, is explained by the disorder engendered by a political and social body which can only valorize, confer life on energy in the form of capital. And the analysis of these mechanisms leads to conscientious efforts, political and literary, to restore to the "corps politique" its lost equilibrium.

At the same time Balzac imbues this dying world with a rare poetry and lyricism, almost as though the very artistic power of his evocation will help restore it to life. But we must realize that this poetry of the historically doomed develops simultaneously with the vision of the true movement of contemporary life.

In *Eugénie Grandet* (1833) and *Le Père Goriot* (1835), Balzac is consciously writing "drame bourgeois." He has found the locus of modern tragedy.[19] Inheritances, marriage, the problems of women, of the son-in-law, the degradation of the family, and social relationships, are no longer "scènes de la vie privée" — they have become the point of departure, the paradigmatic experiences through which the real dimensions of bourgeois tragedy reveal themselves. Nor does it seem coincidental that the axis around which will be coordinated the multiple effects of the *Comédie Humaine*, develops simultaneously with the discovery that the "drame bourgeois" begins, constitutes itself and develops at that moment when there is *danger of non-reproduction*.

Eugénie Grandet illustrates perfectly the pattern of all the later novels. Eugenie and her father have lived harmoniously together, each in his own sphere, since her childhood. It is only when the question of her marriage arises, that the conflict between the two antagonistic systems of values which they incarnate, Christianity and capitalism, becomes a problem. Eugenie's marriage brings to the surface the incompatibility of their two philosophies of life (which is the "tragédie bourgeoise" itself) because, though each of their "religions" has been powerful enough to sustain their individual existences up to this point, in order to develop and reproduce themselves integrally, one must destroy the other. And in this struggle between the religion of love and charity, and the religion of money, we see the fate of all natural non-reified virtues in capitalist society; namely, that the principles of existence by which such people live can only serve as useful fodder for those who want to exploit them. Eugenie, like her treasure, incarnates intrinsic values, and what happens in her attempt to preserve her own code of life is that the code is revealed to be full of self-contradictions and conflicting obligations. Her noble and stoic effort to obey her father and be loyal to Charles leads ultimately to martyrdom and illusion, and most tragically to sterility and the drying up of all her vital energy. Her simple and genuine qualities, which Balzac constantly compares to the processes of physical nature and the instinctual sources of natural fecundity,[20] that "passion vraie" which unfolds like a flower, joyously realizing its own nature and harmony with the world, is destined to perish without even the natural consolation of maternity. "Rien de grand, ni de noble ne peut subsister plus longtemps de par ses propres vertus."[21] The tragedy of naive simplicity and genuine Christian values is that *they do not have the power to regenerate themselves*.[22] On the contrary, Grandet's "religion" is powerful enough to kill the natural principle of reproduction, both Eugenie's maternity and family continuity, because money as capital has the unnatural property of self-reproduction.[23] That is why money plays the central role in bourgeois drama. Grandet epitomizes the transformation from the patriarchal to capitalist bourgeoisie and with it, the dissolution of all the natural and religious bonds which have held society together because he has discovered the secret of the eternal life of capital. "The immortality which money strove to achieve by setting itself negatively against circulation, by withdrawing from it, is achieved by capital, which preserves itself precisely by abandoning itself to circulation." [Marx, *Grundrisse*, p. 26]

Eugenie, like all the sources of natural life and regeneration, is condemned to sterility because the self-expanding quality of money means that it can multiply and reproduce itself independently of natural existence.[24] In brief, as Marx comments, value "has acquired the occult quality of being able to add value to itself ("enfanter la valeur" in French). It brings forth living offspring, or at the least lays golden eggs." [*Capital*, Vol. I, p. 154]

The deforming power of money therefore assumes its full personal and social significance in this novel, because Balzac has found the link between the unnatural reproduction of capital and its effect, i. e. the incapacity of both the individual and the society (family, wealth, spiritual and material resources) to reproduce themselves naturally in the circulatory system of capitalist society. And it is this new dimension, fully explicated in Eugenie's fate which I believe is decisive. Grandet's capacity qua capitalist to bypass, do completely without Eugenie, defines a new relationship to natural value. His triumph, which Balzac deliberately bases on his complete unity with the "forces réelles" of post-revolutionary society, signifies simultaneously the victory of an entire society which can live without Eugenie, that is, for whom the "occult property of capital" has severed all bonds between the production of wealth and its source in human needs in favor of the production of wealth for its own sake. In short, the significance of money's newly acquired power to reproduce itself unnaturally is that once value, detached totally from its natural relation to use-value and endowed with all the qualities traditionally associated with human and organic nature, takes on a life of its own, what is left to bind society together? For Balzac, the threat to humanistic values and social cohesion inherent in this evolution of the bourgeoisie is all too apparent. So it is that the exploitation of Eugenie's natural resources and naive simplicity begun by Grandet-pere is completed by Charles Grandet, the archetype of the new capitalist, whose brutality and cynicism on an imperial scale make old father Grandet's avarice a monstrous comedy compared to what will come.

As an ironic commentary on the meaning of Eugenie's tragedy, Balzac showers one fortune after another on his "pauvre hérétière" — proof that the only life to which she can give motion and fecundity in the here-and-now is that of her fructifying capital, whereas for her, the only rebirth possible is in heaven. Thus Eugenie, like all the other "fleurs de son sexe," who maintain their personal integrity even at the price of self-sacrifice and martyrdom, suffers intensely for the repression of her natural, life-giving passions; a crime against nature which ultimately avenges itself by turning the passions themselves into self-consuming forces. Balzac ironically justifies this saintly path in two ways. Charity and Christian righteousness are seen as a form of social compensation for personal impotence, and the non-life on earth is to be rewarded in the hereafter. But if charity has the merit of being consistent with Eugenie's intrinsic values, as a system of "dépense," it is equally unproductive; while eternity, though ideologically consoling, is not much compensation for non-life on earth.

In this light we can see *Le Médecin de campagne* (1833), conceived at the same time, as an effort, to find a form of social activity or sublimation which, unlike personal charity, will be a productive "dépense." But we find here, as later (*Le Curé de village, Le Lys dans la vallée*), that even these heroic attempts to redeem the disequilibrium of the political economy at its natural sources, the land, water, peasants, etc. are frought with inescapable contradictions. Objectively, even where the superhuman force of spiritual faith and love of these reformers is powerful enough to impart life to matter, human and material, the victory is at most temporary. This weakness shows itself most fundamentally in the failure of each of them to establish any principle of continuity, either personal or institutional, which would assure the perpetuation of their labors. Thus their works of social regeneration are undermined from within, while on the wider, external scale, these experiements are unable to outlast their personal existences because the associative values to which they are giving life cannot reproduce themselves in the mainstream of society.

Nor is it fortuitous that Balzac chooses in each of these novels a hero or heroine fleeing from the moral consequences of a love-alliance he or she considers illegitimate. Benassis, Veronique de Graslin, Mme de Mortsauf are all retreating from a society to which they are ill-adapted, a society which represses the legitimate expression and satisfaction of their spiritual and physical "desires." This is so because if society permitted them to realize their love and find happiness is a normal way, i.e., through the legitimate love-alliance of marriage, they would be able to perpetuate themselves integrally. It is therefore their very quality as authentic, noble human beings which excludes them from any love relationship which is both fruitful and spiritually rewarding. Deprived of productive issue, they all attempt to compensate for their social impotence by giving themselves entirely to the constitution of a "corps social," which will substitute for the social existence denied to them. Similarly, they all struggle to sublimate their frustrated passion by a sort of adoptive maternity or paternity which is their form of vicarious existence for the life denied to them. However, subjectively as their confessions, all a return of the repressed, indicate, these acts of personal martyrdom have not assuaged the violence inflicted on their own natures.

It is indeed revealing that Balzac chooses here as elsewhere, the metaphor of unfulfilled sexuality to cast doubt on the efficacy of their personal martyrdom. This constant coupling of the theme of "passions refoulées" with the theme of social regeneration should also be seen as a tacit but *uncontrollable* confession on the part of the author as well. Irresistably, involuntarily, this constant eruption of the "droits de la nature," this sign of the breakdown of reason and repression in characters of the moral stature of Benassis of Mme de Mortsauf, reveals also that they have not overcome the impotence and sterility that the real movement of social life has imposed on their ideologies.

On a broader level, then, we can trace the ambiguity of these experiments in social reform to a common source. Each seeks to go beyond the individualistic, egotistical values upon which liberal political philosophy bases its notion of "community." All of them dream of a form of social organization which will be an organic equilibrium — uniting individual passions and interests with the dynamic well-being of the entire social organism — a natural fusion or alliance (the metaphor is from the *Lys*) capable of reconciling the material and spiritual forces in an order consistent with the overall interest of the perpetuation of society and with the self-conservation and happiness of each of its members. "L'harmonie est la poesie de l'ordre, et les peuples ont un vif besoin de l'ordre. La concordance des choses entre elles, *l'unité, pour tout dire en un mot, n'est-elle pas la plus simple expression de l'ordre?"* (*La Duchesse de Langeais*)

What happens is that these isolated attempts at reform never go beyond the initial stage. They do succeed in bringing undeveloped regions out of their primitive dependence on nature and in showing them that their livelihood depends on transforming nature to their needs. But ironically, instead of pointing to the future, these reforms turn out to be constructive only to the degree that they are a repetition on a small scale of what the bourgeoisie, on an historical scale, has already accomplished. Thus they succeed in the material sphere, just as the crusading and progressive pre-revolutionary bourgeoisie had represented new sources of energy and human enrichment vis-a-vis feudal backwardness, but the spiritual force which animates them is destined to degenerate with the death of their founders. Balzac does not say, but we can guess, that this first elan of material progress will soon give birth to the next stage of the bourgeois revolution — "le règne de l'argent," and of speculation, the reign of individualism and self-interest described in *Les Paysans*.

There is a sense of profound discouragement present in these novels. The hope expressed at the end of *Le Père Goriot*, that some form of struggle, even if morally corrupting, might eventually culminate in a constructive conquest of society, along with the fervent desire that serious reform of the Benassis-type might remedy the sickness of the social organism, cedes continually to Balzac's relentless social observation. More and more, the unnatural effects of bourgeois society are identified with structural contradictions in the capitalist mode of production and exchange itself. At the same time, the preoccupation with the problems of creation continues to express itself in the more philosophical works through probing investigatons of the dynamics of artistic and creative activity. It is no coincidence that all these previous themes culminate in his most mature and comprehensive vision of social reality (*Illusions perdues*), where the problems of creative genius become one with the experience of disillusionment in bourgeois society.

In this novel, the experience of the "intellectuals," David and Lucien, of those "who apply thought to the new production of human forces, to a new combination of natural elements, physical or moral"[25] has become the point of departure for the revelation of the true nature of social reality, because the contradictions emanating from intellectual production are the paradigm of those affecting all human labor and relationships in the new conditions created by industrial capitalism. In other words, the problems of art and spiritual production reflect the contradictions inherent in the bourgeois system of production itself and become those which best reproduce the ensemble of social relations. Similarly the dialectic of "mourir pour vivre," at first (*La Peau de chagrin*) regarded as a symptom of "mal du siecle," then as a sort of permanent disorder (*Le Lys dans la vallée*), now implants itself integrally as the characteristic metabolism of the bourgeois social organism.

A brief glance at the opening of *Illusions perdues* will illustrate how the inadequacy of the natural limits to sustain life, now has its origin in the iron laws of capitalist production. It is the transformation of the means of production and the social relations arising from this change-over, that not only explain "the capitalization of intellectual production" (cf. Lukacs), but also the anomaly of capitalist society — its inability to create, to release its own productive powers without destroying both human nature and its own base for survival.[26] It is the change from wood to iron presses, from manufacture to machinery which contains the ineluctable contradictions on which the entire book is based. The new devouring Stanhope presses "use le caractère," alienate the worker from his former unity with the tools of his trade and the product of his labor, alienate language itself from its source in real activity, institute a new, unnatural rhythm and intensity of work, turn the worker into a commodity who no longer has pride in his own workmanship, etc.[27], but they are also the basis of a positive cultural revolution that will ultimately enrich the lives of more and more people.

> ...the implements of labor become automatic, things moving and working independent of the workman. They are henceforth an industrial *perpetuum mobile*, that would go on producing forever, did it not meet with certain natural obstructions in the weak bodies and the strong wills of its human intendants. The automaton, as capital...is therefore animated by the longing to reduce to a minimum the resistance offered by that repellant yet elastic natural barrier, man. [Marx, *Capital*, Vol. I, p.403]

Unlike the romantics, revolutionary and otherwise, Balzac is not denouncing industry as such. What is agonizing to him is the seemingly inescapable fact that this revolution in society's capacity to produce wealth cannot do so without turning the labor-process itself into an unnatural and alienating activity,[28] that the act of production itself diminishes and destroys man's humanity rather than enlarging, extending his powers. We notice that the antagonistic qualities of the fantastic "peau de chagrin" now reappear, no longer mysteriously veiled in their philosophical dress; they have assumed their true, objective form as the contradictions arising from capital, just as the act of production in bourgeois vital economy is unnatural because it is at once the creation of new sources of human wealth,[29] (the expansion of human powers and capacities) and the destruction of natural human unity due to the alienation of one's natural labor-power to the devouring monster of capital. The contradictions of this dialectic manifest themselves most significantly and essentially in the dilemma of those who regard the act of production-creation as their "natural" destiny.

In the figure of David Séchard we witness the impasse felt by the young generation of post-revolutionary intellectuals and specifically that of the energetic, virtuous, and talented section of the bourgeoisie who considered as their legitimate heritage the right to employ their capacities to transform the means of production for human needs and enrichment. From the outset, both in terms of his father's depraved and anachronistic mentality and of his material heritage itself (the outmoded presses and tools of the printing-shop), David's bourgeois heritage confronts him as "richesse" and "obstacle." It is "richesse," insofar as this store of accumulated labor and skills constitutes real values that could be converted into exchange-value assuring David's daily existence. But it is "obstacle," in that the father chooses to use all his resources, talents, and fortune as a means of preventing him from earning a living and realizing himself as an inventor. Thus David's predicament is that, in order to maintain himself and realize his own nature, that is, both to insure his daily subsistence as a printer, and to valorize his scientific creativity, he must revolutionize the existing means of production. But he cannot transform the wood presses into iron ones, nor reeds into paper without, on the one hand, destroying the old natural harmony associated with manufacture and patriarchal social relations, nor, on the other, without consuming himself. Expansion:contraction; "jouissance":"usure"; "richesse":"obstacle" etc. have now become properties of the bourgeois heritage itself, a heritage which we notice significantly cannot vitalize itself without the intervention of capital.

Balzac's manner of opening the novel, as well as his deliberate choice of David the inventor's story as the cadre for Lucien the poet's, suggest therefore an intention wider than the explicit one of a description of the material base underlying the corresponding transformations in the spiritual or ideological sphere. The ambiguities of his personal and social position are, in fact, the infrastructure of the historical period as well. The dialectic of "mourir pour vivre" which David encounters in the form of his relationship to his material and spiritual heritage characterizes also that of the social praxis of a century in which one cannot exploit, employ, enrich one's heritage, nor create new value, without alienating or selling oneself. Similarly the unnatural father-son realtionship is both a microcosm of what the monstrous social forces of speculation and greed will do to David, i.e. force him to sell his labor-power to the Cointet[30] or kill himself and reduce his family to starvation, and the sign that the bourgeois legacy has turned into an obstacle because it views its own creations as a threat to its survival.

Pere Sechard is of course, like Grandet, a portrait of the ultimate in bourgeois perversion — the transferral of all natural, life-giving qualities to the passion for gold, the calculated destruction or rendering sterile of his own progeny in favor of the immortal life of his fortune, the conservation of which he equates with eternal life. But unlike Grandet, who realizes fully the principles for which he lives by becoming a capitalist, Sechard remains an irrational miser. "The never-ending augmentation of exchange-value, which the miser strives after, by seeking to save his money from circulation, is attained by the more acute capitalist, by constantly throwing it afresh into circulation." (Marx, *Capital*, Vol. I, p. 153)

Sechard-pere distinguishes himself as being at once the living vestige of the past which has not transformed itself to meet the new conditions of capitalist life, and the image of the effect of a revolution halted in its development, the result of which is the rupture of the old harmony on which his existence depended and a passionate clinging to the status quo for fear that any expansion will release powers that threaten his existence.

What I would like to emphasize is that we have in this conflict between father and son, old and new, a critique of bourgeois liberalism that goes far beyond Balzac's previous novels. The focus has now changed from that of capitalism's destruction of the old values to its *incapacity to confer life on its own*. Whereas Grandet-pere for example opposed himself to an ethic and ideology already weakened and undermined by the prevailing forces, David's father poses himself as an obstacle to a son representing the epitome of bourgeois virtue and potential creative capacity. Father and son thus embody two phases of the same revolution whose continuity has been shattered on the one hand by the father's alliance with the Cointet Brothers and on the other by his view of David as a competitor whom he must crush by selling him his own heritage at an exorbitant price.[31] In this respect therefore their mutual relations foreshadow and reproduce the betrayal of the bourgeois heritage, its "illusion perdues" on a socio-historical scale. The bourgeoisie's ideal of a "social contract" has been transformed into a contractual agreement, a debtor-creditor relationship in which in order to exist one must sell one's labor-power. Its desire for gain which once stimulated a measured, progressive development of productive forces, now governs the production of human and social wealth, and this passion for profit, elevated to a social force, has resulted in the rejection of all creative labor which is not value-producing. (In other words, with the evolution from a patriarchal to an industrial-capitalist bourgeoisie, the bourgeoisie itself has renounced all labor which does not produce surplus-value.)

Thus the essential criticism of bourgeois society (and that is why David's experience structures the entire book) is that by transforming the intellectual and material labor-process itself into a mere appendage of capital, an activity totally divorced from all considerations of human value, it has torn man from the potentialities of his own natural existence and the unlimited horizons of his creativity.

It is in this context that the struggle of the intellectual comes to represent that of all qualitative human values and ambitions. The "poete" (artist or scientist) reflects in his condition the disorder of an entire society because his work, his self-activity, is inseparably linked to "Nature." "L'Art est la nature concentree." Both in terms of object: the reformation and recombination of nature — human, social, and physical; and in terms of the labor-process itself, *the laws of art resemble those of nature.* (See speech of D'Arthez in *Illusions perdues*)

The activity of art singles itself out as special 8 both in the sense of a model of bourgeois alienation, and as a source of resistance to bourgeois society — *because the laws of its reproduction are diametrically opposed to the laws of the reproduction of capital*. In other words, the intellectual, understood in the Balzacian sense of anyone who applies thought to the reorganization and production of new forces, is theoretically the only individual in bourgeois society capable of realizing himself without the mediation of social relations. However, what happens in *Illusions perdues* is that this unified vision of the poet and intellectual as originally sharing a common destiny breaks down.[32] To put it briefly, the fact that virtue destroys David, that in his case personal discipline and self-sacrifice make him a victim rather than a conqueror, means that the inventor and the artist are subject to different fates. David has no choice; for him the path of virtue leads to the same results, selling himself, as does the path of vice for Lucien. The difference lies in the object of their work. Because David's reproduction of nature involves the physical consumption of matter, objective, real matter, he cannot maintain his existence without external capital investment. Whatever personal resources, moral and financial, David may possess, he cannot thrive as an inventor independently of the mediation of socially accumulated capital (whether it is in the form of private capital or not). Like the artist, his productive labor is intrinsically satisfying, a non-alienated form of activity, but the price paid for indulging in this non-value-producing act of production is self-consumption and poverty.[33] Both the extent of the forces of speculation and greed, as well as his dependence upon their capital during the process of elaboration and experimentation, make it impossible for the inventor to live and create in capitalist society without selling himself.

The moral of Lucien's experience, as we know, is quite the opposite — that he cannot be a great poet and sell himself. Nor, like David, can he retreat into the sphere of private happiness and find some kind of compromise, like collecting insects which, although it represents a clear resignation from the active, creative life and a social loss of his talents, at least preserves a sphere of purity and natural value in which he can deploy his scientific aptitude. No, Lucien, the poet, is subject to the extremes of heaven and hell, complete triumph or complete rejection — "Tout ou rien est la devise du poète."

The reason, I think, is that, as the contradictions of bourgeois relations become consolidated in more and more domains, and as the political horizon dims, the artist has become for Balzac the only hope for regeneration of society. If the dialectic of "mourir pour vivre" characterizes all productive activity in bourgeois society, *the artist appears to be the only individual whose suffering and self-alienation can ultimately be compensated by social triumph*. Thus the poet alone, in capitalist society, retains the godlike power of *self-reproduction*, of unalienated self activity, because he can simultaneously realize himself and reproduce matter, without metamorphosing himself into an exchange-value, without sacrificing his intrinsic personal and social values. His destiny is to be a Prince or a victim, a God or a fallen angel, because his is the only form of creation-production which cannot alter from nature if it is to be authentic. Nowhere would Balzac have been in more profound agreement with

Marx than on this question. "The writer must, naturally, make a living in order to exist and write, but he must not exist and write in order to make a living...The writer in no way regards his works as a *means*. They are *ends in themselves*; so little are they a means for him and others that, when necessary, he sacrifices *his* existence to theirs..."[34]

Lucien's weakness, like that of all the "artistes manqués" in Balzac, is the consequence, not only of lacking the will to resist, but also of lacking the capacity to transform himself completely into a commodity. What makes his artistic temperamental deformity, his "mobilité de caractère," so fatal is that in order to succeed, he must be one or the other, an artist or a sell-out. Lacking either the force of character needed to resist, or to struggle according to the rules of the bourgeois game, he alienates himself from all possibility of creative production. Apart from these two paths, and this is the moral dilemma for the man of ambition, there is only dissipation and waste or suicide, i.e., no chance of valorizing his creative energy and genius. Since, as I have said, artistic activity is the only form of human productive labor in which self-realization is synonymous with the reproduction of nature, it is also the only one which, in deviation from nature, cannot be itself. That is why Lucien's inability to follow the noble path of art can lead only to death or selling his soul. There are other roads to success, if not to art. If Lucien's experience in society has destroyed his ambition to dominate as a poet, it has not killed his desire to dominate. Thus, Lucien's education in the world, his failure to survive the hardships of the lofty and arduous path of art, not only means the end of his youthful illusions but also the suicide of his natural, poetic self. Only by casting away the mantle of poetry, by the suicide of his artistic ambitions and a confession of this failure, can Lucien be reborn into a new social existence, that of an exchange-value; which he appropriately inaugurates in disguise. [Cf. opening chapter of *Splendeurs et Miseres des Courtisanes*]

For the poet qua poet no compromise is possible, and that is why, for Lucien to become susceptible to Vautrin's temptation, he must finish where Rastignac began. And, in order to be sure that the meaning does not escape us, Balzac has Lucien and Herrara voyage past the home of Rastignac, that young man who has succeeded so well because "il a donné dans le positif" and not "dans la poésie." [*Illusions perdues*]

This passing allusion to Rastignac signifies much more than a reminder of past history. The reappearance of Vautrin at this juncture, this time not as "révélateur," but as confessor, means, among other things, that the significance of the alternatives of conduct formulated by

Vautrin, "l'obéissance" or "la révolte," has also evolved. And, indeed, we shall see that the new metamorphosis of Vautrin corresponds to an evolution of Balzac's concept of Revolt as a viable form of struggle against bourgeois society. In *Le Père Goriot*, the diabolical temptation to sign a pact with Vautrin is only averted by the fact that Rastignac has a socially acceptable, and for that reason infinitely more powerful outlet, in the person of Nucingen, Vautrin's legal counterpart. And, as we know, Balzac's sympathy for Vautrin is based on the latter's clear moral superiority to the legalized crime of bourgeois society. However, what has not been appreciated fully is that Vautrin's superior ethical code of human solidarity, loyalty, honor, friendship, etc., just like all the other precapitalist and "natural" philosophies of existence mentioned earlier, falls prey to the dilemma — *that he cannot reproduce himself alone and creatively*. In fact, we have in Balzac's monstrous but terrifyingly attractive portrait of Vautrin, "cet être qui résume toutes les forces humaines," a mythological incarnation of all the ambiguities of bourgeois society and, most specifically, those of creative productivity and energy alienated from itself and the social organism. In his role outside the social sphere, Vautrin incarnates as "un être extérieur à l'homme et le dominant" (Marx, see p. 495, Fondements, Vol. I), the fantastic shape and proportions that man's natural qualities and powers assume in their alienated form. Similarly, in his attempt to overcome his alienation to "se faire valoir" in capitalist society, Vautrin's dilemma summarizes, in a negative form, that of the fate of all natural, authentic human values and qualities. His essential contradiction is that, as long as he remains true to his values and his theory of opposition, the Vautrin "valeur-en-soi," so to speak, he cannot realize or reproduce himself in the social sphere. Thus, isolated from the "forces vives" of social movement, his activity is confined to the dark undercurrents of social life and the destructive and individualistic methods of re-establishing the social equilibrium. This social impotence has its psychological counterpart in his sexual depravity — his homosexuality representing a sterile retreat from normal productive sexual relationships. In short, like all those characters in the *Comédie Humaine* who refuse the modern bourgeois world of reified and dehumanized values, Vautrin suffers from his incapacity to reproduce himself integrally in the diseased and unnatural, but rapidly expanding capitalist organism. And like all these characters, he attempts to compensate for his own impotence, by procuring himself "un accomplice de sa destinée," a mediator whose possession of the very social virtues and mobility that he lacks, will enable him to "revivre dans une forme sociale..." [*Splendeurs et Miseres des Courtisanes*], that is to purchase himself a soul in whose commodity-form he can invest all the treasures, both sentimental and monetary which, as long as he lives authentically, he can only detain in a non-productive form. But that is not all. Vautrin is an "homme double," a realist and a romantic — a man of good and evil, a "sauvage" and a superman.[35] Though he may emotionally experience the world in terms of a pre-capitalist moral code, his vast intelligence is that of a man without illusion who observes and understands the real forces responsible for the "desordre social." It is this schism between his realistic understanding of the world and his emotions that accounts for the irreconcilable tensions in his personality: on the one hand, his fanatic desire to retain his integrity as the incarnation of revolt which leads to the ironic contradiction that he cannot be himself, without revealing, betraying himself. On the other hand, the knowledge of his own impotence drives him to push the very bourgeois relationships which he detests to their logical conclusion, i.e., assume the mask and disguise for his social activity of the personages to whom he is the most ideologically opposed — a bourgeois rentier, a priest, and chief of police.

We see that the chief weakness of Vautrin's path of revolt, which is in a sense but the conscious example of what other people undergo in a state of illusion, lies in the fact that the isolation from the real domain of human activity, society, transforms all the positive and natural resources of life into their opposite. It is for this reason, I think, that the Vautrin of *Le Pere Goriot*, whose alternative of revolt at the threshold of the world still remained an ambiguous possibility, because there was no other alternative of resistance in the social sphere, cedes to another vision in *Illusions perdues*. In between, Balzac has discovered another path of resistance to bourgeois society — D'Arthez and the Cenacle. This allows him, at least imaginatively, to oppose to the negative and destructive, but morally superior natural fraternity of Vautrin and "le bagne," the image of a fraternity, similarly animated by non-reified and anti-bourgeois values, but also committed to the positive and constructive activity of the regeneration of society. The writer, in particular, is charged with the holy mission of reforming a vision of humanity which will be at once the expression of authentic human nature and a going beyond it to a creation of new forms. This is because art is the only domain in which *thought* alone can successfully achieve a reproduction of nature which is also a transformation of it; or in other words, the only sphere where creation is possible without mediation.

It is in this context that the figure of Vautrin assumes a new meaning. The existence of D'Arthez, of a form of meaningful opposition which is not "une lutte insensée contre l'ordre social," enables Balzac to minimize the justice of his revolt and concentrate on his negativity and evil. Thus, in *Illusions perdues*, Vautrin becomes the negative incarnation of the alienated powers of the artist, the point by point perverted double of the qualities and powers required for creative production. Like the artist, he is a priest, "avant tout un artiste est l'apôtre de quelque verité," whose cult imposes a monastic, chaste life, a rigid discipline in the service of an ultimate faith. This "poète du mal" who employs his vast powers of comprehension and intuition in the service of vengence and, ultimately, of repression and reaction, is now the alternative to D'Arthez. And just as the artist's activity incarnates the last realm where self-reproduction corresponds to the laws of nature, so Vautrin, in his negativity, realizes his full potentiality as the image of alienated social power, of natural creative power denied social issue.

Art becomes the answer to both the impotence and negativity of revolt and to the dehumanization and reification of bourgeois society. Balzac's realism of observation leads him thus to a romanticizaton and idealization of the artist — a dichotomy which manifests itself clearly in the fact that in all his realistic portraits, the artist cannot live without social mediation.

But then there is his own example!

In this all too brief exposition, I have tried to show that the reason Marx and Engels learned more from Balzac than from all the political and social experts put together can be found in the fact that all three located the crucial contradiction in bourgeois society in its inability to reproduce itself naturally; an impasse which Balzac, for ideological and personal reasons, could only sublimate idealistically through a recourse to Art. Unable to change the world, he reproduced and interpreted it, but remaining forever true to his own dictum, in a manner which gives us the keys to "un avenir inconnu dont (il prépare) l'oeuvre."[36]

NOTES

1. It goes without saying that Marx and Balzac resemble (and differ from each other in more ways than this paper can indicate. One aspect which particularly merits study is the striking similarity of metaphor, vocabulary, images, etc. Globally of great importance is the weight, both quantitative and qualitative, that each attaches to images drawn from the biological and physical sciences. I have tried to

choose citations from Marx which indicate this conceptual affinity. Unfortunately the English translations of the French do not always bring out these correspondences which is why in some cases I have kept the quotations in French, prefering to translate them only when necessary. One such notion for example is Balzac's usage of the ordinary French expression "se faire valoir" which in French means both "to valorize" in the ordinary sense of "to make the most of something or some quality," "to enhance," "to make the most of" and also in the economic sense, "to be worth," "to put a value on," etc. A close study of Balzac's use of this expression reveals a truly pre-marxist anticipation of Marx's theory of value in capitalist society. See my study of *Le Pere Goriot*, "Pour une Lecture Nouvelle du *Pere Goriot*," in *La Pensee*, Avril, 1973.

2. See Marx's and Engels' statements regarding his method and purpose in *Capital*: "...it is the ultimate aim of this work to lay bare the economic law of motion of modern society." (Vol. I, p. 10) "As soon as society has outlived a given period of development, and is passing from one given stage to another, it begins to be subject also to other laws. In a word, economic life offers us a phenomenon analogous to the history of evolution in other branches of biology..." (p. 18) Karl Marx, *Capital*, Foreign Languages Publishing House, Moscow, 1959. All future quotations from *Capital* will be drawn from this edition. See also Balzac's stated intentions in his "Avant-Propos de *La Comédie Humaine*," 1842: "Il a donc existé, il existera donc de tout temps des Espèces Sociales comme il y a des Espèces Zoologiques. Si Buffon a fait un magnifique ouvrage en essayant de représenter dans un livre l'ensemble de la zoologie, n'y avait-il pas une oeuvre de ce genre a faire pour la Societé...ne devais-je pas étudier les raisons ou la raison de ces effets sociaux, surprendre le sens caché dans cet immense assemblage de figures, de passions, et d'évenéments....Ainsi dépeinte, la Societé devait porter avec elle la raison de son mouvement."

3. For reasons of space, only Balzac's mature works can be considered here. Anyone interested in pursuing the genesis of these ideas should consult Pierre Barberis, *Aux Sources de Balzac: Les Romans de Jeunesse*, Paris, Les Bibliophiles de l'Originale, 1965.

4. For a more detailed analysis of this problem, see my article, "Une Interprétation de la Peau de Chagrin," in *L'Année Balzacienne*, Paris, 1971.

5. Cf. Balzac, "Avant-Propos": "L'animal a peu de mobilier, il n'a ni arts ni sciences; tandis que l'homme, par une loi qui est à rechercher, tend à representer ses moeurs, sa pensée et sa vie dans tout ce qu'il approprie à ses besoins.". "Les habitudes de chaque animal sont, à nos yeux au moins, constamment semblables, en tout temps; tandis que les habitudes, les vetements, les paroles, les demeures d'un prince, d'un banquier, d'un artiste, d'un bourgeois, d'un prêtre et d'un pauvre sont entièrement dissemblables et changent au gré des civilisations."

6. Pierre Barbéris in his monumental work *Balzac et le Mal du siecle*, Paris, Gallimard, 1970, has exhaustively shown how the *Peau de Chagrin* and Balzac's work in general reflects his disenchantment with the revolution of 1830, and the entire contraction of hopes, ideals, and outlets suffered by his post-revolutionary generation.

7. Cf. Balzac in his *Lettres sur Paris*, 20 fevrier 1831: "Le résultat du mouvement social pendant quarante annees a été d'appeler aux bénéfices de l'instruction un million d'hommes de plus en France, de créer un million de proprietaires nouveaux et de former trente mille industriels, tout au plus....Cette conquete *du bien sur le mal* nous a coûté la vie de deux millions d'hommes et deux milliards de dettes."

8. For Balzac's ideas on this subject, see the "Avant-Propos à *La Comédie Humaine*."

9. This and all the following quotations regarding Paris are taken from *La Fille aux yeux d'Or*.

10. "Use-values become a reality only by use or consumption; they also constitute the substance of all wealth, whatever may be the social form of that wealth. In the form of society we are about to talk about (capitalism), they are in addition the material depositories of exchange-value." (Marx, *Capital*, Vol. I, p. 36.)

11. "To become a commodity a product must be transferred to another, whom it will serve as a use-value, by means of an exchange." (Marx, *ibid*., p. 41) "...value can only manifest itself in the social relation of commodity to commodity," (*Ibid*., p.47)

12. "Objects that in themselves are no commodities such as conscience, honor, etc. are capable of being offered for sale by their holders, and of thus acquiring through their price, the form of commodities" (Marx, *ibid*., p. 103)

13. "As an exchange-value it (the commodity) differs from itself as a natural material thing. A mediation is required to posit it as an exchange-value." (Marx, *Grundrisse, Introduction to the Critique of Political Economy*, translated by Martin Nicolaus, Penguin Books, 1973, p. 188. All quotations from the *Grundrisse* refer to this edition.)

14. "The first quality of capital is, then, this: that exchange-value deriving from circulation and presupposing circulation preserves itself within it and by means of it; does not lose itself by entering into it; that circulation is not the movement of its disappearance, but rather the movement of its real self-positing as exchange-value, its self-realization as exchange-value." (Marx, *Grundrisse*, p. 260) In French the organic quality of capital is even more clear. "La prémiére caractéristique du capital, est que la valeur d'échange qui est issue de la circulation *se conserve* en elle et par elle; qu'elle ne se perd pas en y entrant, et qu'elle n'est pas le mouvement de sa disparition, mais de sa propre mainifestation et de sa propre realisation en tant que valeur d'echange."

15. As the case of Victorine Taillefer in *Le Père Goriot* illustrates, innocence does not protect one from the universal crime on which bourgeois society is based. All fortunes including the one that she eventually inherits are based on a "crime properly done." The illusion of innocence thus has the double disadvantage that one is always the victim and one can never prevent further crime.

16. "Au lieu que l'homme soit lui-même l'intérmédiare pour l'homme, l'homme considère sa volonté, son activité et son rapport avec les autres, comme autant de puissances indépendantes de lui et des autres." (Marx, quoted in the French

edition of *Grundrisse, Fondements de la critique de l'economie politique*, Editions Anthropos, Vol. I, p. 194.)

17. For a detailed discussion of Balzac's increasing disenchantment with the bourgeoisie and the motivations behind his public adherence to the monarchist cause see Pierre Barberis' book.

18. For an excellent study of the internal dynamics of Balzac's work see Jean-Pierre Richard, *Etudes sur le Romantisme*, Seuil, 1971.

19. Balzac in *Eugenie Grandet*: "La tragédie bourgeoise (est) relativement aux acteurs plus cruelle que les drames accomplis dans l'illustre famille des Atrides."

20. Here as elsewhere in Balzac, characters not touched by the modern capitalist mentality are compared to nature. And unlike those struggling to exist in a world totally mediated by exchange-value, they live in equilibrium with their own natures and their milieu.

21. Marx, *Grundrisse*, French edition, p. 366.

22. It is for this reason, I think, that modern tragedy is more tragic than Greek tragedy. Modern capitalism deprives the individual of all hope, all transcendance, and all sense of community. In the past, man's conflict with nature, with forces greater than himself, resulted in a greater affirmation and understanding of his humanity. Out of his resistances to "forces maléfiques" (evil forces), man forged the principles of his life, out of his unhappiness and condition he found the true inspiration for being and activity. But now that the "forces maléfiques" have become the very principles of social life, all the natural principles of human life dry up, become petrified, turn into "vestiges." Only capitalism has robbed people of the power to renew themselves.

23. "The circulation of capital is at the same time its becoming, its growth, its vital process. If anything needed to be compared with the circulation of the blood, it was not the formal circulation of money, but the content-filled circulation of capital." (Marx, *Grundrisse*, p. 517)

24. Marx, *Capital*, Vol. I, p. 75: "The consumption of commodities is not included in the circuit of the capital from which they originated." P. 78: "The entire character of capitalist production is determined by the self-expansion of the advanced capital-value, i.e. in the first instance by the production of as much surplus-value as possible"... secondly "by the production of capital, hence by the transformation of surplus-value into capital."

25. Balzac, "Lettre aux Ecrivains Francais."

26. "Capital posits the production of wealth itself and hence the universal development of the productive forces, the constant overthrow of its prevailing presuppositions, as the presupposition of its reproduction. Value excludes no use-value; i.e. includes no particular kind of consumption etc. of intercourse etc., as absolute condition; and likewise every degree of the development of the social forces of production, of intercourse, of knowledge etc. appears to it only as a barrier which it strives to overpower." (*Grundrisse*, p. 541)

27. Listen to Balzac on wage-slavery: "L'escalvage réduit à sa plus simple expression est le travail d'un homme devolu tout entier à un autre. Si l'on croit avoir aboli l'esclavage, on se trompe étrangement. Il existe sous nos yeux des esclaves innomes, plus malheureux que les esclaves nommés, que l'esclave chez les Turcs, que l'esclave chez les anciens, que le nègre. Ces trois sortes d'esclaves vivaient. L'industrie moderne ne nourrit pas ses esclaves. L'antiquité tuait ses esclaves coupables. Le fabricant laisse mourir son esclave innocent..." (Catechisme Social)

28. "The means of production are at once changed into means for the absorbtion of the labor of others. It is no longer the laborer that emloys the means of production, but the means of production that employ the laborer. Instead of being consumed by him as material elements of his productive activity, they consume his as the ferment necessary to their own life-process, and the life-process of capital consists only in its movement as value constantly expanding, constantly multiplying itself." (Marx, *Capital*, Vol. I, p. 310)

29. "The barrier to *capital* is that this entire development proceeds in a contradictory way, and that the working-out of the productive forces, of general wealth etc., knowledge etc., appears in such a way that the working individual *alienates* himself; relates to the conditions brought out of him by his labor as those not of his *own*, but of an *alien wealth* and of his own poverty. (Marx, *Grundrisse*, p. 541)

30. "Whereas the labor-power is a commodity only in the hands of its seller, the wage-laborer, it becomes capital only in the hands of its buyer, the capitalist, who acquires the temporary use of it. The means of production do not become the material forms of productive capital, or productive capital, until labor-power, the personal form of existence of productive capital is capable of being embodied in them. Human labor-power is by nature no more capital than are the means of production." (Marx, *Capital*, Vol. II, p. 35)

31. In order to understand *Illusions perdues* more profoundly all the various "ventes" or acts of sale should be analyzed.

32. Balzac, like the eighteenth century encyclopedists, cherished the belief in the unity of manual and spiritual labor, and his portrait of the breakdown of this unity was extremely painful to him.

33. Of course the artist too suffers from the fact that his creative labor is not immediately value-producing; but his independence from the need for capital investment means that individual control, resistance, etc. are possible.

34. Marx, "Debatten uber Pressefreiheit," in *Literature and Art by Marx and Engels: Selections from their Writings*, International Publishers, New York, 1947, p. 63.

35. In this aspect Vautrin obviously reflects Balzac himself.

36. A French version of this article has been accepted for publication in *La Lecture Sociocritique du Texte Romanesque* — to appear shortly in Canada and France.

13

POE AND DOSTOEVSKY:
A Case of Affinity

Louis Harap

The prevailing mood of Poe's work is one of intense suffering of the sensitive individual who cannot reconcile himself with society or the world as it is. Poe's alienation is well-nigh total: a chasm separates him from other people, from the vital love of women, from a hostile society as a whole and from a physical world that is inadequate to his dreams of perfect beauty. He rejects *in toto* this world he never made, denies its reality, strives to destroy it and reconstruct in imagination a supernal realm of beauty and exquisite sensation. The dehumanized world where people and ideas are counters in a market place of commodities he replaces with an equally dehumanized world of dreams whose inhabitants are not human but angelic or demonic.

That Poe's outlook was consonant with long-range trends in Western society receives striking confirmation from the discovery of certain affinities with the viewpoint of Dostoevsky. This is quite specific in *Notes from the Underground*, a pivotal work of modern literature. The Russian master was born in 1821, half a generation after Poe. The wide differences in the backgrounds of the two men, in their environments and traditions and in their temperaments and talents, are clear. Poe stemmed from the slave-owning section of a nation that was rapidly becoming industrialized; Dostoevsky emerged from a serf society (before liberation in 1861) within an underdeveloped economic order in which the intellectuals and writers lived in an urbanized milieu under powerful western European influences. The two writers occupied this common ground: they were responding in new ways to socio-economic and ideological tendencies working themselves out in western society as a whole.

The intellectual and ideological ambiance of both writers was in large part, with local differences and peculiarities, the complex of ideas that originated largely in Western Europe, ideas born under the impact of the most radical economic and social revolutions mankind had known up to that time. While it is true that capitalism had scarcely as yet touched Dostoevsky's Russia, it was equally true that her most advanced intelligensia lived intellectually in the shadow of ideologies that grew out of the industrial capitalist society of Western Europe. The Byronism of Pushkin, the realism of Gogol, the revolutionary ideas of Belinsky and Chernyshevsky suggest the dependence of the Russian literature of Dostoevsky's time on West European trends. Just as Dostoevsky's intellectual atmosphere was drenched in ideas drawn from the bourgeois world, so also were Poe's ideas, despite the fact that he gave allegiance to the plantation system. And the ideas they absorbed and those they repelled were symptomatic of the alienated consciousness that the industrial, scientific and technologi-cal developments of capitalism were bringing about.

In his study of *Notes from the Underground* and its influence on Russian literature, Robert Louis Jackson writes: "In the figure of the Underground Man, alienated consciousness becomes aware of its alienation and adopts a consciously belligerent posture. The revolt of the Underground Man's entire life is a repulsion from impotence, from an overpowering and humiliating reality. The Underground Man's entire life is one continuous attempt to make contact with the world and with himself; isolated, unable to act, he is a social zero."[1] Dostoevsky's conception of the alienated man in the *Notes* is surely one of the most drastic ever conceived. It has struck a responsive chord in large numbers of influential writers and artists since his time and particularly in our own period, such as Kafka, Hesse, Gide, Camus, Sartre, down to Ralph Ellison and Saul Bellow, among many. The affinities of Poe with the Underground Man, as we shall see, throw into high relief the modernity of the American writer and testify to his significance as an exemplar of the alienated man. Both writers, quite independently of one another, were suffering from the wounded consciousness that is the hallmark of the alienated man and were fighting, as they thought, a last-ditch battle for the integrity and freedom of the individual. One can interpret their response to their times as a defensive action against the growing alienation of man.

The most immediate point of contact between Poe and Dostoevsky is to be found in the likeness of certain features of *Notes from the Underground* with two of Poe's tales, "The Black Cat" and "The Imp of the Perverse." The former tale, it will be recalled, is the story of a man who first gouges out the eye of his cat, then hangs the animal; acquires a second cat like the first which enrages him to the point where, in his effort to kill it with an axe, he murders his wife instead; the wife is walled up in his cellar, but the cat has disappeared; and when the police come to search for his wife, in sheer bravado he taps the wall where he has buried her and the piercing wail of the cat, which had been walled up with the wife, betrays the murderer to the police.

Early in the tale Poe interrupts the narrative to expound the notion of the Imp of the Perverse. How did he come by this idea? An examination of the source of the tale reveals that the idea was original with Poe and illustrates how his originality operated beyond his sources. Edith Smith Krappe has suggested with much cogency that the twin stories, "The Tell-Tale Heart" and "The Black Cat," were derived from "The Clock-Case" incident in *Master Humphrey's Clock*.[2] Dickens' story is a murder confession penned in prison the night before execution, as are both of Poe's tales. In the Dickens story the narrator is greatly disturbed by the "fixed and steady" look habitually trained on him by his sister-in-law; she dies after giving birth to a son who then comes to live with the murderer-to-be and his wife. But the son, he soon discovers, pierces him with that same sinister look as his mother and the idea of killing the boy grows upon him. Additional motivation comes from the fact that he is heir to the boy's inheritance. He finally strangles the boy and buries him in the garden. Later, as he is sitting on a chair directly over the grave, a police bloodhound enters the garden, discovers the grave to the wild confusion of the murderer; the grave is unearthed and the culprit is condemned to die.

In both of Poe's stories, the eye of the murdered ones (an old man and a cat) figures in a crucial way, perhaps as a dreaded Evil Eye. Miss Krappe suggests that the idea of murder in both cases arises like that in the Dickens story: it is obscure in origin, gradual in taking shape and finally "irresistible." In "The Tell-Tale Heart" the murderer does say, "It is impossible to say how first the idea entered my brain; but once conceived, it haunted me day and night."[3] Yet there is no suggestion of the specific idea of the perverse in the Dickens story. It is in "The Black Cat" that the "Imp of the Perverse" first appears. The narrator there attributes to the "Imp of the Perverse" — personification of perversity — the impulse to gouge out the cat's eye and subsequently to hang the cat. Poe describes the Imp. "Perverseness," Poe reasons, is one of the irreducible, unanalyzable "Primitive impulses" which, he says, "give direction to the character of Man." The Imp impels men to act contrary to accepted judgment and standards of behavior. The perverse is committed with malice aforethought: it is a deliberate act of the soul of doing "violence to its own nature — to do wrong for wrong's sake only."[4] The narrator hanged the cat, says Poe, *because* he knew the cat had loved him and despite his awareness that the act would destroy his soul eternally.

Poe was facinated by the concept, for he returned to it two years later, in 1845, in a story called "The Imp of the Perverse." Actually, the piece is more nearly an essay than a story. The narrative takes up only the last third of the piece while the first two-thirds are a discourse on the nature of the Imp of the Perverse. This radical, primitive, prime mover of behavior, says Poe, has hitherto been neglected and gone unrecognized because of "the pure arrogance of reason." Phrenology, which Poe otherwise accepted as the science of psychology, he impugns here as a rationalistic construction based on man's arbitrary assumption that God's design for humanity has no place for perversity. His own approach, he says, is inductive, empirical, founded rather on how man actually behaves. It is observation that yields for him the existence of the prime impulse of "perverseness."

This impulse is paradoxical in that it is unmotivated and has no object. "Through its promptings," he says, "we act, for the reason that we should *not*." He describes the sensations of a man poised at the brink of the precipice and seized with an irresistible impulse to jump, anticipating the sensations of the fall with a fierce "delight of its horror." Unless one allows reason to intervene, one submits to the overwhelming impulse to jump to destruction. Thus we perpetrate perverse acts merely "because we feel that we should *not*."[5] Then follows the story climaxed by a perverse act. The narrator commits an ingenious murder for which he goes undetected and gains the inheritance of his victim. Years afterward, it suddenly occurs to him one day as he walks in the street that he is safe unless he himself confesses. The perverse impulse to cry out his confession takes hold of him until it becomes irresistible. He gives himself away on the street and is condemned to die.

If one holds Poe's notion of the perverse in suspension as one reads Dostoevsky's *Notes from the Underground*, a striking similarity of theme emerges. The man ridden by the Imp acts irrationally in the sense that he does what he knows he should not — even *because* he should not — and commits wrong for its own sake. A similar theme runs through Dostoevsky's *Notes*. The Underground Man is throughout actuated by malice or spite. The Russian word *zloi* or its cognates and synonyms, meaning evil, spite, malice or wrong-doing, recur throughout. He opens his confessional with the phrase, "I am a spiteful (*zloi*) man"[6] and he returns over and over again to his malicious or spiteful motivation. Though he is aware, he says, of "every refinement of all that is 'good and beautiful,' " he nevertheless acts "as though purposely" to commit such acts "as occurred to me at the very time when I was most conscious that they ought not to be committed."[7]

The general ideas that guide the Underground Man's mode of life are expounded in Part I of the *Notes* and their working out in certain incidents in his life is narrated in Part II. His relationships with his former fellow-students and with the prostitute Liza some fifteen years earlier are shown to be permeated with malicious perversity and to cause him the most exquisite suffering. For instance, after he has awkwardly invited himself to a dinner given by his former fellow-students for the officer Zvyerkov, he debates with himself whether he should appear at the dinner after all, since they are all patently displeased at the prospect of his presence. "The more wrong, the more tactless it was for me to go, the more certainly I'd do so," he muses. As the dinner hour draws near, he iterates: "Of course, it would have been best not to go at all. But that was out of the question. When something drew me, it really drew me head first."[8] This thought is reminiscent of Poe's statement of the irresistibility of the perverse, once it takes hold on the mind. Like Poe's view of the objectlessness of the perverse, too, is the Underground Man's observation that he broods "on the fact that there is no one even for you to feel vindictive against, that you have not, and perhaps never will have, an object for your spite."[9]

Towards Liza he behaves with terrifying psychological cruelty. He deliberately plays on her finer feelings out of sheer malice. He inspires love in her and invites her to come to visit him. He is tortured by the thought that she might come. When she does call on him several days later, he lacerates her spirit with the most humiliating words and brutally drives her away. His last act as she is about to go is to force money into her hand. Why did he do this? Was it, he says, done "accidentally, not knowing what I was doing, acting in a sort of daze?" "But I don't want to lie," he confesses, "so I say candidly that I opened her hand, and it was spite that made me put that into it."[10] His "sheer malice" is psychologically equivalent to Poe's "wrong for wrong's sake." The Underground Man's statement of his position at the opening of Chapter VII of Part I bears a striking similarity, up to a point, with Poe's theory of the irrationality of the perverse. Dostoevsky begins, as Poe does, by polemicizing with those who believe that men do not act contrary to their own interests. "What is to be done," says Dostoevsky, "with the millions of facts that bear witness that men, *consciously*, that is fully understanding their real interests, have left them in the background and have rushed headlong on another path, to meet peril and danger, compelled to this course by nobody and nothing, but, as it were, simply disliking the beaten track, and have obstinately, wilfully struck out another difficult, absurd way, seeking it almost in the darkness. So, I suppose, this obstinacy and perversity were pleasanter to them than any advantage."[11]

Thus far, Poe's idea of the Imp of the Perverse is similar to the malicious motivation of the Underground Man. Poe explained this mode of behavior as "a radical, a primitive impulse." But he could not analyze it any further: "We perpetrate them [perverse acts] merely because we feel that we should *not*. Beyond or behind this, there is no intelligible principle."[12] But what was unintelligible to Poe was given penetrating analysis by Dostoevsky. In the two stories dealing with the Imp of the Perverse, Poe treats this psychological phenomenon as isolated and unanalyzable. If we connect it with relevant material elsewhere in Poe's thought, we may discover the meaning of the Imp in its full context. For his part, Dostoevsky brought together in the *Notes* one comprehensive statement of the malaise of the intellectual and the artist in modern society.

Both men rejected the dominant trends of their century. Poe took every occasion to vent his scorn on the social and political movements of the nineteenth century. He specifically ridicules industrial development, reform movements and democracy itself. Dostoevsky, for his part, locates the type of the Underground Man in the nineteenth century. The malaise of the Underground Man, he writes, had set in "twenty years" earlier than the time of writing, that is, in the eighteen forties. This is the very time when Poe was expounding his theory of the Imp of the Perverse. In a footnote at the beginning of the *Notes* Dostoevsky even goes so far as to attribute the plight of the Underground Man to environmental influences. Such a man, he writes, "may and indeed, must, exist in our society, if we think of the *circumstances under which that society has been formed.*"[13] (Emphasis added) Again and again he bemoans "the lot of a cultivated man of our unhappy nineteenth century."*[14]

* While Dostoevsky continually reiterates that his Underground Man is "an educated man of the nineteenth century," it should be noted that he also affirmed that "man everywhere and at all times, whoever he may be, has preferred to act as he chose and not in the least as his reason and advantage dictated."[15]

The malicious and perverse behavior of his "anti-hero," as Dostoevsky called the Underground Man, is not unintelligible, as Poe suggested. It stems from a deliberate revolt against reason and science which would rob man of his freedom and individuality and reduce him "from a human being to an organ stop."[16] Dostoevsky especially aimed at what he considered the rationalism and "scientism," as we should say today, of the revolutionary movement in Russia, particularly as exemplified in the ideas of its then leading exponent, Chernyshevsky. That writer had hailed the Crystal Palace, the technically revolutionary structure of steel and glass built for the London Exposition of 1851, as the symbol of the possibilities for fulfilling the needs of all the people, especially the working people. Dostoevsky had himself seen the Crystal Palace on a visit to London and was repelled by the rationalized, dehumanized effects of the mechanical civilization that this symbolized to him.

However, it is important to observe that Dostoevsky was repelled not only by the revolutionaries' rational utopias: it was also the mechanized existence in an industrial society that he abhorred. The "educated man of the nineteenth century," he wrote, "is one affected by progress and European civilization, a man who is 'divorced from the soil and the national elements,' as they express it nowadays."[17] One must include not only revolutionary social ideas but industrialism as well in the indictment that Dostoevsky drew up. He even faintly prophesied cybernetics and "game theory," those consummate products of rationalization, mathematics, science and industry, in his complaint that, "And as all choice and reasoning can really be calculated — because there will some day be discovered the laws of our so-called freewill — so, joking apart, there may one day be something like a table constructed of them, so that we really shall choose in accordance with it."[18] This sort of life, he feared, would reduce man to an "insect."[19] (Kafka was later to draw out this apprehension literally in his "Metamorphosis.") Suffering, he passionately believed, was essential to the spiritual life; the Crystal Palace and all that it implied would eliminate suffering and hence deprive man of his humanness.

He ridiculed Chernyshevsky's view that enlightened self-interest would issue in the common good. The Underground Man — and Poe's victim of the Imp of the Perverse — apparently acted quite deliberately against their own interests. But was this really so? Poe had replied simply that the perverse was irresistible and even afforded a "delight of its horror." But Dostoevsky challenges the assumption that perverse behavior is antagonistic to man's interest. Behavior in apparent contradiction to one's interest, he believed, can be explained by the presence of an interest far more commanding and one that overshadows all others in the nineteenth century dispensation. This interest is the assertion of individual freedom, the exercise of personal will as the only countervailing force to the deadening, fragmentizing influence of the Crystal Palace. The Underground Man insists: "But I repeat for the hundredth time that there is one case, and one only, when man may consciously, purposely, desire what is injurious to himself, what is stupid, very stupid — simply in order to have the right to desire for himself what is very stupid and not to be bound by obligation to desire what is sensible. Of course, this very stupid thing, this caprice of ours, may be in reality, gentlemen, more advantageous than anything else on earth, especially in certain cases. And in particular it may be more advantageous than any advantage even when it does us obvious harm, and contradicts the soundest conclusions of our reason concerning advantage — *for in any circumstances it preserves for us what is most precious and most important — that is, our personality, our individuality.*"[20] [Emphasis added]

What Poe was groping toward in his concept of the perverse, Dostoevsky realized in all its implications. The impersonal rationalization and mechanization of life that industry and social relations enforced were draining man of his humanity and making of him a fragmented, disintegrated personality. Neither writer saw any possibility that man's condition could be meliorated by social change. Hope lay only in the free activity of each individual. But how deal with an oppressive social reality? Common to both men was rejection of the prevailing accomodation to society and acceptance of reason and science. "What do I care for the laws of nature and arithmetic," asks the Underground Man, "when, for some reason, I dislike those laws and the fact that twice two makes four?"[21] Even though he cannot refute them, he will flout them and act as he pleases without being reconciled to them. We should observe that it was the effect of the application of these laws of nature in industrial technology and what he considered erroneous theories based on them that drove him to defiance and to embrace irrational attitudes. In frustration the Underground Man will strike back irrationally and maliciously even if "you have not, and perhaps never will have, an object for your spite."

Poe's Imp was an almost unconscious manifestation of the same frustration. More generally, Poe took out his frustration in the destructive motifs that pervade his writing. Like Dostoevsky he was repelled by the mechanizing implications of science, as he made clear in "Sonnet to Science." He there charged science with having destroyed poetry and driven the poet "To seek shelter in some happier star." If Poe used the laws of science, as in *Eureka*, it was only to create a cosmic myth of the basically *esthetic* nature of the universe. The source of his discontents, the alienating conditions of modern society, was basically the same as that of Dostoevsky.

Both writers were deeply influenced, directly or indirectly, by German Romanticism of the first few decades of their century in the work of writers like Tieck, Novalis and Hoffmann. The tortured awareness of conflicts within consciousness, of the tensions between the conscious and subconscious that were central to the writings of these Germans — later to be given systematic definition by Freud — received literary expression in the theme of the *Doppelgänger*. The Underground Man is a mass of contradictions: he behaves maliciously and is tortured by remorse; he has a half-suppressed envy of the self-confidence and self-assurance of a Zvyerkov that he himself lacks, and at the same time feels contempt for that type's conventionality and insensitivity. He is basically repelled by the false values he sees around him and he strikes out almost blindly in irrational and impotent protest. His ingrown consciousness is torn by ambivalence and he is ridden by an obsessive subjectivity that disturbs his mental balance. He inveighs against the "accursed laws of consciousness."[22] He is a mental hypochondriac who prides himself on his tortured consciousness. "I am firmly persuaded," he says, "that a great deal of consciousness, every sort of consciousness, in fact, is a disease."[23] He wallows in the ambivalence of his feelings: he enjoys the suffering entailed in deep regret for his depravity and he absolves himself by ascribing his misbehavior to his diseased consciousness, yet tears at himself for scoundrelly actions.

With Poe, too, consciousness of the real world is intolerable. Everyday reality is repulsive to him; science, the most rational mode of consciousness, is dull and robs one of imagination; the actual world is this "damned Earth." His self-analysis, however, does not have the profound insight, nor is it so drastically thorough as that of the Underground Man. He is "tortured" and "destroyed"[24] by his perverse acts in "The Black Cat"; but he attempts no self-flagellating analysis to justify such acts beyond the bare statement that he was driven to them by the "primal" impulse to perversity. Instead, he flees to the borders of consciousness where truth and morality are irrelevant. While the Underground Man analyzes his condition without mercy, Poe seeks consolation in resort to the intermediate state between sleep and waking, between life and death, in which state he may enjoy sensation and pleasure free of any human responsibility whatsoever.

The Underground Man was speaking for Poe as well when he says, "we've all lost touch with life and we're all cripples to some degree. We've lost touch to such an extent that we feel a disgust for life as it is really lived and cannot bear to be reminded of it."[25] Both men responded irrationally. The one suffered — and enjoyed — an ambivalent and intensely acute flagellation of his mental state. The other, too, was riven by conflict but created — and enjoyed — a subjective world perceived at the borders of consciousness through destructive transcendence.* Poe in fact identified perversity with the movement toward the world of the "indefinite," as he suggests in "The Imp of the Perverse." In straining to describe the transition from perception of a perverse act to its execution, he writes, "We tremble with the violence of the conflict within us, — of the definite with the indefinite — of the substance with the shadow."[26]

Both men were horrified by the truth about themselves. In the *Marginalia*, where Poe set down some of his crucial ideas, he suggests that one could startle the world with a little book entitled, "My Heart Laid Bare." But a book that is worthy of this title, he adds, cannot be written: "No man dare write it. No man ever will dare write it. No man *could* write it, even if he dared. The paper would shrivel and blaze at every touch of the fiery pen."[27] Baudelaire was later to attempt it in *Mon Coeur Mis à Nu*. Dostoevsky not only dared write it in the *Notes*: he elaborated it in the great novels that followed. At the end of Part I of the *Notes* the Underground Man pretends that he has written the book for himself alone. "I want to try the experiment," he says, "whether one can, even with oneself, be perfectly open and not take fright of the whole truth." He observes that Heine had said "that a true autobiography is almost an impossibility, and that man is bound to lie about himself." Heine, he says, is right. But he, the Underground Man, he slyly adds, did not write for the public but for himself and therefore implies that he had written the full truth about himself.[28]

The heightened self-consciousness of the age brought with it a tendency to recoil from what it revealed about the self. Although the ambivalence of consciousness pervaded the work of both writers, the problem is specifically explored in Dostoevsky's "The Double" and Poe's "William Wilson."

---

* This concept of "destructive transcendence" is expounded by Richard Wilbur in his edition of Poe's poetry [*Poe*, ed. Richard Wilbur, The Laurel Poetry Series (New York, 1959), pp. 17ff].

There is an interesting difference between the two suggested by a comment of Thomas Mann. " 'The Double,' " he thought, "certainly did not surpass Edgar Allan Poe's 'William Wilson,' where the same arch-romantic motif is treated in a morally more profound manner."[29] In both stories the two selves within the individual (the "arch-romantic motif") are embodied in a vaguely unreal way in two physical men in implacable conflict. What Mann means, I think, is that the Poe story contains a more specifically ethical element than that of Dostoevsky. Both stories represent alter egos as psychologically opposed in terms of a conflict as to socially acceptable qualities. One self is more ambitious or deals more successfully with conventional social situations and receives greater social approval. The opposition of the two selves is between socially eligible and ineligible behavior within the tortured consciousness. While the Dostoevsky story is almost entirely played out on the neutrally psychological plane, a strong element of ethical conflict is present in the Poe story. The virtuous alter ego of "William Wilson" is represented as the voice of conscience, symbolized by his "singular whisper"; "his moral sense . . . was far keener than my own."[30] And the latter part of the tale is taken up with the alter ego's disapproval of Wilson's immoral, dissolute conduct. The contrast emerges fully at the conclusions of the two stories. At the end of "The Double," Golyadkin goes completely mad — a psychological climax. But when the evil William Wilson finally kills his ethically superior alter ego, the last words of the murdered conscience are ethically oriented: "Henceforward art thou also dead — dead to the World, to Heaven and to Hope! In me didst thou exist — and, in my death, see by this image, which is thine own, how utterly thou hast murdered thyself."[31] The Dostoevsky story ends with total psychological disintegration; the Poe story ends not only with the breakdown of consciousness, but also of the moral self.

Dostoevsky's treatment is more "modern" than that of Poe, although the latter is also colored by the suffering of the ambivalent consciousness.* Despite the differences however, Poe remains essentially in the

---

* The difference is reflected in the sources of the two stories. Charles E. Passage has shown how fully "The Double" is influenced by several tales of Hoffmann, in which the tensions of consciousness are explored.[32] But "William Wilson" derives from Calderon's "El Purgatorio de San Patricio."[33] The theme of the conflict of good and evil within the self is, of course, as old as ethical thought. German Romanticism, however, shifted the emphasis from ethical conflict to the psychological plane of consciousness. Though Poe retained the ethical orientation in this story, he too was influenced by the Romantic emphasis, for it too contains psychological analysis. And it is likely that Hoffmann's influence is present in the story. At the end, for instance, Wilson's alter

same stream of tendency as Dostoevsky. They both were artists who had "lost touch with life" and were tormented by mental strife. They were separated from their fellow-men. Dostoevsky sought salvation in fervent faith in the Russian Orthodox God and in a mystical union with the Russian people; Poe turned his back on reality and looked for solace to a subjectively created world of supernal beauty.

By this rejection of reality Poe signified that the world was alien to him. In his story, "The Man of the Crowd" — pregnant title — Poe gives us a parable of alienation. The narrator sits at the window of a coffee house in a crowded section of London one evening in an observant and receptive mood, in a mood "of the keenest appetency, when the film from the mental vision departs,"[34] and watches the scene as people of various classes and types pass before him. He describes each in turn in a hard, realistic manner. An old man suddenly comes within his focus and on his face the narrator reads traits that might in many respects characterize the Underground Man: "of vast mental power, of caution, of penuriousness, of avarice, of coolness, of malice, of bloodthirstiness, of triumph, of merriment, of excessive terror, of intense — of supreme despair."[35] His interest and curiosity aroused, the narrator follows the old man for many hours through various parts of the city. Throughout the period the man is never seen to speak to a single person.

The ensuing journey is reminiscent of the street-wanderings of the Underground Man or of the despairing Golyadkin of "The Double." The old man passes to a crowded side street. He "walked slowly and with less object than before. . . . He crossed and recrossed the way repeatedly, without apparent aim." In a brilliantly lighted square: "His chin fell upon his breast, while his eyes rolled wildly from under his knit brows, in every direction, upon those who hemmed him in. . . . [In] a large and busy bazaar . . . he forced his way to and fro, without aim, among the host of buyers and sellers. . . . He entered shop after shop, priced nothing, spoke no word, and looked at all objects with a wild and vacant stare. . . . A shop-keeper . . . jostled the old man, and, at the instant I saw a strong shudder come over his frame." After more wandering, the old man mingles with an after-theater crowd and "followed closely a party of some ten or twelve roisterers." He then goes to "the most noisome quarter of London, where everything wore the worst impress of the most deplorable poverty, and of the most desperate crime. . . . The whole

---

ego, gored by his evil counterpart's sword, suddenly appears as a mirror-image. This device of the mirror-image had also been used by Hoffmann in *Kreisleriana* as a reflection in the water and it also appears in that form in "The Double."

atmosphere teemed with desolation." They arrive at "one of the palaces of the fiend, Gin . . . With a half shriek of joy" the old man goes in, walks about "without apparent object, among the throng." The narrator thus trails the old man until the next evening, when, weary of the game, he stops in front of the old man. But the old man does not notice him and passes on. The narrator concludes that "This old man is the type and genius of deep crime. He refuses to be alone. *He is the man of the crowd. . . . 'er lasst sich nicht lesen.'* "[36]

The sketch is enigmatic and not easily susceptible of interpretation. Does it epitomize simply the criminal type in the conventional sense? Why doesn't the man allow himself to be probed? Is it because his evil is too deep to be fathomed? The answer to these questions seems to me — no. In the opening paragraph Poe gives us a clue as to what he means by the criminal. He is the man of ambivalent consciousness. "Now and then, alas," says Poe, "the conscience of man takes up a burthen so heavy in horror that it can be thrown down only into the grave."[37] The criminal element here may be interpreted in the sense of the profound malice of the Underground Man. Like the latter, Poe's old man is not only alone, but incapable of establishing contact with his fellow beings. Indeed, if the old man were the narrator of the story, one can imagine him opening his narrative with something like this passage from the *Notes*: "In the recesses of my heart and conscience there seemed to be working something which would not die — a sort of mysterious feeling which hurt me even as a burn might have done. Generally, on such occasions, I directed my footsteps toward the most crowded and most populous thorough-fares — especially at dusk, at the hour when the throng of hurrying workmen and artisans (their faces worn almost to brutality) becomes denser, and daily toil has reached its end."[38]

The sense of alienation is implicit in the citation from La Bruyère that Poe placed at the head of the story. It is the same as that with which he began his first story, "Metzengerstein," though the wording is not identical: "*Ce grand malheur, de ne pouvoir etre seul*." The man of the crowd — and the Underground Man — *cannot* be alone. At the end of the story Poe says that the man of the crowd "refuses to be alone." But it is clear from the recital of his wandering among crowds that he *is* in fact alone and never succeeds in establishing contact with others. His desperate need and desire are frustrated: he is an alienated man. We can interpret as irony Poe's assertion that the old man cannot be read. We can read him as one who has "lost touch with reality," as the Underground Man said of himself, and is desperately seeking reunion with the people. He cannot be alone because he is human and being human in the fullest sense requires rapport with one's fellow-men. The lack of such rapport has a crippling effect. The desire to be whole drives one to seek others, even if the effort is frustrated. It is the old man, and not the narrator, who is Poe himself. The perpetual search to reach others, to live humanly with the opposite sex, is Poe's own. In his writing, Poe lets himself be read. His frustrations with the real world led him to create a more congenial world in his alienated condition by a destructive transcendence of a real world that will not allow him an integrated life. He projects an unreal realm of beauty that justifies the destruction of the real world. This is Poe's ultimate rendering of the Gothic escape from a hostile, commodity-dominated society.

NOTES

1. Robert Louis Jackson, *Dostoevsky's Underground Man in Russian Literature* (The Hague, 1958), p. 14.

2. Edith Smith Krappe, "A Possible Source for Poe's 'The Tell-Tale Heart' and 'The Black Cat,' " *American Literature* (1940), XII, pp. 84-88.

3. *Complete Works of Edgar Allan Poe*, ed. James A. Harrison, 17 vols. (New York, 1902), V, p. 88. Hereafter cited as "Harr."

4. *Ibid.*, p. 146.

5. *Ibid.*, VI, pp. 145, 147, 149, 150.

6. F. Dostoevsky, "Notes from the Undergound" in *Existentialism from Dostoevsky to Sartre*, selected and introduced by Walter Kaufmann (Cleveland, 1956), p. 53, hereafter cited as "Kaufmann." This work includes only Part I of the *Notes*. Citations from Part II are from *Notes from the Underground*, trans. Andrew R. MacAndrew, (New York, 1961), hereafter cited as "MacAndrew."

7. Kaufmann, p. 56

8. MacAndrew, p. 148.

9. Kaufmann, p. 62.

10. McAndrew, p. 200.

11. Kaufmann, p. 67.

12. Harr., VI, pp. 147, 150.

13. MacAndrew, p. 90n.

14. Kaufmann, p. 56.

15. *Ibid.*, pp. 63, 71.

16. *Ibid.*, p. 72.

17. *Ibid.*, p. 63.

18. *Ibid.*, pp. 72-73.

19. *Ibid.*, p. 56.

20. *Ibid.*, pp. 73-74.

21. *Ibid.*, p. 61.

22. *Ibid.*, p. 65.

23. *Ibid.*, p.56.

24. Harr., V, p. 143.

25. MacAndrew, p. 202.

26. Harr., VI, pp. 148-149.

27. Harr., XVI, p. 128.

28. Kaufmann, p. 82.

29. Thomas Mann, "Preface," *The Short Stories of Dostoevsky* (New York, 1945), p. xvii.

30. Harr., III, pp. 309, 310.

31. *Ibid.*, p. 325.

32. Charles E. Passage, *Dostoevsky the Adapter* (Chapel Hill, 1954).

33. See Horace Horner, "Hawthorne, Poe and a Literary Ghost," *New England Quarterly*, VII (1934), pp. 146-154.

34. Harr., IV, p. 134.

35. *Ibid.*, p. 140.

36. *Ibid.*, pp. 141, 142, 143, 144, 145.

37. *Ibid.*, p. 134.

38. F. Dostoevsky, *Letters from the Underground*, trans. C.J. Hogarth, Everyman Edition, p. 124.

39. Dostoevsky's introduction to the three Poe stories is translated by V. Astrov, "Dostoevsky on Edgar Allan Poe," *AL*, XIV (1942), pp. 70-73, and by C.E. Passage, op. cit., pp. 191-192. Our citations are from the Passage translation.

40. Passage, p. 191.

41. *The Letters of Edgar Allan Poe*, ed. John Ward Ostrom, 2 vols. (Cambridge, 1948), I, p. 257.

42. Kaufmann, p. 78.

43. F.M. Dostoevsky, *Polnoe Sobranie Sochinenia*, 23-vols.-in-13 (St. Petersburg, 1911-1918), XXII, pp. 226-227.

44. H. Braddy, *Glorious Incense, the Fulfillment of Edgar Allan Poe* (Washington, D.C., 1953), p. 128.

14

HERMAN MELVILLE:
Artist of the Worker's world

Bruce Franklin

Herman Melville began life as the son of a prosperous merchant. But his father died, bankrupt, raving, deeply in debt, when Melville was a young boy. So at the age of twelve, he was forced to go to work. At nineteen, he shipped out as a merchant seaman. Then in 1841, at the age of twenty one, he left America on the crew of a whaleship. He returned, almost four years later, as a foretopman on a U.S. warship. He had been a whaler, a deserter, a mutineer, a sailor who had lived in terror of his captain's whip, and a man who had shared the life of the Pacific islanders being subjugated by Europe and America. He was now ready to become one of America's greatest writers.

If Herman Melville had not fallen from a petty bourgeois family into the proletariat, if he had not worked in the most oppressive conditions inflicted on white workers in the mid-nineteenth century, and if he had not rebelled against these conditions with the "crimes" of desertion and mutiny, he might still have been an artist. But he would not be the artist we know as Herman Melville, an artist whose creative imagination was forged in the furnace of proletarian experience, an artist who saw the world of nineteenth-century U.S. society and its commercial empire through the eyes of a class-conscious worker.

But at this point in U.S. history, when you approach Herman Melville as a proletarian artist, you expose yourself to the ridicule of the academic literary establishment, the professors who "earn" $15,000 to $40,000 a year by misrepresenting literature. To them, all great literature is without class content, for it "transcends" class struggle. Great literature exists to be appreciated — by them and their best students — for its greatnes. That is, they reduce literature to a pleasant amenity of their own affluent existence.

Melville understood that he was doomed by his times to write to an audience mainly composed of people of the same social class as the professors of today. The people who then read novels and romances, and of course particularly those who read them to see whether they should be published and whether they should be recommended in reviews, mainly consisted of petty-bourgeois gentlemen and ladies with leisure and education. So Melville begins his career as a literary artist by defining the class relation of himself, and his art, to this audience. He ends the very first paragraph of his first romance, *Typee*, with these words, a defiant statement of an oppressed worker to the people he serves:

> Oh! ye state-room sailors, who make so much ado about a fourteen-days' passage across the Atlantic; who so pathetically relate the privations and hardships of the seas, where, after a day of breakfasting, lunching, dining off five courses, chatting, playing whist, and drinking champaign-punch, it was your hard lot to be shut up in little cabinets of mahogany and maple, and sleep for ten hours, with nothing to disturb you but "those good-for-nothing tars, shouting and tramping over your head," — what would ye say to our six months out of sight of land?[1]

The petty bourgeois critics and other literati of Melville's day were much less sophisticated, or at least more brazen, than our professors. They recognized Melville for what he was, which was certainly not a professor or one of their "cultured" proteges. Within a year, *Typee* was issued in a new, highly censored edition. Melville's publisher forced him to delete the entire passage I have quoted, as well as the anti-imperialist guts of the book. As Mao Tse-Tung puts it in *Talks at the Yenan Forum on Literature and Art*, "All classes in all class societies invariably put the political criterion first and the artistic criterion second. The bourgeoisie always shuts out proletarian literature and art, however great their literary merit."

Melville recognized right away that his art would be perceived by much of his audience as just more "shouting and tramping" by one of "those good-for-nothing tars" disturbing their slumber. Some of the petty-bourgeois intellectuals of his time at first indulged in a certain amount of amusement at the spectacle of this "reading sailor spinning a yarn" with "nothing to indicate the student or the scholar." It was as if one of those chimpanzees we have taught to read were to write his autobiography. But they were quick to point out that this ignorant sailor should not be taken seriously, because "Mr. Melville's mind, though vigorous enough, has not been trained in those studies which enable men to observe with profit." [*The Spectator*, February 28, 1846.]

But Melville persisted in exposing the essence of capitalist society. The more deeply he went into his vision of this world, the more outraged was the response from the literati. His second book, *Omoo*, described the hideous conditions on a whaleship, the mutiny Melville helped to lead, his experience as a prisoner of British imperialists, and the savage destruction of Pacific societies by European and U.S. imperialism. His next book, *Mardi* (1849), a philosophical and political allegory, induced the reviewers to demand that he go back to writing South Sea romances, stripped of such arrogant pretentiousness. In *Redburn* (1849) he describes the exploitation and oppression of sailors on a merchant ship, and the terrifying poverty of Liverpool. *White-Jacket* (1850) tells of the vicious dictatorship that American seamen live under; like *Typee*, *Omoo*, and *Redburn* it is largely autobiographical. Then came *Moby-Dick* (1851), a book most of the reviewers admired for its "wildness," though almost all found it "obscure," if not downright "incomprehensible." But the judgment soon to be put into effect was advanced most clearly by the *United States Magazine and Democratic Review* (January, 1852):

> "Typee" was undoubtedly a very proper book for the parlor, and we have seen it in company with "Omoo," lying upon tables from which Byron was strictly prohibited, although we were unable to fathom those niceties of logic by which one was patronized, and the other proscribed. But these were Mr. Melville's triumphs. "Redburn" was a stupid failure, "Mardi" was hopelessly dull, "White-Jacket" was worse than either; and, in fact, it was such a very bad book, that, until the appearance of "Moby-Dick," we had set it down as the very ultimatum of weakness to which its author could attain. It seems, however, that we were mistaken.

When *Pierre* appeared in 1852, the reviewers were shocked by Melville's subversiveness, although they claimed not to understand the book. They now realized that they had been too lenient and careless in their toleration of Melville's work. Even people he considered his friends among the New York literati deserted him and rallied to the cause of silencing this rude barbarian before he could do any more damage. Leading the frenzied chickens was George Washington Peck, who began his article in the *American Whig Review* (November, 1852) with the words, "A bad book!" Peck explains that he is not concerned if Melville falsely depicts

"South Sea savages" and sailors, but Melville's vision of polite society cannot be tolerated any longer:

> We can afford Mr. Melville full license to do what he likes with "Omoo" and its inhabitants; it is only when he presumes to thrust his tragic *Fantoccini* upon us, as representatives of our own race, that we feel compelled to turn our critical Aegis upon him, and freeze him into silence....he strikes with an impious, though, happily, weak hand, at the very foundations of society....
>
> We have, we think, said sufficient to show our readers that Mr. Melville is a man wholly unfitted for the task of writing wholesome fictions; that he possesses none of the faculties necessary for such work; that his fancy is diseased, his morality vitiated, his style nonsensical and ungrammatical, and his characters as far removed from our sympathies as they are from nature.
>
> Let him continue, then, if he must write, his pleasant sea and island tales. We will always be happy to hear Mr. Melville discourse about savages....

The critical aegis of polite society was partly successful. Melville was driven underground, forced to write for several years anonymously and under pseudonyms. Then, on April 1st, 1857, Herman Melville published under his own name the last work of prose fiction to see print in his life, though he lived for another thirty-four years. It was entitled *The Confidence-Man: His Masquerade*. It depicts capitalist society as the world of a riverboat perilously floating down the Mississippi into total darkness, a world in which every waking moment of every passenger is spent trying to fleece somebody or trying to keep from being fleeced.

Melville was rescued from oblivion after World War I, when he was rediscovered and his works reprinted. Until World War II, the prevailing critical opinion summed up his career as three stages: First came some fine romances of life in the South Seas and on ships. Then suddenly came his masterpiece, *Moby-Dick*. Then, burned-out and more than half crazy, he lapsed into incomprehensible attempts to recapture his artistry, ending with the obscure "fragment," *The Confidence-Man*. After World War II, the magnificent short fiction of the 1852-1855 period, particularly "Bartleby the Scrivener: A Story of Wall Street," "Benito Cereno," and "The Encantadas," began to receive recognition, and one or two critics even began to acknowledge *The Confidence-Man* as a "great book." After the Korean War, the beginning of the Indochina War, and the birth of a revolutionary movement inside the United States, some people, including myself, began to argue that *The Confidence-Man* is Melville's masterpiece.

Although Melville has been unfrozen from the silence and obscurity imposed on him by the petty-bourgeois authorities of the cultural world of his own time, though his works are now taught in every college and university, and though the United States government has even issued a Moby Dick postage stamp, what is most vital and relevant about Melville is still suppressed and buried. For the Melville that is taught is a Melville redesigned in the image of the professors.

There is a tremendous irony in this fact, for Melville was keenly aware of his alienation from the academic world of higher education. And he saw a fundamental contradiction between that academic world and the world in which he received his true education, his artistic training, and all that was worthy about him as a human being — the world of the worker. As he puts it in *Moby-Dick*, speaking with the thinnest of disguises through his persona Ishmael:

> And, as for me, if, by any possibility, there be any as yet undiscovered prime thing in me; if I shall ever deserve any real repute in that small but high hushed world which I might not be unreasonably ambitious of; if hereafter I shall do anything that, upon the whole, a man might rather have done than to have left undone; if at my death, my executors or more properly my creditors, find any precious MSS. in my desk, then here I prospectively ascribe all the honor and glory to whaling; for a whale-ship was my Yale College and my Harvard. [156]2

Melville perceived social reality in terms of class contradictions. In *White Jacket; Or, The World in a Man-of-War*, he presents capitalist society in microcosm as the world of a warship. His explanation of class conflict in the larger society emerges as he explores the reactions of the two main classes of men on the ship to the rumor of an impending war. All the seamen on board, "almost to a man," "abhorred the idea of going into action." Would the seaman's "wages be raised? Not a cent." "What, then, has he to expect from war? What but harder work, and harder usage than in peace; a wooden leg or arm; mortal wounds, and death?" But the opposing class has an opposite response: "But with the officers of the quarter-deck it was just the reverse." To them it offered the possibility of "glory" and "promotion." Hence they had an objective interest in the "slaughtering of their fellow-men." Melville then generalizes from this example:

> This hostile contrast between the feelings with which the common seamen and the officers of the *Neversink* looked forward to this more

than possible war, is one of many instances that might be quoted to show the antagonism of their interests, the incurable antagonism in which they dwell. But can men, whose interests are diverse, ever hope to live together in a harmony uncoerced? Can the brotherhood of the race of mankind ever hope to prevail in a man-of-war, where one man's bane is almost another man's blessing? By abolishing the scourge, shall we do away with tyranny; *that* tyranny which must ever prevail, where of two essentially antagonistic classes in perpetual contact, one is immeasurably the stronger? [203-204][3]

Melville does not offer this as a picture of *all* human society, or as an inevitable consequence of human nature. It is capitalist society he is talking about. In fact, *Typee*, his somewhat fictionalized account of the period he passed with the people of the Marquesas Islands, takes precisely the same view of the origin of classes, private property, and the state as Engels' *Origin of the Family, Private Property, and the State*, which was published almost forty years later. The society of the Typee Valley is what Marx and Engels call primitive communism. There are no social classes in this society, but rather a single extended family, living in the "harmony uncoerced," the "brotherhood of the race of mankind" that Melville cannot find in the "civilized" world:

During my whole stay on the island I never witnessed a single quarrel, nor anything that in the slightest degree approached even to a dispute. The natives appeared to form one household, whose members were bound together by the ties of strong affection. The love of kindred I did not so much perceive, for it seemed blended in the general love; and where all were treated as bothers and sisters, it was hard to tell who were actually related to each other by blood. [230]

In a passage censored out of the second edition, Melville singles out for his special admiration the unanimity of view that flows from this communality:

There was one admirable trait in the general character of the Typees which, more than anything else, secured my admiration: it was the unanimity of feeling they displayed on every occasion. With them there hardly appeared to be any difference of opinion upon any subject whatever. They all thought and acted alike. . . . They showed this spirit of unanimity in every action of life: everything was done in concert and good-fellowship. [229]

There is no "state" and no "estalished law," Melville observes in another passage censored from the second edition [225-226], and yet every person lived without fear of crime: "in the darkest nights they slept securely." [226] There is personal property, such as hand-carved artifacts, but no socially produced private property. In still another passage censored from the second edition, Melville pointedly contrasts this communism with capitalist society:

> There were no foreclosures of mortgages, no protested notes, no bills payable, no debts of honor in Typee; no unreasonable tailors and shoemakers, perversely bent on being paid; no duns of any description; no assault-and-battery attorneys to foment discord, backing their clients up to a quarrel, and then knocking their heads together; no poor relations, everlastingly occupying the spare bedchamber, and diminishing the elbowroom at the family table; no destitute widows with their children starving on the cold charities of the world; no beggars; no debtors' prisons; no proud and hardhearted nabobs in Typee; or to sum up all in one word — no Money! "That root of all evil" was not to be found in the valley. [146]

Existence in Typee is Edenic, and "There seemed to be no cares, griefs, troubles, or vexations in all Typee." [146]

Melville, however, does not sentimentalize life in Typee, and he is not a utopian. He realizes that a person whose being is shaped by capitalist society cannot live in the society of Typee, nor in some utopian community (like Brook Farm) trying to recreate such a society as an island in the midst of capitalism. In fact, the very presence of the narrator begins to tear apart the structure of Typee society, and the last image we have of it is a violent argument about him culminating in the symbolic end of Eden: "Blows were struck, wounds were given, and blood flowed."

The actual end of this society, and of the other stable societies of the Pacific, are described at length in *Omoo* and *Typee* in passage after passage delineating the hideous features of European and U.S. imperialism. Needless to say, almost every one of these passages was deleted from the second edition of *Typee*. Melville describes the conscious destruction of the natives' culture by the Christian missionaries, the looting of their resources, the spurious claim to sovereignty over them imposed by fleets of warships and marines landing to burn down their villages, the establishment of puppet rulers, the pretexts used to impose more and more direct colonial rule, the investment of capital, and the starvation, disease, wage and chattel slavery, and utter misery and degradation imposed by "civilization" and carried out by "the most ferocious animal on the face of the earth": "the white civilized man." [145]

The ship which brings the narrator to the Marquesas contains the basic class relationships of capitalism, the class relationships being extended throughout the Pacific by the various empires' ships of commerce and war. The purpose of the voyage is to kill whales in order to make money for the owners of the ship. The people who do the work are the super-exploited and oppressed sailors. The agent of authority is the captain, for whom justice resides in "the butt end of a hand-spike." The narrator commits the "crime" of desertion, a crime peculiar to this group of workers, whose condition lies about midway between wage and chattel slavery. He contemplates the more serious crime of organized resistance, but gives it up because "our crew was composed of a parcel of dastardly and mean-spirited wretches, divided among themselves, and only united in enduring without resistance the unmitigated tyranny of the captain. It would have been mere madness for any two or three of the number, unassisted by the rest, to attempt making a stand against his ill-usage."

The ship on which Melville left the Marquesas, the Australian whaleship *Lucy Ann*, had quite a different sort of crew, as described in *Omoo*. Eating rotten food on a rotting ship commanded by an incompetent gentleman and swarming with cockroaches and rats, the crew eventually refuse to work, and they sign a bill of complaints drawn up by the narrator. When the British consul at Tahiti tries to browbeat them back to work, they rise up, led by a knife-wielding sailor who proclaims that now "we're all a parcel of mutineers and pirates!" For this "crime" of refusal to work, Melville and the rest of the crew were incarcerated by the British.

The most serious crime Melville contemplates against lawful authority is murder. In *White Jacket*, the captain of the ship orders the narrator to be flogged for unintentionally missing an assignment. In an apparently autobiographical passage, one of fine physical and emotional detail, the narrator carefully calculates the force, time, distance, and moral choice necessary to rush at the captain and carry him overboard to their mutual death:

> The captain stood on the weather-side of the deck. Sideways, on an unobstructed line with him, was the opening of the lee-gangway, where the side-ladders are suspended in port. Nothing but a slight bit of sinnate-stuff served to rail in this opening, which was cut right down to the level of the captain's feet, showing the far sea beyond. I stood a little to windward of him, and, though he was a large, powerful man, it was certain that a sudden rush against him, along the slanting deck, would infallibly pitch him head-foremost into the ocean, though he who so rushed must needs go over with him. My blood seemed clotting in

my veins; I felt icy cold at the tips of my fingers, and a dimness was before my eyes. But through that dimness the boatswain's mate, scourge in hand, loomed like a giant, and Captain Claret, and the blue sea seen through the opening at the gangway, showed with an awful vividness. I cannot analyze my heart, though it then stood still within me. But the thing that swayed me to my purpose was not altogether the thought that Captain Claret was about to degrade me, and that I had taken an oath with my soul that he should not. No, I felt my man's manhood so bottomless within me, that no word, no blow, no scourge of Captain Claret would cut me deep enough for that. I but swung to an instinct in me — the instinct diffused through all animated nature, the same that prompts even a worm to turn under the heel.

I have quoted this passage at length because it shows with burning clarity how Melville's artistic imagination was shaped by his work experience. Whether or not it is literally autobiographical, the narrator's position — and his vision — are certainly Melville's own.

White Jacket was Melville's fifth book. In each of these, except for the experimental narrative in the latter sections of *Mardi*, Melville narrates the action from the point of view of a common sailor. This common sailor is in each case a fictionalized self portrait. True, this sailor is also exceptional. Although he is part of the most oppressed sector of the working class, he has fallen into that class from above, and he figures he has a good chance of climbing back out again. That is, like Melville, this worker is doubly declassed, and no longer belongs simply either to the petty bourgeoisie, into which he was born and to which he hopes to return, nor to the working class, into which he has fallen. But to comprehend Melville's art, we must see that he chooses to present the world from the point of view of an oppressed and exploited worker. Most other mid-nineteenth century American authors commonly taught in the academy today saw the world from an opposite class point of view. For them workers either did not exist at all, or, if they did, they existed as objects, as exotic creatures, or, at best, poor wretches. Melvile's art is a projection of the human universe through the eyes of an articulate, self-educated, passionate, philosophic, outraged, and extremely creative worker.

Melville's next book was *Moby-Dick; Or, The Whale*. Here the sailor narrator expands to become Ishmael, the sailor-philosopher. The tremendous creative achievement of *Moby-Dick* flows from Melville's proletarian view of the most important experience of his life, as I am attempting to describe in another article. Suffice it to say here that if it were not for the physicality of the narrative, the facts and details of the actual working life of the whaling industry, *Moby-Dick* would be, as Ishmael himself says, nothing but "a monstrous fable, or still worse and more detestable, a hideous and intolerable allegory." Whatever the White Whale may symbolize, he is one thing for sure: a whale hunted to be turned into dollars. And whatever that hunt may symbolize, it is a very real, dangerous, filthy, and physical form of labor. Without the actual bones and blubber of the whales brutally slain "to light the gay bridals and other merry-makings of men," without the real-life stove boats and drowned men, without Melville's personal experience of all this, *Moby-Dick* would be as abstract and boring as *The Faerie Queene*. The central philosophical exploration of *Moby-Dick* is the relation between our subjective world and the objective world in which we live and which shapes our perception of it. It is here that Melville seeks an answer to the central question of the bourgeois historical epoch: Is freedom possible? This question is not resolved from the point of view of Ahab, the mad individualist, superhero, universe-threatening captain, who thinks he can impose his will and ego on all of objective reality, nor from the point of view of the pious capitalist owners and their reasonable, obedient first mate, Starbuck. It is answered from the point of view of the workers themselves: Queequeg, the South Sea cannibal who is the true savior on board; Pip, the mad, oracular Black cabin-boy; the sagacious Black cook; the grizzled old Manxman; and so on to the most intellectual of the crew, Ishmael.

What scandalized the bourgeois critics most about Melville's next book, *Pierre*, was its wildly honest look at sexual aberration in civilized society. As Melville was subsequently driven underground into anonymous and pseudonymous writing, he went much further in this exploration. Unlike Freud, he recognized clearly that particular sexual impulses, especially the "aberrant" or "perverted" ones, show much more about the particular society than they do about the individuals experiencing them. In fact, he shows that the most essential and most grotesque sexual perversion of our society is merely an expression and product of capitalist social relations. In the same vision he places Satan more accurately than do some of our more recent sensationalist excursions into diabolism, such as E. Howard Hunt's novel *Coven* or the film *The Exorcist*. To Melville, Satan is none other than the factory-owning capitalist, and the underlying sexual perversion of our society is ripping off the creativity of human beings to enslave them to machines working to enrich the handful of parasites who own the means of production.

On April Fool's Day, 1855, *Harper's New Monthly Magazine* published a pair of anonymous sketches entitled "The Paradise of Bachelors and the Tartarus of Maids." These are trick stories, with hidden meanings intended to expose the unwitting polite readers of *Harper's*. They display Melville's view of the two main classes in capitalist society, the working class and the owning class, in the form of a grotesque sexual allegory.

In "The Tartarus of Maids," Melville assumes the voice of a seedsman who visits the factory that produces his seed envelopes. A nice germinous, procreative job. But what the seedsman represents is a perverted male sexuality entering a woman's genitals in the quest of dollars, and these woman's genitals have been captured and enslaved by the archetypal Satanic capitalist. All creativity, including procreativity, has been perverted to produce nothing but blank paper and profits.

The seedsman himself may be considered a view of the creative writer within capitalist society, who, like Melville himself, must sell his art as a commodity in order to live. ("Dollars damn me!" Melville said succinctly.) On another level, his business represents the expansion of industrial capitalism and wage slavery in the pre-Civil War United States: "Having embarked on a large scale in the seedsman's business (so extensive and broadcast, indeed, that at length my seeds were distributed through all the Eastern and Northern States, and even fell into the far soil of Missouri and the Carolinas). . . ."

The seedsman enters a valley, passing "the Mad Maid's Bellowspipe." He enters "a Dantean gateway": "From the steepness of the walls here, their strangely ebon hue, and the sudden contraction of the gorge, this particular point is called the Black Notch." He passes a "strange-colored torrent" called "Blood River." He finally arrives at the factory, which looks "like some great whited sepulchre." It is located in "the Devil's Dungeon."

All the workers in the factory are women, referred to consistently as "girls." The narrator asks why:

> "The girls," echoed I, glancing round at their silent forms. "Why is it, sir, that in most factories, female operatives, of whatever age, are indiscriminately called girls, never women?"
>
> "Oh! as to that — why, I suppose, the fact of their being generally unmarried — that's the reason, I should think. But it never struck me before. For our factory here, we will not have married women; they are apt to be off-and-on too much. We want none but steady workers: twelve hours to the day, day after day, through the three hundred and

sixty-five days, excepting Sundays, Thanksgiving, and Fast-days.
That's our rule. And so, having no married women, what females we
have are rightly enough called girls."[4]

Birth, menstruation, child care — none can be permitted to interfere
with the production of blank paper and profits. The name of the young
man who knows this process from inside is Cupid.

Cupid takes the narrator on a tour of the factory. He shows him "two
great round vats...full of a white, wet, woolly-looking stuff, not unlike
the albuminous part of an egg, soft-boiled." Cupid tells him that this
"white pulp" is "the first beginnings" of the paper. He then takes the
narrator into a room, "stifling with a strange, blood-like, abdominal
heat" where "the germinous particles" were being "developed." The
power for the factory comes from Blood River. A "girl" meekly tends "a
vertical thing like a piston periodically rising and falling." An elderly
woman, formerly a wet nurse, has come to work here because the
"business" of a wet nurse "is poor in these parts." "Poisonous particles"
dart from all sides through the air into the lungs. Only machinery can be
heard, because "the human voice was banished." A woman looks at the
narrator with "a face pale with work, and blue with cold; an eye supernatural with unrelated misery." The narrator proclaims the essential perversion and sterility of the factory:

> Machinery — that vaunted slave of humanity — here stood menially
> served by human beings, who served mutely and cringingly as the slave
> serves the Sultan. The girls did not so much seem accessory wheels to
> the general machinery as mere cogs to the wheels.

And he apprehends the essential deadliness of this factory in the Devil's
Dungeon: "So, through consumptive pallors of this blank, raggy life, go
these white girls to death."

The factory is owned by a "dark-complexioned man" known as "Old
Bach." The narrator doesn't notice that these are both names for the
Devil, but naively inquires whether he is a bachelor. When he finds this is
so, his memory takes him back to "The Paradise of Bachelors," the
subject of the first sketch.

The entrance to the Paradise of Bachelors is not far from another
symbolic phallus, "Temple Bar." It is an anus. To reach it, the narrator
turns, "soiled with the mud of Fleet Street," site of filthy London jour-
nalism, to "glide down a dim, monastic way, flanked by dark, sedate,
and solemn piles," a word signifying then, as now, a morbid dilatation of

the veins of the lower rectum. Inside, in the "honey-comb of offices and domiciles," like "any cheese...quite perforated through and through with the snug cells of bachelors," he enjoys a huge feast of gluttony and good fellowships with nine bachelors, men of business and law. Beginning with "ox-tail soup," which reminds the narrator at first of "teamsters' gads and the raw-hides of ushers," they pass through a course of turbot, "just gelatinous enough, not too turtlish in its unctuousness," to cloy themselves on "a saddle of mutton, a fat turkey, a chicken-pie, and endless other savory things" washed down with round after round of wines and ale. As they give way to "unconstraint," they now bring out, "like choice brands of Moselle or Rhenish," the "choice experiences in their private lives." For instance, "one told us how mellowly he lived when a student at Oxford; with various spicy anecdotes of most frank-hearted noble lords, his liberal comapnions." Another tells "a strange anecdote of the private life of the Iron Duke, never printed, and never before announced in any public or private company." After dinner, they all descend to the courtyard, "two by two, and arm-in-arm." Then they divide, "some going to their neighboring chambers to turn over the *Decameron* ere retiring for the night."

For these men of wealth, pain and trouble simply do not exist:

> The thing called pain, the bugbear styled trouble — those two legends seemed preposterous to their bachelor imaginations. How could men of liberal sense, ripe scholarship in the world, and capacious philosophical and convivial understandings — how could they suffer themselves to be imposed upon by such monkish fables? Pain! Trouble! As well talk of Catholic miracles. No such thing. — Pass the sherry, sir. — Pooh, pooh! Can't be!

These "easy-hearted men had no wives or children to give an anxious thought." They are as barren and sterile as the maids in the Tartarus they own and control.

In "Bartleby, the Scrivener: A Story of Wall Street." Melville probes deeper into the sterile world of capitalism. The narrator of this story is also a bachelor, a Wall Street lawyer, who, "in the cool tranquillity of a snug retreat" does "a snug business among rich men's bonds, and mortgages, and title-deeds." He is "a conveyancer and title-hunter, and drawer-up of recondite documents of all sorts." The paper mill of "The Tartarus of Maids" produces nothing but blank paper, and "all sorts of writings would be writ on those now vacant things — sermons, lawyers' briefs, physicians' prescriptions, love-letters, marriage certificates, bills of divorce, registers of birth, death-warrants, and so on, without end." The narrator of "Bartleby" is the man who converts these blank pieces of paper into the documents upon which capitalism rests: bonds, titles, and mortgages which declare that all the means of production, including that very paper mill, and all the products coming from it, including the pieces of paper themselves, do not belong to the people who produced them with their entire life's creativity, but instead are the private property of a handful of rich parasites.

The narrator is not an unkind, much less a Satanic, man. But he is an employer. Hence he sees his office workers as objects, whose existence is to serve the function he assigns them. He considers one of his two scriveners "a most valuable person to me," and the other "a very useful man to me." His Wall-Street office is made of walls surrounded by other walls. In one direction, his office "looked upon the white wall of the interior of a spacious sky-light shaft," providing a view "deficient in what landscape painters call 'life.'" In the other direction, "my windows commanded an unobstructed view of a lofty brick wall, black by age and everlasting shade."

His business becomes considerably increased when he receives the office of Master in Chancery, a kind of judgeship:"There was now great work for scriveners. Not only must I push the clerks already with me, but I must have additional help." In answer to his advertisement for "help," there arrives at his office a mysterious stranger named Bartleby.

Bartleby is informed of his duties as a scrivener, and at first "did an extraordinary quantity of writing," "copying by sunlight and by candle-light." But when the narrator off-handedly orders Bartleby to compare copy, "a request made according to common usage and common sense," Bartleby calmly responds, "I would prefer not to."

Gradually Bartleby withdraws more and more of his labor from the commands of the narrator, at each point merely stating "I would prefer not to" go to the post office, help tie a package, examine papers, or even do any more copying. The narrator originally had considered him "a valuable acquisition." But as Bartleby's mysterious strike lengthens, the narrator finds this rebellion of "my hired clerk" shattering to all his customary assumptions, first about the relations between employers and employees, then about private property itself, and finally about the entire human condition in this society. Bartleby's "crime" is a mild quiet version of Melville's own crimes of desertion and mutiny: it too is a refusal to work.

Bartleby's strike becomes a strange, mute sit-in, as he "prefers not to" leave the office at all, though he no longer does any work for his employer. The narrator finds himself "sort of unmanned when he tranquilly permits his hired clerk to dictate to him, and order him away from his own premises," not perceiving that his own workers might be similarly "unmanned' by the dictates and orders of their employer. But in fact what is happening is almost the opposite of what the narrator here perceives. By confronting the underlying ethos of Wall Street, Bartleby offers to the narrator the possibility of becoming a human being, with feeling and emotional ties to other human beings. Struck by the discovery of Bartleby's cosmic loneliness and solitude, the narrator's bachelor privacy and smugness disintegrates, and he finds a revelation denied to the bachelor hedonists of "The Paradise of Bachelors":

> For the first time in my life, a feeling of overpowering stinging melancholy seized me. Before, I had never experienced aught but a not unpleasing sadness. The bond of a common humanity now drew me irresistibly to gloom. A fraternal melancholy! For both I and Bartleby were sons of Adam. I remembered the bright silks and sparkling faces I had seen that day, in gala trim, swan-like sailing down the Mississippi of Broadway; and I contrasted them with the pallid copyist, and thought to myself, Ah, happiness courts the light, so we deem the world is gay; but misery hides aloof, so we deem that misery there is none.

But business sense gets the upper hand again, and the narrator orders Bartleby to "quit me." When Bartleby announces that he would prefer not to, the narrator responds as the very essence of capitalist society, reducing all human relationships to money relationships:

> I would prefer *not* to quite you," he replied, gently emphasizing the *not*.
> "What earthy right have you to stay here? Do you pay any rent? Do you pay my taxes? Or is this property yours?"

But gradually the narrator begins to perceive something unearthly, something perhaps even divine, radiating from Bartleby, "this forlornest of mankind." He feels that "Bartleby was billeted upon me for some mysterious purpose of an all-wise Providence, which it was not for a mere mortal like me to fathom." He glimpses the message of Matthew 25, in which Christ identifies himself with all those most miserable — strangers, the poor, the sick, the needy, prisoners — and in which Christ promises to judge each person on how he or she responds to these wretched of the earth:

At last I see it, I feel it; I penetrate to the predestinated purpose of my life. I am content. Others may have loftier parts to enact; but my mission in this world, Bartleby, is to furnish you with office-room for such period as you may see fit to remain.

But the customs and usages of Wall Street overcome this resolve. The narrator buckles under "the unsolicited and uncharitable remarks obtruded upon me by professional friends." He flees from his own office, leaving Bartleby to the tender mercies of the landlord and the new tenant. Then he denies Bartleby three times, in words echoing Peter's three denials of Christ.

Then, "fearful...of being exposed in the papers," he returns in an attempt to help the other functionaries of capitalism to get rid of this "nuisance." He decides to offer Bartleby the choice of other things to do in this society. They range the gamut of the opportunities open to white-collar workers:

"Whould you like to re-engage in copying for some one?"

"Would you like a clerkship in a dry-goods store?"

"'how would a bar-tender's business suit you?"

"Well, then, would you like to travel through the country collecting bills bills for the merchants?"

"How, then, would going as a companion to Europe, to entertain some young gentleman with your conversation — how would that suit you?"

Bartleby prefers not to spend his life doing any of these things.

As a result, he is placed in the New York City prison then, as now, known as "the Tombs, or, to speak more properly, the Halls of Justice." He is charged with being a vagrant, precisely because he refuses to become one. The walls and physical environment of the prison, as the narrator notes, are no more unpleasant than the office world of Wall Street. There Bartleby, whoever he is, completes his withdrawal from this grotesque world, curling up and dying.

At one end of pre-Civil War capitalist America stood the brick walls of the financial district of the Empire State. At the other, Black slaves produced the main cash export of the country, King Cotton, which was providing the capital base for industrial capitalism. "Bartleby" shows one white-collar worker threatening the very existence of Wall Street with a mysterious, individual, mild-mannered withdrawal of labor and refusal to disperse. This form of what his boss calls "passive resistance" succeeds finally in destroying only himself. *Benito Cereno*, another great story of this period, describes a different response, a highly organized and bloody revolt by Black slaves. Melville locates this in the past, but his vision is clearly intended to be prophetic.

The story is based on an actual slave revolt that took place on a Spanish slave ship sailing between two Spanish colonies in the New World. It is told from the point of view of Amasa Delano, the practical, materialist, Yankee captain of the American ship that eventually recaptures the slaver and its human cargo. His ship is the *Bachelor's Delight*, name of a famous pirate vessel, and emblematic of its bland, narrow-minded, optimistic, capitalistic, Yankee bachelor captain. On one level, the rotting old Spanish ship represents the dying Spanish empire, about to be taken over by the vigorous, rising young Yankee empire. The main focus is on the material basis of both these empires: Black slavery. And central to that is the consciousness of slaves and masters.

The slaves are able to take over the Spanish ship because their owner made the fatal error of thinking they were content with their condition and therefore didn't need to be in chains. When the slaves see the American ship, they force what is left of the Spanish crew to assume their original roles. So when Captain Delano comes on board, he enters the scene of an elaborate masquerade, the Black slaves, now in control, pretending to be slaves again, the Spanish crew, now cringing in terror, pretending to be the masters of the ship and the Blacks.

Captain Delano cannot comprehend what is going on, because to him the slaves are primarily "valuable freight," and secondarily pleasant animals who enjoy bright colors, are content with their servile lot, and are "too stupid" to organize a revolt. When he is told the real state of affairs, he organizes the recapture of the ship. His main goal is to take over the valuable slaves, killing and injuring as few as possible. This is for profits, not mercy, a fact made clear by the Americans murdering two of the Spanish sailors incorrectly believed to have in "some way favored the cause of the negroes." But even after all is revealed to Captain Delano, he still does not comprehend that Blacks, just like whites, will kill for their freedom, and that Black slavery contains the seed of the destruction of his own society.

The Confidence-Man displays the diseased heart of capitalist society and prophesies its end. A meek mysterious figure resembling Bartleby opens the book by attracting the curiosity of the more well-to-do passengers on the riverboat. His place is then mysteriously assumed by the seemingly fawning figure of Black Guinea, "a grotesque negro cripple" who, "opening his mouth like an elephant for tossed apples," catches the smallest pieces of money, copper pennies. Black Guinea transmutes into form after form of the Confidence Man, who stalks the decks of the riverboat bringing out the money, and money relationships, which constitute this inhuman society.[5]

At the end the Confidence Man becomes the cosmic figure of the Destroyer, appearing simultaneously as the extravagantly dressed Cosmopolitan and a boy in rags with a face covered with grime. The boy is selling locks to keep thieves out, moneybelts to wear in case they get in, and counterfeit detectors to see if the money was worth protecting in the first place.

This final scene of Melville's last fiction to be published in his lifetime recalls that scene of the first paragraph of his first book. It is a "gentlemen's cabin," in which most of the passengers are still trying to sleep. Melville, that noisy sailor, is still keeping them awake, or trying to. All the lights but one have now died out, and voices call out from the berths protesting that the verbal quest for wisdom is "keeping wiser men awake": "And if you want to know what wisdom is, go find it under your blankets."

The last passenger awake is a "clean, comely" and "well-to-do" old man. He is left with only one activity before being led away into the deepening darkness: he must sit there studying a banknote to determine whether it is counterfeit. His best clue may be a wild goose chase, a symbol, perhaps vaguely outlined on this symbolic piece of paper: "the figure of a goose, very small, indeed, all but microscopic; and, for added precaution...not observable, even if magnified, unless the attention is directed to it." Unknown to this affluent professional gentleman, the bank that issued the bill was part of the Mississippi Bubble, and had already gone bankrupt.

This Mississippi riverboat is steaming toward the same state. Its voyage had begun at sunrise in the slave city of St. Louis, just across the river from the "free" state of Illinois. The first half of the book takes place in daylight, and the boat glides between Illinois and the slave state of Missouri. Twilight comes in a chapter which divides the book precisely into two equal halves. It takes place as the boat lies still at Cairo, the last point on the journey south without Black chattel slavery; from here on there is slave territory on both sides of the river and darkness continues to intensify on board.

Identities shift amidst the deepening ambiguities of action in *The*

Confidence-Man, but Melville's values burn clearly. His quest for truth and the possibility of freedom strips mask after hypocritical mask from the smiling faces of polite society. One of the most revealing exchanges takes place between a gruff, eccentric, rifle-toting, slavery-hating and freedom-loving Missourian on one hand and the Confidence Man in the guise of an affable herb doctor on the other. The Missourian, named Pitch, before revealing his own opinions, demands to know where the herb-doctor stands on the question of slavery:

> "You are an abolitionist, ain't you?" he added, squaring himself with both hands on his rifle, used for a staff, and gazing in the herb-doctor's face with no more reverence than if it were a target. "You are an abolitionist, ain't you?"

Although we readers may not know the fictional identity of the herb-doctor, his answer tells us what he represents, for we have heard his voice again and again in response to the demands of every movement for liberation:

> "As to that, I cannot so readily answer. If by abolitionist you mean a zealot, I am none; but if you mean a man, who, being a man, feels for all men, slaves included, and by any lawful act, opposed to nobody's interest, and therefore, rousing nobody's enmity, would willingly abolish suffering (supposing it, in its degree, to exist) from among mankind, irrespective of color, then am I what you say."

Pitch, still wielding his rifle, the instrument that was shortly to be used to abolish Black slavery, then accurately labels this liberal:

> "Picked and prudent sentiments. You are the moderate man, the invaluable understrapper of the wicked man. You, the moderate man, may be used for wrong, but are useless for right."

Pitch comes from Missouri. In 1820-1821, the liberal northern capitalists had reached a convenient compromise with the southern plantation owners known as the Missouri Compromise, which provided that Missouri would be the only slave state in the Louisiana Purchase north of 36° 30'. But in 1854, three years before the publication of *The Confidence-Man*, Congress had reached a new compromise, the Kansas-Nebraska Bill, which explicitly repealed the Missouri Compromise and opened up the possibility of slavery in Kansas. In 1856, pro-slavery forces conducted a massacre in Lawrence, Kansas. In response there emerged a figure resembling Melville's fictional rifle-toting abolitionist, a man named John Brown.

Two years after *The Confidence-Man*, John Brown led the attack on Harper's Ferry. Brown was convicted of treason against the United States of America, and of urging and inciting slaves to treason and murder. He was hanged in December, 1859, by the government of the United States. In 1861, the Civil War began, with the government of the United States still firmly committed to the support of slavery.

In 1866, the year after the war ended, the slaves now officially freed, Melville published a volume of Civil War poems entitled *Battle Pieces*. The first poem, entitled 'The Portent," is a memorial to John Brown. It begins by describing Brown "Hanging from the beam,/Slowly swaying (such the law). . ." Melville died in 1891, leaving one last work of fiction, published decades later. It also deals with a heroic man hanged because of the law.

Billy Budd opens with another metamorphosis of Black and White. First we see a Black African as the Handsome Sailor, a god-like man, combining "strength and beauty," the "champion" and "spokesman" of his shipmates, workers of "such an assortment of tribes and complexions" they could serve as "Representatives of the Human Race." His figure merges into that of Billy Budd, an Anglo-Saxon version of the same heroic sailor.[6]

Billy Budd is Adam before the Fall, a man of natural goodness and innocence. He is loved by all his shipmates on the merchant ship *The Rights of Man*. Symbolically kidnapped from *The Rights of Man*, he is impressed into service on the aptly named warship of the British empire, H.M.S. *Bellipotent*. The time is shortly after the American and French Revolutions and the British crown, representing the center of reaction in the western world, is faced with rebellions by the sailors of its own fleet.

Claggart, the head of the secret police on board the *Bellipotent*, a human version of a "snake" or "torpedo-fish," falsely accuses Budd of fomenting mutiny. Budd, whose only defect is that he stutters in highly emotional situations, becomes too choked to speak in his own defense. He involuntarily strikes out with his fist, accidentally killing Claggart with that one blow.

This confrontation had been arranged by the captain, with himself as the sole witness, to test the truth of the accusation. He is an intellectual, somewhat bookish, staunchly tory officer aptly named "Vere" (the original spelling for the nautical term for shifting before the wind). Captain Vere knows that Budd is morally and legally innocent of murder and mutiny, but decides immediately that he must be hanged as an example to the rest of the crew. So he calls together a drumhead court, hand-picked — by himself — from among the officers of the ship. When the three officers hear the evidence, they do not want to convict Budd. So Vere takes over the "trial," essentially dictating the verdict he had already reached. He argues they must convict, though it is obviously against nature, because they serve the king, as opposed to nature. He further argues that they should disregard both their "heart" and their "private conscience," because their only loyalty as the King's officers is to the "imperial. . .code." Accordingly, the best man and the truest sailor on the ship is hanged.

Much of the criticism of *Billy Budd* has consisted of a debate about Captain Vere, as if the key issue of the story was to decide whether Melville was condemning or approving of his action. I am not going to restate the correct side of this argument, for there is overwhelming evidence in the story, and throughout all of Melville's other works, that Vere stands for all Melville found most detestable, inhuman, and menacing: arbitrary authority; oppression; military tyranny; legalism; the officer class and its objective interest in war; hypocrisy; loyalty to kings and empire; legalized murder; disregard of nature, the human heart, and the dictates of conscience.

The real issue about Vere is not whether he is right or wrong, but whether he is sane or mad. I do not believe that Melville wrote *Billy Budd* to convince readers not to hang innocent people, nor to argue they should rebel against eighteenth-century British monarchy and imperialism. *Billy Budd* assumes these values, and insofar as it focuses on Vere, who is, after all, quite secondary to Billy Budd himself, it is a psychological study, the tale of a diseased mind that can argue with learning, calmness, and plausibility that the best thing to do is murder the best person in your world.

The question of Vere's insanity is raised privately by the ship's surgeon, and Melville then asks each reader to answer "by such light as this narrative may afford." He provides the answer in a philosophical disquisition on "Natural Depravity." Talking in particular about the obvious example of Claggart, he frames a general definition which fits Captain Vere even more precisely. The best examples of this depravity "invariably are dominated by intellectuality." "Civilization, especially if of the austerer sort, is auspicious to it. It folds itself in the mantle of respectability."

But the thing which in eminent instances signalizes so exceptional a nature is this: Though the man's even temper and discreet bearing would seem to intimate a mind peculiarly subject to the law of reason, not the less in heart he would seem to riot in complete exemption from that law, having apparently little to do with reason further than to employ it as an ambidexter implement for effecting the irrational. That is to say: Toward the accomplishment of an aim which in wantonness of atrocity would seem to partake of the insane, he will direct a judgment sagacious and sound. These men are madmen, and of the most danger-ous sort, for their lunacy is not continuous, but occasional, evoked by some special object; it is protectively secretive, which is as much to say it is self-contained, so that when, moreover, most active it is to the average mind not distinguishable from sanity, and for the reason above suggested: that whatever its aims may be — and the aim is never declared — the method and the outward proceeding are always perfect-ly rational.

Essential to these men is a secret passion, a force driving their *will*, which dominates their conscience. Using as metaphor the profession Melville finds most contemptible, the very one Vere assumes at the critical moment, he tells us that "Claggart's conscience" was "but the lawyer to his will." And what was Vere's secret passion, that degrades his conscience to the role of lawyer? Vere's "spirit...'spite its philosophic austerity may yet have indulged in the most secret of all passions, ambition." Vere is Claggart in the most subtle form.

Melville is now largely in the hands of academic gentlemen who are so blind to their own motives, but so aware of how to serve their own ambition, that they can uphold Vere as a good man. In fact some have actually written that Vere is Melville's one true "hero," and the one character in all his fiction with whom Melville can best be identified. This is appalling, but it should be no great surprise. It is only fitting that these gentlemen, profiting handsomely as they do from the status quo by intellectual jugglery, should identify themselves with this intellectual captain who so skillfully veers in the service of his empire.

On the other side are the oppressed people. When Billy Budd is hanged, in his death he becomes a kind of god to the sailors of the entire fleet. Any chip from the spar from which Billy was hanged is for them "as a piece of the Cross." The last words of the story — and the last words of Melville's life as an artist — are in the form of a "rude" ballad, made by the "tarry hand" of "another foretopman...gifted, as some sailors are, with an artless *poetic* temperament." The poem, narrated by Billy, is of course really Melville's. For Melville himself was a foretopman.

NOTES

1. Herman Melville, *Typee*, ed. Harrison Hayford, Signet, New York, 1964.

2. Melville, *Moby-Dick*, ed. Charles Feidelson, Bobbs-Merrill, New York, 1964.

3. Melville, *White Jacket: Or, the World in a Man-of-War*, Grove Press, New York, 1956.

4. *Herman Melville* (the short fiction), ed. R. W. B. Lewis, Dell, Laurel, New York, 1962.

5. Melville, *The Confidence-Man*, ed. H. Bruce Franklin, Bobbs-Merrill, Indianapolis, 1967.

6. Melville, *Billy Budd, Sailor*, ed. Hayford and Sealts, University of Chicago Press, Phoenix Books, Chicago, 1962.

15

HENRY JAMES, AMERICAN NOVELIST
or: Isabel Archer, Emerson's Grand-daughter

Annette T. Rubinstein

Parrington's casual dismissal of Henry James, expatriate, is today generally accepted as one of the few outright errors in his remarkably ambitious pioneering survey of American intellectual history. The best of the critical studies which followed this lead — Van Wyck Brooks' book, *The Pilgrimage of Henry James* — contains some very perceptive analyses of James' growing disillusionment with the English society he had chosen, and is still worth reading. It is, unfortunately, less known in detail than for its overstated conclusion that, lacking native roots, James was finally, with all his great talent, only a novelist manque or might-have-been. It is interesting to recall that Brooks himself was haunted by a sense of this injustice; one of the most moving passages of his autobiographical *Days of the Phoenix* tells of a recurrent impression, during the years of a mental breakdown which followed the completion of his book, that James' "fine eyes" were fixed on him, mournfully and reproachfully, from some point just beneath the ceiling.

Neither of these eminently democratic American critics demonstrate any of the holy hatred or zeal for excommunication which animates Maxwell Geismar's ill-judged attack; but then neither of them had been exposed to the exasperating cult of the Jacobites with their insistence on interpreting every failure of the master as a new profundity, every excess as a stroke of felicitous perfection, and, above all, every critical idea, expressed or exemplified, as an absolute standard by which to measure and form or demolish later novelists.

But despite engulfing adulation and hysterical response we can, I

think, now take it for granted that James *is* an important novelist in
terms both of his own writing and of his influence, and that there is, therefore, something of unique value in his work. It would, I believe, be interesting to consider this in the light of somewhat different prepossessions than
those with which he is usually approached by friends as well as enemies. I
would like, that is, to consider him not as an exception, but as an
example of the peculiar American tradition of the novel developed
unconsciously by Cooper, consciously if involuntarily by Hawthorne, and
with deliberate intention by Melville.

By speaking of James as a representative American novelist I mean
something more, and something more controversial, than emphasis on his
choice of subject matter or specific viewpoint. His characteristic subject
was unquestionably the impact of Europe on Americans, and of American ideas and mores on Europeans; almost all his major figures were
Americans; his own point of view was, all but invariably, that of a
cosmopolitan American. True, his protagonists are largely domiciled in
Europe, as he himself was, and their observation is restricted to the
by-no-means-random sample of their countrymen with money and leisure
to travel or live abroad. But James was not unaware of the true center of
the American scene in the United States. His awareness is, in fact, a
much fuller one than that of any contemporary writer, with the possible
exception of Mark Twain.

His early editor and lifelong friend, William Dean Howells, was the
first American novelist to deal seriously with the all-important figure of
the rising businessman. Yet compare the gentle interpretation of American business in *Silas Lapham* with the insight expressed in James'
explanation of the literary failure to grapple with the subject. In a series
of *American Letters* written for magazine publication in 1898 James said,
in part:

> . . . the typical American figure is above all that businessman whom
> the novelist and the dramatist have scarce yet seriously touched. . . .
> He is often an obscure, but not less often an epic, hero, seamed all over
> with the wounds of the market and the dangers of the field, launched
> into action and passion by the immensity and complexity of the general
> struggle, a boundless ferocity of battle. . . . The difficulty, doubtless, is
> that the world of affairs, as affairs are understood in the panting cities,
> though around us all the while, before us, behind us, beside us, and
> under our feet, is as special and occult a one to the outsider as the
> world, say of Arctic exploration — as impenetrable save as a result of
> special training. Those who know it are not the men to paint it; those

who might attempt it are not the men who know it. . . . The romance of fact, indeed, has touched him [the American businessman] in a way that quite puts to shame the romance of fiction. It gives his measure for purposes of art that it was he, essentially, who embarked in the great war of 1861-4, and who, carrying it on in the North to a triumphant conclusion, went back, since business was his standpoint, to his very "own" with an undimmed capacity to mind it.

The rather ambiguous compliment in the last sentence hints that James' perception of American political reality was also unblurred by distance. This hint is reinforced in such comments as the following two — one on the prewar New England scene, written in 1887, and the other on the postwar South, written in 1906 when he revisited the United States at the beginning of the twentieth century.

(1)

Nothing is more perceptible today than that their criticism produced no fruit — that it was little else than a very decent and innocent recreation — a kind of Puritan carnival. The New England world was for the most part very busy, but the Dial and Fruitlands and Brook Farm were the amusement of the leisure-class.

(2)

. . . It is the vacancy that is a thing by itself, a thing that makes us endlessly wonder. How, in an at all complex, a "great political" Society can *everything* so have gone? — assuming indeed that, under this aegis, very much had ever come. How can everything so have gone that the only "Southern" book of any distinction published for many a year is *The Souls of Black Folk,* by that most accomplished of members of the Negro race, Mr. W.E.B. DuBois? Had the *only* focus of life then been Slavery? — from the point onward that Slavery had reached a quarter of a century before the War, so that with the extinction of that interest none other of any sort was left.

But these passages, and a hundred similar ones which might be cited from *The American Scene* alone, testify only to James' personal understanding of the United States, not to the vision expressed in his novels. I use them merely to indicate that we must look further than any assumption of ignorance or insensitivity to account for the novelist's concentration on certain kinds of people leading special kinds of lives.

One fundamental reason is fairly obvious, and has been stated in quite different ways by many critics, including several Marxists. James begins by assuming that consciousness is the supreme human quality and that free choice, exercised responsibly with a full awareness of its implications, is correspondingly the most typical human function (typical in Lukacs' sense of essential, not average). Stated thus abstractly, this philosophy might serve as the starting point for either a socialist or an existentialist, but James was, of course, neither, and the concrete form these assumptions take in his work is quite a different thing.

The consciousness he envisions is always a highly cultivated, articulate sensibility which obviously presupposes great leisure and relative immunity from distracting practical demands on its owner's attention; the free choice is always a choice among *already existing alternatives* and its freedom seems measurable by the number of possibilities actually available to its possessor. Furthermore, except for the artist-protagonist, who is a frequent figure in the short stories but appears only twice, and then rather unconvincingly, in the center of a novel, the material on which both consciousness and choice is almost exclusively exercised is that of personal relationship. The people dealt with must, then, almost invariably be members of a leisure class with all that that implies. Even the artists are, characteristically, either portrait painters or novelists who deal with such people and their relationships.

Shakespeare, with a different scale of values, made the same kind of choice when he selected as his most typical or representative human beings kings, lords and generals — those who by virtue of their background and opportunities were most able to influence large numbers of their fellows. Nor is there necessarily any *a priori* reason why James' selection should not be, within the limits of his imagination, equally successful. And James does, of course, have many brilliant successes. But it is notable that the best of these involve, in varying degrees, a kind of symbolism, running all the way from morality play to myth, which makes the individuals involved stand for some group or force quite beyond their personal selves, and thus allows James to break out of the claustrophobic circle of a consumers' value system into which at his worst he often falls.

It is curious that this sort of super-personal non-psychological abstract philosophic approach, which James as a critic detested in fiction, should so often come to his aid when all his interest and ability in rendering the social scene, as his admired predecessors Jane Austen or George Eliot had done, did not quite enable him to succeed in writing their kind of novel. For I must be presumptuous enough to say, in defiance not only of most Jamesian critics but of the highly conscious author himself, that James was *not*, essentially, the sort of traditional realistic novelist he wished and thought himself to be.

Hawthorne too had yearned to be a part of the great English tradition of social realism, although his expressed ambition soared no higher than the novel of manners exemplified by Trollope. But he had early realized that that was not his genius and had coined the somewhat inept term "a romance" to distinguish his great masterpiece, *The Scarlet Letter*, and others of its genre. James deeply regretted Hawthorne's compromise, much preferred *The House of Seven Gables* for its greater thickness of observed background, and deplored, in terms very similar to those used by Cooper and Hawthorne himself, the bare stage with which his predecessor had been forced to make do.

James' own stage was far from bare, and there are few scenes in literature which would compensate for the loss of tea on the lawn at Grandcourt, Millie's confrontation with her portrait at the great house party in which her English visit culminates, Strether's meal at the small French inn, the purchase of the golden bowl, and a dozen others. These are certainly comparable in kind as well as degree to many in Tolstoi, Turgenieff, Austen, Eliot, and, for that matter, Scott, Balzac or Dickens. But the sense of history which distinguishes every one of these writers was a sense which James — never more typically American than in that lack — completely lacked.

He had a sense of tradition, which is quite another thing, and a deep love of the mellow dignity imparted to life by beautiful old belongings. But he had absolutely no sense of social life as *becoming*, either in the past or in the future. His sense of present realities was keen, as the letter on American businessmen quoted above, or the whole magnificent picture of *The Bostonians*, clearly shows. But even there he has little feeling of any serious causal sequence, and takes people, situations and beliefs as simple givens which might just as well come into being by a process of spontaneous generation.

If we compare him in this respect with his closest analogue, Jane Austen, we find Darcy's Pembroke a pale shadow beside Mr. Touchett's Gardencourt or even Adam Verver's Fawns, and Darcy himself quite insignificant beside Lord Warburton, to say nothing of Maggie's Prince. But if we explore the sense of an organic society or coherent community in any books by the two authors, our judgments are inescapably reversed.

True, James had no such stable society to deal with as Miss Austen did, and a great part of his increasing insistence on objects, whether in so poor a book as *The Spoils of Poynton* or in so good a one as *The Golden Bowl*, may well be explained by his increasing awareness that these beautiful artifacts were finally the only aspects of his high civilization

which did not crumble when firmly grasped. But a sense of disintegration
and collapse, such as Turgenieff or Proust gives us, is also a sense of
history, and James imagines no real growth or decay — no real direction
for any large social unit.

It is interesting to see how frequently, for him, a phenomenon which is
merely an almost accidental symptom outweighs one which is a germinal
cause, although both are observed with accuracy and reported with
precision. For example, in quoting his magnificent picture of the American
tycoon-in-the-making above, we omitted a sentence and a half. His
description of the

> epic hero, seamed all over with the wounds of the market and the
> dangers of the field, launched into action and passion by the immensity
> and complexity of the general struggle, a boundless ferocity of battle

concludes

> driven above all by the extraordinary, the unique relation in which he,
> for the most part, stands to the life of his lawful, his immitigable woman-
> kind, the wives and daughters who float, who splash on the surface and
> ride the waves, his terrific link with civilization, his social substitutes and
> representatives, while, like a diver for shipwrecked treasure, he gasps in
> the depths and breathes through an air-tube.

The final sentence of the paragraph, also omitted in our quotation
above, points the way to James' own special use of the American
businessman in wealthy retirement in Europe. It reads:

> When, in imagination, you give the type, as it exists today, the benefit of
> its great double luster — that of these recorded antecedents and that of
> its preoccupied, systematic, and magnanimous abasement before the
> other sex — you will easily feel your sense of what may be done with its
> overflow.

There could hardly be a greater descent from a sense of "the causes of
things" to a preoccupation with the surface phenomena than is here illustrated.

This complete lack of historical imagination occasionally leads to
something very like an inadvertent parody. For example, Adam Verver of
The Golden Bowl, who is presented as preternaturally rich, capable and
wise, with an infallible sense of genuineness and value in people as well as
objects of art, has spent untold millions and all the years of his retirement
on an art collection which he plans to house in his native mid-western city.
This carefully selected concrete embodiment of all the traditions of Europe

is intended to be more than a museum — it is to make possible the flowering of that same rich European culture in the very heart of the United States! This is not presented as an absurdity but as a serious project which James, as well as Verver, feels justifies the earlier years spent in amassing a fortune.

Even in James' consideration of the lives of certain key individuals we sometimes find the same sort of inconsequence. This is almost always true of the father figure — the retired millionaires whom we watch emerge with minds and characters totally unaffected by the lifelong activity which won them their millions. Not one of these fictional characters remotely resembles the "epic hero, seamed all over with the wounds of the market and the dangers of the field." The best and most plausible is also the youngest and earliest — Christopher Newman — but he is neither as rich nor as passive as the later father figures and plays the part generally assigned to heiresses in the later books.

It is interesting to note the accuracy of James' social and psychological observation in this quick change to an heiress as the center of almost all his subsequent novels. Of course it takes no great penetration to see the difficulties which would be incurred by positing a whole series of self-made millionaires young and unambitious enough to retire, even temporarily, to a European life of leisure. Yet a less perspicacious novelist might simply have substituted their Harvard-bred sons. Indeed, that was precisely the pattern set in James' own family. His grandfather had made a considerable fortune and settled it on Henry James Sr. to free him from material considerations and subsidize his lifelong pursuit of truth, goodness and culture. But James was far too keenly aware that the American mores in general had no room for a masculine leisure class. The typical tycoon's son was forced to attempt, however weakly, imitation or emulation of his father and rarely earned that father's respect. Daughters were another matter. Freed from any such demand, they often won awestruck admiration by their success in carrying on the conspicuous display which crowned and proclaimed their fathers' achievement. This feminine function which an older bourgeois society expected of wives was here more often relegated to the next generation, since the wife of a self-made millionaire's youth was unlikely to be above him in breeding or education and even more unlikely to equal him in force and imagination. (Wasserstrom's *The Golden Heiress* offers a fascinating full-length study of this aspect of late nineteenth century American life in fact and in fiction.)

By thus centering his novel about the petted indulged self-assured and wilful daughter, with or without attendant parents, James was able to take a spacious self-determined way of life as a given, ignoring all questions of how it had come to be or what effect the struggle to win it had had upon the victor.

It is time, however, that we turned from these fragmentary remarks on the kind of novelist James is not, to some consideration of what he so strongly and, in nineteenth century English terms, almost uniquely is. (The only exception to this uniqueness which I can think of in those terms is Emily Bronte's *Wuthering Heights.*)

I do not mean to use the adjective as a term of denigration, although James would certainly so have used it, when I suggest that James at his best was, like Cooper, Hawthorne and Melville, and unlike Defoe, Fielding, Austen, Dickens and Eliot, an abstract or metaphysical novelist. It is easy for us to see that so naive a novelist as Cooper still lives not because of, but rather in spite of, his clumsy dialogue, romantic Indians and creaky plots. Though he does undeniably have a real flair for presenting scenes of crowded violent action, there would be little loss if we were to ignore virtually everything but the heroic myth of Deerslayer. This fixed in a moment of pure poetry the new man, without forbears or descendants, face to face with the virgin forests of a new world — forests and a world that were doomed to vanish almost as rapidly as he himself did.

It is even easier to see, as Hawthorne himself realized, that *The Scarlet Letter* owes none of its importance to the plausible reconstruction of a historic scene, or even to the imaginative creation of Hester, Dimmesdale and Chillingworth as individual characters, but takes its place in our literary history solely on its merits as a highly sophisticated moral fable. It lives because of the new resources of subtle observation and profound analysis it brought to its study of guilt, penance, concealment, remorse and the one unforgivable sin — that of coldblooded tampering with another human soul.

But James deplored this semi-genre which Hawthorne called "a romance," urged allegiance to the European tradition of the realistic social novel, and is, in his own traditional sense of the word, a very important novelist. He has created such great, if imperfect, monuments of that form as the serious cultural studies in *The Ambassadors, The Wings of the Dove, The Golden Bowl;* had achieved a more completely typical, if secondary, example in *The Tragic Muse;* and did manage at least one extraordinarily powerful socio-psychological novel — *The Bostonians.*

Yet many of his best shorter fictions and at least one superb full length novel, as well as parts of those just mentioned, are really centered about a metaphysical question rather than a concern with psychology or social mores. *The Portrait of a Lady* depends almost as little for its inner meaning on the proper conduct of a marriage or a house party as *Moby Dick* does, ultimately, on the discipline of a whaler.

The greatest of the works which belong, in this sense, to the American rather than the English tradition, is appropriately the one which takes for its theme an examination of the indigenous American philosophy of transcendentalism. Specifically it poses the question of perfect freedom, a question earlier posed in one way by Emerson and Thoreau, and examined in another by Melville.

Emerson's simplest and best known statement of this theme is, of course, that which concludes his famous essay, "Self-Reliance." Here he says:

> There is a time in every man's education when he arrives at the conviction that envy is ignorance; that imitation is suicide; that he must take himself for better or worse as his portion; that though the wide universe is full of good, no kernel of nourishing corn can come to him but through his own toil bestowed on that plot of ground which is given him to till. The power which resides in him is new in nature, and none but he knows what that is which he can do, nor does he know until he has tried. . . Trust thyself: every heart vibrates to that iron string. . . Whoso would be a man must be a nonconformist. . . I remember an answer which when quite young I was prompted to make to a valued adviser who was wont to importune me with the dear old doctrines of the church. On my saying, "What have I to do with the sacredness of traditions, if I live wholly from within?" my friend suggested — "But these impulses may be from below, not from above." I replied, "They do not seem to me to be such; but if I am the Devil's child, then I will live from the Devil." No law can be sacred to me but that of my nature. Good and bad are but names very readily transferable to that or this; the only right is what is after my constitution; the only wrong is what is against it.

Of course Emerson could speak so blithely because it was impossible for him really to imagine what it would mean to be the devil's child. It took another transcendentalist, a greater and more realistic artist if not a more profound thinker, to explore that possibility concretely with Captain Ahab. In *Moby Dick,* one of the earliest and still, many people feel, the greatest of American novels, Herman Melville set himself this central problem: an examination of the full meaning and possible consequences of such an absolute reliance on one's own individual intuition of significance and value in the universe.

Captain Ahab is a man of enormous personal force and of iron determination, with a profound need to assert human dignity in the face of an indifferent or antagonistic universe. His monomaniacal hatred for the white whale is based on no childish superstition or ignorant deification of the enormous beast which has crippled him. He sees it rather as a symbol of universal evil and feels that in his relentless pursuit of this powerful animal he is striking, as a man must, at the tangible and visible appearance of all that is inimical to him in an often destructive, inhuman, world. He himself clearly sees this, and says that one must, for his own honor and for the honor of mankind, strike at or through the veil of appearances by which he is surrounded wherever a point of attack offers itself, concluding: "Be the white whale agent or be the white whale principal, it is through him that my own attack must be launched."

But it is not only in envisaging the inhuman suicidal course on which Captain Ahab is impelled by his conscience that Melville examines the implications of an utter ethical individualism. The realistic imagination of a great novelist which so often enables its possessor to "grasp the future in the instant" made Melville fully aware of a vital truth to which Emerson and his other contemporaries remained blind.

Melville realized, as the early philosophers of individualism did not, that the consequences of a ruthless individualism in action cannot be confined to their effect on the individualist himself. Real power in our world must mean the power to control others; absolute individualism, unchecked, must also mean absolute slavery; and so we find Captain Ahab, in an ecstatic climax, explicitly demanding that the crew of his ship serve him as his own arms and legs, losing their individual beings entirely to become the very extension of his.

Less socially minded than Melville's examination of the implications of an unbridled Emersonian individualism, James' experiment seeks to determine the results for his heroine herself rather than for others. Superficially, therefore, Isabel Archer's experience may seem to resemble Jane Austen's education of Emma, or George Eliot's history of Dorothea's development in *Middlemarch*. But despite all the obvious resemblances in action, circumstance and even presentation to these older sisters, whom her author much admired, Isabel Archer is more essentially related to Captain Ahab, of whom James was probably altogether unaware. They had a New England grandfather in common — Ralph Waldo Emerson — and he might more easily have traced his lineaments in the granddaughter than in the grandson.

Emerson would, of course, have colored a self-portrait very differently, but he could hardly have doubted whom James' first formal picture of Isabel intentionally brings to mind. (There are many lighter touches to the same effect from Isabel's first appearance, but this is the first full length study.)

> In matters of opinion she had had her own way, and it had led her into a thousand ridiculous zigzags. At moments she discovered she was grotesquely wrong, and then she treated herself to a week of passionate humility. After this she held her head higher than ever again; for it was of no use, she had an unquenchable desire to think well of herself. She had a theory that it was only under this provision life was worth living; that one should be one of the best, should be conscious of a fine organization (she couldn't help knowing her organization was fine), should move in a realm of light, of natural wisdom, of happy impulse, of inspiration gracefully chronic. It was almost as unnecessary to cultivate doubt of one's self as to cultivate doubt of one's best friend: one should try to be one's own best friend and to give one's self, in this manner, distinguished company. The girl had a certain nobleness of imagination which rendered her a good many services and played her a great many tricks. She spent half her time thinking of beauty and bravery and magnanimity; she had a fixed determination to regard the world as a piece of brightness, of free expansion, of irresistible action: she held it must be detestable to be afraid or ashamed.

> . . . Altogether, with her meagre knowledge, her inflated ideals, her confidence at once innocent and dogmatic, her temper at once exacting and indulgent, her mixture of curiosity and fastidiousness, of vivacity and indifference, her desire to look very well and to be if possible even better, her determination to see, to try, to know, her combination of the delicate, desultory, flamelike spirit and the eager and personal creature of conditions:she would be an easy victim of scientific criticism if she were not intended to awaken on the reader's part an impulse more tender and more purely expectant.

James' father was accustomed to refer to Emerson as his "unfallen friend," and there are many passages which emphasize that aspect of Isabel's philosophy. In fact, in the passage just quoted I omitted:

> . . . on the whole, reflectively, she was in no uncertainty about the things that were wrong. She had no love of their look, but when she fixed them she recognized them. It was wrong to be mean, to be jealous, to be false, to be cruel; . . . Her life should always be in harmony with the most pleasing impression she should produce; she would be what she appeared and she would appear what she was.

A few pages earlier there had been a jesting discussion of the ghosts supposed to haunt great mansions, which concluded:

> Charming as he [Ralph] found her, she had struck him as rather presumptuous — indeed it was part of her charm; and he wondered what she would say. "I'm not afraid, you know," she said: which seemed quite presumptuous enough.
>
> "You're not afraid of suffering?"
>
> "Yes, I'm afraid of suffering. But I'm not afraid of ghosts. And I think people suffer too easily," she added.
>
> "I don't believe you do," said Ralph, looking at her with his hands in his pockets.
>
> "I don't think that's a fault," she answered. "It's not absolutely necessary to suffer; we were not made for that."

In *Emma* or *Middlemarch* such an exchange would have justified us in expecting the heroine to learn, through sad experience, a more adequate comprehension of evil; we might also have anticipated some variation of the idea of the "fortunate fall" — an idea explicitly discussed by Hawthorne in his conclusion to *The Marble Faun* and bitterly, if cryptically, rejected by Melville in his enigmatic *Pierre*.

But James' orientation here is not Austen's or Eliot's. As in *Moby Dick* or *The Scarlet Letter*, it is primarily the reader, not Isabel, who is being educated; it is the author, not the heroine, who is carrying on a philosophical inquiry.

Toward the end of the book Isabel, after learning thoroughly to understand and hate her husband's way of life, suddenly receives specific knowledge of the guilt he had earlier shared with Madame Merle, and of the duplicity her most intimate friend had practised upon her in order to arrange her marriage. How little her basic philosophy of life is affected by the shock of this recognition is clear. James says:

> She asked herself, with an almost childlike horror of the supposition, whether to this intimate friend of several years the great historical epithet of *wicked* were to be applied. She knew the idea only by the Bible and other literary works; to the best of her belief she had no personal acquaintance with wickedness. She had desired a large acquaintance with human life, and in spite of her having flattered herself that she

cultivated it with some success this elementary privilege had been denied her. Perhaps it was not wicked — in the historic sense — to be even deeply false; for that was what Madame Merle had been — deeply, deeply, deeply.

Clearly it is not any fundamental change in a specific transcendentalist with which James is concerned, but transcendentalism's adequacy as an interpretation of life. It is, in fact, poor Ralph rather than his cousin with whom we can most readily identify ourselves.

He is no transcendentalist but he feels the same wistful attraction toward that state of heroic innocence that James himself did. All too clearly in his semi-invalid state a thrall to necessity, Ralph would like to believe that Isabel could exemplify perfect freedom; it is he who sets the experiment in motion by securing for her use an independent fortune so that she may be able completely to realize herself.

He is not at all cynical in making this provision, and means no reflection upon her courage or disinterestedness. Isabel has already, at this point, rejected two highly desirable suitors without any such material security to fall back upon.

One of these proposals is a quite phenomenally good offer ardently urged by a handsome, intelligent, considerate and liberal lord. Isabel likes him very much, but is firm in her refusal.

What she felt was that a territorial, a political, a social magnate had conceived the design of drawing her into the system in which he rather invidiously lived and moved. A certain instinct, not imperious, but persuasive, told her to resist — murmured to her that virtually she had a system and an orbit of her own.

One is reminded of Thoreau's response to a friend's suggestion that he accompany him on a world tour. He refused politely enough, but confided to his journal his indignation that anyone should suppose that another adult did not already have his own course marked out and his own path to explore.

Her other suitor, an American buisnessman by whom she is simultaneously more strongly attracted and more deeply antagonized than she is by Lord Warburton would, she feels, similarly circumscribe her life by the very force of an intense personal relationship. When Madame Merle hears of Mr. Goodwood's proposal she asks Isabel how his house compares with Lockleigh castle. James scrupulously refrains from taking sides in the ensuing discussion, but again we must note how firmly he centers our attention on a consideration of two opposing philosophies:

"I don't care anything about his house," said Isabel.

"That's very crude of you. When you've lived as long as I you'll see that every human being has his shell and that you must take the shell into account. By the shell I mean the whole envelope of circumstances. There's no such thing as an isolated man or woman; we're each of us made up of some cluster of appurtenances. What shall we call our 'self'? Where does it begin? Where does it end? It overflows into everything that belongs to us — and then it flows back again. I know a large part of myself is in the clothes I choose to wear. I've a great respect for *things*! One's self — for other people — is one's expression of one's self; and one's house, one's furniture, one's garments, the books one reads, the company one keeps — these things are all expressive."

. . . "I don't agree with you. I think just the other way. I don't know whether I succeed in expressing myself, but I know that nothing else expresses me. Nothing that belongs to me is any measure of me; everything's on the contrary a limit, a barrier, and a perfectly arbitrary one. Certainly the clothes which, as you say, I choose to wear, don't express me; and heaven forbid they should!"

"You dress very well," Madame Merle lightly interposed.

"Possibly; but I don't care to be judged by that. My clothes may express the dressmaker, but they don't express me. To begin with, it's not my own choice that I wear them; they're imposed upon me by society."

While this conversation takes place in the drawing room, Ralph, at his father's bedside, is urging the old man to alter his will so as to make Isabel rich. His father, who has intended a legacy of five thousand pounds, asks him, "What do you mean by rich?" And Ralph answers, for James as well, "I call people rich when they're able to meet the requirements of their imagination. Isabel has a great deal of imagination."

Later, when Isabel has for several years been in possession of such a fortune — specifically, the income from seventy thousand pounds — she finds herself increasingly unable to imagine anything worth doing with it. As much for that as for any other reason she decides to accept a most undesirable offer of marriage. Ralph, dismayed, attempts to dissuade her. James in this scene clearly indorses Ralph's judgment, but not his surprise. For him the open question has never been the scope of Isabel's imagination but the validity of a determination to approach life with absolute intransigence. Of course Ralph, hopelessly in love with his cousin, and clinging to his interest in her as the only personal one left by his rapid physical decline, cannot take the failure of his experiment with such intellectual satisfaction.

"I had treated myself to a charming vision of your future," Ralph observed; "I had amused myself with planning out a high destiny for you. There was to be nothing of this sort in it. You were not to come down so easily or so soon."

"Come down, you say?"

"Well, that renders my sense of what has happened to you. You seemed to me to be soaring far up in the blue — to be, sailing in the bright light, over the heads of men. Suddenly some one tosses up a faded rosebud — a missile that should never have reached you — and straight you drop to the ground. It hurts me," said Ralph audaciously, "hurts me as if I had fallen myself!"

The marriage is even worse than Ralph has foreseen, and Isabel is far more unhappy than she could have imagined. But her attitude toward suffering in the last pages of the book varies philosophically not a jot from the lighthearted disapproval of it she manifested at the very beginning six years earlier.

When Isabel was unhappy she always looked about her — partly from impulse and partly by theory — for some sort of positive exertion. She could never rid herself of the sense that unhappiness was a state of disease — of suffering as opposed to doing. To "do" — it hardly mattered what — would therefore be an escape, perhaps in some degree a remedy.

One might, just for fun, select a dozen other significant passages and pair them with parallel Emerson quotes. For example, his well known comment, "Books are for the scholar's idle times," which continues to discuss the harmony of the motions of the real scholar's spirit with the structure of the universe, is immediately suggested by James' remark:

She had a great desire for knowledge, but she really preferred almost any source of information to the printed page; she had an immense curiosity about life and was constantly staring and wondering. She carried within herself a great fund of life, and her deepest enjoyment was to feel the continuity between the movements of her own soul and the agitations of the world.

Similarly, Emerson's verse beginning

> I like a church; I like a cowl;
> I love a prophet of the soul;
>
>   . . .
>
> Why should the vest on him allure,
> Which I could not on me endure?

and his aphorism, "Consistency is the hobgoblin of little minds" are called
to mind as we read:

> "Ah," said Isabel with a kind of joyous sigh, "I like so many things! If a
> thing strikes me with a certain intensity I accept it. . . . So long as I look
> at the Misses Molyneux they seem to me to answer a kind of ideal. Then
> Henrietta presents herself, and I'm straightway convinced by her."

When Isabel is in Rome, James tells us that "The sense of the terrible
human past was heavy to her, but that of something altogether contemporary would give it wings that it could wave in the blue." Again we recognize
a favorite attitude of Emerson's and recall his urgent emphasis on the
contemporary. "The foregoing generations beheld God and nature face to
face; we, through their eyes. Why should not we also enjoy an original relation to the universe? Why should not we have a poetry and philosophy of
insight and not of tradition?"

But actually this is unnecessary, except as a game, for James himself
summarized the intention of the book as an exploration of the transcen-
dental thesis. Twenty years after its first publication, he said in his
retrospective preface that its entire meaning, for him, lay in the conception
of a "young woman affronting her destiny." This was, he continued,
originally:

> all my outfit for the large building of *The Portrait of a Lady*. It came to
> be a square and spacious house — or has at least seemed so to me in this
> going over it again, but such as it is, it had to be put up round my young
> woman while she stood there in perfect isolation.

"All history is biography," said Emerson, and Thoreau amended this
dictum to read, "All history is autobiography." "Is that so?" asked the
novelist, and designed an experiment to test its truth.

16

The Incest Theme in *The Great Gatsby*: An Exploration of the False Poetry of Petty Bourgeois Consciousness

Stephen Zelnick

> *For it is no easy matter to look stark reality in the face and no one succeeds in achieving this at the first attempt. What is required for this is not merely a great deal of hard work, but also a serious moral effort. In the first phase of such a change of heart most people will look back regretfully to the false but 'poetic' dream of reality which they are about to relinquish. Only later does it grow clear how much more genuine humanity — and hence genuine poetry — attaches to the acceptance of truth with all its inexorable reality and to acting in accordance with it.*

> — Lukács in *Studies in European Realism*

I

The Great Gatsby was written nearly fifty years ago by a young man in what has to appear to Americans in the nineteen-seventies as a young age. It has been a very special novel to American readers. Fitzgerald was justified in seeing *The Great Gatsby* as an important technical achievement for him: it is a remarkably well-constructed novel. Beyond that, *The Great Gatsby* has been taught and read enthusiastically more than any other novel in America. And yet to a new sensibility arising out of our present historical situation, there is something essentially wrong with *The Great Gatsby*. Teaching it in the nineteen-seventies, one finds that its vision of America does not take us far enough and that its characters and lyrical effusions belong to a different way of feeling about the world. Especially after the experiences of the last decade in which the raw power of American imperialism has revealed itself openly and in all its systematic strength to effect every phase of our lives, *The Great Gatsby* seems increasingly to be, as in Mencken's judgment, a mere anecdote. The problem with Fitzgerald's novel has, in the final analysis, a great deal to do with the narrow vision of America it achieves. It is not simply that *The Great Gatsby* is now fifty years old, but that it represents exclusively the world-view of the petty bourgeoisie and is colored throughout by the extravagant illusions that are a dominant feature of that social class.

Marxist social analysis of the class system in capitalist society provides a useful analytical tool for understanding how literature reflects and interprets the world. The capitalist world is founded on class antagonisms. The bourgeoisie owns and controls the means of production and accrues vast wealth and power through the exploitation of the proletariat. The antagonism between capital and labor is the central fact of the bourgeois world, and much of our literature — not merely proletarian or explicitly political novels — deals with this essential matrix of reality. The manner of this treatment is certainly diverse, ranging from conscious partisanship in the class struggle to the unconscious reflection of the effects of capitalist society. The latter situation is most often the case with petty bourgeois writers, who find themselves somewhere in the midst of the class struggle but unable to orient themselves clearly. They may, as in the case of Fitzgerald, feel contempt and hatred for the bourgeoisie, but they are usually unable to free themselves from the illusions generated by capitalism. The petty bourgeoisie, because it is in an anomalous position in society, is least able to grasp the central facts of history clearly. Even its advanced members, and Fitzgerald is one, see the world through the illusions which belong to their position in society.

The petty bourgeoisie is the social class which neither owns the means of production nor is dependent upon the sale of its labor power for survival. Members of this class tend to associate their interests with those of the bourgeoisie proper. But they do not control its power and wealth. At the same time, the petty bourgeoisie fears and despises the proletariat. They fear desperately the prospect of falling into the proletariat (a fear justified by the contingent nature of their social position) and they are threatened by the collectivized effort of the proletariat to advance its interests. The petty bourgeoisie includes small businessmen (who in many cases must struggle daily in a highly competitive market for survival), salesmen who depend substantially on their commissions (and the illusive achievements of personality), professionals and technicians who are in a position to contract individually for their special skills (often in a marketplace that is phasing out old skills and replacing them with new ones), and artists who, in the decay of capitalism, must often depend upon their personalities and salesmanship as much as on their skills. As a class, the petty bourgeoisie experiences the most prospects for mobility up or down. It depends most upon radical individualism — it can neither be corporatized nor collectivized. And because of its identification with the ruling class to which it does not belong, it produces the most illusory thinking, the most wayward imaginings, and experiences the most intense neurotic problems.

The petty bourgeoisie is especially likely to think, imagine, and feel in a fantastic manner because it does not participate directly in determining the essential course of reality. It is not in a position to determine the management of society nor does it produce wealth directly. And yet its members think of themselves as the measure of truth, as a norm against which both the bourgeoisie proper and the proletariat are extremes. At the same time, because its relation to the mode of production is anomalous and because its security tends to be threatened by the full realization of the actual relation between capital and labor (something we are experiencing today), it perceives the world through exhilarating fantasy alternating with nervous anticipations of doom. The petty bourgeoisie is not rooted firmly in social process, and so it goes its way lonely and embattled, tense and expectant, alternatingly reckless and cautious. The radical individualism of the petty bourgeoisie forces it to make the world up as it goes along, suspicious all the while that there exists a harder and more stern reality that may come crashing down at any moment.

This is what *The Great Gatsby* portrays so well. Fitzgerald's novel is neither the story of East and West which Nick takes it to be, nor the story of America as a whole, nor certainly the story of man's universal quest as so many critics see it.[1] It is, rather, a specific and historically definite portrayal of the American nineteen-twenties as it was perceived by a humane and talented writer, whose theme, although he was finally unable to grasp it firmly, is the tortuous contradicitions of his own petty bourgeois class.

The Great Gatsby is usually appreciated as a bitter critique of the insidiously alluring American Dream. Certainly Fitzgerald devastates the Horatio Alger ideology of success and sees the destruction of Emersonian optimism in an increasingly corrupt America. But at the same time, Fitzgerald is never quite able to step outside his own class perspectives in order to discover what lies behind this destruction of ideals. He has no adequate grasp of the forces which direct American society — as, for example, Dreiser and Dos Passos do — and, consequently, between the exotic aspirations of his petty bourgeois characters and the cosmic fulfillment they seek, stand only the restraints of social manners and personal morals. Real social power is never at issue. The network of actual social, economic, and political forces that explain American society is overlooked. This remarkable omission affects the novel from its racism and mysogyny to its central passion, the pathetically neurotic insistence on the incest fantasy.

To be sure, Fitzgerald condemns the bourgeoisie in the persons of the Buchanans and their elite crowd, but he does not condemn them for exploiting masses of workers, but rather for being vulgar and treacherous in their personal relations. By the same token, he has Nick characterize Gatsby's dream as "vast, vulgar, and meretricious," but he cannot finally overcome the same sort of unattainable desires. The proletariat appears only as the grey denizens of the anonymous valley of ashes. Their actual role in America, their character, their history, and their future simply do not exist in the novel.

Fitzgerald's failure to achieve a critical distance from the contradictions of his own petty bourgeois heritage results in more than a sociological and historical falsification of America. He also has difficulty in depicting and evaluating his central character, Gatsby himself, who remains only a schematic figure and cannot be fleshed out without revealing his essential contradictions.[2] Gatsby remains a figure of phenomenal ignorance and lack of depth, a character who both in terms of his corrupted taste and abysmal lack of intelligence seems to deserve everything that happens to him. Only Nick, neither a thoughtful nor an active man but rather a sentimental/cynical lyricist, is capable of making something of Gatsby. But Nick (and he speaks for Fitzgerald) represents the petty bourgeois qualities of illusion and self-delusion most clearly.

Much has been written about Nick as an example of a well-handled point-of-view character, a well-placed and well-executed central consciousness for the novel. But it is crucial to understand that Nick is a classic petty bourgeois character and that his judgments display the values and habits of mind of his class. Christopher Caudwell, in *Studies in a Dying Culture,* describes the petty bourgeois character as "rootless, individualist, lonely, and perpetually facing, with its hackles up, an antagonistic world. It can never know the security of the rich bourgeoisie or the companionship of the worker."[3] Nick is a restless spirit, hungry for experience because his real circumstances as son of a midwestern merchant family are so restrictively conventional. He is ripe for the romantic idealism, new lifestyle adventurism, and bohemian fantasies that he finds in the East, precisely because his true class circumstances deny him all that. But, as most Blacks and white working-class observers of the middle-class hippie of our own day know, the petty bourgeois "adventurer" is free to return to his relatively secure foundations whenever he becomes confused, bored, or hurt. He is on a "trip" and is really only passing through. This rootlessness makes Nick seem to be an objective observer for the events of the novel since he is, as Nick says of himself, "within and without, simultaneously enchanted and repelled by the inexhaustible variety of life" [p. 36].[4]

It is a curious commentary on our critical habits that Nick has been thought of as a suitable interpreter of the events he reports precisely because he is not committed to anything and has no firm set of values to assert other than a generalized sense of the need for common decency. One should consider that after he has experienced the corruption of the East, Nick's adolescent mentality sends him rushing back to his family demanding that the world "be in uniform and at a sort of moral attention forever" [p. 2]. His normalcy includes pursuing fashionable women through the streets of New York weaving anonymous erotic fantasies about them, standing aloof from every situation he finds himself in, having no job pressures, no responsibilities, no strong desires, and no philosophical commitments. His vacillation between romantic extravagance and stern moral scruples is normal only for the rootless petty bourgeoisie. In the same regard, his special honesty which he calls his "cardinal virtue" is totally conditioned by that outlook. Rather than see the events he has experienced in the East as fundamentally a drama of social class in the decay of capitalism, he will venture any number of interpretations and hypotheses: he will suggest that the world is an inescapable wasteland, that social warfare is an individual struggle depending upon bio-chemical forces, that the story is a story of East and West, that the rhythm of desire transcends time and history, and so on. His "honesty" and eclecticism (another "virtue" of the petty bourgeoisie) allows him to be totally random in his interpretations of the meaning of the experiences he describes. For social analysis he gives us personalities; for historical analysis he gives us the lyrical reverie on the universal, timeless pattern of the ebb and flow of desire delivered in what Fitzgerald himself admitted to be obscuring "blankets of excellent prose."[5]

In the end, Nick's lyricism (it is the measure of Fitzgerald's sensibility) obscures the meaning of the events of the novel rather than illuminating them. The tragic confusion of petty bourgeois life in America, which is the point of the novel, is buried in lyrical effusions that point towards emotional infantilism rather than historical clarification. The strength of *The Great Gatsby* is its presentation of the social class drama and particularly the crisis of the petty bourgeoisie. Its notable weakness is the emotional infantilism revolving about a deeply-held incest fantasy which Fitzgerald fuses with the self-destructive dreams of his characters. Finally, the novel urges us to participate in the despair of the petty bourgeoisie, to accept the notion that because the fantastic dreams of the petty bourgeois adventurer are ultimately unattainable, existence is a cruel joke and we are all doomed to a hideous cycle of delusion.

II

The social class drama in the novel depicts the relation between the bourgeoisie and the petty bourgeoisie. As Caudwell explains the ruling desire of the petty bourgeoisie, its "whole existence is based on a lie. . . . It has only one value in life, that of bettering itself, of getting a step nearer the good bourgeois things so far above it" [p. 76]. Such a pursuit is doomed to failure and, as *The Great Gatsby* demonstrates, leads to personal disintegration when developed to its full expression.

In the class drama of the novel, Tom, Daisy, and Jordan are the bourgeoisie. Tom Buchanan represents the raw power of solid wealth in America. He is physically brutal, wilfully aggressive, and threatening; he covers this brute force with comically thin pretensions to aristocratic manners and intellectuality and, in moments of personal threat, with an adventitious sentimentality that substitutes for moral idealism. Daisy, while she seems to have brought some Southern gentility to the carnival of the East — her stereotypical gracious youthfulness and vulnerable passivity — is revealed to be amoral, cynical, and fearfully empty. Her beauty, mystery, and romantic promise turn out to be nothing more than stage gestures. In fact, she is Tom in all essentials. Jordan Baker is brighter than Tom but just as ruthless. She is hard, underhanded, and exceedingly cool. She is, as is all the bourgeoisie, above the middle-class moral scruples of Nick.

The most dynamic social group in the novel is the petty bourgeoisie. Besides Nick, this group includes Myrtle Wilson, Meyer Wolfsheim, and Mr. McKee, and they all point to Gatsby himself. Myrtle Wilson is hungry for a life which her poverty denies her. Her sensual energy demands expression which cannot be found, Fitzgerald believes, in the wasteland of the defeated working poor and can only be realized in the bourgeoisie. As a parvenu she is comic, but also grotesque and frightening. Her elaborate gestures of elegance are vulgar and preposterous. Her raw force is the force of Tom Buchanan, but without his class prerogatives it can only destroy her. She is a creature of his whim and thus pitiable. Mr. McKee's wished-for road to prominence is through art. He is weak and ineffectual, like George Wilson and, in a parodic way, like Gatsby. McKee aspires to move in the big world. His manners are courtly and dignified, but his art is a pathetic effort to emulate an outmoded impressionism. In all his innocence, and very much like Gatsby, he still believes that genteel accomplishments can survive in a world of brute power. The only successful man on the rise is Meyer Wolfsheim, the ethnic parvenu (as in *The Beautiful and Damned,* the condemned heir to "nobility" in America). Wolfsheim's corruption is the source of his crude power, and, as with Tom Buchanan, this power is ludicrously disguised by his concern with propriety and his gross sentimentality.

All these characters help interpret Gatsby. Gatsby has the drive and desire of Myrtle — in his case the product of imaginative rather than sensual energy. He also shares with her an elaborate pretentiousness, a grotesque imitation of the bourgeoisie. Like McKee, Gatsby is essentially childlike, a victim of his own innocence and gentility. Like Wolfsheim, he is corrupt, an operator, but believes too much in the genteel romantic tradition to make his business his life. Gatsby shares with all of them a desire to become bourgeois but is both more pitiful and grand than any of them because he truly believes that the bourgeoisie commands the finest traditions of America.

All these characters maintain their aspirations with an awareness of their own contingency. Unlike the true bourgeoisie, their pretensions are vulnerable, always a pin prick away from explosion into thin air. Myrtle's fantastic aspirations depend upon Buchanan's whim and hasty largesse. McKee's dignity deflates at a rude remark. Wolfsheim, for all his success, is only a phone call away from prison. And Gatsby's elaborate dreams depend merely on "a promise that the rock of the world was founded securely on a fairy's wing" [p. 100]. In all cases, these characters are at a decided disadvantage in their struggle for realization. The reality they seek is only to be had in the ruling class, and they are all ill-equipped to get it.

Whereas these variously mobile characters display some degree of effort and vitality, Fitzgerald also portrays the purely defeated. Mr. Wilson is the prominent example. Wilson exists on the treacherous borderline between petty bourgeois loneliness and proletarian want. Though he is self-employed, he is a member of the working poor and vulnerable to all the vicissitudes of his failing business. The pressures at this lower level of the petty bourgeoisie are enormous and are clearly destroying him. He is fearful, lonely, routinized, constantly worried, utterly devitalized, and more than a bit crazed. His possession of his wife is the last mark of his manhood, but, as Fitzgerald shows, he is totally at the mercy of Buchanan both for his business and for his wife. Mr. Wilson represents one of the alternatives in an America dominated by bourgeois power. However, Fitzgerald seems to understand failure only in the crude categories of Social Darwinism. As Nick puts it, "there are only the pursued, the pursuing, the busy, and the tired" [p. 81]; and elsewhere, "There was no difference between men, in intelligence or race, so profound as the difference between the sick and the well" [p. 124]. Wilson, like Gatsby's father, belongs to the sick and tired. Their realities too harsh to support the hope for their fantastic dreaming, they live in desperation on the border of the ashen wasteland of failure in America.

In his portrayal of the social class drama Fitzgerald reveals the absurdity of petty bourgeois pretensions. Not only are these pretensions ludicrously transparent, but they imitate a bourgeoisie that itself is second-hand. The Buchanans themselves live on the stage set modelled on European aristocracy. Their wealth does allow them to carry off the illusion much more convincingly than those who would emulate them. However, their personal lives are mean, empty, and unimaginative. Though it may not be the most significant thing to know about the bourgeoisie in its relation to society, Fitzgerald does portray their personal emptiness and treachery effectively. His treatment of this odd relation between the petty bourgeoisie and the bourgeoisie proper is a progressive critique of one of the major contradictions in American society.

III

In Gatsby we are shown the wildest illusions of the petty bourgeois dream. Fitzgerald emphasizes the shimmering glamour, the magic of perpetual youth and social grace that his dreamer associates with the bourgeoisie. But it is here that Fitzgerald reveals his essential ambivalence for he is finally incapable of freeing himself from the idealizations that elaborate this dream. The incest pattern which rules the emotional force of the novel is sustained rather than being discarded as a horrible distortion that results from the treacherous social confusion of the bourgeois world. In the end, Fitzgerald's insistence on the false poetry of the incest fantasy serves only to mystify the experiences of the novel.

A number of critics have remarked on the curious sexual attitudes in *The Great Gatsby,* and D. S. Savage in particular has emphasized the regressive character of the central fantasies of the novel. Savage portrays this fantasy in the following way: "In the dark enchantment of the incestuous regression, life flows back to its own origins, history is dissolved into nature. . . . With money . . . you could *possess* — your girl, the *mater*ials for the earthly paradise, Mother Earth, your mother . . ."[Savage's italics].[6] What critics have not clarified is how such fantastic dreams are bound up with the social class drama.

Gatsby begins his drive to the top by disowning his family roots and inventing for himself a new identity. He changes his name from the rough German "Gatz" to the ruling-class British "Gatsby". His first mentor-father is Dan Cody, a wealthy old roughneck whose gaudy display and loose living associate him with the first-generation rich of the frontier. But Gatsby's elaborate aspirations require more than mere wealth. Daisy Fay of Louisville introduces him to genteel wealth, the world of families with respectable names. He discovers romantic promise in her youthful glamour and fixes his dream on being adopted into this world of wealth and gentility. His new family becomes the bourgeoisie and not as they actually are but as his idealizations fashion them. They come to exist for him as creatures of a special grace which protects them from the hard realities of other people's lives. They become for him gods who have escaped the powers of time and change and of the flesh. Their world is enchanted, and it is in this world that Gatsby wishes to discover his "true"family and the identity he fashioned for himself out of story-books years earlier.

The scene that presents the incarnation of Gatsby's ideal in the figure of Daisy is a useful example of how the incest fantasy becomes entangled with the facts of social climbing. Fitzgerald's rhapsodic prose sets loose the dominant fantasy which underlies Gatsby's aspirations. The fantasy is of mergence with the mother, the peaceful union at her breast. Nick tells us that "out of the corner of his eye Gatsby saw that the blocks of the sidewalk really formed a ladder and mounted to a secret place above the trees — he could climb it, if he climbed alone, and once there he could suck on the pap of life, gulp down the incomparable milk of wonder" [p. 112]. When Nick thinks about Gatsby's incarnation, he is taken back to something in the past that he can barely remember: "For a moment a lost phrase tried to take shape in my mouth and my lips parted like a dumb man's, as though there was more struggling upon them than a wisp of startled air. But they made no sound, and what I had almost remembered was incommunicable forever" [p. 112]. Nick's reaction emphasizes the regression which motivates Gatsby's extravagant desires, the obsessive infantile fantasy of the breast. Daisy becomes an *imago* for Gatsby, a figure who reawakens infantile desires in the context of maturity. Union with her is perceived as a return to the blessed paradise of infancy.

Gatsby's vision of Daisy casts her in the light of the idealized mother. She is seen as capable and complete, "safe and proud above the hot struggles of the poor" [p. 150]. Gatsby is portrayed as a son, imaginative and devoted, and claiming a special relation to her that transcends personality and the changes of time. Daisy herself seems to perceive this fantasy when she visits Gatsby's story-book mansion. Rather than responding to the power and mastery that Gatsby's display might hope to evoke, Daisy is protective. She remarks, "I'd love to just get one of those pink clouds and put you in it and push you around" [p. 95]. He is her sweet imaginative boy, and she will provide him all the tender caring of a pink nursery and a perambulator.

Gatsby's idealization places Daisy above such earthly realities as sexual desire. Daisy is portrayed throughout most of the novel as ethereal. We first see her floating in the breeze and seeming to have "just been blown back in after a short flight around the house" [p. 8]. Fitzgerald introduces Daisy as she exists in her lover's de-sexualized fantasy, as the ethereal dream-woman. Throughout most of the novel Daisy is nothing but a face and a voice. Only at a later moment [p. 116] does she acquire an actual bosom and that is a prelude to the destruction of the dream. In Gatsby's imagination sexuality belongs to the lower classes, to Myrtle Wilson, who cannot be idealized. Daisy, however, must be "pure" if she is to be the goddess-mother, the Madonna figure who will discover in Gatsby her proper son-lover.

The incest motif in *The Great Gatsby* is best explained through the strategies that Freud detailed in his description of the family romance.[7] The family romance is a set of emotional and psychological strategems through which the son hopes to usurp the position of the father by claiming his own very special relation with the mother. He considers his relation to the mother as absolute. After all, he was at one time part of her, she sustained him, and at her breast there was once an absolute union. By comparison, the relation between husband and wife is "just personal".[8] The adult relation does contain the special feature of sexuality, but the son denies this by idealizing the mother and denying her sexual reality. The relation the son wishes to offer, based upon his sensitivity, romantic imagination, and idealized purity, is far superior. In *The Great Gatsby*, the family romance, and particularly the aspect of the usurpation of the father, becomes the central expression of the petty bourgeois adventurer's dream of class usurpation.[9] In this odd reification of the social class drama into the metaphors of the family romance, the bourgeoisie become parents whose wealth and power allow them an untrammled and irresponsible will; all others are children doomed to live in Cinderella fantasies.

The family romance explains not only the extreme idealization of Daisy but also the consistent portrayal of Tom Buchanan as paternal. When Tom is first introduced, along with his physical power and threatening aggressiveness, his voice impresses Nick with its "paternal contempt" and seems to be saying "I'm stronger and more of a man than you are" [p. 7]. His eyes are "flashing about restlessly" as if he anticipates a challenge to his power and possessions. Much later, when Tom becomes aware of Gatsby's intentions to take Daisy from him, his "voice groped unsuccessfully for the paternal note" [p. 131]. Tom finally crushes Gatsby by insisting that his mature "personal " relation with Daisy is superior to Gatsby's idealizations: "Why — they're things between Daisy and me that you'll never know, things that neither of us can ever forget" [p. 133]. Tom is successfully paternal and superior. His wife is his by right of sexual possession and an intimacy that Gatsby's fantasizing cannot erase.

The role of Myrtle Wilson in the working out of this fantasy requires special attention. Myrtle Wilson is associated with the valley of ashes and lives precariously at the edge of working-class exigencies. She represents the sexual animality Fitzgerald associates with the poor. She is a debased Venus whose sexual energies are portrayed as grotesque.

She is measured against Daisy's ethereal image. In the "logic" of the incest fantasy, Myrtle comes to represent everything that is not supposed to be true about Daisy.[10]

In this light, Myrtle's death, coming immediately after the discovery of Daisy's sexual bond with Tom, clarifies a confusion in Gatsby's realization. When Myrtle is killed her breast is torn [p. 138]. The wonderful promise of the "pap of life" and the "fresh green breast" has been blasted. The dichotomy which allowed Gatsby to dream such ideal dreams of virgin purity in a mature woman is no longer possible. The death of Myrtle means that Daisy must be perceived as a sexual woman.

What Fitzgerald has done is to provide his petty bourgeois hero with the most unreal dream to guide him. Finally, Gatsby wants much more than a grand house, a luxurious car, acquaintance with the "best people", and so on. He wants his fantastic illusions of eternal youth, freshness, gayety, romance, and the eternal moment of his rhapsodic incarnation at the "pap of life." Gatsby believes, and Nick assents to this belief, that his capacity to dream so extravagantly somehow entitles him to membership in the bourgeoisie where such freedom is perceived to be attainable.

IV

Finally, neither Nick nor Fitzgerald can extricate himself from the fatal allure of what the bourgeoisie promises. The coda to the novel asserts the necessity to desire the impossible fulfillment of infantile fantasies. The final page of the novel reaffirms the petty bourgeois need to maintain desperate illusions in order to sustain itself. At the same time, Nick is aware that the mystic communion with a power beyond the facts of the world and of history is impossible. The pursuit of adolescent dreams of the past into the adult world is hopeless. However, Fitzgerald establishes a total ambivalence at this point. Although Nick is aware that such wondrous contemplations are doomed, he also suggests that we are doomed without them. We will "beat on, boats against the current, borne back ceaselessly into the past" precisely because for the petty bourgeois dreamer there is no place else to go. History becomes a mirror maze in which the present is a channel to a future that, in turn, is merely a ghostly reflection of the past.

Nick's closing reverie is meant to be universally applicable and is not presented in a context which allows us to recognize it as the illusory world-view of a particular class. For Nick, the last pure moment in history was when man first set eyes on this continent, where he was "face to face for the last time in history with something commensurate to his capacity for wonder." The passing of the pure moment, the ensuing violation of the "green breast" of the virgin land, indicates for Nick the end of mankind's vitality. Ever after, mankind is doomed to pursue the orgiastic future which is "already behind him, somewhere back in the vast obscurity beyond the city, where the dark fields of the republic rolled on under the night." For Nick there is no future. There is only the paradisal past and the purgatorial vision of man's fevered pursuit of a lost moment. Such historical despair is the bleak heritage of the petty bourgeoisie, whose dream of emergence into the rich, clear atmosphere identified with the bourgeoisie is doomed from the beginning. Caudwell's judgment of the prospects of the petty bourgeoisie offers a fitting summary. Caudwell wrote that "of all the products of capitalism, none is more unlovely than this class. Whoever does not escape from it is certainly damned" [p. 76].

Fitzgerald — unlike Melville, Twain, Whitman, Dreiser, London, and Thomas Wolfe — is incapable of viewing the values of the working class as anything but hopeless because the working class lacks the high-reaching illusions that his class survives on. Their grasp of the real material forces that condition reality and their heroic collectivized effort to challenge the power of the bourgeoisie that has been a major theme in the actual history of America is a perfect blank to Fitzgerald. He prefers, as a long list of his critics have, to be "ecstasized" by the delicious defeat expressed in the lyricism of Nick's reverie. *The Great Gatsby* condemns the bourgeoisie and the American Dream, but because Fitzgerald cannot extricate himself from the most extravagant illusions of his class, he ends with no hope for history, no belief in the resources of the human spirit for the struggle to gain social freedom and dignity.

NOTES

1. Robert Sklar typifies this universalizing tendency. He argues that "Gatsby stands for essential qualities of America; and so he stands above time and history, a symbol of eternally recurring hopes and dreams. For all of its insights into history, *The Great Gatsby* is basically an ahistorical novel." In *F. Scott Fitzgerald: The Last Laocoon* (New York, 1967), p. 224. Cf. also James E. Miller, *F. Scott Fitzgerald: His Art and His Technique* (New York, 1967), p. 78; A.E. Dyson, *"The Great*

Gatsby: Thirty-six Years After," in *F. Scott Fitzgerald: A Collection of Critical Essays*, ed. Arthur Mizener (New York, 1967), p. 102; and Maxwell Perkins, *Editor to Author: the Letters of Maxwell E. Perkins*, ed. John Hall Wheelock (New York, 1950), p. 41.

2. In a letter to John Peale Bishop (August 9, 1925), Fitzgerald wrote: "Also you are right about Gatsby being blurred and patchy. I never at any one time saw him clear myself — for he started as one man I knew and then changed into myself — the amalgam was never complete in my mind." In *The Letters of F. Scott Fitzgerald*, ed. Andrew Turnball (New York, 1965), p. 383.

3. In "H.G. Wells: A Study in Utopianism," *Studies in a Dying Culture* (New York, 1971), p. 77. All further citations to Caudwell will be given in the text.

4. All citations are to the Scribner paperback edition and will be given in the text.

5. In a letter to Edmund Wilson (Spring, 1925), in *Letters*, ed. Turnball, p. 367.

6. "The Significance of F. Scott Fitzgerald," in Mizener, p. 153.

7. Freud's discussion of the family romance can be found especially in "A Special Type of Choice of Object Made by Men" (1910); and "The Most Prevalent Form of Degradation in Erotic Life" (1912): in *On Creativity and the Unconscious: Papers on the Psychology of Art, Literature, Love, Religion*, ed. Benjamin Nelson, New York, 1958.

8. Gatsby's "curious remark" that Daisy's relation to Tom is "just personal" (p. 152) is explained by Freud's observation that "the feature of overestimation by which the loved one becomes the unique, the irreplaceable one, fits . . . into the infantile set of ideas, for no one posesses more than one mother, and the relation to her rests on an experience which is assured beyond all doubt and can never be repeated again." In "Object Choice," p. 167.

9. Freud explains that the son shows his gratitude to his mother "by wishing to have a son by his mother that shall be like himself; in the rescue phantasy, that is, he identifies himself completely with the father. All the instincts, the loving, the grateful, the sensual, the defiant, the self-assertive and independent — all are gratified in the wish to be *the father of himself*" [Freud's italics]. In "Object Choice," p. 171.

10. Freud discusses the relation between the love for the mother and the fascination with the harlot figure: "The grown man's conscious mind likes to regard the mother as a personification of impeccable moral purity. . . . This very relation, however, of sharpest possible contrast between the 'mother' and the 'harlot' would prompt us to study the developmental history of the two complexes and unconscious relation between them, since we long ago discovered that a thing which in consciousness makes its appearance as two contraries is often in the unconscious a united whole." In "Object Choice," p. 168.

17

Brecht's *Caucasian Chalk Circle* and Marxist Figuralism: Open Dramaturgy as Open History

Darko Suvin

> Let us not forget for one instant the point which we occupy in space and in duration, and let us extend our view to the coming centuries, the furthest regions, and the peoples yet to be born.
>
> *Denis Diderot*

> Die Weltgeschichte ist das Weltgericht (The history of the world is its Last Judgment).
>
> *Friedrich Schiller*

> Now doth the peerless poet perform both: for whatsoever the philosopher saith should be done, he giveth a perfect picture of it in some one by whom he presupposeth it was done; so as he coupleth the general notion with the particular example. A perfect picture I say, for he yieldeth to the powers of the mind an image of that whereof the philosopher bestoweth but a wordish description. . .
>
> *Philip Sidney*

I

The opus of the German poet and playwright Bertolt Brecht (1898-1956) is a particularly clear case of concern for the historical fate of Man informing and shaping a highly significant aesthetic whole of our times. It has been sufficiently noted by criticism of Brecht[1] how deep-seated that concern was. I have myself argued elsewhere that all of his major plays evince a strong tension between the implied "look backward" from the historical vantage point of an anticipated friendly, classless humanity and his intimate understanding of the bloody history of the 20th Century with its class and national warfare; I have argued that Brecht's basic stance is a utopian blend of intellectual and plebeian alienation from the inhuman contradictions of our times.[2] From such a point of view he effects his whole system of "estrangements" (*Verfremdungen*). From its heights he judges the world that forces a truly good person to develop a tough competitive Alter Ego that will protect the tender and friendly Ego (*The Good Woman of Setzuan*), the world that uses the humor and shrewdness of a mother only for the petty pursuits of a "hyena of the battlefields" trying — and failing — to nourish her own family by cooperating with the warmongers (*Mother Courage and Her Children*), the world that forces a passion for reason into officially approved channels of an exploitative science (*The Life of Galileo*). That is why all major plays by Brecht contain an explicit or implicit judgment scene: the basic stance of the author is thus thematized and brought clearly into the open.

However, even among Brecht's major plays, *The Caucasian Chalk Circle* (further *CCC*) has, I contend, a privileged position. It shares the concern for history as manmade destiny, the tension and the utopian "look backward" described above, with his other plays. But it was written in 1944, at the brightest and most open moment of history in the last fifty years — the moment of victory over Nazism. Only in *CCC* — and in *The Mother*, his play of the early 1930's, written during the decisive battle of the German Left against Hitler's rise to power — is an approximation to Brecht's utopian standpoint concretized on the stage at any length, and brought into explicit and victorious collision with inhuman history.

CCC is thus a glaring exception among Brecht's plays that realistically could not but be plays of stark defeat. However, it also poses complex exegetic problems. These do not seem to have been dealt with fully by Brechtian criticism, and yet they are basic to an understanding of how his open dramaturgy relates and is complementary to his vision of an open history. I propose therefore to examine first the basic motifs which constitute the play into a meaningful unity, and then Brecht's philosophy of history which makes sense of such a composition — and is therefore not a body extrinsic to literary analysis but central to it. This should enable a final discussion of the relationship between Brecht's dramaturgy and historiosophy to be based on the evidence of the play itself; it should also enable reaching toward some general conclusions about the import of the

Brechtian method that blends historiosophy and aesthetics into a significant creative method.

1.

At first glance, *CCC* has an unusually complicated fable, consisting of
three stories distributed in two levels, plus a number of epico-lyrical interventions by the Singer and his accompanying Musicians as well as several
"songs" by some other characters. We can distinguish the opening
"kolkhoz story," the "Grusha story" and the "Azdak story," the latter two
coming together in the "chalk circle judgment." The kolkhoz story is
supposed to happen at the end of World War II, it is chronologically nearer
to the audience, and it acts as a frame to the "chalk circle" nucleus which
is supposed to happen in the depth of Middle Ages.

The center toward which the play converges is indicated by its title: it
is the legendary decision about the future of a Noble Child, placed between
a false and a true mother. However, in a subversion of dominant social
ideologies — such as the one affirmed in the Biblical story of Solomon's
sword judgment in an analogous dispute — the theme of motherhood in
the "Grusha story" is used to demystify the alleged primacy of the "call of
the blood," of the biological motherhood represented by the rapacious
upper-class bitch Natella, in favour of the "social motherhood" of the
dumb servant Grusha, who at a time of political upheaval saved the
Noble Child left at the mercy of killers by its biological mother. Yet if this
were the whole import of the play, it is scarcely explainable why it would be
necessary to supplement this plebeian fairy tale with the whole history of
the judge who hands down the wise chalk-circle judgment. Still less is it
clear why this whole nucleus must be performed as a play-within-the-play
presented for and by the kolkhoz litigants over the use of a valley. And in
fact, the bourgeois theatre has often treated the Grusha story as a sentimental fable, supplemented in a pseudo-Shakespearean way by the comic
relief of a hammy Azdak; logically the kolkhoz story was then seen as a
piece of "socialist-realist" propaganda on the virtues of Soviet society and
performed with great embarrassment or completely dropped. I want to
argue here that such a sundering procedure is false, since it violates the
basic presumption of unity and economy in a significant work of art.

In order to show the unity of the play, it is necessary to analyze more
closely the themes of the various "stories" and see whether they have a
common set of references. To go back to the Grusha story, we saw that
even a first attempt at formulating its theme was impossible without

entering into the universe of social relationships in that story. That
universe is, right from the beginning, clearly identified as a world of
topsy-turvy human relations passing for normal and indeed hallowed,
where basic human values are polar opposites to the official ones:

> In olden times, in a bloody time
> There ruled in a Caucasian city —
> Men called it the City of the Damned —
> A Governor.
> His name was Georgi Abashwili.
> He was rich as Croesus
> He had a beautiful wife
> He had a healthy baby.
> No other governor in Grusinia
> Had so many horses in his stable
> So many beggars on his doorstep
> So many soldiers in his service
> So many petitioners in his courtyard. [27]

This world is a world of war, of class oppression of the poor and powerless
by the rich and powerful, and of internecine Hobbesian warfare of each
against each in the upper class, engendering a system in which the lower
class also has to choose between kindness and survival (for example — the
peasant selling milk to Grusha, or her brother). Grusha saves the infant
because she is, as Brecht noted, an exceptional "sucker" — that is, she
responds to norms of human kindness although they threaten her with
death in the unnatural class society. Obviously, behind the old legend, the
basic Brechtian questioning of what is "normal," of the alienating effect of
social power-relations on human potentialities, insidiously reemerges.
Appearances deceive, the reality is fraught with murderous contradictions,
and any peaceful moment is only an interlude:

> The City lies still
> But why are there armed men?
> The Governor's palace is at peace
> But why is it a fortress?
> And the Governor returned to his palace
> And the fortress was a trap...
> And noon was no longer the hour to eat:
> Noon was the hour to die. [33]

When Grusha succumbs to the "terrible temptation of goodness" to help a helpless human being, though she is helpless herself, she has to flee through the Northern Mountains, encountering in that epic anabasis all kinds of trials and surmounting them by means of a slowly developing sense of motherhood. To the killings of the princes and the egotist insensitivity of Natella she opposes a principle which is as important as the all-pervading destructiveness of the upper classes; the principle of *productivity* or *creativity*. If it were not sufficiently clear from the language and style of the play, its use of stylized scenery, masks for the upper-class characters, etc., even this first approach to the fable might be sufficient to show that Grusha's actions, putting as they do into question the norm (e.g., of "true motherhood"), are super-individual. As other major figures of Brecht's, she is both a precisely personalized character and allegorical in a sense yet to be explored, but more akin to the Shakespearean synthesis of allegory and realism than to the individualist 18-20th Century drama. Thus, a child in Brecht's plays usually carries his basic motif of *posteri*, the future generations whose forebears we are. The tug-of-war between the biological upper-class mother and the plebeian "social mother" over the Noble Child is an *exemplum*, standing for a decision which social orientation shall prevail as the parent of posterity, future ages (see the song "Had he golden shoes," 125). Grusha's social maternity is characterologically earned by her labors and dangers, but it is also the sign of a potential coming into existence of a new set of human relations, a new normality, which is attained by standing the topsy-turvy universe of the Chalk Circle nucleus on its head — i.e., by subverting it.

Thus, the maternity motif is here — as different from other plays by Brecht such as *The Good Woman of Setzuan* — explicitly collocated within the theme of a reasonable and humanized *ultimate goal (telos) of history*[3] envisaged as a system of human actions and interactions. The goal toward which class history is moving is, in fact, the main theme of the whole play. Therefore, developing the "Azdak story" at some length is not only autonomously enjoyable but also essential in order to bring out its theme of an advent of Justice as a *temporary* reversal of historically "normal" (i.e. alienated) power and jurisprudence. As an intercalary short-lived exception at the time of a power-vacuum, Azdak can rid the chalk-circle judgment of a non-cognitively fantastic or fairy-tale character. Placed into the Saturnalian tradition of the Oriental and European Lord of Misrule, "Roi pour rire," whose interregnum momentarily replaces and cancels out the class world and its inhuman laws, the "Azdak story" validates the outcome of the "Grusha story" (and by that token itself, too) as more than escapism — as an incident exemplary by its very exceptionalness, and thus in a roundabout, but logically unassailable way, reintegrated into a theory which sees history as the development of humanity through class conflicts. The combination of Grusha and Azdak, plebeian emotion and plebeian intelligence, revolt against old laws and power over the enforcing of new laws, is necessary for a cognitively credible outcome of the chalk-circle test as an interaction of human wills — where man's destiny is man.

The parallels between the Grusha and Azdak stories, which happen simultaneously but are developed successively on the stage, show up their similarities and differences. Both derive their function from an initial impulsive, "abnormal" humanist action (the saving of the child and of the Grand Duke). This lands them first into trouble, so that they try to back-slide into their old ways, but finally educates them into true motherhood and judgeship respectively. As opposed to the upper class, both Grusha and Azdak show by such acts that they are in harmony with nature, outer or inner. Grusha extends her awakened maternal feeling to the wind:

> *Grusha* (*turning to the Child*): You mustn't be afraid of the wind. He's a poor thing too. He has to push the clouds along and he gets quite cold doing it. (*Snow starts falling*) And the snow isn't so bad either, Michael. It covers the little fir trees so they won't die in winter.[61]

Azdak, on the other hand, is an Epicurean, in the double sense of hedonist and of a radical intellectual for whom his own sensual nature, perceptions and concepts are the only genuinely human touchstone remaining in the desensualized, calculated, brutal world around him. Both Grusha as the herald of a new Nature and Azdak as the herald of a new Wisdom could fail only by selfishness or cowardice, and they both grow by having assumed responsibilities contrary to such temptations of conforming. Without Azdak, Grusha would have been simply a somewhat more violent and expressive Kattrin from *Mother Courage and her Children*, barely beginning to speak and reverting to mutism at times of complex stresses involving both emotion and rationality — a frustrated and barren Mother of the New. Without Grusha, Azdak would be only a Saturnalian Falstaff, Schweik, or Groucho Marx supplying anarchist entertainment but having no significant, historical "bearing on our problem" (as the peasant woman in the kolkhoz scene defines the compositional method of the play) — a freak without insertion into historical processes. As it is, Azdak can be remembered by the people as an anti-judge whose term was "a brief golden age,/Almost an age of justice." Azdak's anabasis is a flight *toward power* (the Ironshirts) used in a new way, complementary to Grusha's flight *from power* used in the old way. During it, Azdak has grown from a disaffected bohemian, first to somebody reducing the old justice to its absurd conclusions by anarchist parody, and finally to the allegorical herald of a new justice, of the new and coming Golden Age which shall "transform justice/Into passion" (Brecht's *Address to Danish Worker-Actors*).

The hypothesis that this is a play thematically centered on a theory which sees history as a conflict of social alienations with strivings toward de-alienation, can also account for the unusual "kolkhoz story" and framework. Its "new wisdom" of peaceful resolution of the dispute over the valley finds a Common Denominator with the Subversive "old wisdom" of Azdak's decision in the concluding verses:

That what there is shall go to those who are good for it:
Children to the motherly, that they prosper.
Carriages to good drivers, that they be driven well,
And the valley to the waterers, that it yield fruit.

This also makes of the central action of *CCC* a performance for an exemplary audience, poetically validating its settling of conflicts of interest without the violence of each against each by inserting it into a historical and philosophical sequence. As Aristotle knew, poetry is more philosophical than historiography.

2.

Brecht's philosophy of history and the compositional method in this play is *Marxist figuralism*.

In his essay "Figura", Erich Auerbach has outlined the medieval figural interpretation of history. A *figura* was a real historical person or event of the Old Testament reaching fulfillment in another real historical person or event of the New Testament — say Moses and Jesus. Neither figure nor fulfillment were spiritualist moral allegories; the allegorical aspect in this process was the *intellectus spiritualis* which recognized figure in fulfillment. Augustine refined this to the point where things and people could "prefigure" abstract fulfillments — e.g., Noah's ark prefigured the Christian church, or the pair Hagar-Sarah prefigured the opposition Old Testament vs. New Testament, also *civitas terrena* (terrestrial Jerusalem) vs. *civitas Dei* (heavenly Jerusalem). Brecht does the same when the boy Michael prefigures the future, so that his redemption from class bondage of his "terrene," biological mother is *figurally* connected with the fate of the valley redeemed from private property and its concomitant warfare-type settlement of disputes.

In Auerbach's definition "figural interpretation establishes a connection between two events or persons, the first of which signifies not only itself but also the second, while the second encompasses and fulfills the first. The two poles of the figure are separate in time, but both, being real events or figures, are within time, within the stream of historical life."[4] This is an allegorical approach which retains and encourages the historicity of events but inserts them within a formal process participating both of historiographic facticity and of utopian expectation. Auerbach observes that "figural interpretation is a product of late cultures, far more indirect, complex, and charged with history than the symbol or the myth"; on the other hand, complementary to the interpretation of venerable, indeed legendary matter, it is "youthful and newborn as a purposive, creative, concrete interpretation of universal history" [57]. These observations seem to me to apply with full force to Brecht's theory of history in *CCC*. Just as the Christian figural interpretation absorbed characters from the Old Testament as well as from lay authors (*teste David cum Sibylla,* as the *Dies irae* has it) down to the Grail legends, so Brecht's Marxist figuralism absorbed configurations from the New Testament and the old folk legends, generally recognized as the two principal sources of his tradition. It is not difficult to find in the Grusha story the archetype of the hierogamic Holy Family, blasphemously complete with a virgin mother (*figlia del tuo figlio* — Dante, *Paradiso* 33) an exalted child, an official father (or two) who does not know how he came by the child, a flight from soldiers sent to massacre the child, etc. In the same way, Azdak's decision is a forerunner of a subversive final judgment. If Michael has overtones of the Christ Child, Azdak finally assumes overtones of Christ as the messianic fulfiller of Moses' leading his people out of bondage: he is beaten and stripped, he tours the country with the sacrament of a new Law —

> And he broke the rules to save them.
> Broken law like bread he gave them,
> Brought them to shore upon his crooked back. . . [107]

As for the folk legends, the use of the Chinese chalk-circle story, the Egyptian Song of the Chaos, the Judgment of Solomon and the legend-imbued location on Caucasus may be sufficient testimonials.

No doubt, differences between the Medieval Christian and the Marxist figuralism are no less pronounced, and homologous with the differences in the main import of these two major systematic non-individualistic philosophies of our civilization. Christian figuralism aims at a super-temporal, theistic resolution, where horizontal temporal prefiguration is possible only because all times refer vertically to divine providence, in whose eye past and future are simultaneous. Marxism takes from secularized (rationalist and Hegelian) historiography a real pluritemporality; the orientation toward earthly historicity that began with the Gothic and Renaissance ages grows into the axiological sovereignty of earthly, human reality, in all its sensory and historically differentiated multiplicity. Following Feuerbach, Marxism stood the god-man relation on its ear: god is an emanation made in the image of man. Therefore, instead of an incarnation of the Word (Logos), a Marxist dramatist will start from a verbalization and rationalization of the flesh, from a canonization of ethically exemplary human relations where the sensual and the visionary are not sundered. Grusha and Azdak behave thus: Grusha's motivation for picking up the child is dumb in terms of Individualist experience (each for himself and the devil take the hindmost), but it affirms a radical humanist *sapientia* as touchstone for the whole play:

> *Older Woman (amiably):* Grusha, you're a good soul, but you're not very bright, and you know it. I tell you, if he had the plague he couldn't be more dangerous.
> *Grusha (stubbornly):* He hasn't got the plague. He looks at me. He's human! [44]

Parallel to Grusha, Azdak can unite the dramaturgic function of a figure of new Justice with the character of a comically sensual, anarchistic parodist of old justice. In short, radical religious prefiguration is in Brecht replaced by radical humanist prefiguration, whose historiography is taken from the *Communist Manifesto* with its succeeding stages of class society identified as human "prehistory" which should lead to a classless and warless brotherhood of man on Earth. The specific ideational characteristic of *CCC* is the encounter of this historiography with radical Marxist and Anarchist anthropology in the tradition of young Marx and Rimbaud (forgotten by much official Marxism).

The Marxist theory of history can be envisaged as a Hegelian synthesis fusing the useful aspects of the feudal and bourgeois historiosophies. As in the medieval Christian theory of history, the Marxist one has a privileged point of convergence in the future which is the saving *telos* of human history (thesis); but as in the rationalist liberal theory of history (antithesis), this point is to be reached by a chain of development based exclusively on human interactions (synthesis). The anticipated Golden Age or Terrestrial Paradise is prefigured by a series of more or less short-lived revolutionary and utopian endeavours and visions throughout history from the equality of tribal society (the "primitive communism" of Marxist historiography) through lower-class revolts (such as the one of Spartacus, Wat Tyler, or the German Anabaptists) and through artistic, scientific, religious, or philosophical prefigurations, to revolutions such as the Bolshevik one. The sequence in the play: the Persian Weavers' revolt — Azdak's judgeship — cooperative socialism of Soviet kolkhozes, is an obvious example of such prefigurational, humanist salvation-history.

However, this is not to be taken to mean that the kolkhoz scene is the final privileged point of convergence, a static utopia of perfection. Beside Brecht's reserves on the development within the Soviet Union, the usual static confrontation of two (only sometimes three) points in Christian history (figure and one or two fulfillments) is here replaced by a dynamic development along an infinite curve of succeeding prefigurations hopefully ever closer to fulfillment. On this asymptotic curve, the chalk-circle point and the kolkhoz point serve merely as dramatically powerful examples and determinants. The "chalk-circle," inner part of the play has to be much longer than the kolkhoz frame because it focuses on the human potentialities of Grusha and Azdak as opposed to powerful social alienations in the barbaric class system; their success can then be transferred *a fortiori* to the more rational kolkhoz situation. But the quote from Mayakovsky characterizing the kolkhoz situation says: "The home of the Soviet people shall also be the home of Reason", prefiguring a further future (the German original "soll auch sein" is formally an imperative but also with future-bearing function). Then too, and more obviously, as in the inner play there is still war in the kolkhoz story (although it is a just one, as opposed to the unjust one about which Azdak sings the "Song of Injustice in Persia"). Also, the frame story itself is a dispute about stewardship of possessions which recalls the fierce ownership battle around the Noble Child, the inheritor of the Abashwili estates (although the battle is now fought with a pencil and not with a pistol). The social differentiation between the direct producers (the peasants and the artist) on one hand and on the other a centralized State apparatus, represented by a Delegate from the nearby town, still exists — and Brecht was very aware of its degenerative potentialities. In fact, the type of decision reached by the kolkhoz villagers without a court situation and by mutual agreement, which acts as a fulfillment of the unorthodox Azdak judging, would be illegal in the Soviet Union of 1944 as of today (though not of 1920), as the Soviet critics of Brecht have clearly stated. Another pointer is the deliberate onomastic mixture: Grusha is a Russian name with Dostoevskian (or anti-Dostoevskian) echoes of the humble being exalted, Azdak an Iranian one with radical and salvational echoes.[5] Also, the mixture or indeed mix-up of mostly Grusinian place-names with Russian and Azerbaidjani ones makes out of the kolkhoz situation a very stylized reality indeed (in "real life" the Nazi army came only to the border of the Grusinian Republic, and never to Azerbaidjan). The kolkhoz in the play is thus more of a model-like fulfillment of the legendary Azdakian Golden Age than a "socialist-realist" reflection of 1944 Transcaucasia. This too is of a piece with the figural method. As Auerback noted, there is always a certain contradiction between figure and history: history (*historia* or *littera*) "is the literal sense or the event related; *figura* is the same literal meaning or event in reference to the fulfillment cloaked in it, and this fulfillment itself is *veritas*" [47]. The human relationships in the Grusinian kolkhozes are thus not to be taken either literally or as a final truth, but as Auerbach's "middle term" [47] between their historical literality and dynamic fulfillment: they are themselves another, more advanced figure.

In the same way, the figural parallels of the disputed valley to young Michael are clear: the fruit-growers have a better right to it partly because they fought for it against the Nazis, just as Grusha did against the Iron-shirts and other vicissitudes, but mainly because they propose to use it more productively. The question which Azdak decides in the chalk-circle judgment is not at all who should "possess" Michael, and by implication "own" the future. As his questions and the final verse show, the decision hinges on who will be better *for the child*. Not the child to his mother, but the child "to the motherly," the maternal ones, says the Singer in the quoted conclusion — a stylistic device taken over by Brecht from the Luther-Bible style which substitutes the nominalized adjectival quality for a static, fixed substantive. The child and the valley-area are not objects to be allocated to subject-possessors — they are entities, subjects in their own right, and the users have only rights of stewardship over them in the name of human productivity. The formal analogies to the medieval theory of property and just dealing in the name of divine justice are clear. Such analogies are not syllogistic proofs, since a prefigurational parallel is never complete: a certain tension between *figura* and fulfillment is immanent to this approach. Yet, like the fruit-growers, Grusha too had to earn her right to motherhood, and indeed parts II and III of the Grusha story show the

birth of Grusha as a "motherly one." Her nascent capacities for feeling are
criminal in the chaotic world around her:

> She sat too long, too long she saw
> The soft breathing, the small clenched fists,
> Till toward the morning the seduction was complete.
>
> . . .
>
> As if it was stolen goods she picked it up.
> As if she was a thief she crept away. [46]

Yet such feelings grow into justification of Grusha's right to be the Noble
Child's parents — hers is the true nobility, and the blood-and-water
baptism of Michael and changing of his clothes are initiation rites for
Mother Grusha:

> *Corporal:* Fine linen!
> *Grusha dashes at him to pull him away. He throws her off and again
> bends over the crib. Again looking round in despair, she sees a log
> of wood, seizes it, and hits the Corporal over the head from behind.
> The Corporal collapses. She quickly picks up the Child and rushes
> off.*
> *Singer:* And in her flight from the Ironshirts
> After twenty-two days of journeying
> At the Foot of the Janga-Tau Glacier
> Grusha Vachnadze decided to adopt the child.
> *Chorus:* The helpless girl adopted the helpless child.
> *Grusha squats over a half-frozen stream to get the Child water in
> the hollow of her hand.*
> *Grusha:* Since no one else will take you, son,
> I must take you.
> Since no one else will take you, son,
> You must take me.
> O black day in a lean, lean year,
> The trip was long, the milk was dear,
> My legs are tired, my feet are sore;
> But I wouldn't be without you any more.
> I'll throw your silken shirt away,
> And wrap you in rags and tatters,
> I'll wash you, son, and christen you in glacier water.
> We'll see it through together.
> *She has taken off the child's fine linen and wrapped it in a rag.*
>
> [57-58]

The *telos* of Marxist figuralism is indeed, notwithstanding dogmatic vulgarizations, not to be found in any particular, arrested point. Though in its dynamic theory of historical equilibrium the direction of humanity is always clear, each point should also be the starting point for new contradictions and resolutions: Judgment Day is also Genesis. It might seem curious that Brecht at some moments insisted that the inner play in *CCC* is not a parable — though its story is told in order to clarify the kolkhozes' decision about the valley — but another (undefined) kind of exemplary narration, to whose "practicability and also genesis" the kolkhoz story "assigns a historical localization."[6] In fact, this is an aesthetic correlative to a salvational perspective in which history has no end, so that the "kolkhoz story" is simply a *presently possible* society in which Azdak's exceptional drawing of a chalk circle has become the normative or dominant use of pencils instead of pistols.

3.

The curve of prefiguration leads thus not only from the chalk circle nucleus to the kolkhoz frame, but also from the Singer's final verses to the temporal point of the audience — 1975, or any time at which the prefiguration of a Golden Age has not been fulfilled although it is felt as absolutely necessary. The play is fully relevant only for such an audience, and it becomes clear why for an audience with a different attitude it must seem a chaotic mixture of fairy tale, clowning and propaganda. It is no accident that the first prefiguration of such a fulfillment has been written by Brecht in 1944, at the most promising moment of modern history, the moment of the victory of the anti-fascist coalition, and that he placed at least the frame story into the year in which he wrote it (an extraordinary exception rarely paralleled in modern drama). Drama and history touched in a privileged moment, an epiphany, that lent its effulgence to both. History is here shown as open-ended though clearly not value-free: there is a fixed provisional goal, but it will be reached only if the spectators learn what it means to become parents of the New, of the Future (as Grusha and Simon learned), and if they realize that the victory of the Golden Age of justice depends on the ability of later Grushas to act and later Azdaks to be in the arbiter's seat. Whether the historical horizon of a just, classless humanity will be reached depends on a further powerful conjunction of subversive emotion and subversive reason. For this change of the times ("thou hope of the people," 35) the play is a dynamic *exemplum*. Fittlingly, its structure as an open drama exemplifies its message of an open history.

The open structure of the play is communicated through a number of devices. I have already touched on some effects of the play-within-the-play form which results in two audiences. We watch the kolkhoz both act out the chalk-circle story and function as its audience, in a prefiguration of the participatory or doing-your-own-thing theatre, of politics as theatre rather than theatre as politics; and we see the kolkhoz members obtaining insights which justify their decision about the valley as a step in the necessary humanization of humanity. By watching this, we as the "outer" audience gain not only the "moral of the story" but also the reasons why and ways how it is moral. We see, as Brecht wrote in his *Address to Danish Worker-Actors* that "only he who knows that the fate of man is man/Can see his fellow man keenly with accuracy"; and we see this cognition presented as delight.

One could embark upon a discussion of songs, and many other devices in the play, but I want finally to consider here only the Singer-narrator. He seems to me to be much more than a formal trick, in fact a semiotic model which not only signifies but is significant in his own right as showing Brecht's theatre esthetics in action. As with almost all major modern dramatists (and indeed artists in general) the theatre's reflection about life is at the same time a reflection about itself. The play — and its performance — is a seduction to goodness in the exemplary type of Grusha, and to justice in that of Azdak. It seduces through a method uniting in its allegorizing the corporeal and spiritual (in)sight, *eros* and *agape*; it warns against the difficulties on the road to goodness and justice presented in Grusha's archetypal flight and Azdak's tempestuous ups and downs, the small-scale landlocked *Odyssey* and *Iliad* of this stage narration.

Parallel to this, the Singer personifies the right type of theatre for an audience interested in the delightful didactics of history; the Chalk-Circle nucleus which he narrates and his approach to its narration and performance are supposed to represent the proper message and the proper style of a plebeian, liberating theatre. The Singer is the only stage figure participating in both the kolkhoz frame (as character) and the chalk-circle nucleus (as narrator and commentator). He mediates between the stage and the audience (both the stage audience and the "real" one); he makes it impossible to forget that the kolkhoz audience is (that we are) seeing the exemplary reality of a performance and not illusionistic slices of life. Like a novel narrator, he manipulates time and space rhythm at his will, he knows the motives and thoughts of all characters. His comments suggest to the audience the most economical attitude proper to the play and its unified understanding. Similar to a Greek chorus, or to Hamlet in the Mousetrap play-within-a-play, he unites epic coolness and lyrical emotion, such as in "O blindness of the great":

> O blindness of the great!
> They go their way like gods,
> Great over bent backs,
> Sure of hired fists,
> Trusting in the power
> Which has lasted so long. But long is not forever.
> O change from age to age!
> Thou hope of the people! [35]

Compared to Bob Dylan's "The times they are a-changing" this singer-narrator (*cantastorie*) is obviously better trained in philosophy and sociology, but he is turned much in the same direction. His arsenal of devices ranges from narrative interjection to the equivalent of operatic arias such as the one just quoted, and encompasses the stichomythic questions-and-answers he exchanges with his attendants and gnomic fixations of pantomimic events such as Grusha's seduction by the Child. With Grusha and Azdak, the Singer is the third, and perhaps central character of this rich tapestry in time and space: he too, besides being Arkadi Cheidze, is the New Theatre — a male plebeian Thalia, an open, liberating dramaturgy which has assimilated manifold devices of written and oral literature, spectacle and cinema, in order to present us with a useful and delightful lesson about our existence.

The basic tension between utopia and history, humanity and class alienation, results here in a vision of open history transmitted through open dramaturgic structures. I have discussed above how history can be open yet meaningful in a mature Marxist figuralism. The dramaturgy is open in a double sense. First of all, it openly shows its artificial nature, from the fact that it is an art-form consisting of scenic signs of reality and not reproducing it, right to the particular techniques used — beginning with the fact that a particular kind of people (actors) portray other "iconic" people (characters). Further, its structure is open toward the spectators' reality, in which such drama finds its culmination and resolution. It becomes a significant unity only by its effect on the spectators' reality, whose change it wants to help along by esthetic exemplarity. Based on a similarly grand sweep of historical and philosophical horizons as the medieval drama, the Brechtian one differs from it mainly in the imaginary ideal onlooker for whom it is written. In the Middle Ages, that ideal onlooker was he to whom all unfamiliar events were familiar because he saw their eternal essence through surface differences — i.e., God. For *CCC*, the ideal onlooker is he to whom all familiar events are unfamiliar because he looks for the unrealized potentialities in each historical stage of man's humanization — i.e., A Man prefiguring the ethics of a blassed classless Future. This ideal onlooker is both demanded and shaped by Brecht's play. Showing us an open drama correlative to open history, the play itself contributes to such opening.

NOTES

1. See Reinhold Grimm's excellent bibliographical handbook *Bertolt Brecht*, 3d ed. (Stuttgart: Metzler, 1971). A long select bibliography which I contributed to *Brecht*, ed. Erika Munk (New York: Bantam, 1972) indicates perhaps how conscious I am of trying to stand on the shoulders of other viewers of Brecht's opus, beginning with his own. Yet to total drowning in a sea of footnotes I have preferred the *terra firma* of concentrating on the text and the implicit performance, trusting that my use of insights by, say, Ernst Bloch, Hans Mayer, Reinhold Grimm, Hans J. Bunge, Bernard Dort or Albrecht Schoene is readily apparent. This essay was first presented as a lecture at Toronto University in 1970, and then as a paper in the Forum "Perspectives of Marxist Scholarship" on the margins of the 1972 MLA meeting. I am grateful to my colleagues Don Bouchard and Yehudy Lindeman from McGill University and David Stratman from Colby College for suggestions how to improve it. All quotations from *The Caucasian Chalk Circle* are from Eric Bentley's translation (New York: Grove, 1972), and will be indicated by page number in parenthesis.

2. See D. Suvin, "The Mirror and the Dynamo: On Brecht's Aesthetic Point of View", in *Brecht*, ed. Munk, op. cit. I have tried to examine a crucial phase of Brecht's arriving at such a stance in an essay on Brecht's *Saint Joan of the Slaughterhouses*, in print in *Brecht: Themes and Figures* ed. H. Knust and S. Mews (Chapel Hill: University of North Carolina Press).

3. Georg Lukacs's definition in *History and Class Consciousness* supplies a Marxist approach pertinent to this discussion: "The ultimate goal [*Endziel*] is rather that relation *to the totality* (to the whole of society seen as a process) through which every aspect of the struggle acquires its revolutionary significance. This relation *dwells within* every moment in its simple and sober ordinariness, but it only *becomes real by becoming conscious,* and . . . raises the moment of daily struggle to *reality* out of *mere factuality*" — *Geschichte und Klassenbewusstsein* (Berlin: Malik, 1923), pp. 36-37, trans. D. S. (see also the translation by Rodney Livingstone, London: Merlin, 1971). This opposition between factuality and an ontologically and axiologically more significant "reality" seems analogous to the

medieval opposition between *historia* and *figura*, just as the "ultimate aim" is analogous to the fulfillment which is the only real truth or *veritas* — see later discussions in this essay, and Auerbach's discussions in the work cited in note 3. An argument parallel to Lukacs's but better known to Brecht is in Karl Korsch, *Marxismus und Philosophie* (Leipzig, 1923; rptd. Frankfurt a.M.: Europaische Verlagsanstalt, 1966).

4. Erich Auerbach, "figura," *Scenes from the Drama of European Literature* (New York: Meridian, n.d.), p. 53; further quoted in text by page number in parenthesis.

5. Mazdak was a communist Zoroastrian heresiarch and leader of a plebeian revolt in 6th Century Iran — see Firdusi's epic *Shah-name*, also A. E. Christensen, *Le Regne du roi Kawadh I et le communisme Mazdakite* (Copenhagen, 1925), N. Pigulevskaia, *Goroda Irana v rannem srednevekov'e* (Moskva-Leningrad: AN SSSR, 1956), and on Mazdak's later influence Ziia Buniatov, *Azerbaidzhan v VIIIX vv.* (Baku, 1965), and Dzhamel Mustafaev, "Priroda sotsial'nykh utopii stran Blizhnego Vostoka", *Voprosy filosofii* No. 8 (1968), 115-24.

6. Brecht's note in *Materialien zu Brechts "Der kaukasische Kreide-kreis,"* ed. Werner Hecht (Frankfurt a.M.: Suhrkamp, 1966), p. 18, trans. D.S.

7. This essay was accepted for publication by *Clio* magazine.

18

Decolonization and Social Classes in *The Tragedy of King Christophe* by Aimé Césaire

Herve and *Nicole Fuyet, Guy* and *Mary Levilain*

> I write to help me take possession of myself.
> — Aimé Césaire

To write about *The Tragedy of King Christophe*[1] is a challenging task given Césaire's controversiality and the wide gap that exists between his world and ours. As did Diderot's Jacques le Fataliste, we hesitate to write about authors who are still living, as they are constantly changing. And Césaire is alive and well. His numerous literary, cultural and political activities prove it. He is also Black and we are not, although one of us is of American Indian ancestry and another of Vietnamese origin, our experience is not that of Césaire.

We will thus have to be very cautious in our analysis and constantly go back to the environment in which the play was written, as Cesaire often refers to ill known social and cultural forms and also because the context of the play is morally and historically very peculiar.

The two summers we spent in Martinique in 1968 and 1970 have helped us greatly; in particular meetings and discussions we had with Aimé Césaire, Edouard Glissant, with local intellectuals and politicians, and the invaluable contribution of the Martiniquese workers, humble "masters of the dew", who, without false folklore, added to our understanding of the beautiful and complex Caribbean soul.

We shall approach *The Tragedy of King Christophe* by adopting as a hypothesis Gorki's formula that any theatrical play is an artistic co-production.[2] For Gorki, a work of art contains a view of the world objectively existing and the subjective element brought by the author and the public. As we hold all literary texts to be fundamentally allusive, we shall try, in this case, to bring out the dimensions of the play as revealed by its constituent elements. Our analysis will not be positivist or determinist, but rather an attempt at a dialectical study. We hope to establish between these three elements the lines of interaction that will expose the richness of the play, particularly the historical and social structure, the character of Christophe and the relation between form and content.

The Tragedy of King Christophe is Césaire's second play. According to Raoul Bernabé, political leader, literary critic and professor of literature in Martinique, it is a step forward from Césaire's first play *Et les chiens se taisaient*: ". . . there is precisely between the two plays the gap that one finds between the work of a beginner and that of a mature author, between a cutting, biting work with only two characters of which the essential quality is the chant and the cry, and an elaborate work, truly dramatic, full of substance and of characters who speak and act. . . *The Tragedy of King Christophe* is part of history, especially that of Haiti, and takes place around a character, a crowd and a citadel, historical in all respects."[3]

As it would be impossible to speak of the French Revolution of 1789 without mentioning the class struggle between the decadent nobility and the rising bourgeoisie, so it would be unthinkable to study *The Tragedy of King Christophe* without exploring the role of the social forces at the time of Haiti's independence.

In the case of Haiti, such an analysis is even more necessary, since her history is not well known. With the first independence of Haiti in 1804, "power was in the hands of the feudal landlords who were divided in two camps, the clan of the 'former freemen', i.e. the freedmen of the colonial period, most of whom were 'mulattoes', former slaveowners for the most part, who understood that their demands for equality with the whites would never come about under the colonial regime and who finally allied themselves with the masses of former slaves to conquer independence; opposed to them were the clan of the feudal 'newly freemen' freed during the struggle, great leaders of the liberating army, and now big landowners. These two factions of the ruling classes fought to grab land left by fleeing or massacred French settlers and were opposed to a large distribution of the lands."[4]

Dessalines, liberator of Haiti, wanted to establish a society based on large property, privately and state owned, as well as on small peasant property, but he was murdered and a secession took place.

"Each clan was occupying a portion of the territory and as a result there were two states: a kingdom in the North led by Henry Christophe and a republic in the West and South led by Alexandre Pétion. There was never a real allocation of land. Part of the peasantry did not submit and took refuge in the mountains. . . Therefore, since independence, the feudal landlords have been opposed to the realization of deep social changes."[5] Unfortunately, today the situation has not changed. . .

We will mainly speak of the social structure of Christophe's monarchy as the play barely mentions Pétion's Republic. According to the opposition leader of the Republic, the two states were equally ridiculous: "Yes, gentlemen, there is one thing of which I am sure, of which we are all sure, to wit, that Christophe's monarchy is a caricature. But I am beginning to wonder whether we ourselves cut a better figure, whether this Republic of ours is not a caricature of a republic and our Parliament a caricature of a parliament."[p. 34]

The element of caricature characterizing these two regimes is more evident for us today than it was for the Haitians of the last century, especially for the poor agricultural workers crushed under the heel of the "Royal-Dahomets", forerunners of the "Tonton-Macoutes", gestapo of Papa Doc Duvalier.[6]

Césaire mentions many times in the play that Pétion's regime was composed of "mulattoes" and Christophe's of "negroes". It was the French, before independence, who divided to conquer. They created three social strata in Haiti: the white settlers, who had civil and political rights, the "mulattoes", who had only civil rights, and the "negroes", who had no rights at all. So, the conflict is not between a democratic bourgeois republic led by "mulattoes" and a "negro" kingdom, but between two feudal groups historically divided along racial lines and fighting to have land. Metellus, leader of the *jacquerie*, gives some indications of the feudal rivalry that is ruining the social revolution which embodies the aspirations of the rural proletariat:

> We were going to build a country all of us together!
> Not just to stake out this island!
> A country open to all the islands!
> To Black men everywhere. To Blacks of the whole world!
> But then came politicos

cutting the house in two
laying hands on our mother
disfiguring her in the eyes of the world
making her into a pitiful puppet.
Christophe! Pétion!
Double tyranny, I reject them both. . . [p. 30]

Metellus is executed shortly after and his plan of agrarian reforms dies with him. . . In another passage, a peasant in his field complains: ". . . when we threw the whites into the sea, it was to have this land for ourselves, not to slave for other people, even if they're as black as we are, but to have the land for ourselves like a wife." [p.48] We are somewhat aware of the deep social malaise, but unfortunately this is suggested by secondary characters whom Césaire seems to have thrown in for the sake of adding a folkloric flavor.

Regarding the vast promotion of labor, a statement by Christophe seems to be essential. The king is between life and death, he opens his eyes and says to his doctor: "Steward, I'm not fool enough to believe what my courtiers tell me. If I am King, it's not by the grace of God or the will of the people, but by the will and the grace of my two fists." [p. 80-81]

This confession enables us to understand better the objective meaning of this re-education campaign for the masses and also the lack of an enthusiastic response from the whole population. The theme of labor must be interpreted in relation to the nature of Christophe's power. This theme will in turn enable us to analyze the dynamics of the social structure of the kingdom. According to Christophe: "This people's enemy is its indolence, its effrontery, its hatred of discipline, its self-indulgence, its lethargy." [p. 18] Christophe sees only "Shit and dust!" [p. 36] He concludes that the material is to be reshaped.

Césaire, who sees himself as a Marxist, although he left the Communist Party in 1956, expresses through Christophe his belief in Engels' theory that labor creates man. In this vein Christophe declares: "That's what I want to be, the builder of this people." [p. 44] With this goal in mind he will bend his people under the yoke of hard labor: "And that's why I have to ask more of blacks than of other people, more faith, more enthusiasm." [p. 42]*

The notion of a common suffering of Black peoples in history, one of the fundamental elements of the concept of *négritude* is linked by

---

*Manheim does not capitalize the word Black.

Christophe to the notion of the regenerative value of labor. But isn't *negritude*, which strengthened the struggle against white colonialism, anachronistic here in a context of decolonization? True decolonization necessitates the abolition of economic and social structures built under colonialism to serve exclusively the interests of the "mother country" and to divide the enslaved nation. Decolonization necessitates a total revolutionary change in the regime such as the steps being taken in the liberated countries which are building socialism. And decolonization does not mean a simple shift of power, an "Africanization" of the ruling class that would leave unchanged a structure serving the interests of the local elite and neo-colonialism.

Christophe's exhortation is addressed to all Black people, but in fact applies only to the peasants who do not own any land and are forced to work for the feudal landlords. Instead of regenerative labor we have in fact an alienating one which mortifies body and soul. Consequently, "the path of freedom and slavery are identical" [p. 53], as a Lady of Christophe's court says. Hence, Christophe's surprising proclamation:

"Article 1: All overseers and farm workers are under obligation to perform their duties with the same exactitude, obedience, and willingness as the members of the armed forces.

Article 2: All overseers and farm workers who do not scrupulously perform their agricultural duties will be apprehended and punished with the same severity as soldiers who fall short of their duties.

Article 3: . . . freedom cannot endure without labor." [p. 49]

So we may ask "Whose work?", "Whose freedom?" We realize that Christophe attempts to mask a class struggle by posing the problem in terms of color and *négritude*. In the same way today, the Duvalier dictatorship uses this idea of *négritude* to try to convince us that this reactionary regime is conforming to "ancestral traditions" and "Black nature". In this perspective, we can understand the criticisms of *négritude* raised by Boukman and Memmi, who consider the concept obsolete, sterile and mystifying after national independence. Boukman stated in 1966 that "One does not serve African culture by clinging like an oyster to notions historically obsolete. The concept of *négritude*, revolutionary between 1940 and 1950, is good today for the museum of literature."[7] In the same vein, Memmi wrote: "The tom-tom of Cesario-Senghorian negritude sounds like a cracked pan."[8]

This analysis should be carried further by using Hegel's master-slave couple, which represents the two stages of consciousness. In the first stage, the master will use the slave as an extension of his own body to transform nature through labor. Therefore, the master only relates with nature through an intermediary, through the mediation of the slave, and loses any direct relationship with nature. He does not change nature any more through his own labor to give it a form that will satisfy his needs, all he does is enjoy it, without any transformations of his own, as an animal would do. The development of the master's consciousness is stopped at this point. "The great way of man's development is through the consciousness of the slave."9

The slave's choice to live is the first phase of liberation. Labor will be the second phase of this liberation. By confronting the object, the slave explores its structure and his labor is the origin of all science. In the play we see that the King's body is paralyzed: "You will be my limbs, since nature denies me the use of my own. Me, the head, I swore to build the nation . . . with obedience for its plumbline, the Kingdom will endure by our power." [p. 82] We know that Christophe is doomed to failure, while there is a birth of political consciousness among the peasants. This rising consciousness, in spite of oppression, enables the peasants to become part of a dynamic force which will one day challenge the system.

Christophe expresses the humanism of *négritude* which is Césaire's concept, at least the Césaire of *Return to my Native Land*, but at the same time, Christophe by his actions, and also the peasants, negate its progressive character in the context of decolonization. Christophe becomes unable to move, while we see that the peasantry, though a victim, is a force of transformation and creation.

The other elements of this Haitian society are the feudal lords, who elected their king and then betrayed him, a newly created nobility, courtiers and the Catholic Church, the natural ally of feudal regimes.

Our analysis of the historic and social structure in the play places King Christophe in the position of exploiter of the people. But does such an interpretation make the play meaningless? Menil sees Christophe differently: "Christophe's romanticism? Generosity and passion mobilize him at all times, at each breath, for the good of his nation in a stormy climate of rage and fire. Is there anything Christophe would not do to give his people a strong state, a new dignity, a new soul? His enthusiasm is a fire ready to devour everything, and which changes each defeat into a new reason to fight for the pride of the race."10

We believe that these two points of view, far from contradicting each other, are complementary and together constitute the key to Christophe's character.

"Yes, Christophe was King. King like Louis XIII, Louis XIV, Louis XV and a few others", says the commentator at the beginning of the play.

[p.9] We must note that Césaire chose to compare Christophe to the Kings of France who created the concept of absolute monarchy of divine right and not someone like Hugues Capet, who was only the leader among the feudal lords who elected him. "I am the State", declared Louis XIV, "I am democracy", dared to say Duvalier. Christophe is more poetic: "I clench the fist of my race, yesterday enslaved! I clench! Our fists!" [p. 28]. We are here at the beginning of the play and we believe in Christophe's good faith. He conceives of the growth of his race in the framework of a nation: ". . . something that will enable this transplanted people to strike roots, to burgeon and flower, to fling the fruits and perfumes of this flowering into the face of the world . . ." [p. 13]

Such is Christophe at the beginning of the play but praxis will change him. Through a dialectical process of multiple interaction, Christophe acts on events which show him all the romanticism of his venture and the fundamental exploitative character of his regime. The creation of a nobility which was to establish the prestige of the kingdom only creates a class of parasites. The Church crowned Christophe (as it crowned Napoleon who also created a nobility) and plays the same reactionary role which it is still playing in Haiti today. Christophe crushes peasants revolts such as the one led by Metellus and maintains "law and order" in the kingdom. He establishes a very blunt code of labor, a parody of justice, but at the same time, he becomes aware of some fundamental problems: "It's time to teach those niggers a lesson who think the revolution means taking the place of white men and behaving the same way." [p. 56] But this attempt at self-criticism is too little and too late. His people get tired and do not follow him any more. Peasants, members of the royal family, senators and dignitaries all say "enough" to the king. Christophe is more and more isolated from his people. Madame Christophe foresees intuitively what will happen: " . . . if only the day does not come when the misery of the children tells the story of a father's immoderation. Our children, Christophe, think of our children. Oh God! How will it end?" [p. 41] It is only when Christophe is the victim of an attack of paralysis that he becomes fully conscious of the fact that he is king only by the grace of his fists and he wishes then "the swift cleaver of death" [p. 81]. The feudal lords abandon him. Fully aware of his failure, Christophe commits suicide, demanding that he be buried upright.

We feel that it is in this sense that the realism of the play is inseparable from Christophe's romanticism. The generosity of his initial project, his growing solitude, the increasing awareness he has of his failure make Christophe a very romantic and sympathetic character, even though his objective actions, in a reality understood too late, are of a reactionary nature.

Jaspers wrote: "The manner in which man experiences failure determines what he will become".[11] Christophe dies standing upright and Vastey addressing the King says:

> And here you are again a king erect
> holding your own memorial tablet over the abyss.
> O fragile-hearted stars
> born of the pyre of Ethiopian Memnon
> O pollen-swarming birds
> fashion for him imperishable arms:
> on azure field red phoenix crowned with gold. [pp. 95-96].

We see here the birth of a real myth of Christophe. Is this the message of the play? It is not sure. According to Sartre: "it is the conjoined effort of the author and the reader that will bring about this concrete and imaginary object, the work of the mind".[12] It seems doubtful that *The Tragedy of King Christophe* will lead the public to the same conclusions we have reached in this analysis.

It should be noted that this play premiered in Salzburg, Austria in August 1964, before a white public not generally familiar with Haitian history. The play has also been performed before Black audiences as at Dakar Festival where, as Césaire told us, it was particularly enjoyed by the common people. But, whether the public is Black or white, we believe Césaire should not have limited himself to allusions. He should have been more explicit in order to reveal the true tragic message of the play, beyond the historical setting and the romantic drama.

It seems that, if the author had shown Haiti through the viewpoint of the class struggle instead of comparing the rivalry between Christophe and Pétion to a cock-fight, it would have been easier to understand the solitude of Christophe, his relationship to his people and even the creation of a nobility.

It is also hardly possible for a spectator who has a limited knowledge of Haitian history to understand, on the basis of the elements given in the play, that the opposition between "mulattoes" and "negroes" is fundamentally an opposition between feudal lords, historically divided by French settlers along racial lines. The average spectator will rather see a rivalry which is not only racial, but also motivated by pre-existing racism. As for the peasants, who express the growing dissatisfaction of the masses, they are secondary characters, more or less blended in the Haitian landscape.

Women also are secondary, nameless characters, whether they are market women, ladies of the court or women working at the Citadel. The sole exception is Madame Christophe, who, it is true, is the only character in the play to have perceived the real essence of the tragedy.

On the other hand, a great portion of the play deals with the relations between the feudal lords, especially with the creation of the nobility and with the clergy. The ridiculous aspects are emphasized to the detriment of the harsh ones. We do not think that the peasants, who had to deal with the Royal-Dahomets, ancestors of the Tonton-Macoutes, particularly appreciated the comical character of the new regime. We have not insisted much on this side of Christophe's Haitian society, as it is omnipresent in the play, but the white public of today is sensitive to it. Communication between the writer and his public therefore tends to be on a superficial level. As for the "substantive marrow" of the play, it is like a message of a shipwrecked sailor floating in a bottle. Not only does Césaire offer no solution, but he does not define the problem clearly. Let us refer to the interview he granted us in August 1970.

In our conversation, Césaire told us he left the form of the poem for the play in order to reach the "people in the streets". He stated that he is now writing for the people of the Antilles, for Black people in general, but also to "gain possession of himself".[13] We could therefore say that in *The Tragedy of King Christophe,* Césaire does not convey any message, because he has not found a solution to the problem. He has not written a problematic play because he has not yet defined the problem. In fact, we are dealing with a search, a public quest before an audience that is not of his choosing. All this leads to an aborted communication; and it is possible to say that in some of its dimensions the play has only a virtual existence.

How could it be otherwise, when the author himself is committed as a politician to the tumultuous process of decolonization, when he addresses himself to a public, either part of the neo-colonialist world, or part of those who also search for the path of disalienation. As Goldmann once said: "All great literary and poetic works are a social product and can be apprehended in their dialectical unity only on the basis of historical reality."[14]

The relation between Césaire and his epoch, Césaire and his work, is quite complex. Certain elements of his work and of his life, certain structures common to both, should be stressed. We should not forget that Césaire is a socialist, founder of the *Parti Progressiste Martiniquais* (PPM), elected representative of Martinique to the French National Assembly and mayor of Fort-de-France.

In literature, Césaire moved away from surrealism. In politics, he left the French Communist Party in 1956. Putting the future of Martinique not only in the Caribbean community, but also in Pan-Africanism, he seems to share Fanon's views and believes in an "active African solidarity", political form of the concept of *négritude*.[15] According to his new political way of thinking, Césaire substitutes the notion of class with that of "global people", thus trying to analyze political and economical questions in terms of race rather than of class. This heritage of *négritude* is, as we have mentioned earlier, anachronistic in the context of decolonization. If, racially united for the expressed purpose of overthrowing colonialism, the "global people" were able to accomplish this goal, it would rapidly disintegrate, exposing the reality of social classes and their conflicts of interests. Today, in Martinique colonialism has been partially replaced by neo-colonialism.

After an initial success in the late 50's, primarily due to his anti-communist policy, Césaire had to come to grips with his own contradictions. The government, the big *béké* bourgeoisie and the Church supported the PPM in its campaign against the Communist Party of Martinique (CPM), but these same allies showed some reservations and open hostility when the PPM dared to challenge the political leaders who endorsed the colonial policy. Having promoted a fusion of all classes without first defining the terms of this solidarity, Césaire had not forseen that the "anti-colonialism" of his allies was limited. The civil servants and the petty-bourgeoisie, his last allies, eventually withdrew their support to become Gaullists, and Cesaire found himself neutralized and isolated from the masses.

Today, Césaire has analyzed his socialism and measured the extent of his historical error, which was based on such a conception of *negritude* that it went beyond the limits of the cultural sphere to politics.

One hears in Martinique that Christophe is Césaire; this is only partially true. It is rather the whole play that would be a Cesairian psychodrama. Like Christophe, Césaire is aware of his failure but only partially of what caused it. Moreover, we should ask, regarding Césaire's play, the question asked by Goldmann about the theater of Jean Genet: "Is it simply an individual perspective or, as it is the case for most literary masterpieces, a vision of the world of a social group, elaborated partly consciously, partly unconsciously to such a degree of coherence that it offers the poet structured categories that will be the foundation of his literary transposition"?[16]

We could say that *The Tragedy of King Christophe* is the tragedy of the petty-bourgeoisie of Martinique, for, in literary criticism or in litera-ture, as Aragon said bluntly "ideas never come from one man, but from a group of men . . . soul is to be replaced by social class."[17]

We have tried to determine what Marxist critics call "the intention of the play". According to Lukacs: "it is the view of the world, the ideology or *Weltanschauung* underlying a writer's work that counts. And it is the writer's attempt to reproduce this view of the world which constitutes his 'intention' and is the formative principle underlying the style of a given piece of writing. Looked at this way, style ceases to be a formalistic category. Rather it is rooted in the content; it is the specific form of a specific content."[18]

What is the bond between form and content in *The Tragedy of King Christophe*? It is a quite complex analysis given the "bastardized" inten-tion of the play. There is a romantic overtone, at least with respect to the main protagonist, Christophe, who himself represents an aspect of Césaire. With romanticism, the writer loses more and more interest in the object, and conversely the subject, the ego, assumes an ever growing importance. The work of art is aimed less at explaining the world than at expressing and embodying the dreams of the artist. Surrealism is also an evasion. Andre Breton tried to counter the oppressive and crushing world of his youth with a burning desire for marvel: "Neither the priorities nor the values of this world could be ours . . . We countered them with love, poetry and freedom."[19]

Romanticism tends to reduce the outside world to folkloric elements, while surrealistic individualism demands a complete break from the yoke of "barbarians" with its oppressive categories: space, time and concrete goals. Christophe indeed occupies the scene for the most part of the play, and he is always preoccupied with himself. To use Sartre's distinction, he would rather be a pessimistic hero using a cause than a militant who serves it. "When you see an arrow that's not going to miss you, throw out your chest and meet it head on." [p. 88] His world outlook is not all-encompassing; the emphasis is rather on local folklore.

The play starts with a cock fight; we see a market scene; rum, the national beverage, is praised. The use of proverbs provides an additional local touch: "You'll always find flies in the ointment if you look too closely" [p. 11], or "When you teach a monkey to throw stones, there's a good chance he'll pick one up and bash your head in" [p. 13]. Christophe often uses very colorful expressions: "If it's a bitter crab-apple to you, why would it be a juicy pear to me?" [p. 12].

We may add to this, buffoonish jokes and popular puns: Pétion is a "drag ass" [p. 17]; the king is a lecher, yet he admonishes his subjects not to run around "with their flies open" [p. 57]; Hugonin, speaking of feathers, says:"it's better to have them on your head than sticking out of your ass" [p. 71]. The creation of the court is also full of clownish and folkloric details. It should be noted here that the language and the customs are not linked to the plot, but constitute only a setting for Christophe.

Time is treated in a surrealistic way. There is an ever-present revolutionary urgency. Christophe is impatient when faced with the slowness of the peasants: "Time! Time! But how can we wait when time is holding a knife to our throat?" [p. 40]. For him "either we smash everything, or we put the country on its feet." [p. 59].

The Citadel Christophe want to build is revealing: "Exactly. This people has to want, to gain, to achieve something. Against fate, against history, against nature. That's it . . . The Citadel, the freedom of a whole people." [p. 44] At the end of this magnificent passage, Christophe is spellbound and, seeing the Citadel, he shouts: "Let my people, my Black people, salute the tide smell of the future" [p. 45]. This Citadel, the construction of which is out of context in time and reality, symbolizes the "extreme point" of Césaire when, as Breton said, the real and the imaginary, the past and the future, cease to be perceived in a contradictory way. Christophe wants his Citadel at once, like the magician or the child. He does not back up before nature and he is ready to challenge her when she gets in his way: "Let the great horn answer the thunder with cannon, thunder to thunder, face to face. Strike the cymbals. Answer lightning with lightning. Blow the visceral conch. We'll answer blind violence with the controlled violence of our lungs" [p. 70]. And Christophe challenges the heavens with his sword . . .

There is an apocalyptic atmosphere in the play, a burning desire for metamorphosis which does not conform to revolutionary action. The dying Christophe calls to mother Africa for help, but only to "go home"; the king knows a lonely death.

Césaire's concept of *négritude*, his Pan-Africanism, differs greatly from that of Jacques Roumain, the internationalist, who identifies not only with Africa but with all the wretched of the earth.

Can we say that *The Tragedy of King Christophe* gives us a pessimistic point of view? We do not believe so, for if Christophe's death is the failure of a character, it is also the birth of a myth. For Christophe, literally, *natura facit saltus*.

As with the characters of *No Exit*, Christophe *is* only when the moment of truth gives a meaning to his life; having chosen to die willingly after becoming conscious of his failure, he *lives* and bears witness. First a blind and deaf agent of mysteries, Christophe, in freely *choosing* to die (in the Sartrian sense of the word), identifies himself with his destiny. Although harmful when alive, by his suicide he has heroically embodied the myth of the failure characteristic of revolutionary petty-bourgeois romanticism.

Because of its social origin, we believe that Césaire's public does not generally see the play from our point of view. Because it is ill-informed about the history of Haiti, unaware of the problems of decolonization and unable to take a class approach when analyzing social problems, the general public establishes only a superficial level of communication with the author.

Césaire does not have an ideologically enlightened public in the West as yet, although experiments in popular theater in France and in Martinique as well have produced encouraging results. As Gorki said, literature is always the end result of an epoch, a country, a class; it is to society what consciousness is to the individual. With the birth of a new public in the West whose class origin and class position does not tend to a literature of evasion, the divorce between literature and reality will disappear. Only then will we have a demystified public, enlightened by the knowledge acquired in confronting political and social questions, capable of discerning the meaning of a play like *The Tragedy of King Christophe*.

Sartre saw clearly what the core of such a public to come will be when he wrote: "The proletariat is made of men, just and unjust, who may get lost and be often mystified. But one must not hesitate to say that the future of literature is linked with the future of the working class."[20]

NOTES

1. This study is based on Aimé Césaire, *La Tragedie du Roi Christophe*, Presence Africaine, Paris 1963. We use the English translation *The Tragedy of King Christophe* by Ralph Manheim, Grove Press 1970, when we quote passages from the play.

2. Quoted by A. Kharchev, "Aesthetics and Morality", *Art and Society*, Moscow 1968, p. 96.

3. Raoul Bernabé, "La Tragédie du Roi Christophe d'Aimé Césaire", *Action*, Martinique (september 1964), p. 88.

4. Roger Tilandique, "La Dictature duvaliériste et le peuple haitien", *Action*, Martinique (september 1964), p. 56.

5. idem, p. 57.

6. In Haiti today, the per capita income is under $70 a year. The Catholic Church controls education and 80% of the population is illiterate. Out of a population of 4.5 million, the regime has an army of 5500 men and a secret police (Tonton-Macoutes) of 25,000. Since the death of Francois Duvalier (April 23, 1971), the U.S. Navy has established the blocade of Haiti to prevent any attempt to restore democracy and endanger the Duvalier dynasty perpetuated by Jean-Claude Duvalier, a nineteen year old playboy. The State is responsible for the "trade of blood and corpses" in Haiti: blood is bought for $1 a pint from the poor peasants and sold to the U.S. for $17. The bodies of indigents are sold to the U.S. for $350 each.

7. Boukman, "A propos du Festival des Arts Nègres de Dakar", *Partisan* (Paris, mai-juin 1966), p. 120.

8. A. Memmi, *L'Homme dominé*, (NRF 1968), p. 42

9. R. Garaudy, *Hegel*, (Bordas 1966), p. 55.

10. R. Menil, "Le Romanesque et le realismé dans la *Tragédie du Roi Christophe*", *Action*, Martinique (janvier 1965), p. 52.

11. K. Jaspers, *Introduction à la philosophie*, Coll.10/18 (Paris 1965), p. 21.

12. J.-P. Sartre, *Qu'est-ce que la littérature?* (NRF, Idees, 1966), p. 55

13. Interview with Aimé Césaire, Fort-de-France, August 11, 1970.

14. Lucien Goldmann, "Le Théatre de Genet", *Cahiers Renaud-Barrault* (novembre 1966), p. 115.

15. The expression is by Patrice Lumumba.

16. L. Goldmann, *ibid.*, p. 115.

17. Louis Aragon, *Victor Hugo, poète réaliste*, Editions Sociales 1952, p. 29.

18. G. Lukacs, *Realism in our time*, (New York: Harper and Row, 1962), p. 19.

19. A. Breton, *Entretiens*, (Gallimard, 1952), p. 92.

20. J.-P. Sartre, *op. cit.*, p. 305.

CONTRIBUTORS' NOTES

LEE BAXANDALL compiled and edited the highly regarded volume *Marxism and Aesthetics: A Bibliography* (1968). He has published many critical and historical essays on literature, art, theater, and aesthetic inquiry, in journals such as *The Drama Review, Encore, Journal of Aesthetics and Art Criticism, Temps Modernes, Partisan Review,* and *Studies on the Left,* the pioneer theory organ of the New Left, on which he served as an editor. Mr. Baxandall's theater pieces have been performed at La Mama and elsewhere. He has also translated plays by Bertolt Brecht and Peter Weiss. He has recently edited *Radical Perspectives in the Arts,* a collection of theoretical and critical essays on literature, and co-edited *Marx and Engels on Literature and Art,* which brings together the fundamental texts scattered throughout the works of the founders, concerning their views on matters of artistic value.

SHEILA DELANY received her B. A. from Wellesley College and her Ph. D. in English and Comparative Literature from Columbia University. She has taught at Queen's College and now teaches at Simon Fraser University in Canada. She is the editor of *Counter-Tradition: A Reader in the Literature of Dissent and Alternatives* (Basic Books, New York, 1971) and the author of *Chaucer's House of Fame: The Poetics of Skeptical Fideism* (University of Chicago Press, 1972). Ms. Delany has published in numerous professional journals on medieval literature, and most recently in *Science and Society.* She has written political and literary reviews and articles on various topics, e.g. on Rosa Luxemburg, science fiction, and Salinger.

SIDNEY FINKELSTEIN (1909-1974), the eminent Marxist scholar and critic of music, painting, and literature will be missed by all those who had the good fortune of working with him. His best-known works are *Composer and Nation, Art and Society, Jazz: A People's Music,* and, most recently, *Who Needs Shakespeare?.* Two art books, one on the young Picasso and the other on the black painter Charles White, have recently appeared in the GDR. The essay "Beauty and Truth," which he wrote for this volume two years ago, is thus the fruit of a life-time of reflection on human creativity. He was one of the founders of the American Institute for Marxist Studies.

H. BRUCE FRANKLIN is a graduate of Amherst College (1955) and holds a Ph.D from Stanford University. He has taught at Stanford, Johns Hopkins University and was a lecturer at the Free University of Paris in 1967. He is the author of several works, among them: *The Wake of the Gods: Melville's Mythology, Future Perfect: American Science Fiction of the Nineteenth Century, Back Where You Came From,* and two works which are forthcoming: *Red, White, and Other Colors: Communism vs. Capitalism in Russian and Anglo-American Science Fiction,* and *The Victim as Criminal and Artist* which will include his essay on Melville. He has published many articles, worked on several films, and participated in a variety of forums devoted to political and cultural questions. He is now Professor of English and American Literature at Rutgers University, Newark New Jersey.

HERVE FUYET was born in Paris, France. He studied at the Sorbonne and at the University of Montreal where he obtained his Ph. D. in 1966. He conducted research in Africa, in Martinique, Yugoslavia, and the Soviet Union. He has written and lectured on Marxism and on literary criticism on campuses in Europe, Canada, and the United States, and is presently teaching at Saint Cloud State College, Minnesota.

NICOLE FUYET was born in Montreal of French Canadian and Indian background. She studied in French Canada, the United States, and Martinique, and is currently doing journalistic work.

LOUIS HARAP holds a B. A. and a Ph. D. from Harvard University and was librarian of the Library of Philosophy and Psychology there until 1939. He was managing editor of *Jewish Survey* until 1942 and *Jewish Life* until 1957 and has published numerous articles and reviews in both journals, as well as in *Jewish Currents,* of which he is presently an editor. Mr. Harap served as the librarian of the New Lincoln School in New York from 1960-1969 and is presently retired and living in Vermont. He is the author of *Social Roots of the Arts* and the forthcoming *Image of the Jew in American Literature.*

FREDRIC JAMESON is a professor of literature at the University of California at San Diego. He is the author of *Marxism and Form: Twentieth-Century Dialectical Theories of Literature* and *The Prison-House of Language: A Critical Account of Structuralism and Russian Formalism.* He has also published essays in many distinguished journals.

GAYLORD C. LeROY is a professor of English at Temple University. He is the author of *Perplexed Prophets,* a study of Victorian literature, and a co-editor (with Ursula Beitz) of *Preserve and Create: Essays in Marxist Literary Criticism.* He is a member of the American Institute for Marxist Studies and the Committee for Marxist Education.

GUY LEVILAIN was born in Hanoi, Vietnam. He was educated in Vietnam, France, and the United States. He knew colonialist oppression at first hand. This led him to take a deep interest in Black literature of Africa and the Caribbean. He has taught Afro-French writers at the Saint Cloud Reformatory, Antioch (Minneapolis) Communiversity, and Saint Cloud State College. He has lectured extensively on the Vietnam War and national liberation movements. Mr. Levilain's interest in Black culture includes music, as well as literature. He is a jazz trombonist and has performed with leading Black musicians in France, Canada, and the United States.

MARY C. LEVILAIN, born in Saint Cloud, Minnesota, has an interest in reading and writing poetry.

LILLIAN S. ROBINSON is a graduate of Brown University, where she received a B. A. and an M. A. in English. She did M. A. work in art history at the N. Y. U. Institute of Fine Arts before earning a Ph. D. in Comparative Literature at Columbia University. Her publications include several essays in cultural theory from a Marxist and feminist perspective, and she has lectured widely on literature, women's studies, and mass culture. She has been active in the women's liberation movement, as well as in New Left and post-New Left Marxist organizations. During her current leave of absence from SUNY/Buffalo, where she is an assistant professor of American Studies, she is writing a book about television and putting together a collection of her poems called *Good Politics.*

ANNETTE T. RUBINSTEIN taught philosophy at New York University for some years, and then served first as chairman of the English Department and later as principal of the Robert Louis Stevenson School in Manhattan until forced to leave the shool system because of her active opposition to the Korean War. After half a dozen transcontinental university lecture tours in Canada and the United States, she spent several years as visiting professor and guest lecturer in Czechoslovakia, the German Democratic Republic, Hungary, Poland, and the Soviet Union. Her published works include *Realistic Ethics, The Great Tradition in English Literature: From Shakespeare to Shaw, I Vote My Conscience* (editor), and *Schools Against Children* (editor). She is at present an editor of *Science and Society*, an independent Marxist quarterly, and on the advisory board of *Jewish Currents*, a radical monthly magazine. She is now completing a critical history tentatively entitled *American, Not English, Literature,* which has been frequently interrupted by time off to write and use such agitational pamphlets as "The Not-So-Strange Case of the Harlem 6," "The Black Panther Party and the Case of the New York 21," and "Suicide on Rikers Island — A Cry for Help!"

LINDA RUDICH has a B. A. from Hunter College and an M. A. T. from Wesleyan University. She has been writing a book on Balzac in French for many years. Future chapters have been published in such eminent French journals as *La Pensee* and *L'Annee Balzacienne*.

NORMAN RUDICH, the editor of the present volume, is a professor of letters and Romance languages at Wesleyan University, where he has taught French and comparative literature for many years in the Romance Language Department and the College of Letters, an interdisciplinary program of literary studies. He has published various articles and essays on Marxist literary theory, the early writings of Diderot, Baudelaire, and Wittgenstein. He was chariman of the literary discussion group of the American Institute for Marxist Studies, of which he is a board member, and of the first Marxist Forum of the Modern Language Association, sponsored by the Radical Caucus.

E. SAN JUAN, JR. was born in Manila, in the Philippines and received his B. A. from the University of the Philippines and his M. A. and Ph. D. from Harvard University. He has taught at Harvard, the University of California, and now gives courses in Third World literature at the University of Connecticut at Storrs. Among his recent works are *The Radical Tradition in Philippine Literature* and *Carlos Bulosan and the Imagination of the Class Struggle*. He has also edited *Marxism and Human Liberation*, a selection of Georg Lukacs' writings, and *Introduction to Modern Philippino Literature*. He is at present completing a book on Mao Tsetung's poetics.

PAUL SIEGEL holds a Ph. D. from Harvard University and has taught at the University of Connecticut, City College of New York, Ripon College, and Long Island University. He is the author of *Shakespearean Tragedy and the Elizabethan Compromise* and *Shakespeare in His Time and Ours* and the editor of *His Infinite Variety: Major Shakespearean Criticism Since Johnson* and *Leon Trotsky on Literature and Art*. He has published scores of articles and has contributed to many international Shakespeare conferences. He is at present working on a book on the theme of revolution in the modern novel.

DAVID STRATMAN took a degree in Classical Languages from Xavier University in 1966 and a Ph. D. in English from the University of North Carolina, where he studied on an NDEA Fellowship, in 1969. After four years as an assistant professor of English at Colby College, he moved to Boston where he plans to attend law school.

DARKO R. SUVIN was born and educated in Zagreb, Yugoslavia. In addition, he studied at the University of Bristol, England, and at the Sorbonne. He holds a Ph. D. from Zagreb University and has taught there, as well as at the University of Massachusetts and the University of Indiana as a visiting lecturer. He has been active in organizing student theater in Zagreb and Zurich, Switzerland and has participated in a number of conferences on science fiction.

He is presently an associate professor of English at McGill University in Montreal. He is the author of several works in Serbo-Croatian on Krleza, Brecht, science fiction, utopias, and the theater, and many more in English, among them: *Other Worlds, Other Seas: Science Fiction from Socialist Countries* and *Russian Science Fiction Literature and Criticism 1956-1970: A Bibliography.* He has also published numerous articles on drama.

FRED WHITEHEAD is a native of Kansas and comes from a railroad and farming family. He studied at the University of Kansas, University College in London, and Columbia University, from which he received his Ph. D. in 1972. He now works as a welder in Kansas. He is also at work on a comprehensive study of Blake's epics.

STEPHEN ZELNICK received his B. A. from Temple University in 1963. He went to the University of Illinois on a University Felllowship and received his Ph. D. in 1969. He is now an assistant professor at Temple University teaching courses in Marxism and literature and in Victorian Studies. He has co-authored a pamphlet, "The Closed Classroom," sponsored by the Radical Caucus of the Modern Language Association. He is currently doing work on the question of social class in Charlotte Bronte's *Villette.* He has served as director of the Thomas Nabried Center for Marxist-Leninist Education in Philadelphia. He has also delivered papers on Literature and Revolution, Drugs and Capitalism, Normal Mailer, and Thomas Carlyle.

ACKNOWLEDGMENTS

My first thanks must go to the Louis M. Rabinowitz Foundation which twice (1963 and 1966-67) generously supported my growing interest in the Marxist theory of literature. The background studies, thinking, and writing, which these grants permitted me to carry out in the United States and Europe, gave the indispensable first impulse to the activities leading to the present publication. An expression of appreciation is also due Wesleyan University for its enlightened support of research through regular grants to its faculty and a sound sabbatical policy. In addition, Wesleyan has always responded with generous understanding to the special costs entailed by my research.

The discussion group sponsored by the American Institute for Marxist Studies made it clear that the time was ripe for American Marxist literary thought to make itself heard more coherently, concertedly, and aggressively in the confused cultural strife of the 60's. The first idea for this book arose from those discussions and was projected as an AIMS volume. The formation of the Marxist Forum of the Modern Language Association under the aegis of the Radical Caucus in the early 70's decisively broadened our perspectives, both in theoretical and practical criticism, by giving voice to many ideological tendencies representing the Marxist approach and method of analysis and evaluation of literature. Special thanks to Alan Weiss, Julius Buchwald, and H. Black.

Individual acknowledgments are of course too numerous to mention. Here are a few: to my patient contributors, some of whose manuscripts were submitted as long ago as 1969, and who then had to bear with the errors of an inexperienced editor; to my readers, research assistants, and friends, in particular Anne Vinnicombe, Vinod Busjeet, Susan Petersen, Carl Lesnor, Hugh and Laura Aitken, Lyn Thurber, Josette Sayers, and Richard Gilberg; to my Wesleyan colleagues for their indispensable intellectual challenge, especially Manfred Stassen, but also Victor Gourevitch, Hayden White, Stephen Crites, David Konstan, Richard Vann, Paul Schwaber, Howard Needler, Edward Zlotkowski, and Jan Miel; to the Wesleyan College of Letters because its interdisciplinary philosophy of education, experimental boldness, international perspectives, and independent students have made teaching, learning, and writing a rewarding way of life. Thanks also to Linda Rudich, whose Balzacian labors have importantly contributed to my understanding of literature. Finally, I wish to express my loving gratitude to Linda, Steven, and Suzanne Rudich, who have borne with an extraordinary good will the physical and mental absences of their ambulatory *political-scholar-pater-familias*.

INDEX

academic: gentlemen, 306; literary establishment, 287
academicism, 52
Achebe, Chinua, 155
Adamic, Louis, 78
Adams, Henry, 86, 88
Adorno, T.W., 47
aesthetes, 151
aesthetic: creation, 21, 25; production, 22; value of, 22, 25
Africanization, 363
Agee, James, 78; *Let Us Now Praise Famous Men*, 77, 79
alienating: labor, 363; social relations, 149
alienation, 68, 69, 72, 124, 126, 132, 152; industry, 251; urban, 130
allegory, 347, 354
ambiguity, of works of art, 120, 122
American: Dream, 330; P. E. N. (Poets, Essayists, Novelists), 154; Revolution, 306
Anabaptists, 350
Anatomy of Criticism, The, see Frye, Northrup
Anderson, Sherwood, 77, 78
anti-hero, 277
appearance, 95
Aragon, Louis, 25
architecture, 123, 124
archetypal criticism, 98
archetype of the new capitalist, 254
Aristotle, 64, 196, 197
Arnold, Matthew, 83; tradition, 36
art: and beauty, 54, 58; and labor, 22; and material production, 140; and politics, science, 22; and the individual, 23; as property, 149; as social performance, 156; as such, 52, 57, 58; imitates life, 60; of late capitalism, 25; of modern era, 24; pictorial, 78; pour l'art, 17, 52, 57, 58, 148; the task of, 25

artist: 261; as the Elect, 151; in undeveloped countries, 147
artistic: heritage, 120, 126; tradition, 120, 122; values, 119, 120
"atomized society", 154
Auerbach, Eric, 33, 347, 348, 351
Augustine, Saint, 347
Austen, Jane, 314, 315, 318, 320, 322
Azerbaidjan, 351

Bakhtin, Mikhail, 49
Baldwin, James, 78
Ball, John, 199
Balzac, Honore de, 24, 26, 93, 123, 243-265, 315; concept of Revolt, 263; critique of bourgeois relations, 246, 248; energetique, 248; social observations, 253, 256;
  works: *Ceux qui Dispariassment a Paris*, 243; *Comede Humaine*, 243, 245, 249, 252, 263; *Eugenie Grandet*, 252; *La Peau de chagrin*, 245, 257; *Le Cabinet Antiques*, 251; *Le Cure de Village*, 254; *Le Lysdans la vallie*, 254, 256, 257; *Le Medecin de Campagne*, 254; *Le Pere Goriot*, 250, 252, 256, 263, 264; *Les Paysans*, 256; *Splendeurs et Miseres de Courtisanes*, 262, 264
Bartok, Bela, 73
Baudelaire, Charles, *Mon Couer Mis a Nu*, 280
Baxandall, Lee, 90, 119-131
beatnik, 89
Beautiful and Damned, The, 333
beauty: and truth, 51; laws of, 51, 52, 57; perception of, 57
Beckett, Samuel, 153; *Waiting for Godot*, 90
Beer, J. B., 224, 225, 234-237; *Coleridge the Visionary*, 218
Beethoven, Ludwig von, 64, 121

THE SAN FRANCISCO MIME TROUPE:
The First 10 Years
R. G. Davis

"Written by the group's founder and longtime leader, this book offers an interesting and easygoing account of the first 10 years in the life of one of America's most vital and important left-wing theaters. The San Francisco Mime Troupe played the streets and parks and campuses during the great ferment of the past decade and Davis was there in the thick of it. The viewpoint is personal, perhaps a little biased at times, . . . But the essential facts are there — along with a detailed chronology . . . Important for theater libraries and useful for junior college and undergraduate collections. Photographs and excellent drawings."

— *Choice*

LC 74-19943 220 pp., photos, append., index 14.00 (cloth) 3.95 (paper)

THE TROJAN HORSE: A Radical Look at Foreign Aid
Steve Weissman, PSC, NACLA   1975 Edition

"Highly recommended to those who would understand why and how dollars buy influence."   — *Publishers Weekly*

LC 74-32606 250 pp., append., tables, notes   10.00 (cloth) 3.95 (paper)

LATIN AMERICA REVIEW 1 OF BOOKS
Edited by *Colin Harding and Christopher Roper*

"A veritable mine of information, critique, and bibliography. Briefly put, it is a collection of annotated book reviews of books on Latin America, and the number of books considered (well over 100) is remarkable. . . . Both general and college libraries should posess this volume, and college libraries could do with several copies."   — *Choice*

At your bookstore, or order direct from:
Ramparts Press, Box 10128, Palo Alto, CA 94303.
Enclose check with order, California residents add 6% sales tax.
Write for complete catalog of Ramparts Press books.